Building Renaissance Venice

The Scuola Grande di San Marco: detail of the façade, by Pietro Lombardo and assistants, c.1489–91, restored in 2004–5

Richard J. Goy

Building Renaissance Venice

Patrons, Architects and Builders
c. 1430–1500

Yale University Press
New Haven and London

Designed by Emily Lees

Printed in Singapore

Library of Congress Cataloging-in-Publication Data

Goy, Richard J. (Richard John), 1947–
The building of Renaissance Venice : patrons, architects, and builders,
c. 1430-1500 / Richard J. Goy.
p. cm.
Includes bibliographical references and index.
ISBN 0-300-11292-0 (alk. paper)
1. Architects and patrons–Italy–Venice–History–15th century.
2. Architects and builders–Italy–Venice–History–15th century.
3. Architecture, Renaissance–Italy–Venice. 4. Venice (Italy)–Buildings,
structures, etc. I. Title.
NA1121.V4G677 2006
720.945'3109024–dc22
2005028846

A catalogue record for this book is available from
The British Library

Contents

Appendices

Acknowledgements

DURING THE LONG GESTATION OF THIS BOOK, I have been frequently aware of the dangers of drawing broad conclusions from a picture that remains fragmentary and incomplete. It is important to note, too, that I have limited this study to the institutional aspects of the city's remarkable development in the fifteenth century, and have not discussed the equally ambitious – and far more numerous – private developments by the nobility and the wealthier citizenry. Fine Gothic and then Renaissance palaces appeared – as we can see today – in every major *campo* in the city, and on many sites down the course of the Grand Canal. Sadly, though, as readers of my earlier study of the Ca' d'Oro will be aware, documentary evidence for their construction is even more fragmented and elusive than it is for the great public works of *renovatio urbis*.

I have made extensive use of original sources, a good number of which have been published in Italy, but very few in English. Much of this vital primary material was first identified in the seminal studies of the great Paoletti, a century ago, and has more recently been investigated by Susan Connell, Philip Sohm and a handful of others; but I believe that little of this documentation has as yet been sufficiently analysed 'from the foundations to the roof', that is, with a practical understanding of the construction process that lay behind these lists of payments for wages and materials.

Nevertheless, the more specialised scholar will undoubtedly recognise my indebtedness to some who have navigated these elusive channels before me. Pietro Paoletti still remains a benchmark against which all later efforts must be measured, and I have also drawn on the equally pioneering work of Nicolò Erizzo at the Torre dell'Orologio and of Giambattista Lorenzi at the Palazzo Ducale.

Among more recent scholars in these fields, I have derived great benefit from Philip Sohm's very fine work at the Scuola Grande di San Marco, to Lionello and Loredana Olivato Puppi's perceptive study of Codussi; and to John McAndrew's acutely observant eye. Several important works, principally on sculpture, have also been published by Ann Markham Schulz and, on the construction industry, particularly stonemasons, by Susan Connell. Recent collections of essays have also explored specific aspects of Venetian civilisation, particularly that edited by John Martin and Dennis Romano.

Regarding the construction process, the essential secondary work is the richly illustrated study by Giovanni Caniato and Michela dal Borgo, *Le arti edili a Venezia*, which also contains a great deal of primary material; 'minor Venice', first examined by the pioneering studies of Egle Renata Trincanato in the 1940s, has more recently been analysed by the meticulous and sensitive approach of Nubar Gianighian and Paolina Pavanini in *Dietro i palazzi* and elsewhere. The papers published by the Istituto Veneto, as *L'architettura gotica veneziana*, following the conference of 1996, also contain much of great importance, as does the Istituto's magnificent recent monograph on Santa Maria dei Miracoli, edited by Mario Piana and Wolfgang Wolters. I have concluded that this fine work (together with the earlier study by Ralph Lieberman) renders any detailed further discussion in the present book superfluous.

Two further important recent books have surveyed Venice's cultural inheritance within a broader context of space and time: first, Patricia Fortini Brown's *Venice and Antiquity*, and then Deborah Howard's *Venice and the East*, the scope of both of which has added greatly to our understanding of the depth and range of these respective influences.

With the outstanding exceptions of the above, particularly the immense practical knowledge of Piana, Gianighian and Pavanini, few have attempted to comprehend the realities of life on the *quattrocento* scaffolding, with its all-too-frequent difficulties of funding, of the weather, of the acquisition of materials, of hierarchies and responsibilities, of physical danger: in short, comprehension of the entire process that transformed a sketch on a piece of paper or parchment, often over years of vicissitudes, into some of the greatest works of architecture of the Italian Renaissance. It is this lacuna that I hope to make a small contribution towards rectifying.

The original research for this book was undertaken, intermittently, and over a period of some years, at the Archivio di Stato at the Frari, and I am greatly indebted to the unfailing patience, advice and courtesy of the staff there, particularly the initial enthusiasm and encouragement of Dottoressa Maria Francesca Tiepolo. I am also delighted to acknowledge the guidance,

support and company of many other friends, colleagues and associates over the years, especially Frances Clarke, Richard MacKenney, Nick and Shearer Davidson, David Chambers, Brian Pullan, Michael Mallett, James Stitt, Wolfgang Wolters, Alex Cowan, John Law, Paul Holberton, Mary Laven, Mario Piana, Sheila Hale, and the late Peter Laven and Walter Gobbetto.

I owe a great debt of thanks to Deborah Howard, who has spent a great deal of her very valuable time reading (and re-reading) the manuscript, and who has made many invaluable and constructive suggestions, as well as correcting a considerable number of factual errors (some of them minor, but some not so!). I do, of course, take full responsibility for those that remain.

Very special thanks must also be given to Barbara, who (yet again) has seen me disappearing into my study-eyrie for months on end, only to emerge at sundown with grateful thanks for offers of *aperitivi*, and to Catherine, who has been equally patient with her much-too-elusive father.

I must acknowledge here, too, the generosity and enormous practical assistance offered by Giulio Vianello over many years, and more recently of Claudio, too; the countless offers of refreshment by the finest *osto* in the city, Primo Zambon, his daughter Caterina and his colleagues; and the seemingly inexhaustible hospitality and unfailing kindness of my dear friends Paolina Pavanini and Nubar Gianighian, on occasions far too numerous to mention.

This book is dedicated to the memory of John Hale, mentor, colleague and friend.

The Arsenale: the Porta Magna: one of the stone lions at the bases of the columns

1   Palazzo Bernardo, *circa* 1442, one of the last florid Gothic palaces built in Venice

Introduction

VENICE WAS TRANSFORMED DURING the course of the fifteenth century by the construction of an extraordinary quantity of new buildings, representative of an era of imperial expansion and wealth. What is doubly remarkable about this transformation is not simply the quantity of this new building activity but also its quality. This was the era of the great Gothic *palazzo*, that quintessentially Venetian typology (fig. 1); but the second half of the century was also a period of radical stylistic change, the era of Codussi and Pietro Lombardo, the era of the Renaissance.

The chief purpose of this book is to discuss some aspects of this transformation during Venice's period as imperial capital, from around 1430 to about the end of the century. Its focus is a discussion of some of the practical results of the patronage of the three principal groups of institutional patrons in the city: the Church, the unique Venetian organisations known as the Scuole Grandi and, finally, the Most Serene Republic itself. By concentrating on a handful of significant building projects, and by a discussion of the professional careers of some of the principal masters associated with them, a number of crucial issues are addressed. How were these projects conceived by their patrons, and what was their primary purpose? How were the masters who designed them commissioned, and what were the terms of their employment? How did they go about the organisation of the site and procurement of building materials? What were the salaries and living conditions of those who worked under them? And underlying all of these issues, perhaps the most significant matter of all: how did these patrons perceive the masters whom they employed in this flourishing era of Renaissance urban renewal: primarily as practical chief masons? Or essentially as experienced, efficient contract administrators? Or – finally to address that elusive title – did they select them primarily, and most importantly, as creative architects?

For this period was not only a pivotal one in the emergence of Venice as a truly imperial capital city. It was a period of fundamental cultural change; but it was also the era in which the role of the architect finally emerges as something like that which we recognise today. This study therefore tries to trace some of the subtle, elusive shifts in responsibilities and in the perceptions of patrons that facilitated the emergence of the modern architect.

Although the fifteenth century is a vital period in Venice's history for many reasons – in the establishment and consolidation of the Terraferma empire; in its political relationship with the rest of Italy and Europe, as well as the Ottoman empire of the east; in its economic and cultural development (the astonishing growth of the printing industry being a single example) – it remains one of considerable difficulty for the researcher in architectural history. Detailed documentary evidence for studying the chief monuments is at best fairly patchy (with a few outstanding exceptions), and at worst – and all too frequently – non-existent.

The selection of buildings on which to base such a study, therefore, is largely determined by chance survivals, and I have made use of many surviving documentary sources of the era. Fortunately, they do enable us to draw a sketch, if not a fully rendered perspective, of the way in which Renaissance Venice came to be built. The selection of 'case studies' that constitute the latter part of the book has thus been made on the basis that these projects are not only of great importance in themselves, and in the architectural history of the city; but they are also reasonably well served by original documentation, from an analysis of which we are thereby able to draw some useful and, I think, important lessons regarding the patronage of the works, the organisation of the construction site, and the relations among the protagonists in the process. Each of the buildings discussed represents a significant aspect of the Republic's political and cultural structure: together they provide insights into the practical patronage of the principal institutions of the Serenissima in this period. Unfortunately, there is little or no surviving documentation for a number of other important public buildings in this period; these buildings have already endured several centuries of speculation as a result of this paucity of documentation, and since further speculation will serve little purpose, I have reluctantly omitted these works from detailed discussion.

My approach has two principal threads. The first is to a large extent a practical, 'bricks and mortar' analysis. That is to say, I have placed considerable emphasis on the 'how' of patronage: how were aims and wishes translated into walls and floors, balconies and roofs? How, too, were the materials obtained, and from whom? Why did it take only a few months to complete some construction works, while others took a decade or more? And most important of all, what were the relationships among patrons, architects, master masons, carpenters and bricklayers? More specifically, how did the essentially medieval, craft-based organisation of the construction industry allow for the development of one particular type of master, who emerges towards the century's close not only as the principal designer of a project, but who also maintained continuity by supervising the entire process of its construction? These are aspects of early Renaissance architecture that, for Venice, at least, have so far received insufficient attention.

Nevertheless, I have not neglected the aesthetic and symbolic aspects of these works, and an understanding of their iconographic significance is equally essential: this is my second thread. Structures such as the great gate at the Arsenale and the Porta della Carta cannot

2 The lion of St Mark: Doge Ziani's column on the Molo, erected *circa* 1172

be understood, other than on a fairly superficial stylistic level, without some comprehension of the heavy iconographic and symbolic load that they had to bear, of the complex hidden agenda that frequently lay behind their representative imagery. Parallel to the study of the building of these monuments, therefore, is a discussion of this iconographic role in the context of Venice's *imago urbis*.

In the central figure of the emerging architect, too, we see two threads coming together: the creative master whose design skills were put at the service of his patrons was often at the same time the practical administrator and site manager. He was thus charged with the execution of a detailed iconographic programme, which, in a broader sense, also represented the image that this patron wished to project to the world. And this public image was not only intended to reflect or represent the achievements and aspirations of the commissioning body, but, on the wider stage, it served to enhance further the reputation of the city as a whole, to exemplify the Renaissance principles of *renovatio urbis*, all ultimately in honour of the Most Serene Republic, the Republic of Mark the Evangelist (fig. 2).

Chapter One provides a brief political and cultural background to the context in which these buildings were to be set, and sketches the urban condition of Venice in the fifteenth century as one of the great conurbations of western Europe; Jacopo de' Barbari's famous image of the city in 1500 serves as a *terminus ante quem* for the period under discussion. There follow a few observations regarding the elusive matter of routes of influence in terms of evolving architectural style. The final section outlines the roles of the various institutional bodies in the Republic that were responsible not only for the administration of the state, but also commissioned many of the city's principal monuments.

Chapter Two begins with a brief sketch of the patronage of the Republic in the particular case of Rialto, the commercial heart of the capital. A series of laws during the fifteenth century clearly illustrate the role of several departments of government as they attempted to control the urban development of the capital by direct intervention. Following this 'case study', there is a discussion of the unique role played by the Procurators of San Marco, one of whose functions, as estates commissioners, had an important influence over development in the city.

Chapter Three and Four discuss the design and construction process, beginning with a summary of the approaches that patron bodies used to commission their architects. We then look at the construction industry: first, the building trade guilds, their roles, organisation and relationship to each other; then we discuss building materials, where they were obtained, and how the supply industry was organised. Finally, we analyse contracts and methods of payment to the numerous suppliers and craftsmen.

The following chapters discuss the professional careers of some of the chief masters who transformed the city; these biographical studies are closely linked to the projects for which they were responsible, and the roles of these men and their teams of craftsmen are examined in detail.

The first is the prolific career of Bartolomeo Bon, from his earliest work at the Ca' d'Oro in the 1420s through to the two fine portals for the churches of the Madonna dell'Orto and Santi Giovanni e Paolo, which ended his career in the 1460s. Bon was the last great master of the *ancien régime*, fulcrum of an extensive network of other craftsmen, and with whose career their own frequently intersected. Bon's masterpiece, the Porta della Carta, was followed by contributions to the Carità church in the 1440s, the building of which allows us to draw a valuable comparison with

Antonio Gambello's slightly later reconstruction of San Zaccaria. Bon's later career is epitomised by the two church portals, a late flowering of a master in whose work we can just detect the beginnings of new influences.

Chapter Six attempts to identify that elusive period of stylistic transition just after mid-century by reference to one crucial example, the great gate of the Arsenale, the pivotal work of the 1460s.

Chapter Seven is entitled 'The Era of Codussi'. In many ways the career of Mauro Codussi (fig. 3) epitomises an era in which roles were still in flux. It is clear today that his primary importance is as an architect, a master possessed of strong, individual design skills, and whose appointment by several institutional bodies directly reflected the value that they attached to those skills and that individuality. On the other hand, the industry itself had changed very little in its organisational structure over the previous decades; Codussi's career thus essentially spans a peroid of both change and continuity.

A brief introduction to San Michele is followed in chapter Eight by a more detailed discussion of the long, complex history of San Zaccaria, begun by Antonio Gambello and completed, after his death, by Codussi himself. San Zaccaria is probably the most important building of the late fifteenth century in Venice: not only is it a crucial work stylistically, but the manner of its design and construction enables us to identify the central role played by the *protomaestro* (the 'chief master') in regularising and 'professionalising' the construction process. In chapter Nine we turn to the Scuola Grande di San Marco, another project whose design was begun by one master, Pietro Lombardo, and again was completed by Codussi. Some notes in chapter Ten regarding the later stages of the construction of the east wing of the Palazzo Ducale (Doge's Palace) after the fire of 1483 permit us to record how such an important state-funded project was organised, and allow us to trace the roles of the two *proti* in succession, Antonio Rizzo and Pietro Lombardo.

The final 'case study' in chapter Eleven discusses the Torre dell'Orologio, a highly prominent work, the discussion of which brings together several strands that will have emerged from earlier chapters: the developing concepts of Renaissance *civitas* and *renovatio urbis*; the embracing of complex new technology and its application towards those same ends; the Republic's sophisticated fusion of a range of iconographic symbols. The Torre epitomises the stylistic condition of the city's public architecture at the very end of the century; it

3 Detail of the façade of San Michele in Isola, by Mauro Codussi, 1469–75

also stands as a metaphor for the Republic's *renovatio urbis* more clearly than any other project of the fifteenth century.

Finally, I have attempted to draw all the foregoing to some kind of conclusion. A final footnote, rather ambitiously headed 'the New Rome', makes a few summarising observations as to the way in which this republican conceit was indeed transformed into concrete (or rather marble and stone) reality during the late fifteenth century, as the Republic and its various institutions imposed their varied notions of the Renaissance *città ideale* onto this medieval metropolis.

A Note on the Text

The Venetian year began on 1 March; all dates have been modernised. The issue of spelling is less straightforward: almost all the documentary sources are in Venetian, not Italian, and spellings varied widely in this period. In general I have retained original spellings, for authenticity, but have regularised those encountered most frequently: thus Bartolomeo Bon throughout, rather than Bortolomio Bom, Buon or any other combination. Zan, Zuan or Zane are the Venetian forms of Giovanni; Alvise (usually written Alvixe) is the Venetian form of Luigi, Zorzi is that of Giorgio and Viellmo is Guglielmo. Again I have retained the most usual recorded spelling, which sometimes also helps in distinguishing between a 'Zan' and a 'Zuane'. References to money systems always refer to the day-to-day coinage of lire, soldi and piccoli (pounds, shillings and pence) rather than the money of account, the lira *di grosso*. In this system there are 12 piccoli (pence) to one soldo and 20 soldi (shillings) to one lira, the same system that was formerly used in the United Kingdom. The value of the gold ducat in relation to the lira *di piccoli* varied with the exchange rate between the two metals, gold and silver. In 1421 there were exactly 5 lire (100 soldi) to 1 ducat, but by 1455 the rate had shifted to L. 6.4.0 (124 soldi) per ducat. From 1472 it again remained constant at 124 soldi to the end of the century. For further detail of these fluctuating exchange rates (and many others), see the works of Reinhold Mueller cited in the bibliography, as well as P. Spufford, *Handbook of Medieval Exchange* (London, 1986), especially pp. 80–86. The Venetian unit of length was the piede or foot (347 mm); five feet constituted one passo (1.735 m).

Chapter One

THE BACKGROUND:
VENICE AS A METROPOLITAN CAPITAL

The Urban and Political Background

ON 22 JULY 1400 A CONTRACT WAS SIGNED for the carving of the great Molo window on the façade of the Palazzo Ducale (figs 4, 5). This highly symbolic work, richly carved and adorned with the eastern saints Theodore (Todaro) and George, and with the Theological and Cardinal Virtues, represented the apotheosis of the Venetian state. The great window itself was an external expression of the vast chamber of the Maggior Consiglio that stood within, the bedrock of the governance of the Most Serene Republic. Its balcony formed a vantage point, physically and metaphorically linking the great hall with the Bacino outside, in which were clustered at anchor the ships of empire, source of the Serenissima's fame and wealth. The two saints, too, emphasised the Republic's links with the Eastern Empire, whence much of that wealth derived; while stylistically this boldly carved work epitomised the native *gotico fiorito*, rich in sculpted form and imagery, rich in stone and marble, and rich in pecuniary investment. It was a singularly appropriate metaphor for the Serenissima as the new century turned.

For Venice was about to embark on a new role, and with the expansion and consolidation of the Terraferma empire in the decades that followed, was to become more and more clearly an imperial power in both elements, land and sea; the traditional maritime web of shipping lanes, coastal forts and safe anchorages was to be balanced by a land empire of wealthy Terraferma cities, rich farmland and upland forests.[1]

The city's fabric was to develop dramatically over the course of the fifteenth century, reflecting these momentous political and economic events. The dominant building typology, the noble *palazzo* or palace, reached a stage of highly sophisticated perfection; the great monastic houses finally completed their own imposing new churches, while the Scuole Grandi began to invest huge sums in lavishly decorated halls for themselves.

5   The Palazzo Ducale: the Molo façade, begun in 1340

4   The Palazzo Ducale: the central window on the Molo façade, by Pier Paolo dalle Masegne, begun in 1400

commercial activity and banking at Rialto, and the great Arsenale, seat of the Serenissima's Mediterranean power.

The first two decades of the century were a period of economic consolidation, following the final great victory over Genoa in 1380.[2] With the rapid re-establishment of maritime trading routes, and with the acquisition of Padua in 1405 (fig. 7) marking the first stage in the development of the Terraferma empire, the decision in 1422 to rebuild the Piazzetta wing of the Palazzo Ducale was one among many signs of this refound confidence, and an affirmation of the role of the government in the patronage of building works appropriate to this new era of expansionism. It was no coincidence, either, that, only months after the decision was made to rebuild the ancient Ziani palace, in April 1423 Doge Tommaso Mocenigo was to address the Republic's noble administrators with his famous vale-dictory 'state of the nation' speech, in which, *inter alia*, he proudly summarised the impressive statistics of the Serenissima's naval might and economic strength. Among the achievements during Mocenigo's term of office was the reduction of the national debt from 10 million to 6 million ducats; annual receipts from taxa-tion stood at 1,600,000 ducats; the mint coined 1,200,000 gold ducats per year; and maritime exports were valued at 10 million ducats per year, yielding no less than 4 million in profits. Equally imposing was the size and capacity of the merchant fleet (fig. 8): 45 great and light galleys, of 250 to 450 tonnes, manned by 8,000 mariners; 300 other commercial ships larger than 100 tonnes; and 3,000 smaller vessels. To build and service this great fleet, 3,000 carpenters and 3,000 caulkers were employed in the Arsenale.[3]

6 The Palazzo Ducale: the sculpted figure of St Michael, the warrior archangel, on the corner of the Molo and Piazzetta façades, after recent cleaning

7 The Venetian winged lion in the Piazza dei Signori, Padua. The city became a Venetian subject in 1405

Venice was one of the greatest cities of western Europe, a capital defined by its unique environmental context, and politically defined by its equally unique form of government. The city's form contained three 'hearts' or hubs and one world-famous principal artery. The last was, of course, the Grand Canal, whose sinuous form became ever more imposingly lined by noble *palazzi* over the fifteenth century. Extraordinary though the Canalazzo was, it was perhaps the city's three hearts that rendered its structure so highly distinctive: they were the seat of government at San Marco, the hub of

8 Jacopo de' Barbari: detail of ships and boatyards on the south shore of the city; the Zattere were later constructed here

By now, the Venetian economy comprised three well-defined component parts: the traditional empire *da mar*, the more recently acquired mainland empire, and lastly the wealth produced by the city itself. For the capital was far more than a hub of administration and international finance: it was also one of the largest manufacturing centres in Europe.[4] Among the chief of these domestically produced goods were glass, metal products of almost every conceivable type and, above all, textiles (fig. 6). Glassmaking, the dominant feature of the satellite island of Murano, was one element of a large sector of industry that transformed natural raw materials into saleable commodities of greatly increased value. In this same broad grouping we can also locate the textile industry, principally wool and silk, including the production of dyes for fabrics, and the manufacture of soap. The substantial construction industry, too, extracted natural products (sand, lime, clay, stone) either for use directly, or for transformation into essential bricks and mortar. Much of this production took place in the flatlands around Mestre, which contained large numbers of kilns and brickyards.[5]

Glassmaking was particularly important: not only was the process closely controlled by the government, but the finished products generated very high increases in value over the costs of the raw materials; they were exported over most of Europe, from Germany to Sicily, and as far eastwards as Constantinople. The glassworks also produced window glass for the city's palaces on a scale unseen elsewhere in the western world (fig. 9).

Metalworkers produced a vast range of goods in copper, iron and steel, from cooking utensils to weapons of war. At a more rarefied level were specialised craftsmen working with precious metals, gold and silver,

9 Murano: detail from Jacopo de' Barbari's view of 1500

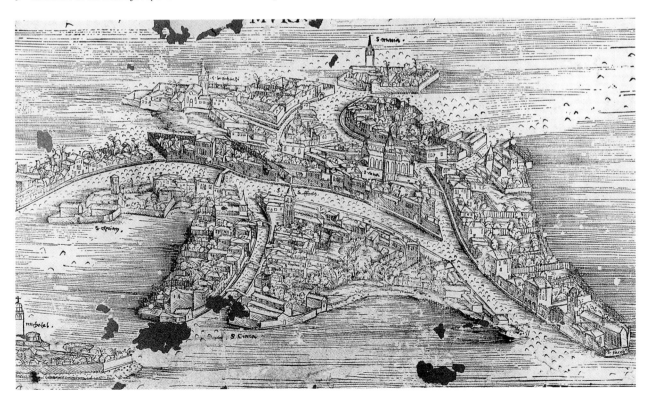

10   The Arsenale: detail of houses along the Riello dell' Arsenale, formerly occupied by the Provveditori dell'Arsenale

which were refined not only for the great quantity of coins produced by the mint every year, but also for jewellery and luxury goods, again much of it for export.

Venice was therefore a highly industrialised centre for the production of goods. Most such enterprises were individually small in scale but large in numbers, scattered over many parts of the city, although certain concentrations were noteworthy, and many can still be identified in street names today: goldsmiths at Rialto, arrow-makers in the Frezzeria, smiths in the Calle dei Fabbri, and so on. Despite the highly localised scale of most individual operations, therefore – the great shipyards of the Arsenale were a unique exception – collectively they rendered Venice a major industrial city.

The three hearts evinced the greatest concentration of specific activities, and each served a clearly defined function. Fundamental to the urban development of all three locations, though, was the Republic's direct ownership of the land, and hence its power to develop it as it saw fit.

The Arsenale is perhaps the simplest of the three to analyse, since it was dedicated essentially to a single function, or rather, a collection of closely related functions: the building, maintenance and victualling of the most powerful navy in the Mediterranean. The history of the Arsenale is a centuries-long process of enlargement, change and refinement, each stage reflecting both technological developments and political exigencies. It remained a working dockyard from its modest inception in the small basin of the Darsena Vecchia in 1104 until our own day, nine centuries later, finally occupying an area of more than 40 hectares. Even by 1400 the original small basin had been expanded by the construction of the much larger Arsenale Nuovo to the east, and the complex was already the most prominent feature of the eastern quarter of Castello. Around the outside of its imposing perimeter walls were a number of support facilities, such as bakeries for supplying the fleets, and the housing of the shipyard workers, the *arsenalotti*.[6]

The Arsenale became the overwhelmingly dominant element in the eastern part of the city (fig. 10), and the urban texture around it directly reflected its presence; there are few noble *palazzi* here, and the district was (and to a large extent remains) characterised by modest terraces of houses, together with a 'green fringe' of monasteries, with their gardens and orchards.

If the Arsenale represents something of a monoculture, the role of Rialto is considerably more complex. As the legendary nucleus from which Venice was said to have come into existence, the islet of Rialto had profound symbolic and metaphorical resonance for the

11   Rialto: the Ruga dei Oresi (Orefici), towards the Rialto bridge, with the campanile of San Bartolomeo; the Fabbriche Vecchie (right) were rebuilt after the fire of 1514 by Scarpagnino

Serenissima's government. San Giacomo or Giacometto, the very first church founded in the archipelago (on 21 March 421, according to legend), itself represented the misty, mystical origins of the great capital city: its true, original heart.[7]

As Rialto developed, the functions concentrated there were many and complex. Its location in the precise centre of the archipelago ensured its permanent role as a meeting place of routes, and a natural location for a market. These market functions grew to embrace almost every aspect and level of human commercial exchange, from the purchase of a day's domestic provisions of bread, fruit and wine to international banking, from shipping insurance to brothels, from goldsmiths to fish-gutting. Most (if not quite all) of those activities still take place here today.

Far less well known is Rialto's role as a centre of administration (fig. 11). Indeed, there may have been more government departments here than there were at

San Marco. Nearly all of those offices that administered the city itself (as distinct from the Republic as a whole) were located here, and the adjacent quays were the sole location where bulk commodities – iron, flour, wine, coal, oil – had to be unloaded and assessed for tax.

Many departments divided their time between Rialto and San Marco. Rialto was the only other location where there was a nobles' loggia; and in the little square in front of San Giacometto there also stood the only other public proclamation pillar (the *gobbo*) where government decrees were made. Here, too, galley fleets were auctioned, and here, of course, were banks and shipping and insurance offices. The many conflicts that these complex functions generated represented an apparently irremovable thorn in the flesh of the Republic, as it frequently attempted to reconcile these conflicting practical requirements with the need to enhance the status and dignity of this hub of the city's fabric.

The role of the third and final heart, San Marco, is in a sense simpler to define. The large island of the patronal shrine contained all the highest organs of the government of the Republic, as well as the chapel of St Mark itself, and the offices of those responsible for its maintenance and administration, the Procurators of San Marco. The complex of buildings at San Marco evolved into two sub-groups, each with their own spaces and functions. The first hub is the Piazza itself, dominated by San Marco, and around which the offices of the Procurators were built. As the numbers of Procurators slowly increased, so, too, did their requirements for more accommodation, such that, finally, by the seventeenth century, the Procurators' apartments occupied almost the entire circumference of the Piazza. The role of the Piazza has always been essentially to form a parvis for the shrine itself, and was thus seen as an essentially ecclesiastical space.[8]

The adjacent Piazzetta (fig. 12), on the other hand, was essentially the square of the Republic's government, and the manner in which it, too, was developed over the centuries enhanced and concentrated these practical and symbolic functions. In its form at the end of the fifteenth century, and as recorded by de' Barbari, the Piazzetta was flanked on one side by the Palazzo Ducale (and specifically, the wing from which justice was dispensed), and on the other by a rather miscellaneous collection of structures, which included, just around the corner in the Piazza, the well-known Ospizio Orseolo, a 'hostel' for pilgrims on their way to the Holy Land. There was also a meat market in the Piazzetta, while along the waterfront, where the present Giardinetti are located, stood the vast warehouses of the

Granai di Terranova, four huge storage blocks, built in pairs. The Piazzetta remained defined on the seaward side by Doge Ziani's great pair of columns, symbolic on several levels. Forming the gateway to the city, they were crowned by the Republic's two patrons, St Mark and St Theodore, but they also represented the physical results of the justice meted out in the adjacent Palazzo, when malefactors were strung up between them.

The characteristic L-shaped configuration of these two great squares, with the campanile as the 'hinge' between them, meant that there remained a considerable difference between them, both in form and function: each represented a crucial aspect of the identity of the Republic.

The two 'hearts', Rialto and San Marco, were also linked by the customs house at the Punta della Dogana, where goods were taxed before being taken to Rialto for unloading and sale.

The city thus revolved around these three nuclei, together with the great artery of the Grand Canal. Although Venice was one of the largest cities in Europe, with the exception of these nuclei the detailed urban structure devolved, as to a large extent it still does, to the level of the island-parish, that fundamental building block of the city's fabric. Although much of the city's perimeter was not fully developed, and remained occupied by monastic houses and their gardens, the central districts were all highly urbanised, with a dense matrix of *calli*, *campielli* and *rami*, each island parish centred on the *campo* in front of the church. Each parish, too, retained a high degree of autonomy in the daily life of its inhabitants.

Construction activity during the fifteenth century closely mirrored the general condition of the Republic's finances and the broader political situation; since the financial interests of the patriciate were inextricably linked with the political and economic fortunes of the state itself, there was an inevitably close correlation between noble construction activity and the economic climate in which they all lived. As always, the level of building activity was an acute and sensitive mirror of the age.

Midway through the century, 'the worst news of all for Christendom' (in Nicol's memorable phrase) reached Venice: the fall of Constantinople to the Ottoman Turks, in 1453.[9] The advent of Francesco Sforza as the new duke of Milan posed a virtually simultaneous military threat from precisely the opposite direction, so that the

12 San Marco: the approach to the Molo, with Doge Ziani's two columns, surmounted by the Republic's patrons, St Theodore and St Mark

Republic's priorities in the last few years of the reign of the formidable doge Francesco Foscari were rapidly diverted to military issues of attack and defence. The failure of the Soranzo bank in the same year of 1453 added to the sense of crisis.

The Republic took drastic fiscal measures. For one full year, all state receipts were allocated to military preparations; even the salaries of government officials were suspended for a year, and in this way between 700,000 and 1,000,000 ducats were made available for military needs: a striking example of the direct and immediate effect of geopolitical issues on the financing of public works within the city itself.[10]

A further example of this close interdependence can be seen in the financially turbulent 1490s. In 1492 Christopher Columbus had made landfall in the 'New World'; in 1499 news reached Rialto of Vasco da Gama's epic sea journey via the Cape of Good Hope to India. Although both voyages were, in their different ways, epochal, it was the second that provoked the most dramatic effect in Venice. Many merchants reacted by concluding that this new Portuguese route would destroy

Venice's monopoly of the spice trade with the Middle East, and that their prices would be dramatically undercut. The effect of this interpretation was immediate: the crisis of confidence led to a run on the Venetian banks and a spectacular crash. Of the four noble banks trading at the start of 1499, two collapsed immediately, the Garzoni and the Lippomani; the Pisani bank fell in 1500; and only the Agostini survived unscathed until, finally, it too ceased trading in 1508. After this initial crisis, though, the Pisani bank reopened in 1504, but the Lippomani and Garzoni did not reappear, and it was only in 1507 that two new foundations, the Priuli and the Cappello-Vendramin banks, once again provided the city's merchant nobility with a full range of financial services.[11]

The trading rivalry with Portugal was far from resolved by the time of the formidable alliance of the League of Cambrai against the Republic and the subsequent debacle at Agnadello in 1509. The League itself was a short-lived alliance of the great western powers – principally the Emperor Maximilian and King Louis XII of France, joined later by Pope Julius II – to destroy

13

the Terraferma empire of the Venetians. At Agnadello the Venetians were comprehensively routed. At the end of the period of this study, therefore, crises both political and economic rendered the Republic doubly unstable, and drastically affected investment in construction projects both by the state itself and by other institutions.[12]

In fact, in the years after Cambrai, the trade war with Portugal developed to Venice's advantage. Clashes between the Portuguese and the sultan of Egypt resulted in the resumption of trading agreements between Venice and Egypt; and while Portugal began distributing spices via Lisbon, Venice wisely returned to her Middle East routes across the Mediterranean, a trade which was consolidated and flourished. It increased further as a result of the expansion of the Ottoman empire into Egypt, offering Venice a larger, more unified eastern market. Such international mercantile interests, and the profits derived from them, directly affected urban development and new building projects in Venice as surely as these events were disseminated as news on the Rialto.[13]

If the last decade of the fifteenth century was defined by crisis and uncertainty, the previous decades had been marked generally by stability and prosperity. This stability was directly reflected in the widespread construction programmes of the Venetian patriciate; many new noble *palazzi*, particularly in the 1450s and 1460s, redefined much of the urban texture of the city, and represented not only the maturation of a long-established typology, but also reinforced the character of the Grand Canal as well as that of many of the city *campi*. These palaces were larger, more rigorously symmetrical, and more harmonious and refined in appearance than almost all of their immediate forerunners; they established a new scale and dignity in the spaces that they now dominated. The genre is exemplified by the imposing *palazzo* that Doge Francesco Foscari began in the 1450s 'in volta dil canal'; monumental and yet refined, it equally represents Foscari's own powerful character and his intention to make his personal mark on one of the most prominent sites along the Canalazzo (fig. 13). Indeed, one of the characteristic developments in this era was the slow continuation of the process of consolidation of the banks of the Grand Canal, a process that had by no means yet been concluded at the century's end, as the ill-defined banks illustrated by de' Barbari attest so clearly.

While Foscari's strong individuality marks one of the defining traits of architectural patronage in the fifteenth century, the other must surely be the determination of institutional patrons – the Church, the Scuole Grandi,

the state itself – to enhance the prestige of the *Dominante* by commissioning a succession of rich, monumental structures that epitomised the concept of Venice as 'the new Rome': that is, a stable republic built on the foundation of justice, and with a capital city that reflected the concepts of order and continuity.

The Architectural Background

Venetian architectural history in the fifteenth century begins and ends, both stylistically and metaphorically, at the Palazzo Ducale. In 1400 the finishing touches were being added to the new Molo façade, including Pier Paolo dalle Masegne's great window. A century later, Antonio Rizzo and his successor, Pietro Lombardo, were in the process of completing the massive new east wing to house the Senate and the other highest institutions of Venice's government. Stylistically, the two projects represent the development from the rich, florid, mature Venetian Gothic to the equally rich, but refined neo-classical relief decorations of the Lombard Renaissance (fig. 16).

Between these two dates the appearance of much of the city had been transformed. In 1400 the overall stylistic matrix was a mixture of many Venetian-Byzantine structures with numerous, more recent Gothic works. By 1500 the emphasis had changed markedly, and the city's dominant aesthetic was the great mature Gothic *palazzo*; by now, though, interspersed with a small but significant scattering of Renaissance jewels, pearls mounted in a textured fabric essentially of brickwork.[14]

The analogy is not merely poetic. The late Gothic *palazzi* were impressive enough, with their elegant façades, their tracery of gleaming white Istrian stone, but the newer façades that had begun to appear, first at San Michele in the 1470s, later at San Zaccaria, Santa Maria dei Miracoli (fig. 15) and the Scuola Grande di San Marco, were not only entirely clad with stone, but most of them also incorporated coloured marbles and rich displays of sculpture.

The most ostentatious early symbol of this era of imperial optimism was Marin Contarini's new palace on the Grand Canal at Santa Sofia, the Ca' d'Oro, completed in the mid-1430s (fig. 14). Although it was to remain the most richly elaborate, it was only one of many such palaces, the construction of which reached an absolute peak of activity in the 1450s and 1460s.[15] The architectural language of all of these *palazzi* remains Gothic, from that of Contarini through to the Giovanelli, Bernardo and Pesaro palaces, some built as late as the 1470s.

13   Ca' Foscari, on the Grand Canal, built by Doge Francesco Foscari *circa* 1453; the two contiguous Giustiniani palaces are of about the same date

above 14 The Ca' d'Oro: detail of façade, by Zane and Bartolomeo Bon, and Matteo Raverti, Niccolò Romanello and others, 1426–31

left 15 Santa Maria dei Miracoli: detail of exterior, by Pietro Lombardo, 1481–9

facing page 16 The Palazzo Ducale: detail of the *cortile* façade of the east wing, by Antonio Rizzo and Pietro Lombardo; begun 1483 and completed in the early 1500s

Although related to the universality of late western European Gothic, Venetian *gotico fiorito* is marked by strong 'dialectal' traits that resulted directly from the city's location, its highly specific social and political structure, its topographical and even geological conditions. As such, too, it formed an essentially Venetian, that is, a 'patriotic' element in the visual history of the city. In the later fifteenth century, when classical and Florentine influences became identifiable, these, too, were to be modified and adapted by these same dialectal forces, moulded into the lagunar way. The use of light and physical lightness, sculpted form and colour, formed the chief components of the Venetian architectural Renaissance; even at the most superficial level, we have only to consider the great Florentine palaces of the Pitti, the Medici and the Strozzi (fig. 17) and compare them with their Venetian equivalents, the Loredan (later Vendramin Calergi), the Trevisan 'in Canonica' and the Dario (fig. 18), to appreciate how little these components of light and colour affected the Florentine Renaissance palace, but how fundamental a part these factors play in the architecture of the lagunar capital (fig. 19).[16]

Deborah Howard has recently published a comprehensive study of the relationship between Venetian architecture, including *gotico fiorito*, and the continuing influences from the Muslim East.[17] These influences varied from the long-established use of decorative, 'moorish' crenellation to *altane* (roof terraces), balconies and courtyard gateways. It is important to realise that the mature magnificence of the native *gotico fiorito* cohabited very happily in Venice for some decades with Renaissance works in the new style, as McAndrew has analysed with great insight. And again, in the design and construction of the Venetian Renaissance *palazzo*, the traditional rhythms and patterns of fenestration and articulation were often retained unchanged, despite the new vocabulary of design: the exquisite façade of Palazzo Grimani at San Polo (*circa* 1520) (fig. 20) offers an excellent example of this reinterpretation of style;

17 Detail of Palazzo Strozzi, Florence, begun in 1489 by Benedetto da Maiano, completed by Cronaca, 1497–1504

18 Façade of Palazzo Dario, *circa* 1487

19 Courtyard of Palazzo Strozzi, Florence: the lower order probably by Benedetto da Maiano, the upper orders by Cronaca

the basic structure of the *palazzo* is quite unchanged from that of its Gothic predecessors, as is the pattern of fenestration.

The philosophical basis for the development of early Renaissance architecture in Venice is a complex one. A strong undercurrent of pragmatism underlies its evolution; indeed, it flows beneath the surface of so much of Venice's intellectual culture. The pivotal works of Leon Battista Alberti initially had only a tangential, indirect influence, although he himself had been educated at Padua, and was in Venice on at least one occasion, when (according to Giorgio Vasari) he painted a perspective view of San Marco, 'one of his best paintings', but now lost.[18] Nevertheless, Alberti influenced many contemporaries in Florence, among them Donatello, who also spent many years in Padua (a Venetian city), and who received commissions from

Venice itself, including the striking *St John the Baptist* for the Florentine chapel at the Frari.

Alberti's *De re aedificatoria* was completed in draft around 1452,[19] about the same time that he was working on the Tempio Malatestiano in Rimini. The great church was probably studied by Mauro Codussi, who worked for the Camaldolesi order at Ravenna, just along the coast, some years later. Alberti was a close friend of Andrea Mantegna, and, like him, was also closely involved with the patronage of the Gonzaga court at Mantua after 1459, first with the church of San Sebastiano, then at Sant'Andrea. Again it is possible that Codussi followed progress on these works; we know that he returned from Venice to his home village in the Bergamasco nearly every winter, and a visit to Mantua was not much of a detour from his route.[20]

20   Palazzo Grimani at San Polo, *circa* 1520s

Nevertheless, such hypotheses remain speculative, and Alberti's seminal text may have been at least as important for its propagation of the civic, public aspects of architecture, and the concept of the *urbs* as a rationally developed, perfectible entity (fig. 21), as it was for the importance of his discussion of individual building typologies. In this, of course, he was highly influential, and we need only mention the works of Bernardo Rossellino at Pienza (1459–62) and Federigo da Montefeltro's development of the castle-palace at Urbino. Both were profoundly influenced by Alberti, particularly by those sections of Books VII and VIII that discuss the civic functions of 'temples' and other public buildings.[21]

Alberti's contemporary Michelozzo, another close associate of Donatello, is known to have visited Venice more than once; possibly *circa* 1423, and again in 1430 and 1433–4, on the last occasion with Cosimo de' Medici, when the latter had been exiled from Florence; the lost library at San Giorgio Maggiore is traditionally attributed to him, and perhaps was where he developed the concept for his spacious, elegant library at San Marco in Florence a few years later. Although Michelozzo's most significant works in Florence (particularly the remodelling at San Marco) are in a refined Tuscan classical idiom, the Venetian library remains enigmatic, its detailed appearance unknown.[22]

Among the outstanding intellectuals of Venetian humanism in the latter part of the fifteenth century, the most influential were three Aristotelian philosophers, Girolamo Donà (or Donato), Ermolao Barbaro and Bernardo Bembo. It was the last who probably made the most significant contribution towards the dissemination of Florentine Renaissance visual theories in Venice. Bembo was a senator and sometime Venetian ambassador to Florence (in the years 1475–6 and 1478–80), where he became a close personal friend of Lorenzo de' Medici. While in Florence Bembo acquired a copy of Alberti's *De re aedificatoria* for his own library, although the text itself was not to be published in its entirety until 1485, thirteen years after Alberti's death. Girolamo Donà, primarily notable as a Platonist and Aristotelian philosopher, was (as we will see later) highly involved with architecture, and he followed very

21   The Renaissance concept of the ideal city: detail from a painting in the Galleria Nazionale, Urbino

closely the rebuilding of Codussi's San Michele; he left 100 ducats in his will towards the completion of this revolutionary new church.[23]

A little after Michelozzo, Antonio Averlino (called Filarete) also visited the lagoons from Florence. His own approach to the philosophy of architecture as described in his *Trattato* in twenty-five 'books' (1461–4) differs markedly from the rather more exalted, neo-classical concepts of Alberti. Filarete spent many years in Rome before returning to Florence in 1448, and then moved north, finally settling in Milan under the patronage of the Sforza. His treatise was written in a robust *volgare* rather than the Latin of Alberti, and is remarkable for the straightforwardness of his approach, illustrated with numerous sketches and plans. His direct influence on Venice, though, is again unclear, although he was closely interested in Bartolomeo Bon's great project for a palace on the Grand Canal for the Corner clan, which was to have been a remarkable work on a monumental scale. Filarete's other lasting legacy was the development of the imaginary ideal city of Sforzinda, specifically developed with his Milanese patron in mind.[24]

Rather closer to the lagoons both physically and culturally was the career of Fra Giocondo, born in Verona in 1433. Giocondo was a true polymath, with interests in engineering, hydraulics, archaeology and the classical inheritance and town planning. He studied the classical ruins of Rome and Naples extensively, and was one of the crucial figures in the dissemination of this legacy in the north of Italy. Giocondo was employed by the Consiglio dei Dieci (Council of Ten) in Venice in 1506, almost certainly on the basis of his knowledge of structural and hydraulic engineering; he spent some time in the Terraferma advising the Republic on engineering matters, and later (1509–11) worked on the fortifications of Padua and Treviso. Although he spent some of his later life in Rome, Giocondo published an edition of Vitruvius in Venice in 1511, and illustrated the treatises of Francesco di Giorgio. He also offered a proposal for the reconstruction of Rialto after the disastrous fire of 1514. The imposing Loggia del Consiglio in Verona (completed *circa* 1493) is often accepted as his only major built work, a remarkable structure combining a refined classical Tuscan lower colonnade with a richly detailed upper storey, the wall surfaces clad with fine sheets of marble and the pilasters equally richly carved with bas-reliefs.[25] Much of this characteristic Lombard aesthetic was to be evinced in the work of Pietro Solari (Lombardo), originally from Carona on Lake Lugano, but who settled in Venice in about 1467, and whose flourishing workshop was to produce many of the city's most characteristically 'Venetian' and yet most typically Lombard works.

Ennio Concina has argued recently that much of the influence for Venice's earliest Renaissance architecture came not – or not exclusively – from the intellectual source of Florence (or from Rome itself) but rather from the classical remains by which Venice was surrounded; the ruins of Altino, for example, were almost within sight of the city, and both there and at Torcello Roman inscriptions were being unearthed in the fifteenth century, much as they still occasionally are today.[26] There were also the remains of the great classical city of Aquileia, which became part of the Terraferma empire in 1420, while not much further afield were the Roman theatre, amphitheatre and triumphal arch at Pola (Pula) across the Golfo di Venezia in Istria, the last of which was much studied by Renaissance architects and theorists. The Venetians had numerous other Terraferma examples to inspire them as well, among which the magnificent Arena, bridge and theatre at Verona were the most remarkable. In Verona, too, stood the Arco dei Gavi and the Porta dei Borsari, the former inscribed by 'Vitruvius' (although not the Vitruvius of the famous *Ten Books*). Concina correctly emphasises the proximity of so many outstanding classical sites, all of them a good deal more accessible than making the arduous journey to Rome.

In mid-century, too, two further events exerted a discernible influence on these cultural developments: one was a deterioration in relations between Venice and Florence, and the other was the loss of Constantinople in 1453. The former was triggered by the formation of the alliance in 1450 between the Venetian Republic, Siena and the Kingdom of the Two Sicilies against a counter-alliance consisting of Milan, Genoa and Florence. Although this political situation disrupted cultural links between Florence and Venice for a time, more significant in the longer term was the loss of the Eastern capital, widely seen by contemporaries as a cataclysmic event not only politically but in both religious and cultural terms as well. Whilst it may be argued that the loss of the eastern capital was perhaps felt more spiritually and symbolically than practically – the short-term economic and practical effects were very limited – nevertheless, in its aftermath Venice saw her own role more and more clearly as a cultural (and mercantile) bridge between east and west, as the natural successor to this now tragically lost capital. In fact, both events assisted in rendering Venice's path of cultural development more clearly distinct from those of either Florence or Rome, while rendering the city more closely conscious of its own eastern inheritance.

It remains notable that many of Venice's most outstanding early Renaissance built works (as distinct from texts or theoretical debates) were – as is so often the case – the result of the direct patronage of strong, influential, individual figures; to a qualified degree, they can be seen in a similar light to the princely patronage of the courts of Mantua, Urbino and the rest, except that in Venice, of course, these particularly enlightened men were at the same time members of a collective form of government, one widely famed abroad for its caution, conservatism and pragmatism. Clearly, within such an overall political structure it was considerably easier to exercise (sometimes daring) individual patronage outside the rather reactionary confines of the Palazzo Ducale than it was within them. There were exceptions: sometimes the doge himself proved to have comparatively adventurous tastes; the Arsenale gate, for example, represented to a significant extent the aesthetic and political philosophies of Doge Pasquale Malipiero, while Codussi's remarkable church at San Michele was the direct result of the patronage of a particularly influential group of humanist intellectuals, among them Pietro Donà and Pietro Delfin. In a similar manner, it was individual patronage by Zorzi (Giorgio) Corner that commissioned the family's chapel at Santi Apostoli, as was that of the Gussoni at San Lio; the latter family had developed a strong taste for rich Renaissance decoration, as the façade of their nearby *palazzetto* clearly evinces (fig. 22).

In a crowded, organic city like Venice, though, there was little opportunity for the execution of entirely new works of rationalised Renaissance planning, such as that which Pope Pius II (Piccolomini) could indulge when transforming his own home village of Corsignano in Tuscany into the miniature Renaissance city of Pienza, under the creative hand of Bernardo Rossellini.[27] Nor was there in Venice the absolutist political structure to allow individual power to be exercised in such a *tabula rasa* manner. It is undoubtedly the case that an enlightened absolutist Renaissance prince was far better positioned to encourage, indeed to execute, such ground-breaking works as Pienza than was the oligarchic gerontocracy that ruled the Most Serene Republic; such virtually unfettered power was invested not only in the papacy, but in the humanist court of the Gonzaga at Mantua, the Este in Ferrara and in Ludovico Sforza in Milan. In each of these cities, too, we can still see the large-scale results of the power of these rulers on the city's fabric, from the vast Sforza castle in Milan to the Addizione Erculea at Ferrara and the works of Alberti and Giulio Romano at Mantua. And while Venice was undoubtedly home to an impressive number of classicists, humanists and philosophers, theologians and intellectuals, all living in a city notable for its relative liberality of expression, substantial clouds of pragmatic caution, that perennial Venetian phenomenon, rolled like mist over the lagoon to obscure the execution of radical large-scale examples of urban Renaissance re-planning. There are no fifteenth-century Venetian equivalents of the profoundly influential Piazza della Santissima Annunziata in Florence (fig. 23),

22 Palazzetto Gussoni at San Lio: detail of façade, sometimes attributed to Pietro Lombardo

or of Ercole d'Este's impressive, rational extension to the city of Ferrara built after *circa* 1499 by Biagio Rossetti. When larger-scale *renovatio urbis* did take place in Venice it was well into the sixteenth century, and was epitomised by the practical, rational reclamations of the Zattere and the Fondamente Nuove, reaching its apogee in the long, phased programme of works by Jacopo Sansovino at San Marco.[28]

There were, however, a series of individual building projects – rather than urban works – of the late fifteenth century through which we can chart the development of Venice's own unique dialect of the early Renaissance. These developments have traditionally been identified as consisting of two broad stylistic approaches. The first is a highly decorative style that makes extensive use of rich detailing, particularly of refined relief decoration and by the application of 'veneers' of decorative marbles to planar wall surfaces. This approach was identified with the projects of the workshop of Pietro Lombardo and his sons (fig. 24), and although often simplistically identified as 'Lombard' also remains strongly indebted to Florence, as well as to Venice's own intrinsic or traditional 'orientalism'.[29] The second approach has been equally traditionally (and equally simplistically) identi-fied with Mauro Codussi, and could be characterised as the 'rational, structural' approach, rather than the more decorative approach of Lombardo. In this approach, the highest priority is given to the structural and architectonic framework.

If we glance at one example, however, the façade of San Michele (fig. 26), we can quickly identify the weaknesses in such simplifications. San Michele was in many ways revolutionary for Venice; but it retains much that is traditional in its relationships of solids and voids, in its tripartite form. Its façade can equally be read as a fairly radical re-evaluation of the traditional Venetian Gothic church façade (fig. 28) as it can as a truly new, revolutionary work. Its interior is axial and basilical, while the language of its internal detailing – although some elements are highly inventive and eclectic – is also in many ways Florentine, classical, simple and refined. Codussi's later interiors of Santa Maria Formosa (fig. 29) and San Giovanni Grisostomo again evince a refined discipline of detailing that make these churches members of the same extended family as, for example, Filippo Brunelleschi's Florentine works (the Pazzi chapel) (fig. 27), and of Sangallo's sacristy at Santo Spirito in Florence and Santa Maria delle Carceri in Prato.

23   Piazza della Santissima Annunziata, Florence, with the homonymous church in the centre, and Brunelleschi's Ospedale degli Innocenti on the right, begun in 1426. In the centre is Giambologna's equestrian statue of Ferdinando I, 1601–8

24   Santa Maria dei Miracoli: detail of exterior, by Pietro Lombardo, begun 1481, completed *circa* 1489

The imprecision and serious limitations of these two traditional stylistic groupings – 'Codussian' and 'Lombard' – can be seen at San Giobbe (fig. 25), where Lombardo himself built a refined west portal as well as a 'Florentine' cupola (complete with roundels in the pendentives) that seems more Codussian than 'Lombard'; and at Codussi's Palazzo Loredan (later Vendramin Calergi) (fig. 30), whose imposing, monumental façade is neither 'Lombard' nor Florentine, but is the most purely 'Roman' Renaissance work yet seen in Venice. Both masters worked in succession at the Scuola Grande di San Marco, and to this day it remains unclear precisely where Lombardo's original design ends and where Codussi took over to complete the remainder.[30]

The point of citing such familiar exemplars as these is simply to emphasise the complex, elusive character of much Venetian work of the early Renaissance, subject as it was to influences from several sources, as well as the powerful continuum of the native stylistic 'heritage'. The strength and vigour of this indigenous tradition was only slowly modified by these external influences, sometimes from this direction, sometimes from that. Above all, we can see the results in the way in which the architecture of Venice from around 1450 to 1500 deals with the elements of colour and of light, those two vital immaterial elements in the art of architecture; elements that in Venice are at least as important as the physical weight and form of the materials themselves.

Organisations: The Organs of Government and its Executive Agencies

Of all the institutional patrons responsible for the transformation of Venice in the fifteenth century, the Republic itself was – despite its gerontocratic, oligarchic nature – the most influential. Although numerous members of the patriciate transformed the banks of the Canalazzo with fine new *palazzi*, they were, of course, all acting individually, their primary motivation (other than housing themselves in an appropriate manner) being the glorification of their own particular clan, and the maximisation of long-term investment in valuable Venetian real estate.

25   San Giobbe: west portal, by Pietro Lombardo, *circa* 1470

facing page (above) 26   San Michele in Isola: façade to the lagoon, with the Miani chapel on the left. The church was begun in 1469 by Codussi, the Miani chapel built by Guglielmo de' Grigi in the years 1528–35

facing page (below) 27   The Pazzi chapel at Santa Croce, Florence, by Filippo Brunelleschi, begun in 1442

28 San Giovanni in Bragora: façade to the *campo, circa* 1475. Almost exactly contemporary with San Michele, Bragora remains typically late Gothic in style

29 Santa Maria Formosa: detail of interior, by Mauro Codussi, begun in 1491, completed *circa* 1504

30 Palazzo Loredan (later Vendramin Calergi): detail of façade, by Mauro Codussi, begun in 1502, completed *circa* 1508–9

Similarly, the monastic houses' decades-long programmes of rebuilding were based on their own physical and spiritual needs, but often invigorated by conscious rivalries between them, particularly between the two orders of mendicant friars, the Franciscans and Dominicans, whose great temples still loom today over their respective halves of the city, kept at a diplomatic distance by the original donation of their sites by the Republic.[31]

And in a similar manner again, the ambitious rebuilding programmes of the Scuole Grandi were fuelled by a somewhat unstable mixture of piety, practical necessity and self-glorification, together with notorious rivalries between them, which became considerably more overt, and even vituperative, than those between the monastic houses.[32]

Only the Republic itself was able to rise above such factional considerations and special interests, and in its role as *fidei defensor*, champion of the winged lion of St Mark, was in the strongest position of all to develop building programmes based on a universal common cause, the *res publica*. Throughout the century, though, this practical patronage waxed and waned considerably, principally for the reasons sketched out above; foreign wars, in particular, imposed a great strain on the exchequer, as did economic crises such as that of 1492. Major building projects were necessary on several occasions as a result of fires, notably those at the Palazzo Ducale and at Rialto, rather than as elements in a predetermined programme of urban renewal; but even in urgent cases such as these, progress was frequently affected, and sometimes brought to a halt entirely, by fiscal stresses on the Republic's exchequer.

On the practical level, there were two principal channels or agencies through which Republican desires and images could be transformed into brick and stone. Before turning to them, it may be helpful to identify the principal elements in the governance of the Republic, and their respective roles in the patronage process.

The doge himself stood at the apex of the pyramid of power (fig. 31). Elected by a complex series of ballots of the Maggior Consiglio, he reigned for life and was the physical representation of the Most Serene Republic of Mark the Evangelist. In addition to his many symbolic and ceremonial roles, the doge presided over sessions of all senior organs of state: the Serenissima Signoria, the Senate (Pregadi), the Maggior Consiglio and the Consiglio dei Dieci. In 1493 Marin Sanudo, the famous diarist, defined his responsibilities in this manner:

The Dose di Veniesia [*sic*], also known as the Prince, is the highest office that our Republic can bestow on its most meritorious gentleman . . . [after his election, in San Marco] the Prince speaks certain words promising to dispense justice objectively, to maintain the Republic at peace and the city in abundance . . . He has a remarkable breadth of jurisdiction, but also heavy responsibilities, as does our present Serene Prince [Agostin Barbarigo] . . . In the mornings he chairs the Collegio and after lunch either the Council of Ten or the Council of the Pregadi, or takes a public audience; on feast days (Sundays) [he chairs] the Gran Conseio [*sic*], so that over the whole year rare are the days when he can rest . . .'[33]

All these bodies were concerned with government at its highest level, and naturally had many matters to deal with that were of far greater political significance than the commissioning of building works. Nevertheless, as we will see, the doge sometimes played an important, direct role in the development of the 'new Rome' during the fifteenth century.

The doge and Serenissima Signoria formed the highest level of government, collectively forming an inner cabinet.[34] The Signoria originally consisted of the doge, his six ducal councillors and the three Capi della Quarantia, ten men in all. Between 1400 and 1430 the addition of three further groups – the Savii Grandi, the Savii ai Ordini and the Savii alla Terraferma – created the body known as the Pien Collegio, or 'full cabinet', with twenty-six members. The Pien Collegio dealt with many matters of state; they also debated reports from the Provveditori al Sal (see below) and the Patroni all'Arsenale.

During the fifteenth century the Signoria seems to have played only a minor role in commissioning state building works, although it did become directly involved with the new Torre dell'Orologio in the 1490s, and instructed works to the hall of the Maggior Consiglio. Apart from the doge himself, members of the Signoria and Pien Collegio served short terms of office, as was the case with most senior government posts. The well-established principle was to ensure frequent shifts of power and prevent the development of factions that might undermine republican stability. But one of its disadvantages was the fact that there was thereby never sufficient continuity of senior office-holders to guide or influence a major construction project from inception to completion, with the concomitant consistency of aims and intentions. We find many examples where this discontinuity became a severe handicap.

The Senate was the chief deliberative and legislative body of the Republic,[35] its name consciously borrowed from ancient Rome, although it was often less formally referred to either as the Pregadi or, in Latin, *rogatis*, since its origin lay in the 'request' for members to attend and advise the Signoria. Elected by the Maggior Consiglio, the Senate originally contained sixty men, who held their posts for one year; it was enlarged to include the forty members of the Quarantia al Criminal, and was later further augmented by an additional sixty members, the Zonta or Aggiunta.

The Senate was 'steered' or directed by the Signoria, and debated all important matters of state, of foreign and domestic policy, as well as more local matters concerning the functioning, appearance and development of the capital. It was the most influential government body for the commissioning of major public works. The land of both nuclei of the city, Rialto and San Marco, was the property of the Republic itself; the Senate thus had ultimate responsibility for development policy in these two zones, for the maintenance of existing structures that stood on them, and, from time to time, for reconstruction.

If we examine the records of meetings of the Senate in the 1480s and 1490s, for example, we find directives for work to the quays at Rialto, where goods were unloaded and assessed for tax duties; for the excavation of the Grand Canal; and for repairs to shops, again at Rialto, which were leased by the state to individual traders. Throughout the 1490s the Senate was also closely involved with the construction of the Torre dell'Orologio, one of the most prominent works of urban improvement undertaken in this period. The Senate passed decrees (*terminazioni*) for such works, which were then executed under the supervision of the Provveditori al Sal, the Salt Commissioners, who were also instructed to fund the works. The Provveditori thus acted as the executive arm of the Senate, and, from time to time, of the Consiglio dei Dieci. After the disgraced Antonio Rizzo had fled his post as master at the Palazzo Ducale, for example, it was the Senate that appointed Pietro Lombardo to replace him, and this appointment was itself ratified by the Dieci, who in turn also decreed that, like Rizzo, he should be paid from the revenues of the Salt Fund.[36]

The Maggior Consiglio[37] was the stratum of bedrock on which all these other elements of the Venetian constitution rested (fig. 32). The Consiglio elected all the other upper organs of state, and represented, on a profoundly symbolic level, the essentially republican nature of the state. Its very large membership was one of the principal reasons for the reconstruction of the Molo

31 Detail of the portrait of Doge Francesco Foscari by Lazzaro Bastiani, 1480s

wing of the Palazzo Ducale after 1340, and the immense council hall has remained for centuries one of the most awe-inspiring sights in the city. In Sanudo's day, the total number of men eligible to attend was approximately 2,600, but he conceded that, although attendance was theoretically compulsory, the numbers actually attending the Sunday afternoon sessions were typically closer to 1,400–1,500. Some members were away on *viazij* (trading voyages) or on embassies; others held posts in the Republic's subject cities and territories; others, still, were too aged or infirm to attend. The council, however, rarely participated directly in decisions regarding major building works in the city, and most such decisions were made by the Senate or the Dieci.[38]

The Dieci stood immediately outside the familiar 'pyramid of power' but became a body of great importance and influence. The Ten were established in 1310 as a consequence of the Baiamonte Tiepolo conspiracy, with the initial responsibility of dealing with treason and crimes against the Republic. The Tiepolo uprising was led, not by common people, but by a group of noble clans, including members of the Querini and

32   The Palazzo Ducale: interior of the hall of the Maggior Consiglio; the fabric was constructed after 1340, but the interior was comprehensively remodelled after a fire in 1577

Badoer who plotted to overthrow the doge, Pietro Gradenigo, and establish a dynastic principality, like those elsewhere in Italy. It was one of very few government bodies to hold its own independent treasury or *cassa*. The Consiglio's powers were broadened significantly during the fifteenth and early sixteenth centuries, although state security remained at their heart. When in session the Ten were always augmented by the doge himself and his six ducal councillors, so that the bench in fact numbered seventeen. They held, or were given, responsibility for the rebuilding and maintaining of palaces and other buildings that were the property of the Republic, including (not surprisingly) the prisons. Usually, though, this responsibility was again, like that of the Senate, devolved at the practical level for implementation by the executive agency of the Provveditori al Sal.

During the fifteenth century the Ten passed a number of important decrees regarding construction activity, most of them with the addition of a further Zonta of fifteen to twenty members. The principal structure over which the Dieci exerted direct control over staffing, labour and expenditure was the Palazzo Ducale itself, particularly the works that were necessary after the fire of 1483. Not only did they issue regular decrees regarding capital expenditure, and stipulate the sources from which this capital was to be raised, but they also decided on appointments and salary levels for the masters working at the palace, including Antonio Rizzo, superintendent for the new east wing, as well as the painters Giovanni Bellini and Alvise Vivarini, who decorated the hall of the Maggior Consiglio in the early 1490s.

Among the Dieci's other responsibilities was the Rialto bridge, which required frequent repair and maintenance; and in 1505 they decreed the rapid and total reconstruction of the Fondaco dei Tedeschi after its destruction by fire in that year. The primary role of the Ten in these and other cases was in passing the initial decree and in voting funds; executive direction was delegated to the Provveditori al Sal.

THE PROCURATORS OF SAN MARCO[39]

It is strictly inaccurate to classify the august figures of the Procurators of San Marco as a government body or agency; they were, among the many institutions of the Republic, *sui generis*, unique in both status and function. They also played an important role in the commissioning of building works. The Procurators were second only to the doge himself in terms of protocol, and the only other noble posts in which office was held for life. This fact alone thus gave them an almost unique continuity, stability and influence by comparison with all other senior state appointees.

The date of the foundation of the office cannot be established with precision; Francesco Sansovino cited Andrea Dandolo's claim that the Procuracy was established by Doge Domenico Contarini in 1042.[40] The origin of the office lay in the necessity to appoint a senior nobleman to take responsibility for the shrine of St Mark, to ensure the upkeep of the basilica, to supervise any necessary building works, to maintain security and to administer its considerable funds. The Procurators thus had a direct involvement in the building process from their inception (fig. 33).

Although there was originally just a single Procurator, after Doge Sebastiano Ziani (d. 1178) had left considerable property to the Republic, and with the steadily increasing size and wealth of the city, Doge Giacomo Tiepolo created a second post in the 1240s, followed by a third in 1259. These three Procurators were given distinct jurisdictions; the original Procurator, now known as *de supra*, retained his responsibilities for San Marco and the state properties around the Piazza. But the other two, known as Procurators *de citra* and *de ultra*, were respectively responsible for the administration of wills, bequests and estates commissions (*commessarie*) respectively on 'this' and 'that' side of the Grand Canal, relative to San Marco. Their numbers, however, increased further. In 1319, under Doge Giovanni Soranzo, they were doubled to six, three pairs for each of the above functions; finally, in 1442, with Doge Francesco Foscari, they were increased to three groups of three, a number that remained constant into the following century (fig. 34).

33 Detail of the main portal of San Marco; the Procurators *de supra* were responsible for the maintenance of the state chapel and all the other buildings on the Piazza

The title of Procurator carried immense prestige, but no direct remuneration. Nevertheless, it came to be perceived as a reflection of such statesmanlike responsibility that it was a natural stepping-stone towards the throne of St Mark; most doges over the course of the fifteenth century had been Procurators before receiving the ducal *corno*.

The three Procurators *de supra* were identified by Sanudo in 1493 as 'Procuratori della chieisia [*sic*] di San Marco', since the church itself remained at the heart of their responsibilities. Their broader responsibility for the fabric of all of the structures around the Piazza, however, had led to an early perception of the need to employ a permanent salaried surveyor of these properties, and he was known as a *protomaestro*, 'chief surveyor', usually abbreviated to *proto*. The first name that has survived seems to be that of Antonio Zelega, who held the post until 1470, when he was replaced by the equally obscure Bartolomeo Gonella, who died in 1505. Gonella seems in turn to have been replaced by Pietro Bon, although until recently there was considerable confusion over the roles and responsibilities (and even the identities) of two Bon, Pietro and Bartolomeo, the Bergamasco. On 7 April 1529, however, the Procurators made the most significant appointment in their history by entrusting the office to Jacopo Sansovino, recently arrived from Rome. He retained the post until his death forty-one years later, by which time he had transformed the appearance of both the Piazza and Piazzetta of San Marco.[41]

34   The Procuratie Vecchie: detail of part of the façade, *circa* 1514–19, probably by Bartolomeo Bon, the Bergamasco

The duties of the *proto de supra*, though, were many and varied, some mundane in the extreme. They ranged from regular surveys and reports on the conditions of the buildings in his charge to occasional major new works of architecture. The Procurators administered funds from a variety of sources, not only from offerings at the shrine, but, more prosaically, from rental income from the shops that occupied the ground floors of the buildings on the Piazza (as they still do today), from taverns and hostelries in the Piazzetta, and stalls in the San Marco meat market. Their more exalted – though rather less clearly defined – responsibilities remained 'to secure and enhance the beauty of the Piazza and the setting and fabric of the shrine of San Marco by their own efforts'.

The other two groups of Procurators had different responsibilities; in one of their most significant roles, as the administrators of estates and bequests, they played a major part in developing the physical fabric of the city, and were directly responsible for a number of construction projects over the course of the century.

THE PROVVEDITORI AL SAL: PALACES FROM SALT

The Salt Commissioners[42] were high-ranking members of the nobility, the roots of whose office began in the thirteenth century, in the administration of the lagunar salt-pans. Salt production had been a major source of revenue for the early Republic, but, over a long period, the Provveditori's duties had gradually expanded to embrace many other responsibilities. They eventually became a kind of executive agency for government-sponsored construction projects, many of which still continued to be funded from salt revenues.

As an indirect result of their responsibilities for the salt-beds, the Provveditori gradually took over the costs of the maintenance of the lagoon and its sea defences, as well as the salt-beds themselves, which from time to time required extensive works of repair. Although income from the salt tax was used to fund many public works, the Provveditori remained a purely executive body, with no powers of their own to raise taxes or to instigate significant new building works. Such initiatives remained the prerogative of the Senate and the Dieci.

Salt production remained a state monopoly. The lagoon around the town of Chioggia remained the chief centre of production, and although its output had slowly declined, the eight *fondamenti* (salt-pans) that survived into the sixteenth century still employed 800 men and generated considerable revenue (fig. 35).[43]

As is the case with most of these government institutions, Sanudo gives us a useful summary of the roles and duties of the Provveditori: 'At present there are six Provveditori, although since 14 [87] . . . under our present Serene Prince [Agostin Barbarigo] a further two were added to the original four; their term of office is 16 months, and they are elected by the *bancha* in two stages'. Sanudo remarks that they were considered important, senior appointments, not least because of the large sums of money for which they were responsible; patricians could only be elected to one of these posts 'if they were at the very least members of the Pregadi'.

He goes on to explain:

One of them is deputed to San Marco where he records all the salt that arrives in the city; one is based at Rialto where he keeps the monthly accounts and registers; one is in charge of the salt warehouses; one goes every morning to the Collegio delle Biave [the grain commissioners], over which he [also] presides; and the last two are in charge of the buildings, both the Palazzo Ducale and those on the island of Rialto, since all of Rialto is under their control. These last are responsible for rents of shops, stalls, warehouses, and vaults on the island of Rialto, and on this account are responsible for large rents for San Marco, that is, for the income of San Marco [i.e., the Republic]. They also lease the public quays at Rialto.[44]

The Provveditori thus had executive responsibility for buildings in the two main poles of the city; like San Marco, the island of Rialto had come under government ownership from an early date, much of it from a bequest in 1097, while its markets had been under direct state control from an even earlier date.

The Provveditori employed a number of officials, reflecting the range of their responsibilities; they employed *soprastanti* (supervisors or surveyors) for the *lidi* and sea defences as far south as Chioggia, as well as craftsmen for construction and maintenance works. The duties of the Provveditori for directly funding works at San Marco were already in place prior to 1422, when the decision was taken to rebuild the

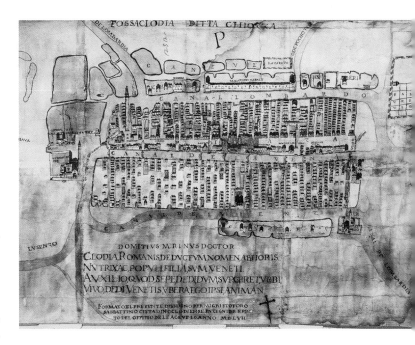

35 Detail of Cristoforo Sabbadino's view of Chioggia, dated 1557. At the top in the centre is the salt warehouse, while on the far right is the salt-pan known as Codevigo

Piazzetta wing of the Palazzo Ducale. The work was to be supervised by the two Procurators of San Marco *de supra*, but funding was provided by the Salt Commissioners. And by 1438, when the Porta della Carta was commissioned, the Provveditori were cited in the contract with Bartolomeo Bon as the employing party, since their own revenues directly funded the works; the overall management of the project as a whole, though, remained the responsibility of the Procurators of San Marco. The Provveditori's direct involvement at the palace continued until 1533, when new posts were created, the Provveditori sopra la fabbrica dil Palazzo.[45]

As Sanudo notes, the Provveditori originally numbered four, but were increased to six in 1487, by decree of the Maggior Consiglio. This was a direct reflection of the increasing amount of work for which they were responsible, and, more specifically, of the need to rebuild the *rio* wing of the Palazzo Ducale, badly damaged by fire in September 1483. It is revealing to read that 500 ducats per month were to be diverted out of the regular budget of 900 ducats allocated to the repair of the sea defences, to fund the rebuilding works directly. The regular annual budget for these sea defences had thus been around 10,000 ducats (more than 60,000 lire), a reflection of the scale of such routine maintenance. Despite its slow decline, even at the end of the century salt tax income still exceeded 100,000 ducats annually, nearly 10 per cent of all of the Republic's revenues.[46]

Among a miscellany of other responsibilities that the Provveditori accumulated was that for the Lazzaretto Vecchio (the quarantine islet); the customs house; the house of the Consiglio dei Dieci on the Lido (used for the Sposalizio festivities on Ascension Day); and a small group of churches that traditionally came under the direct patronage of the doge: San Pietro di Castello, the monastic islet of San Servolo, the Eremiti, as well as the new votive church of Santa Maria dei Miracoli, to which were to be added, in a later period, those of the Redentore and Santa Maria della Salute. From time to time, all of these properties required restoration and maintenance.[47] A much larger drain on funds was the rebuilding of the Fondaco dei Tedeschi after 1505, and on 17 June 1506 the Dieci decreed that 600 ducats per month (instead of the previous 300) should thenceforth be allocated from the Provveditori's revenues towards the rapid completion of this important project.

Like the Procurators, the Provveditori also appointed a *protomaestro* or *proto*, a salaried official responsible for supervising building operations on the properties under their jurisdiction. One of the first *proti* whose name has survived seems to have been Zuan Davanzo, a fairly obscure civil servant who left little of architectural importance. Davanzo held the post until 1470, when he was replaced by Domenico (Meneghin) Bianco, about whom we know little more. In 1473 Meneghin in turn was replaced by Nicolò Pain, who held the post for nearly twenty years, until he, too, was succeeded by the better known Bartolomeo Bon, the Bergamasco. During the latter part of his period in office, Pain was paid an annual salary of 90 ducats, an increase over his earlier income, and this rise was approved by the Provveditori in June 1498, when Pain was also recorded as keeping just one apprentice on a regular basis. He was highly regarded by his employers, since he was given his rise as a result of 'the great efforts that he puts into the execution of his duties'. It was a reasonably good salary, and he was also almost certainly given other benefits, such as free accommodation.[48]

During the latter part of the century, there was considerable construction activity at the Palazzo Ducale, where Antonio Rizzo had effectively worked as a kind of 'sub-*proto*' since 1468. His formal status, though, was not confirmed until 1484, shortly after the serious fire on 14 September 1483. As a result of urgent necessity, therefore, Rizzo was given a distinctly new title, that of *proto dil palazzo*, responsible exclusively for the rebuilding of the east wing, but with no remit beyond the palace walls, where the Provveditori's own *proto* retained

his role. Later, in 1499, Rizzo was both *in absentia* and in disgrace, and was replaced by Pietro Lombardo; later still, in the sixteenth century, the role of *proto dil palazzo* was to be filled by other outstanding masters, such as Scarpagnino and Antonio da Ponte.[49]

In the 1480s and 1490s the Provveditori were instructed to fund a wide variety of building works, and their orders came from all three of the highest levels of the Republic's government, most frequently from the Dieci, but also from the Senate and occasionally from the Signoria. The Provveditori were also empowered to issue their own decrees (*terminazioni*), although the precise extent of these powers is unclear. In addition to the extensive sums derived from the salt tax (which were central government funds), they also had access to a *cassa piccola*, a minor fund, which was used to pay for lesser works of repair and maintenance, without direction by the Senate or Signoria.

AGENCIES OF DEVELOPMENT CONTROL: PIOVEGO, PROVVEDITORI DI COMUN, GIUSTIZIA VECCHIA, MAGISTRATO ALLE ACQUE

General building activity in the city was controlled and monitored by several agencies. Although the Republic itself was a major landowner and developer, the remainder of the city's land and fabric was owned by a large number of different proprietors, chief among them the great noble clans and the many monastic houses.

All potential developers were subject to considerable restrictions on their building activities, some of which were covered by the ancient office of the Piovego.[50] The forerunners of this office had been established in the thirteenth century, with various responsibilities concerned with the maintenance and repair of streets, quays, canals and bridges, but in 1282 and 1290 these responsibilities were codified into statute. Sanudo summarised their posts thus:

> [The Zudesi – Giudici –] are three in number, with a term of office of 16 months, and they are men at least 25 years old; they meet in the mornings, on Mondays, Wednesdays and Fridays, in the hall of the Piovego, or that also known as the Sala dei Signori di Notte [in the south wing of the Palazzo Ducale] . . . in the afternoons they meet at Rialto . . .

The role that concerns us here is their control over construction projects; Sanudo continues:

> They control the public streets so that no person is allowed to impede the public right of way, and they

have the authority to demolish such infringements, and ensure that the Comune retains the land free of buildings, and they set the conditions when one wishes to build a house. They also have custody over the excavation of canals, and keep records of those debtors who have responsibility for paying for excavations, that is, those who have houses in the relevant *contrada*, and must pay at the appropriate rate.

When a landowner applied for permission to construct or rebuild a structure, the Piovego often sent surveyors to the site to establish or confirm building lines, to ensure there were no encroachments on the public street.

The role of the Provveditori di Comun complemented that of the Piovego.[51] They had been established (again according to Sanudo) in the reign of Doge Pietro Tradonico (836–64), one of the almost mythical early doges, although the earliest surviving document dates from 1272, and in this identifiable form they had probably been re-established a couple of decades earlier. Their field of responsibilities embraced commerce and navigation, but they also regulated and supervised many metropolitan activities, including fire-fighting, the maintenance of public wells, ferries, postal services, and the activities of the minor *scuole* or devotional confraternities. They numbered three magistrates, whose offices were at Rialto, and, like most such posts, had a term of duty of sixteen months.

Writing in 1493, Sanudo also recorded that 'they have great authority over matters of the *comune*, being responsible for the paving of streets, because all of the streets of Venice are paved with stone, like the Piazza of San Marco.' Sanudo exaggerates considerably here, perhaps reflecting an over-enthusiastic *campanilismo*, and his claim is not supported by de' Barbari. The Piazza itself was in fact paved with brick, with stone detailing; of the other squares or *campi*, however, some were also paved with brick, but many lesser streets were not yet paved at all.

He continues: 'they also build and maintain the bridges – now also of stone – which were originally built of timber'. The Provveditori also acquired several other miscellaneous responsibilities (rather as did several other agencies), among which was the recording of claims of foreigners living in Venice who wished to become citizens after the requisite period of residence.

The Giustizia Vecchia[52] was another ancient magistracy, established in the reign of Sebastiano Ziani, in 1173. Its responsibilities covered much trading activity, including weights and measures, and setting fair prices for the sale of goods. Sanudo again: 'they set the price of fish and fruit and other foodstuffs that are sold in the city; and establish prices for timber; they also have jurisdiction over almost all of the Arti of Venice'. This last role included superintending the activities of all the building guilds, masons and carpenters. All guilds had formally to register their statutes (*mariegole*) with the Giustizia, which thereafter had responsibility for ensuring that these statutes were adhered to; the magistrates inspected workshops and could levy fines for infringements. The Giustizia also levied a *dazio* or duty on timber brought into the city for the construction industry.

The Magistrato alle Acque[53] was the final body with some involvement in the physical fabric of the city and its surroundings. As the name indicates, the Savii (sages or wise men) of the Magistracy were responsible for monitoring and maintaining the lagoon and its navigable channels. There were again three Savii, again based at Rialto, with a period of office of two years. (Their office is a remarkable example of administrative continuity: it still functions today, still based at Rialto, and still with its ancient responsibilities for the lagoon, although nowadays it forms a specialist section of the national Environment Ministry.)

Although the posts of the Savii were unpaid, their importance was considerable, and they had the right to sit at sessions of the Senate, a reflection of the vital strategic role of the lagoons, channels and sea defences; much of their funding came from revenues raised by the Provveditori al Sal. Various other posts within the Magistracy were consolidated in 1502 by the Dieci, and four years later the 'umbrella' agency of the Collegio alle Acque was formally established, with the power to issue laws and decrees over the heads of several older offices in the department.

Chapter Two

REPUBLICAN RESPONSIBILITIES AND
RENAISSANCE *RENOVATIO URBIS*

IN THE FOLLOWING PAGES TWO ASPECTS of the responsibility of the Republic towards the fabric of the city are discussed. The first part focuses on the district of Rialto, the heart of Venice's banking and mercantile activities. The Republic itself was the landowner of Rialto and thus had total control, at least in theory, over its development; a discussion of this vital urban nucleus gives useful insights not only into the manner in which this control was exercised, but also into its practical limitations. The second part describes some of the activities of the Procurators of San Marco, something of a miscellany of works. The Procurators accumulated responsibility for a wide variety of property in all parts of the city, and in their capacity as estates commissioners were important building patrons during the fifteenth century.

Pro bono comunis: *Public Works and the Fabric of the City*

The city's complex fabric required regular and frequent maintenance by the agencies of the Republic. On a practical level the principal bodies were the Provveditori di Comun and the Piovego. But the primary roles of these agencies were essentially reactive; they were concerned with the enforcement of bye-laws and with maintenance rather than with the instigation of new initiatives. Fifteenth-century records, however, also reveal a second, distinctly proactive attitude on the part of the Republic, which was concerned with initiation and improvement, with Renaissance *renovatio urbis*: works were commissioned with the express purpose of improving the city's fabric for reasons of prestige, physical convenience or from a simple desire to enhance the Republic's revenues; frequently, no doubt, from a mixture of all three motives.

The responsibility of the Republic for the city's fabric, though, was by no means unlimited. It was responsible for the waterways, for bridges and street surfaces, as well as the small number of licensed public quays. But the maintenance of other quays traditionally fell upon those who would derive benefit from them, that is, the owners of the properties that bordered them. The extreme complexity of administering this arrangement, however, later resulted in a simplified collective approach. For example, the dredging of the Grand Canal in 1408 was to be funded by the entire citizenry on the basis of an *estimo* of their relative wealth, and based on the quite reasonable philosophy that the Canalazzo was a facility that benefited the entire population.

As we might expect, the process of urban improvement was to be long, piecemeal and fragmented, ranging in its scope from the straightening of the course of the Mercerie between 1272 and 1340 to attempts to beautify the banks of the Grand Canal by two measures, in 1433 and 1462. The first required the removal of small private boatyards (*squeri*) from its banks, while the latter required stonemasons' yards to be removed a minimum of 8 *passi* (40 feet or 13.88 m) from the edge of the Canal.[1]

There were two principal locations in the city where *renovatio urbis* was to be concentrated in the fifteenth century: Rialto (fig. 37) and San Marco. Although the former was not imbued with the spiritual dignity of the Piazza, as the 'machine' for the generation of wealth through trade, Rialto was even more vital to the prosperity of the Serenissima than was San Marco. Without the sacks of pepper and bolts of silk, the banks and insurance offices, there could be no pageants and processions, no lavish banquets for foreign princes, no ambitious programmes of public works. Hence the Republic's almost obsessive concern with the condition of Rialto and its efficient organisation.[2]

The market district was a complex, densely developed quarter of the city, with many diverse functions concentrated in an extremely small area. These functions embraced the entire social spectrum of the city, from the wealthiest patrician merchants and bankers to the humblest itinerant vendors and prostitutes, as well as wholesale markets for bulk commodities and retail

37   Detail from Jacopo de' Barbari's woodcut of 1500. Rialto: showing the timber bridge and (immediately behind it, to the left) the nobles' loggia. Left again is the church of San Giacometto and the '*piazza*'. Behind the bridge to the right is the old Fondaco dei Tedeschi ('fontico dalamanij'), burnt to the ground in 1505 and replaced by the present Fondaco

markets for foodstuffs: fish, meat, fruit and vegetables; for craftsmen selling rope and cords, leatherware, fabrics of every conceivable kind, pots, pans and utensils, and spices and oriental luxuries. Nearly all were concentrated on one small islet measuring barely 300 metres in both directions; the congestion was almost indescribable.

As a general rule, the more *signorile* activities, that is, the stalls of the bankers, money-changers and insurance offices, and the dealers in luxury goods, were located closer to the foot of the bridge and the market church of San Giacometto. The loggia at the bridge foot (now lost) was in theory reserved for the nobility, although in practice it was frequently encroached upon, and at times overwhelmed by the quotidian activities of the market traders. As far back as 1280 the Signoria had attempted to keep the raucous stallholders at arm's length from these masters of international finance, and the legislation was repeated by the Maggior Consiglio in 1332, a sure sign that the first attempt had either failed or proved impossible to enforce.[3]

The long series of attempts to improve the district really began in 1394, with the commissioning of a clock, at the considerable cost of 140 ducats, and the psychological and practical importance of which was considerable. A degree of order and discipline was now to descend on the markets and banks as everyone at Rialto, regardless of status, now had their professional lives measured and regulated for the first time.[4]

Only a few months later, on 17 December 1394, it was decided to pave the Piazza at Rialto (figs 38, 39). The use of the term *piazza* in contemporary records is significant: the only other *piazza* in Venice was that at San Marco, all the other city squares being merely *campi*. That of San Marco was already paved, and in the perception of the government there was little difference in the prestige of the two locations. Shortly afterwards again, a new loggia was built next to San Giacometto, since the existing one had proved inadequate to house the numbers that gathered here to seek shelter, exchange news and information. Completed in 1397, the loggia was 'assai bella e di grande ornamento' in the records of the Maggior Consiglio.[5]

The year 1396 saw the reconstruction of both the fish and fruit markets in stone instead of timber, a work that not only enhanced the dignity of the district but also reduced future maintenance costs and lowered the risk of fire.[6] Four years later again, in 1400, the campanile of San Giovanni Elemosinario was rebuilt, and also provided with a new clock; in the year of its completion, 1408, the *casaria*, the dairy produce market, was

The Senate, however, was divided. The new loggia was at first rejected on the grounds of cost, although Bon returned with a more modest proposal, suggesting that a smaller one could be built using demolition material from the Palazzo Ducale; this would reduce expenditure to 600 ducats. This thrifty proposal was approved, and although costs inevitably increased in construction, the project could not be halted, it was stated in the Senate, without damaging 'the honour of the State, and the beauty of the district of Rialto, and of the entire city'.[8]

Such sentiments were to be a familiar theme for the rest of the century; fiscal prudence and the need to fund substantial and ever more 'high-profile' public works elsewhere (above all, at the Palazzo Ducale) meant that improvements at Rialto proceeded in a long series of fits and starts, despite the evident appreciation of its importance at San Marco.

By the latter part of the century a long series of measures indicates the Republic's new-found determination to bring further order to this congested district. One of the many fundamental difficulties in maintaining dignity here, though, was the extremely small size of the square of San Giacometto, around which the whole of Rialto revolved. Even Sanudo conceded that it was 'una piazzetta non molto grande', and it was, in truth, far too modest for the great symbolic

38 The Campo San Giacometto, the heart of Rialto, from the colonnade of the Banco Giro. The church clock was installed in 1394

39 Detail of the sixteenth-century *gobbo* ('hunchback') in the Campo San Giacometto, the public proclamation stone of the Republic

also restored. All these works evince the Republic's desire actively to improve the environment at Rialto.

A little later again, attention turned to the highly congested area at the bridgehead. In theory, the quay next to the bridge, the Erbaria (fig. 40), was reserved for the use of ferry boats and for produce to be unloaded for the retail markets; but vessels from the Riva del Vin, on the other side of the bridgehead, had taken over the other quay as well, mooring next to the nobles' loggia. By the 1420s the loggia had been more or less abandoned to the lower – or lower-most – orders of the district. In 1424 Scipione Bon, the government's *proto*, attempted to restore and 'clean up' the area; he proposed demolishing the timber loggia, rebuilding it on a larger scale, in brick, with a commodious approach by steps from the quayside. The construction works themselves would also hopefully sweep away the undesirable elements.[7]

40   The Erberia beyond the colonnades linking the Fabbriche Vecchie (right) with Sansovino's Fabbriche Nuove, begun in 1554

importance that it had to bear, to say nothing of its many practical functions: banking, insurance, public proclamations, religious processions, as well as the market itself.

Legislation similar to that of 1332 was enacted in 1459, the intention again being to separate international mercantile activities from the daily markets. In a particularly long-lasting decision, the fish market (fig. 41) was relocated to a new site, at the north-western end of the island, where it remains today, so that the bridgehead and the Piazza were now exclusively occupied by *signorile* activities.[9] A few years later a new programme of paving was begun, and in 1471 the fish market quay was broadened by reclamation from the Grand Canal, *pro bono comunis*, that is, for the benefit of the city, as the record relates. In 1491 a new covered market was built for the fishmongers, thus completing this stage of Rialto's improvement and rationalisation. Nevertheless, much of the congestion remained.

In 1487 the Republic proposed a new initiative. It was begun by a debate in the Senate in September, the scope of which was initially very broad. Although fully aware of 'the many things that beautify our city, chiefly its buildings', the Senate was deeply concerned over the streets and quays, the essential veins and arteries of the city. Some of the latter were at the point of collapse, 'giving rise to great damage and inconvenience to the inhabitants'; if action were not taken promptly, it would not be possible to circulate either by land or water. The Provveditori di Comun were to be given a new respon-

sibility; already dealing with bridges, they would now also take control over quays and pavements.[10] Funding was to be raised in two ways; the owners of properties on the quays were to be responsible for one quarter of the costs of upkeep and repair, while the remaining three-quarters were to be derived from a levy on the fines that the various magistrates were empowered to impose on misdemeanours, based on a sliding scale.

The difficulties at Rialto, though, remained formidable. Only a month or so after the Senate's decree on the quays, on 20 October 1487 the doge, Agostin Barbarigo, and his ducal councillors debated with the entire Collegio what was to be done. The perceived civic importance of the island is emphasised by the first words of the record of their debate: 'since Rialto is one of the noblest places in our city'.[11] Despite the inevitable noise, dirt and odours of the daily markets, therefore, the principal role of Rialto in the minds of the Signoria remained that of a civic hub, a place of pride and dignity, a role that was certainly failing to be fulfilled.

It was resolved once again to improve the physical environment: two days later the Provveditori al Sal issued a decree that all streets must be cleared of itinerant, unlicensed traders, who had yet again invaded the loggia, 'a place reserved for gentlemen and merchants'. By December firmer measures were already found to be necessary. On 24 December the Signoria decreed (rather unseasonably) that all the stalls between the loggia and the quays 'where vegetable produce from Chioggia is sold' were to be cleared away. The area was now to be 'kept clean and open, free from any activity

41   The Rialto fish market, relocated on its present site in 1459

and impediment'.[12] Four days later, the Pregadi confirmed that the old fish market, the fabric market (tellaria) and even some of the bankers' benches were all to be cleared away 'so that the end of the island of Rialto shall be open, and so that gentlemen merchants and other citizens as well as foreigners may be free to embark and disembark from their boats to unload merchandise, for the benefit of the city'.[13]

Still further measures were introduced on 6 February 1489, again 'for the improvement and beautification of the city', but requiring yet more demolitions and clearances. Many stalls and shops were to be taken down, including not only humble traders' stalls but a shop leased by the doge himself, Agostin Barbarigo. It is not too surprising, however, to learn that he was to be recompensed with a new site in replacement, 'near the ferry [to Santa Sofia], at present held by one Todaro'; the Most Serene Prince would henceforth pay 10 ducats per year rent to the Provveditori.[14]

The state flour warehouse was one of many central facilities located at Rialto; it stood at the far end of the Riva del Vin, near San Silvestro. The *fontego* had been built in the thirteenth century, and was a substantial structure. It had a short façade onto the Grand Canal, with a central arch, and a long flank down the *rio* at the side (the canal was later reclaimed). The warehouse contained thirty stalls or concessions, most of them managed by private citizens, and the leases for which were usually put up at public auction. Although retail prices were regulated, the possession of a *fontegaria* (concession) was generally held to be a sound, reliable way to obtain a reasonable income. On occasion, these concessions were awarded by the Republic (usually for a defined period) to particularly deserving servants of the state, on request to the Consiglio dei Dieci.[15]

In October 1492 the Provveditori began a major restoration of the *fontego*; the quay along the side canal was rebuilt, and new columns and stone vaults were necessary to the stalls themselves, as were the floors to the offices of the three nobles who administered the *fontego*, the Ufficiali al Formento. Doors, stairways and balconies, too, were rebuilt. Despite this extensive and costly operation, however, in 1505 it was necessary for the Dieci to authorise a further 250 ducats on repairs.[16]

STREETS AND CANALS

One of the ways in which enhanced *civitas* could be achieved was in the paving of streets. In Venice this was an extremely protracted process, although the principle of its civilising effect was appreciated long before it was published by Alberti in his *De re aedificatoria*. By the

fifteenth century it was universally accepted that major new streets should be paved from the outset, although Alberti's own assumption that all the streets of a city should be 'handsomely paved and cleanly kept' was clearly something of a counsel of perfection where markets like Rialto were concerned.[17] Nevertheless, the site of the old fish market (near the loggia) was paved in 1471, as was the new fish market in 1511; at the same time the latter was furnished with twenty-five *stantie*, stalls or slabs of stone for the traders. The extent of the paving at Rialto is clearly recorded by de' Barbari in 1500, when it included the square of San Giacometto, but did not apparently yet extend into the surrounding streets and alleys.[18]

Elsewhere in Venice, too, the paving process was still patchy. At San Marco it was fairly extensive; according to Sansovino paving had begun under Doge Renier Zeno in the 1250s, and was completed by Antonio Venier in the 1380s or 1390s. By 1500 it extended along the Molo as far as the Ponte di Paglia, and in the other direction to the far end of the great grain warehouses. In all such cases, the paving consisted of bricks, generally laid in a herringbone pattern and divided into squares by strips of Istrian stone.

Paving was the responsibility of the Provveditori di Comun, but it was funded from a levy of 2 soldi per *sententia* on civil crimes, a revenue that must have allowed for only very limited progress. By the century's end, though, most of the city's main squares were paved, including those of San Zaccaria, the Frari, Santi Giovanni e Paolo and Sant'Angelo. Elsewhere, however, they were paved only in part, usually around the wellhead, such as those of Santa Maria Formosa (fig. 42) and Santi Apostoli. It is no surprise to record

42 Detail from Jacopo de' Barbari: Campo Santa Maria Formosa in 1500, with a small extent of paving around two of the wellheads

that most of the *campi* in the outlying districts (San Geremia, the Madonna dell'Orto) were not yet paved at all.[19]

The city's canals also required regular maintenance; they were all subject to silting and needed (but did not often have) regular re-excavation. Naturally enough, the condition of the Grand Canal was the highest priority; in 1490 the Pregadi decreed that 860 ducats were to be made available from the wine duty and from funds normally allocated for the repair of the sea littoral; it was said to have become impossible for the ducal Bucintoro (state barge) to be moored at the Molo because of silting. In case this was perceived to be a rather narrow interest, however, the Pregadi made it clear that cargo ships were also unable to unload at the Dogana (customs house) for the same reason, the works thus being essential in order that trade was not adversely affected.[20]

In most of the works sketched above, particularly at Rialto, the Signoria and the Dieci acted from a mixture of interrelated motives. Such measures were undertaken for reasons of practical necessity, to enable the financial and mercantile life-blood of the city to flow as smoothly as possible; but equally clear is the intention not simply to maintain or restore but actively to enhance the city's beauty and prestige. Something of the spirit of Renaissance *renovatio* is identifiable in nearly every case.

THE RIALTO BRIDGE

The sole span across the Grand Canal was itself the responsibility of the government, and although essential for the functioning of the markets and for communications throughout the city, was also a considerable liability, since it required repair or restoration on countless occasions.

By the fifteenth century, the ancient timber bridge (or, more accurately, the endless reconstructions of it) had become an essential part of the iconography of the city (fig. 43). Sanudo described it in 1493 as 'a great timber bridge, high and strong, and broad'. He later notes that 'it was built in its present form in 1458, with the shops on top, which obtain a high rent because of their excellent location – and this bridge is divisible in the centre with chains that can be raised, dividing Venice into two parts'. He was as well aware as the rest of the nobility of the costs of its repair, however, and, from time to time, its almost complete reconstruction. It had, in fact, been rebuilt in 1432 at a cost of precisely '2,332 ducats, 6 soldi, 4 grossi and 11 piccoli' as Sanudo himself records.[21]

43 Vettor Carpaccio: detail from *The Miracle of the Cross at Rialto*: part of the old timber bridge, as it appeared in 1494

The 'rebuilding' of 1458 to which Sanudo refers was itself a repair, but it was from that date that the shops on it were completed, with the specific intention of raising revenue towards its upkeep. The proposal had come from the Provveditori al Sal, supported by the Collegio, although when it was referred to the Senate the debate reveals an interesting divergence of opinion as to the merits of the proposal. Nearly half disagreed with it, arguing that not only would the proposed scheme remove the spacious 'balcony' in the centre, from which spectacles could be observed in the canal below, but also that the new shops would 'diminish the value of the shops in the Mercerie'.[22] In the end, a compromise was reached, which allowed for the retention of a 'loggia magna' in the centre; it was, in fact, a drawbridge, which could be opened for shipping. As was often the case, a balance had to be found between the desire to maximise revenue and the perception of enhanced *civitas*.[23]

Nevertheless, it was only forty years before another programme of repairs was necessary. By 1499 the shops were in poor condition, although by now they yielded around 1,800 ducats per year in rent, a substantial sum that rendered their restoration a priority.[24] By 1505 still further works were necessary, and on 15 January the Dieci approved the expenditure of 300–400 ducats, since the upper parts threatened collapse. As usual the work was funded by the Provveditori al Sal, who were required to maintain 'careful and accurate records of all expenses'.[25]

Throughout the fifteenth century, therefore, the bridge was restored, patched, repaired but essentially retained in its basic form: all of timber, with two ramps supported on a small forest of timber columns and piles, and with a drawbridge in the centre. However, this is not to say that the civic and symbolic importance of the bridge was not yet appreciated in the context of Renaissance *renovatio* (fig. 44). Morachiello has pointed out that Doge Cristoforo Moro, who was closely involved with architectural patronage at San Giobbe, left funds in his will (written in 1471) for a new bridge across the Cannaregio Canal, to adorn the city and to improve access to San Giobbe; significantly, and appropriately in his view, the bridge was to be all of stone, a permanent material 'che doveva perpetuare memorie'. It was to be more than eighty years after the repairs of 1505, however, that the daunting challenge of spanning the Canalazzo with a bridge all of stone was to be considered, and – eventually – its own new shops auctioned for rent.[26]

THE FONDACO DEI TEDESCHI

On 28 January 1505 the old Fondaco dei Tedeschi, the Germans' trading base in the city, was destroyed by fire. It had stood near the southern end of the Rialto bridge, and was a rather heterogeneous collection of structures, facing the Grand Canal and bounded down one side by the Rio del Fontego. Its reconstruction was a matter of some urgency for the Republic, since trade with Germany was a vital element of the economy. And indeed, first reactions were swift. As Sanudo records in his dairies, the Collegio decided within barely a week

44 Palazzo dei Camerlenghi (right), probably by Guglielmo de' Grigi, and the Fabbriche Vecchie (left), begun in 1514 by Scarpagnino

that the Fondaco should be rebuilt as quickly as possible: 'refar[lo] presto e bellissimo'.[27]

During the period from 4 February to 19 June 1505 preparatory works and the installation of new foundations were apparently already in hand, under the supervision of Giorgio Spavento. The man principally responsible for the execution of the works was Francesco de' Garzoni, the principal Provveditore al Sal, but Spavento was not the Provveditori's own *proto*, rather he was the salaried *proto* of the Procurators of San Marco. It seems likely that Spavento was employed in this initial phase simply because he was already a salaried government employee. He had a high reputation: Sanudo refers to him as a 'homo di grande inzegno',[28] and in 1500 he had already been appointed 'proto et inzegner' to the Ufficio alle Acque, partly as a result of the influence of Taddeo di Andrea Contarini, one of the Procurators of San Marco. As a 'persona de mazor intelligentia' with a good knowledge of hydraulics and engineering, he was thus probably felt to be an obvious choice for the urgent task of consolidating the site and reinforcing the canal embankments that surrounded the site on two sides. In 1504, in fact, a new post had been created, 'deputato alle fabriche di Rialto e San Marco', and Spavento was then confirmed as the *proto* to this office, in charge of the general maintenance of the government buildings at Rialto and San Marco. The decision was confirmed by the Consiglio dei Dieci and Zonta on 28 July 1505.[29]

Despite – or perhaps partly because of – the perceived urgency of the reconstruction, a number of eminent and highly influential Venetian patricians took a close interest in the development of the new proposals. They included Andrea Gritti, the future doge; Zaccaria Dolfin; Bernardo Bembo, sometime ambassador to Florence, and a leading humanist scholar; Francesco de' Garzoni; Marco da Molin, Procurator of San Marco *de citra*; Andrea Loredan, patron of Mauro Codussi at San Michele and at his own *palazzo* at San Marcuola; and Paolo Trevisan and Antonio Grimani, both of them Codussi's sponsors at Santa Maria Formosa.[30]

In February 1505 an initial 'design ideas' competition was launched for the new Fondaco. Among those known to have submitted proposals were Scarpagnino, Spavento, Fra Giocondo and a certain Gerolamo Tedesco. A possible proposal by Pietro Lombardo is not supported by contemporary documentation, and is in fact only first recorded by Tommaso Temanza in 1778. A great deal of uncertainty still surrounds these initial designs, some of which may have been drawings, some models and some perhaps simply concepts. At one stage,

it appears that the Senate actually approved – in principle – the 'model' of 'Gerolamo Tedesco', but what form that 'model' took we do not know. In June the Collegio held a series of meetings to discuss these alternatives, but around this time the elusive Gerolamo seems to have disappeared from the scene. Spavento and Scarpagnino were in fact appointed jointly to manage the project, regardless of which final design was to be chosen. Shortly afterwards, however, Spavento declined the post, stating that he had too many other commitments elsewhere; he may also have been deterred by the clearly ambitious programme for the reconstruction. On 12 October, therefore, Scarpagnino was appointed the sole supervisor for the execution of the works.[31] Concina has inclined to the view that the final design was basically a compromise or 'confluence' between two or even more of the submitted solutions. Before a few observations on the design as constructed, it is salutary to summarise the extraordinary speed and efficiency with which the works were executed on site. Foundations and 'enabling works' were already complete by the summer of 1505. A year later, by the end of June 1506, all the walls were complete up to the first floor, which was then being installed.[32] By 15 March 1507, less than a year later again, the roof finishes were being completed, and a celebratory inscription on the portal to the Calle del Fontego at the side states proudly: 'Ducatus Leonardi Lauredani inclyti ducis anno sexto', that is, the sixth year of Loredan's tenure of the throne of San Marco.[33] Decorations – both internal and external – continued for some months, but in July 1508 a final solemn mass and benediction was conducted in the central cortile.

The design of the new Fondaco was specified at the outset as being simple and unostentatious. The plan (at all levels) is rational and repetitive, a fact that assisted greatly in speeding up the construction period. Surrounded on two sides by canals, the ground floor was designed to have outward-facing shops on the other two sides, to raise additional revenue from leases; in the middle of both landward façades was an entrance portal. The Grand Canal façade was naturally the most prominent, but was to be detailed simply and repetitively, albeit with a spacious five-bay central loggia at water level for the unloading of goods. There were three upper floors for lodgings and other facilities for the German community in the city. On the first floor were all the main halls and semi-public rooms. In fact, there were two large halls or refectories on the first floor, facing the Grand Canal: that towards the south corner, nearest to the bridge, was the 'summer hall', while that on the north was the Sala della Stua (*stufa*), and was the winter hall, with heating provided. Both halls have long balconies onto the canal.[34]

The Fondaco is a truly Renaissance building in its planning and appearance, and has one or two rather un-Venetian characteristics. The diminishing storey heights, for example, follow directly Alberti's precepts in *De re aedificatoria*. And although the façade has characteristic crenellation to enliven the skyline, the main façade lacks the typical centralised, tripartite composition of the traditional Venetian *palazzo*. It is true that the canal loggia is centralised, but the fenestration to the upper windows is not, and all three upper floors have simple paired lights. As originally built, the *fontego* incorporated a degree of Venetian historicism in the addition of the two little *torreselle* at the two outer corners, small square turrets that rose a further storey above the general roofline, and reminiscent of the *torreselle* of the Venetian-Byzantine palaces of the twelfth century. The façades to the Grand Canal and to the *calle* at the side were also originally enlivened by the famous lost frescos of Titian and Giorgione. The central *cortile* is even more of a model of disciplined, logical restraint: square and regular, with simple repetitive modules of colonnades.[35]

In essence, then, the design is a compromise, and we (with Concina) may suggest a sequence of events that began with an outline design by Gerolamo, later modified by Spavento and perhaps Fra Giocondo. The lack of the traditional Venetian axial *portego* is perhaps attributable to Hieronimo's influence, as may be also the creation of the two large halls on the first floor. Much more clearly Venetian are the spacious water access, the crenellation and the *torreselle*. One particularly Venetian element is the comparatively richly carved land gate; this has a close affinity with the entrance portal of the Palazzo dei Camerlenghi, across the Grand Canal, and both are almost certainly the work of Scarpagnino. The portal here at the Calle del Fontego was, as Concina has also noted, a clear violation of the Republic's forbidding of carved stonework on the façades of the new Fondaco.[36]

A Miscellany of Works: The Procurators of San Marco as Patrons

The Procurators *de supra* were responsible for the patronal shrine and the buildings on the Piazza of San Marco, but it is the other two groups of Procurators to whom we will now turn, those *de citra* and *de ultra*, one of whose duties was the management of estates and bequests, *commessarie*, in the two 'halves' of the city. Most of these duties were clerical, legal and administrative,

but from time to time the Procurators were required by the terms of wills to engage in construction works, which often took the form of building charitable almshouses or the restoration of buildings already in their charge. As examples of the first of these two forms of activity, we have two modest developments of almshouses, one of which survives (although considerably altered) today.

This development, known as Corte Nova alla Tana, was begun in 1429. On 9 March the Procurators *de citra*, Fantin Michiel and Bertuzi Querini, drew up a contract for building a group of almshouses behind the ropeworks of the Arsenale, in Castello. Funding was derived from the estate of Marco Michiel, formerly of San Giovanni Novo, and whose will is dated 14 May 1348, the year of the great plague.[37]

The site was a substantial rectangular plot, one short side of which faced the Rio della Tana, while the other end faced another canal, the Rio di Castello, much later reclaimed to form the present Via Garibaldi. It was broad enough to allow the construction of two rows of cottages, with a spacious courtyard in the centre. Rather unusually, the contract was made with a *maestro* Candio, who was not a builder, but a master carpenter. The description of the works is clear enough: the cottages were to be in two rows, with twelve in each row, and were to be on a single storey. The almost universal, timeless nature of the design of such humble dwellings can be gauged by the fact that they were to be modelled on some earlier almshouses, also built by the Procurators with funds from the estate of Zuan (Giovanni) Ravagnan, on a site in Cannaregio. The Tana cottages, in their turn, were destined to be used as a model for those built by the same *maestro* Candio, this time at the Misericordia, a decade later.

Candio's brief at the Tana was clear: he was responsible for all the doors, windows, ceilings 'and all of the other things that are required of his craft'. The Procurators would provide the timber, and have it delivered to the site for Candio to prepare for building-in. His agreed fee was a flat sum of 10 ducats (52 lire) for each house, that is, 240 ducats in all, with payments made 'from time to time according to my [Candio's] progress on the said houses'. Any additional works requested by the Procurators would attract a further maximum of 4 ducats per house.[38]

Sadly, we have no other records for a further ten years, until November 1439, when we find Candio still working for the Procurators, this time on the adjacent quay. He was well paid (32 soldi a day) for the two weeks of repairs, and reference to the 'chaxe nove' (new houses) confirms that they had been built in the intervening years. However, the project was to require considerable further funding from the Procurators in the following decades, much of it to effect more repairs to the quay. In 1457 alone these works cost 220 ducats, and involved the purchase of piling timber from the friars of San Giobbe, as well as the reconstruction of the canal retaining wall, with nearly 400 feet of coping stones. Much of this funding came from the estate of Zan Moresin (Giovanni Morosini), whose estate the Procurators administered, but the works give us a clear example of the scale and costs of the almost endless cycles of maintenance that the city's many kilometres of canals and quays required.

As to the almshouses themselves, they were built exactly as the specification recorded, with a broad space – still unpaved – in the centre, between the two rows of cottages. At each end the development was enclosed by a high brick wall, surmounted by crenellations, and with a single portal for access, all characteristic features of such projects.[39] Around the end of the century a second, very similar development was built on land almost immediately adjacent, known as Corte dei Preti; it was to serve a similar function, and was built by the Ospedale di Santi Pietro e Paolo.[40]

The present appearance of Corte Nova (fig. 45) differs radically from that when originally built. The enclosing walls at each end are lost, and in the seventeenth century the houses themselves were extended – in fact, virtually reconstructed – by the addition of two upper storeys. Nevertheless, the overall configuration remains, as do the housing units themselves, although today with only ten houses down one side and eleven down the other.

A second development, also known as Corte Nova, and again built by the Procurators, is better documented than the first. This consisted of twenty almshouses, built on land next to the Scuola Vecchia della Misericordia, in Cannaregio. Like the first, it was a charitable development, built as the rather belated result of bequests left in the estates of two citizens, Zorzi, son of Marco Baseggio, of Santa Fosca, and Dardo Signolo. The Procurators carefully balanced the contributions from the two estates, so that in the final account the two were almost identical: L. 179.16.6 from the Baseggio estate and L. 180.9.11 from the other.[41] The cottages were built in the years 1438–45, and were intended to house poor brothers who were members of the adjacent abbey and Scuola; the date of their construction coincides with the modernisation of the Scuola itself, also in the 1440s, and the workshop of Bartolomeo Bon is associated with both developments. The Corte Nova project was approached by a stone

gateway, elements of which have survived today, and have been reused (figs 46, 47). The cottages themselves had been completed by around 1445.

The building accounts are not well organised, and our records consist solely of two lists of expenditure, together with a rather random list of outgoings in a different notebook, this time (surprisingly) in Latin;[42] there are also both arithmetical errors and inaccurate transcriptions of names – Zulian Bon for Zane Bon, for example, as well as a Bortolomio, who came from either Crema or Cremona, but not both: the entire source should therefore be regarded with caution.

The development was very similar to the Castello Corte Nova, with two terraces facing each other across a wide private street, which is always called a *corte* in such developments. The southern end faced the quay of Rio della Sensa, broadly as we see it today, while the northern end was marked by another high wall, beyond which was the Sacca della Misericordia and the open lagoon.

Although the buildings were extremely simple, a large number of masters was involved in the project,

45 Corte Nova alla Tana as it is today: east side

46 Corte Nova alla Misericordia: the arched entrance gate is on the left;
further down the quay is the Scuola Vecchia della Misericordia

and the entire process was more than a little lacking in continuity and coordination. The masons involved were Zane Bon and Luca Taiamonte, with their respective workshops. Bon was almost a neighbour, since his house and yard were at San Marziale, a few minutes' walk away, while Taiamonte was as familiar a figure as Bon on the building sites of the city. He was later associated with Antonio Gambello at San Zaccaria, and (this time with Zane's son Bartolomeo) at the Madonna dell'Orto, again not far away. Several other masons made contributions, including Antonio Foscolo, who had worked at the Ca' d'Oro for Marin Contarini a decade or so earlier (again with the Bon workshop), while the Pantaleon recorded here is almost certainly the same Pantaleon who later became Bartolomeo Bon's partner.

The master builder was Bortolomio da Crema (or Cremona), and the carpenter was Candio, who had built the earlier Corte Nova in Castello. Indeed, his contract required him to build these new cottages in just the same way as the earlier development: 'facere et fabricare domos xx . . . ad formam et condicionem

47 The Scuola Vecchia della Misericordia: detail from Jacopo de' Barbari's woodcut of 1500, showing the Scuola Vecchia and the adjacent monastic house of Santa Maria in Valverde

49

illarum quas habemas in Curia Nova in confinio sancti petri de Castello'.

The Candio were a prominent extended family of both carpenters and builders, active on several Venetian sites in this period, while the various items of metalwork for the cottages were provided by Niccolò Luxe, much of whose working life revolved around the Bon workshop. Luxe's smithy was at Santa Maria Formosa, and he also supplied ironwork for the Carità church (where Bartolomeo Bon was the chief mason) between 1442 and 1452; a little later he provided metalwork for Gambello at San Zaccaria. The chief suppliers of bricks were the equally well-known figures of Marco Corner and Antonio Venier.

The development of this site marks a new stage in the urbanisation of this peripheral zone of the city. It had never been built on before, and was an orchard or market garden; because it was a marginal site, with poor bearing subsoil, it was necessary to stabilise the land and – even for such a modest development as this – to drive new piled foundations. A large number of *tolpi* (stakes for piling) were delivered, as well as many stone bedding slabs. The fabric of the cottages was entirely of brick, and around 150–180,000 were necessary in all.

Pile-driving took place in the summer of 1438, and was complete by October. There were perhaps as many as 15,000 piles, a subterranean forest of stakes under all the structural walls. In the same year, the first stone slabs were ordered for the strip-foundations, and the first record of Bortolomio, the master builder, is found, taking delivery of his first consignment of 28,000 bricks. With a simple, repetitive development such as this, consisting of two rows of identical houses, a good deal of standardisation of components was possible; it was also feasible for Bortolomio to begin bricklaying at one end of the terrace while piling still continued at the other end. Economies of scale, therefore – at least in theory – made such developments easy and quick to build. Progress was slow, however, despite the fact that Bortolomio had a team of up to six men and apprentices with him. The last record of Bortolomio is from July 1440, although Candio continued to work on the roof structure probably in spring 1441 and again in 1443.

Requirements for stonework were simple enough; there was a large number of simple window surrounds, as well as twenty front doorways. Zane Bon's workshop provided much of this routine work, and later he delivered *pozi*, corbels for the roof eaves. The stone was delivered in stages until August 1440, although Bon did not receive his last payment until as late as 1446. After June 1439, however, Luca Taiamonte became the main

stone supplier, and by the end of the summer of 1440 most of the stonework was supplied and fixed; during the same summer the walls were also plastered. It is not clear when the roof was completed, although this was probably carried out in stages, and the first consignment of *copj* (roof tiles) dates from June 1439. Again, it seems that work proceeded in stages down the lengths of the two terraces, much as we would expect.

Large numbers of planks as well as *tavolle* for stairs were delivered as late as April 1447, as were large consignments of laths (*cantinelle*) for internal partitions, indicating that interior fitting-out continued long after the roof was on. The stairs must have been fairly rudimentary affairs; since the cottages were only on one storey they simply gave access to the roof attic.[43]

In 1445 a new cistern was excavated to serve the cottages; built by a master Zuanne, it cost a substantial 170 ducats, almost the same as the cost of one of the cottages themselves.[44] The total cost of constructing the houses was 3,600 ducats or approximately 20,500 lire *di piccoli*, just over 1,000 lire per dwelling. This is a surprisingly large sum for such modest dwellings, and was considerably inflated by the costs of the foundations. Each of the three principal crafts, masons, builders and carpenters, played a roughly equal part in the process, and, as we inferred earlier, there had been no overall contract between the Procurators and a single coordinating master for the project as a whole. There may have been an initial drawing, but drawn information was probably minimal, and the Procurators relied on the experience of the masters who had executed such works before.[45]

Most of the other construction works with which the Procurators became involved were similar in character to these two developments. Often they were smaller and even simpler in scope. In the 1440s, for example, the Procurators *de citra* converted some houses at San Biagio into a 'hospital', that is, a lodging for pilgrims en route to the Holy Land, thus serving the same purpose as the better-known Ospizio Orseolo in the Piazza. The houses were in the estate of India Formenti and stood very close to Corte Nova in Castello; the name of Corte Formenta still survives today. In the necessary conversion works, the Procurators again purchased stone from Bartolomeo Bon. More extensive was the estate of Dandola Caroso, which was administered together with that of Formenti, and consisted chiefly of a group of sixteen cottages at Santa Maria Nova.[46] In 1506 major restorations were undertaken here, amounting to a partial reconstruction, requiring 42,000 new bricks for a new upper storey, fireplaces and chimneys. As at Corte Nova in Cannaregio, the last operation was the excavation of a new cistern in 1507, 20 feet square at the top, 10 feet deep ('or a little more') and 12 feet square at the base.

In all such operations, we see the Procurators fulfilling their role as the administrators of estates, responsible for the maintenance of an extensive colletion of charitable trusts. The fragmentary records of these activities, however, yield one interesting exception to the more routine repairs to almshouses: this is the estate of Francesco, son of the nobleman Marco Giustinian. This branch of the ancient patrician clan lived at San Giovanni in Bragora, and Francesco wrote his will on 13 February 1378; he died four years later.

Among the properties that the Procurators administered was Francesco's former palace on the Grand Canal at San Moisè, which is still known as Palazzo Giustinian today, and was, until recently, the administrative headquarters of the Biennale. A century after Francesco's death, extensive works were required to the palace; although the accounts are entitled 'restauri della Casa grande', the works, executed in two stages, amounted to its virtual reconstruction. Indeed, the detailed expenses refer more accurately to the 'casa refata', that is, rebuilt.[47] These records are extremely valuable since we have very little surviving documentation on the great Gothic palaces with which Venice is so splendidly endowed. The documents cover in detail the second stage of the palace's reconstruction, which began in April 1477, and was completed in about eighteen months.

The Giustinian family was well established in the parish of San Moisè; they were recorded here as early as 1310, and at some time in the fifteenth century they also built the adjacent *palazzetto*. Other property in the family's ownership included several cottages, a house in the Frezzaria, and others in the street nearby, known both then and now as Corte Contarina. Reconstruction of the *casa da stazio* (family seat) had been begun in 1474 (figs 48, 49), by a mason called Paolo di Giacomo;[48] in 1477, though, considerable work still remained. However, the Procurators did not enter into a single contract for the remaining works, but rather employed a range of masters on a day-wage basis.

Many of the building accounts kept by the Procurators are not well organised. Some contain arithmetical errors, and are often fragmented and piecemeal. Those relating to Ca' Giustinian, however, are a rare exception: clear, concise and well arranged, they are grouped according to trade or materials, with each account on a separate folio.[49] As is often the case, we can gauge the extent of the works by the quantities of bricks, sand and lime that were necessary, in this case around 700

48 Palazzo Giustinian: detail from Jacopo de' Barbari (1500), with the *palazzo* on the right

barrels of lime, 54,000 standard bricks and 19,000 small ones. It was a substantial contract, which also included a completely new roof. Most of the façade seems to have been completed in the first phase of the works, and this second stage relates chiefly to the structure of the upper storeys, the internal walls and the roof. The remodelling involved significant demolitions, and no fewer than 157 barge loads of *ruinazj* (demolition materials) were removed between June 1477 and the following March.

Four *mureri* were employed on the reconstruction, Bortolamio from Bergamo and Marco, Bortolamio and Antonio da Torre, all from the same family. The first two were both masters, the last two apprentices, either sons or younger brothers of Marco. Their efforts took about a year, from June 1477 to the following June, when Marco took sole charge of the little work that remained. The work of the carpenters was closely intertwined with that of the *mureri*, and master Tomaso, the

49   Palazzo Giustinian at San Moisè: detail of the façade, rebuilt in the 1470s

marangono (carpenter) was also on site for about a year, from August 1477 to the following summer. Tomaso's timber supplies, much of it for the new roof, came from several sources, including Zacharia di Piero Trevisan, whose family had extensive interests in importing bulk timber.

The small quantity of finished stone for the second phase was initially provided by a master Piero, who came from Alzano, near Bergamo, the home village of the well-known de' Grigi family. It did not amount to much, however: a few door and window surrounds, sills, pilasters, brackets for a fire-surround and finally, four sinks, one for the 'casa granda', the others presumably for the outbuildings, which were also being reconstructed.

Re-roofing with new tiles took place between autumn 1477 and late spring of 1478; special bricks were also required for the characteristic Venetian chimneys, three of which we can see in de' Barbari's view of 1500. Inside the palace, *maestro* Steffano, who lived at the 'ponte dele amchore [sic]' – perhaps near the Calle dei Fabbri – was responsible for laying 1,000 square feet of new terrazzo flooring to the upper great hall. One of the very last finishing operations, in 1479, included the glazing of windows, with 912 panes of glass provided by Vettor of San Luca.[50]

The palace itself had both outbuildings and five adjacent cottages; the latter were also rebuilt in 1481, forming a short terrace along the Calle del Ridotto. Such cottages were characteristic of these back lots; they were sometimes occupied by the servants of the proprietor, and sometimes rented to poor local craftsmen or tradesmen. These cottages, however, like most in the city centre, have long been lost to redevelopment at much higher densities.[51] They were very humble structures, with only the simplest of stonework to door and window surrounds; the master carpenter, Gasparo di Zane, was paid only 27 lire for his work to each cottage, representing perhaps two weeks' work on each. Most of his timber was bought from Lorenzetto Giustinian, a member of Francesco's own clan.

Our final example of the miscellany of works for which the Procurators were responsible is also a special case: indeed, it is unique, a work of great richness and complexity, a sharp contrast not only to the modest almshouses of the two Corte Nova projects, but also to the reconstruction of Ca' Giustinian.

Giovanni Miani, of the parish of San Simon Profeta (San Simon Grando), had married into the Vitturi family. His wife Margherita outlived her husband, and wrote her will on 23 January 1428.[52] By its terms she left instructions for a chapel to be built adjacent to the monastic church on the island of San Michele, with the specific requirement that the chapel should be accessible both from the church and directly from the outside (figs 36, 50, 51). A hundred years later, her wishes were finally to be executed, with the drafting of a *strumento* on 14 January 1529, forming an agreement between the monastery and the Procurators *de citra*, the administrators of the estate.[53]

Over the intervening century, the church of San Michele itself had been completely rebuilt by Mauro Codussi in the years after 1469. The agreement of 1529 made available a rectangular plot of land on the furthermost corner of the islet, facing Murano. It seems highly likely that the reason the site had not been developed already by the monastery itself was the considerable difficulty in stabilising the subsoil and forming a foundation on this vulnerable corner, which was bounded on two sides by deep channels with strong currents.[54] Nevertheless, the site was very prominent, and the chapel would be seen by the hundreds who travelled between Venice and Murano every day.

The architect was the notable Guglielmo (Viellmo) de' Grigi, from Bergamo, and his design was as unusual as the site itself: an irregular hexagonal plan, with its principal faces oriented east and west, and with the other four, shorter faces towards the north-west, north-east, south-west and south-east. The main façade was parallel to Codussi's elegant new church façade, while the south-east face connected directly with the church interior, to conform to the conditions of Miani's bequest. It was thus a centralised form, and was to be a work of rare opulence: clad, like the church itself, entirely with gleaming white Istrian stone, richly ordered with Corinthian columns and encrusted with slabs of rare marble and porphyry. Finally, it was to be roofed with a dome, the only one in Venice constructed entirely of Istrian stone.

Preliminary work began on site even before the agreement had been ratified, but the chapel took seven years to complete, and at considerable cost. Guglielmo de' Grigi also oversaw most of the construction on site; he was one of the most prominent masters of the generation after Pietro Lombardo, and had worked at the Procuratie Vecchie in the Piazza a few years earlier; he

is also associated with the modernisation of the Palazzo dei Camerlenghi at Rialto, with which the Miani chapel has much in common. Both works are characterised by rich, rather fussy detailing, and the liberal use of inlaid marble paterae.[55]

Needless to say, the foundations were extensive and costly. Pile-driving was supervised by Girardo, the master builder, who remained closely involved on site for several years. However, a glance at the chapel today indicates that Girardo's contribution was modest compared to that of Guglielmo and his team of specialised masons, stone polishers and sculptors. Like Pietro Lombardo's famous Miracoli church of a few decades earlier, Girardo's humble brickwork was to be entirely clad, within as well as outside, with stone and marble.

While the piles were being driven (by a master with nine labourers), stone was ordered for the foundation slabs, and by June 1528 Girardo could begin to build the main structural envelope of brick. At the same time we find records of the first acquisition of rare marbles that were to decorate the walls and, later, the internal altars. This first consignment included slabs of porphyry, several *tondi* of porphyry and serpentine, and colonnettes, also of marble. This marble was obtained from various sources and required different treatments to prepare it for building into the work: some was in the form of thin slabs that had to be cut to size and polished; some were colonnettes that had to be cut to length; others were *tondi* or discs sliced from larger columns. All these works kept not only Guglielmo employed, but also stone sawyers (*segadori*), such as Niccolò and Cristofalo, and polishers (*lustradori*), such as *maestro* Altobello.[56]

Floor slabs were installed in the summer of 1528. In the early autumn Guglielmo was paid large sums for purchasing stone and for wages for himself and his team of masons; he had five or six men under his supervision. He was not employed as a salaried *proto*, but on the basis of a weekly wage. Perhaps the most revealing data on the overall costs of the chapel are the comparative totals paid to the *mureri* and the masons under Guglielmo. Over the first two years on site, Girardo the builder and his men were paid a total of 1,707 lire, while the bill for de' Grigi and his own *tagliapietra* (including stone purchases) totalled nearly 10,500 lire.

By the summer of 1529, with works well advanced and the walls more than halfway to completion, the Procurators paid a sculptor, Zuanbattista da Carona, for carving a figure of his namesake, John the Baptist, for one of the niches on the exterior of the chapel.

50 The Miani chapel: section through the interior, from Cicognara, Diedo and Selva

Zuanbattista was yet another of the many migrants from the Lombardy lakes; he came from the same village as Pietro Lombardo himself. Progress continued more slowly for the next three years, but by the summer of 1533 the chapel was complete up to the level of the parapet above the rich Corinthian columns. In June 1533 the Procurators ordered 3,600 Treviso bricks ('of good quality') for the inner shell of the cupola, which seems to have been completed by Girardo by Christmas, when he installed a chain to tie the vault together.[57] In the same summer of 1533

further finishing works included the making of the doors to the chapel; in keeping with the quality of finishes elsewhere, they were all of walnut.

The final structural operation was the building of the outer stone cupola, which is considerably higher than the inner one, rather like the cupolas of San Marco. This outer cupola, unique as it was, seems to have been something of an afterthought, however, since the lower inner dome was originally finished with a pitched timber roof clad with clay tiles. Only after this tiled roof was completed (thus weather-proofing the interior) was the stone cupola built above it. This was the subject of a new agreement with de' Grigi, on the basis of a drawing that he had prepared, and was signed on 18 June 1533; the cost of 380 ducats was to include the vase on top and the six stone balls that adorned the perimeter parapet. Guglielmo was to be paid on a daily basis 'according to how the work progresses'.[58]

The Miani chapel remains a highly unusual example of opulence funded by the Procurators' *commessarie*. From the overall picture sketched in these pages, however, we can draw a few conclusions as to the way in which the Procurators approached their obligations in the field of building construction. These obligations were by their nature random and piecemeal, both in time and in space, dependent entirely on the desires and instructions left in Venetian nobles' and citizens' wills. One clear result was that these Procurators were not able to maintain any permanent staff dedicated to construction works, unlike the Procurators of San Marco itself, who could (and did) employ a full-time

51 The Miani chapel at San Michele: plan from Cicognara, Diedo and Selva

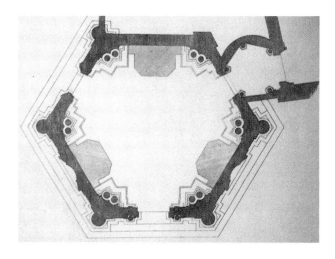

salaried *proto* to manage their estate and supervise their own construction activities. The Procurators *de citra* and *de ultra* had no choice but to approach building works in an ad hoc manner, employing craftsmen when and where necessary, and relying on the expertise of the master builder to coordinate and supervise construction. We have the distinct impression that few, if any, of the Procurators had much knowledge or understanding of the construction process, and were unaccustomed to keeping building accounts in a disciplined manner; doubtless, their strengths lay elsewhere, chiefly in the field of legal administration.

52   Raising stone onto the scaffold: detail (by Bernardino Butinone?) of the *incipit* of Filarete's treatise, *De architectura*, 1488–9

Chapter Three

THE BUILDING PROCESS

The Process of Patronage: Client Bodies and Their Organisation

My use of the word 'process' is intended to emphasise the essentially linear character of building construction, which was often spread over many years. The erection of any major new building, in almost any era, is a long chain of events, often phased and frequently interrupted by many external factors, sometimes by more direct ones. Rare indeed in the fifteenth, as in any other century, was the project that was conceived, funded and executed in a single, seamless operation, from the first conceptual sketch to the 'topping-out' ceremony.

To put the subject of this study more bluntly, building construction is an expensive, messy, long-drawn out series of 'sub-processes', which eventually come to some kind of conclusion, when a building might be said to be 'finished'. It is rather amusing to read in many otherwise highly respected and authoritative books that, say, the Torre dell'Orologio was built in the years 1496–9, or the church of San Zaccaria was constructed from 1458 to 1481, with such convincing (and often quite inappropriate) precision of dating, although the latter example does at least give a hint, in the twenty-three-year time-frame, of the complex process that lay behind these bald dates. Architecture is not like sculpture or painting; a work of marble, positioned on its plinth, can clearly be said to have been completed in a certain year (even within a certain week), and duly handed over to its commissioning patron; in the same way, we can state that a work of art on canvas was com-

pleted, mounted in its frame and positioned above the high altar: both works were finished and handed over. The completion of a major work of architecture is rarely, if ever, so simple, as the studies in this book will graphically show. It is essential that we understand the fragmented nature of the building process if we are to understand the relationships among its chief protagonists: the patron, the architect, the building masters. Then, as now, there were countless opportunities for changes of direction, for 'rethinks', additions or subtractions to what had – perhaps – been the original concept of the design. Another of the numerous modern myths regarding the 'medieval' construction process – that buildings always took a very long time to complete – will, I hope, also be laid to rest, on the evidence of two or three buildings that were constructed with an astonishing rapidity that would be difficult to achieve even today. Sometimes, undeniably, there were protracted *longueurs* as a simple result of the drying-up of funds; occasionally, on the other hand, there were extraordinary bursts of activity, rapid and awesomely efficient, such that, for example, the new *albergo* (meeting room) for the Scuola della Carità could be built in just a few months in 1443,[1] while the very much larger Scuola Grande di San Marco was reconstructed – it is always claimed – in a mere eight months, a truly prodigious feat, in 1437–8.[2] At the other extreme was the example of San Zaccaria noted above, the period – in fact – of more than three decades while the church was slowly, painstakingly reconstructed, and during which time, famously, the very style of the fabric itself evolved from a late, rich example of Venetian *gotico fiorito* to Codussi's elegant Renaissance rationality.

To complete a major construction project rapidly and efficiently, a number of prerequisites were necessary. First, and perhaps most important, there was the will of the commissioning client or body, a strong, sometimes even urgent desire to complete the work as quickly as possible. Perhaps the best example of such single-minded determination is the reconstruction by the state of the Fondaco dei Tedeschi after its destruction by fire in 1505 (figs 53, 54). The Fondaco was an extremely important building to the Republic, hub of the wealthy German community in the capital, and an urgent priority for rapid reconstruction so that transalpine trade could flourish once again. The rebuilding of this imposing edifice took only three years, a remarkable achievement, although it was intentionally rational and repetitive in both its structure and its detailing. Nevertheless, it offers a fine example of what could be achieved with efficient funding and sufficient manpower and patronal will.

The second prerequisite was adequate money to pay for the men and materials. Again, the example of the Fondaco could have been achieved only with the allocation of substantial financial resources. In this case, funding initially came from the revenues of the Provveditori al Sal, but the first tranche proved insufficient, and so, to speed up the process further, Francesco de' Garzoni, one of the Provveditori, proposed that a monthly allocation of 160 ducats from the 'Casse di S. Marco et Rialto' and a further 140 ducats monthly from the Cassa Grande (the main treasury) should be adequate to fund the work to completion; over three years, therefore, 10,800 ducats would be spent. (A little later, it became necessary to augment these funds still further by lesser sums from two other sources; finally, the monthly allowance was doubled to 600 ducats to complete the works as rapidly as possible.)[3]

As important in purely practical terms as the availability of sufficient funds and the necessary political will was the organisation of materials and labour. The Venetian construction industry in this period was fairly large and flourishing, and in most cases seems to have been able to rise to the demands that were placed on it; an exception, though, must be made in the case of stonemasons, who became increasingly scarce and thus in high demand later in the century. There were also undoubtedly occasional shortages of materials (notably bricks) in times of peak activity. But the supply of such bulk materials (including timber, lime and sand) was in general a well-organised and large-scale activity, on a substantial 'proto-industrial' scale.

Finally, however, we come to perhaps the most significant aspect of all in the commissioning and execution of these works: the clarity of the patron's objective and the manner in which that objective was to be achieved. Since institutional projects rather than private works are being discussed, it bears reiterating that Venice was a gerontocracy, both in the government at the Palazzo Ducale and in many other aspects of its institutional administration; again, to be more blunt, most building patrons were old men. Not only that, but most official posts were occupied on a short-term rotational basis, which meant that, during the course of the execution of any major building project, not only was there a strong likelihood that several of those involved in the original commission would die, but there was the certainty of frequent changes in the composition of the commissioning body itself. Few indeed were the large projects in which there was anything like complete continuity of administration, and hence the opportunities for changes of emphasis, even for major alterations of design direction, were almost limitless. This is one of the principal reasons for the pivotal role played by the *protomaestro*, who was often the only person who had a profound knowledge of the project in its entirety, from the initial sketch design through to the 'topping out' ceremony. Indeed, he was often the only one involved from the start who had a reasonable chance of still being alive at this happy conclusion.

Having already sketched the principal governmental commissioning bodies, it may be helpful here if we also outline the structures of the two other principal

53 The Fondaco dei Tedeschi: plan from Cicognara, Diedo and Selva

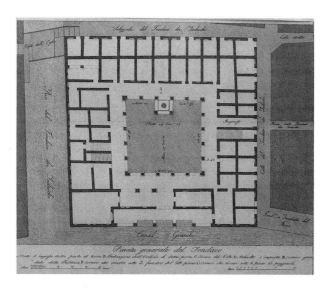

54 The Fondaco dei Tedeschi, reconstructed in the years 1505–8: the façade from the Rialto Bridge

commissioning clients, the Church and the Scuole Grandi.

The ecclesiastical institutions in the city can be sub-divided into two groups, parish foundations and religious houses. Parishes in Venice were small, as were most of their churches, and it was only in the case of the complete reconstruction of a fairly important parochial foundation that the parish priest (*parroco*) found it necessary to resort to formal administrative procedures. Such was the case, for example, at Santa Maria Formosa, a wealthy, prominent parish, when in 1491 the chapter appointed three procurators, all noblemen of distinction, to supervise progress on the reconstruction of the church by Mauro Codussi.[4]

A similar procedure can be seen at the nunnery of San Zaccaria; in this case, the abbess herself took a close personal interest, but she established a *banca*, a 'bench' or committee, to administer the works. The reconstruction works of the great religious houses were, of course, of a different order of magnitude from the reconstruction of a parish church, although the rebuilding of the two largest of these, the Frari and Santi Giovanni e Paolo, was largely complete by the early fifteenth century, and it was left to Bartolomeo Bon to provide the finishing touch to the latter, in the form of its magnificent west portal.

Income for the funding of such monastic projects came from several sources, the largest and most significant being personal donations, most generously (and often more regularly) by families with members within the order itself.[5] Both the Carità church and San Zaccaria received significant donations as the work progressed, although clearly, if this remained their chief source of income, it was by its nature erratic and unreliable. To a large extent, the ability of these religious institutions to raise funds reflected their own importance in the public perception, and their own intrinsic wealth and influence; put simply, a great and ancient foundation like San Zaccaria, traditionally patronised by powerful members of the nobility and by the doge himself, had a far easier task raising funds for its new church than did a minor institution in a distant corner of the city, with few wealthy benefactors.

The last of our institutional patrons are the religious confraternities, the Scuole Grandi. These were a uniquely Venetian institution, voluntary lay confraternities which all classes of society were able to join. They performed many functions and became extremely important patrons of the arts, particularly in the late fifteenth and sixteenth centuries. They also embarked on major construction projects to build accommodation for their spiritual and philanthropic activities. There

were two permanent organs that effectively formed the 'patron' in commissioning new works at the Scuole Grandi, the Capitolo Generale, or general chapter, and the *banca*. The Capitolo Generale had originally consisted of all of the approximately 500 members of a Scuola, but in practical terms a much smaller core of only fifty or so was considered sufficient to form a quorum over issues of policy. These fifty, not surprisingly, tended to be the wealthiest and most influential members; indeed, the poorest members, those in receipt of alms, were specifically excluded from voting rights in the chapter.

Day to day administration was in the hands of the board of governors or *banca*, with sixteen men, who held office, in the typically Venetian manner, for only a year, beginning on 1 March. They were also ineligible for re-election for five years after their term of office, yet again a characteristic Venetian method of preventing the development of factions, but which was almost guaranteed to exacerbate difficulties of administrative continuity over major construction projects.

The *banca* was chaired by the Guardian Grande (Vardian Grando in Venetian dialect), who was also the only member eligible to put forward issues for discussing and voting; he thus wielded considerable influence during his brief tenure of office. The Vardian was further supported by twelve deacons (*degani*), a chaplain (*vicario*) and a secretary (*scrivan*), the last responsible for keeping accounts. For important building works, the *banca* sometimes appointed a *provveditore sopra la fabbrica*, with much the same role as those of the government Provveditori. The membership of the Scuole was eventually (theoretically) stabilised at a maximum of 550 members, but from time to time they approached the Consiglio dei Dieci (to whom they were ultimately accountable) to increase their numbers.[6]

Funding for the large, costly building developments undertaken by the Scuole in the fifteenth century (fig. 55) came from a variety of sources. Bequests left in members' wills represented a fairly minor source, and again were erratic and unpredictable. Interest on investments (chiefly in the Republic itself) also helped, but individual donations from live members were of more substantial benefit, particularly since they were frequently tied to a specific project or element of work. One of the most lucrative ways of raising revenue, though, was by approaching the Dieci to permit an increase in membership, since each new member paid an enrolment fee. The *banca* also sometimes approached the Dieci to request the suspension of their obligation to distribute alms and food to the needy, a sharp reminder of the flexibility with which the Scuole sometimes regarded these (theoretically mandatory) charitable duties.

And finally, on one unique occasion, the Scuola Grande di San Marco made an unprecedented petition to the Republic directly for funds to pay for the reconstruction of their building after a fire in 1485. The Republic responded with the substantial sum of 4,000 ducats, but it was an act of generosity never to be repeated either at San Marco or any of the other Scuole.[7]

These, then, were the institutional bodies that were to be responsible, during the course of the fifteenth century, for the commissioning of some of the most remarkable and beautiful works of architecture ever seen in Venice. We must now consider the first stage in the process that brought these works into being, the appointment of their 'architects' and the design process itself.

The Design Process

Although no construction drawings appear to have survived in Venice from the fifteenth century, there are a number of references to drawings in contemporary documentation, and their vital role in the development of the design of a project. The chief elements in the otherwise almost organically evolving design for the façade of the Ca' d'Oro, for example, were closely based on highly detailed drawings; a drawing formed an essential element in the contract with Pier Paolo dalle Masegne in 1400 for the great Molo window at the Palazzo Ducale, just as it did in the contract of 1438 with Bartolomeo Bon for the Porta della Carta. In addition to the written contractual description or specification, there was one further medium available to the architect or craftsman involved in the creation of a major new work: the architectural model.

One of the most important roles of the architectural model was its use in competitions, and there are examples of this practice in many parts of Italy after about the 1450s. Although considerably more durable than paper drawings, no more than forty or fifty architectural models have survived from this period in Italy out of several times that number that may have been made. All these examples are of wood, often of several different types.

In the case of a design competition (for example, that for Cosimo de' Medici's new palace in Florence, and the later one for the completion of the façade of Santa Maria del Fiore in the same city), the model was clearly intended to be evaluated by direct comparison with

55 The Scuola Grande di San Rocco: main portal to the *campo*, by Pietro Bon (between *circa* 1520 and 1524)

others, and, as Goldthwaite has put it, also acting as a kind of guarantee of what the commissioning client could expect to see at the end of the works, often many years later. A model crystallised the design intentions of the creator in a manner that even a lay committee could easily understand, and it thereby helped to formalise the design process: it became a bench-mark or reference point for the many years of more detailed design development that lay ahead. For obvious reasons of cost and manageability models were generally built to a fairly small scale, although there were some outstanding exceptions, such as Antonio da Sangallo's imposing construction for the new St Peter's in Rome, which is 7.4 metres long and nearly 5 metres high. Generally, though, they were therefore unable to represent all of the most refined small-scale carving or detailing; but they were often extremely skilfully made, works of creative craftsmanship in their own right.

Millon's survey has indicated that architectural models were commonplace in all regions of Italy. There were, for example, models made for the cathedrals of Milan and Bologna, as well as that of Florence; two models of the latter survive, one of the whole of Brunelleschi's cupola, with the drum and apses, the other a detail of the lantern, probably made just before its erection, around 1436.[8] Both are kept at the Museo dell'Opera del Duomo.

The construction of a model, however, can serve different functions from those made for architectural competitions (fig. 56). For Alberti, one of its purposes was simply to indicate the general size, shape and modelling of the proposed building, for which purpose it was not necessary to indicate a great deal of architectural detail. Such a model was a design aid, therefore, for the master himself, rather than a presentational device for communication to others. The other purpose of architectural models, however, was the clear representation of an idea or philosophy, rational and fully resolved. With such motivation, richness of detailing must sometimes have been crucial to the success of the designer in communicating this richness (or any other intended attribute) to his patron. In addition to its role in 'selling' the design, such a model could still also be used as a key or small-scale template for the stonemasons to develop their own more detailed profiles – capitals, pilasters and so on – within an overall defined framework.

Surprisingly, perhaps, there appear to have been few models made in Venice during the fifteenth century, and among the major projects discussed in this book, the reconstruction of San Zaccaria is the only work where there is evidence of a wood model – two, in fact – being commissioned. Their precise function remains unclear. The first was made under the direction of the architect and *proto* Antonio Gambello in 1458, and was complete at the beginning of May, about the same time that he was confirmed in his post. Since substantial foundation works were to begin almost immediately

56 Detail model of the lantern on the top of Brunelleschi's cupola at Santa Maria del Fiore, Florence

after completion of the model, it appears most likely that it was commissioned so that the design of the new church, rendered in three dimensions, should be more clearly comprehensible to laymen, or rather to religious women: that is, to the nuns of the order. The design must have been drawn on paper or parchment already, since it would not have been possible to make the model (let alone begin the building itself) without reasonably accurate drawings. It must also have been clear by now that this was to be a complex and expensive building, which would take many years to complete. The building accounts begin with a list of initial contributions made by the nuns themselves towards the works, and there seems little doubt that a well-made model would be a significant asset in persuading the parents of these ladies (representing many of the Republic's most notable patrician dynasties) to part with more of their ducats in such a worthy cause.[9]

Gambello's model cost 110 lire and took a number of weeks to make. In essence, this must have been the

57   The Fondaco dei Tedeschi: detail of the façade, with its spacious central loggia

definitive scheme, and was to form a design template for some years to come; it was probably also fairly well detailed in execution, and may have proved helpful to Gambello's assistants as a guide, particularly since on more than one occasion he was away from the city for some time. Interestingly, however, a further model was called for some years after this one, perhaps representing some change in the design intentions.[10] One of the most unusual features of the completed church is the apsidal ambulatory, with its radiating chapels; this arrangement remains unique in Venice and it is not unreasonable to speculate that this complex spatial

arrangement was the particular feature that may have called for a model to be made, in order to make Gambello's proposal comprehensible. It is a difficult spatial concept for a layman to grasp from conventional plans and sections, and there were no nearby precedents to inspect.

An example of a model being produced as part of a competitive design process is the reconstruction of the Fondaco dei Tedeschi: in this case, 'design ideas' in model form were requested by the Republic after the devastating fire of 28 January 1505, which destroyed the old Fondaco. Giorgio Spavento produced two alternative proposals, both apparently in the form of physical models, while a native German had also produced a three-dimensional proposal. The elusive Fra Giocondo, too, had proffered advice, although it is not clear whether he produced a model. In any event, and whatever the precise contribution of the equally elusive 'Gerolamo Tedesco', it is clear that the purpose of these models, as distinct from that at San Zaccaria, was to put forward a design concept in direct competition with others. To that end, they probably indicated the overall volume and 'footprint' of the proposed building, and the general distribution of space, perhaps with some indication of the appearance of the façades. Since these offerings were speculative at this stage, therefore, and since it was clear that the Senate wished to see a simple, practical solution to an urgent problem, it is likely that the models were fairly schematic. Indeed, the Senate specified that the new Fondaco was to have no marble, no window tracery and no superfluous ornamentation, a stipulation largely followed in the execution of the successful project (fig. 57).[11]

In general, therefore, models cost money, required considerable skill to make, and were generally produced only for buildings of major architectural importance, or to explain or 'sell' a particularly complex or unusual design proposal. Many important buildings were produced without one, particularly if their design was straightforward and followed a well-established tradition. The church of the Carità is an example of such a project, built largely from a collection of stock or previously used elements, and forming one of a group of late Gothic churches in Venice that were all members of the same broad family: Sant'Andrea della Zirada, San Gregorio, San Giovanni in Bragora, Sant'Aponal, Sant' Elena.

The use of drawings, of course, was different. They were universal in the fifteenth century, but, rather like architectural models, served a number of different purposes. The evolution of drawing and design techniques in the later medieval period has been analysed extensively over the last two or three decades, so my comments here are limited to observations that directly reflect the Venetian experience, rather than rowing once again over familiar waters.[12]

Definitive design drawings were often drawn on parchment, for obvious reasons of durability, the same reason that most legal contracts were also executed on parchment; indeed, such drawings themselves were often legal, or quasi-legal documents, in the same sense that today definitive agreed or 'signed off' drawings form an integral part of a building contract. The drawing for the Molo window at the Palazzo Ducale,

for example, the earliest in this survey, dated 2 October 1400, was on parchment, and appears to have been a fairly detailed elevational representation of this complex collection of architectonic and sculpted forms. It must have been sufficiently detailed to show at least the location of the thirteen sculpted figures 'of good, clean Carrara marble' that the contract required, although since the iconography of these figures is not stated, this was to be the subject of later discussion and agreement.[13]

Bon's Porta della Carta was a rather similar work. Here the written specification is more detailed, although it is still not comprehensive. The drawing (which is not stated as being on parchment, although it probably was) was itself also more detailed than that for the Molo window, since it illustrated such elements as the putti and the foliage decoration that run up the extrados of the main arch of the great window; it also showed the central figure of St Mark 'in the form of a lion'. Here again, however, the iconography of the other principal figures is not stated, and may have still been the subject of debate, with Doge Foscari himself undoubtedly playing a major part in this process.[14]

What is clear from both of these examples (as well as others from the Madonna dell'Orto and elsewhere) is that the drawing and the written contract were both considered essential parts of the agreement. It is, after all, extremely difficult to describe in words alone the required appearance of either of the two examples above, whereas one drawing renders clearly the architect's or sculptor's design intentions.

Such drawings therefore represented the client-approved scheme in terms of the overall design, the compositional structure and at least the number (and sometimes the size) of the principal sculpted elements, which would then be developed in further detail. They were in no sense practical drawings for use in the masons' yard, and were undoubtedly originally held by the client body (again as a reference point, like the model), together with the contract itself, which was sometimes notarised. The master who had produced this drawing, however, would almost certainly have made a second copy for himself as his own reference point, in order to develop more detailed drawings.

Having reached agreement with the client, therefore, as to the general nature and configuration of the work – and its cost – the master was then able to develop what we today identify as shop or production drawings, that is, more detailed, larger-scale drawings, this time on paper. It is not clear from the records whether some of these drawings themselves would have been submitted for the approval of the patron, although they almost certainly were, particularly if the original contract drawing had left some details or iconographic subject matter unresolved.[15] These paper drawings formed an intermediate scale of information production, between the contract drawing and the still larger details that were necessary before stone could be cut.

The final stage in the development of a design was the production of full-size templates or *sagome* for the stones to be carved to the correct profile. Since we are considering major public works of architecture, most of the facing treatment to the exterior of such works was of Istrian stone, and therefore the process is essentially that of the further development of this design by the architect/sculptor/stonemason, with the other principal building craft, that of the *murer* or builder, playing an essentially supportive role.[16]

The Building Crafts and Society

All the men who worked in the construction industry in fifteenth-century Venice had certain features in common, both socially and, in broad terms, economically. From such remarkable masters as Bartolomeo Bon and Mauro Codussi to the more modest but equally essential blacksmiths and pile-drivers, most were members of the same social order, the *minuto popolo* or common people. A few were members of the still highly elusive (and by no means rigidly defined) citizen class; perhaps the most famous of these was the Bellini family of painters, who were not only citizens but claimed to be *cittadini originari*, that is, original citizens of the Republic, and only slightly lower in rank than the nobility. All, however, without exception, were also members of the extensive network of trade guilds or *arti*.

Other than those who were *cittadini*, they played no direct role in the government of the Republic at any level. Nevertheless, the complex, sophisticated structure of that Republic enabled them to fulfil a visible, public role in several respects: they could participate, for example, in all the major festivals of the Venetian calendar, in processions in the Piazza on St Mark's Day, Ascension Day and on the election of a new doge; they could organise, through the statutes (*mariegole*) of their own guilds, systems of charity, of mutual assistance in times of hardship. And as well as membership of the crafts guilds, they could also become members of the Scuole Grandi and the lesser *scuole* of devotion.[17]

Many of them did so. All classes could join the Scuole Grandi, although nobles were not permitted to sit on the governing *banca*, which was reserved for the *cittadini originari*. Affiliation to one of the Scuole Grandi was entirely voluntary (unlike the compulsory membership of one's own trade guild), but carried with it many advantages, from the more elusive patriotic advantage of identification with the city and Republic and the enhancement of a sense of civic duty and responsibility, to the more practical aspects of personal contact with many other Venetians, some them noble – and some of them wealthy – who might patronise new construction works and thus further one's career. Did building masters join the Scuole Grandi partly in order to obtain work and patronage or, conversely, did they obtain work because they were members already? It is difficult to answer such questions definitively, although the careers of a number of leading masters in the second half of the century do reflect a network of patronage and connections.

The Scuola Grande di San Marco played a much more dominant role in the lives of the building craftsmen (and of those of painters and sculptors) than did the other Scuole Grandi; nearly all of the most prominent artists and sculptors of the late fifteenth century were members of this Scuola. The Scuola Grande itself was also particularly active in the 1480s and 1490s in rebuilding its own accommodation, a process that naturally required the skills of many such masters. Indeed, the first building of the Scuola at its new site at Santi Giovanni e Paolo, begun in 1437, was constructed by a master builder, Stefano da Cremona, who was already a 'fradello de scuolla', a member, and this close association between construction masters and membership of the Scuola continued in the great reconstruction programme later in the century.[18]

On some occasions, therefore, masters were already members of the Scuola prior to receiving commissions from it, while others joined after they had completed work for the Scuola. Gentile Bellini and Antonio Scarpagnino were both admitted on acceptance of their first commission, while, much later, both Jacopo Tintoretto and his son Domenico were admitted on condition that they provided four paintings for the Scuola. Others, like Stefano, joined first, and were later given commissions; for example, Giovanni Candio, Alegreto di Damian and the painter Alvise Vivarini were all members for some time before they contributed physically towards the reconstruction works; on the other hand, Antonio Rizzo joined the Scuola in 1477, as did Giovanni Bellini in 1484, both of them after they had already completed works for the institution. Nor was this the end of the roll-call of the Scuola's illustriously creative membership: Bartolomeo Bon also joined, as, in a later generation, did Antonio Lombardo. Among

58 The modest guildhall of the *arte* of the *mureri* (builders), at San Samuele, constructed in the fifteenth century

the other artist members was Lazzaro Bastiani, who contributed towards the painting cycle of the *Miracles of the Cross* for the rival Scuola Grande di San Giovanni Evangelista, but who was deacon (*degan*) at San Marco in 1479.[19]

The role of his contemporary, Giovanni Bellini, offers an example of the 'social bridging' that membership of the Scuole Grandi was intended to foster; Giovanni, fourth child of Jacopo, was no mere member of the *minuto popolo*, however: the family's position among the 'original citizenry' of the Republic endowed them with a number of privileges. Giovanni's son Alvise worked in the ducal chancellery, a post that was open only to citizens, and – despite the possibility that he was illegitimate – Giovanni himself was in many respects a pillar of middle-ranking Venetian society, with a flourishing workshop. He was also a member of the Scuola di San Cristofalo (Cristoforo), a devotional *scuola* based at the church of the Madonna dell'Orto, as, too, were

Zane and Bartolomeo Bon, Alvise Vivarini and Gentile da Fabriano. In 1484 Giovanni Bellini joined the Scuola Grande di San Marco, where he rose to be elected deacon in 1486 and again in 1494.

His brother Gentile played an even more prominent role in the administration of the Scuola. Gentile was deacon in 1476 and again in 1504; he was *guardian da matin* in 1492 and was on the governing board on no fewer than four occasions. Gentile played an influential role in determining the Scuola's artistic policies, and was equally prominent in government circles; as early as 1474 he was given the commission for the pictorial cycle in the great hall of the Maggior Consiglio in the Palazzo Ducale, thus effectively becoming the official portrait-painter to the Republic. Five years later he was sent to Constantinople to paint the sultan, Mehmed II.[20] Clearly, there was a good deal of scope for personal advancement both within the Scuole themselves and by developing an appropriate network of patrons elsewhere, above all, of course, at the Palazzo Ducale.

THE BUILDING CRAFTS

There was little fundamental change within the overall structure of the building industry during the course of the fifteenth century. Despite the introduction of the Renaissance vocabulary in design, and despite the development of the role of the *proto* in certain major new building projects, in general the industry was structured in much the same way in 1500 as it had been in 1400. The recent work of Caniato and Dal Borgo in the field of the Venetian building crafts, their organisation and development, is of enormous importance, and the reader is referred to their definitive study, *Le arti edili*, for far more detail – as well as numerous illustration – than is possible here.

Three principal crafts were responsible for the overwhelming majority of the construction activity over this century: stonemasons, builders and carpenters (fig. 58, 59, 62). All three had been registered with the Giustizia Vecchia, together with their statutes, at an early date, the builders and carpenters both in 1271 and the stonemasons in 1307. They were supported by the materials industry, which provided them with stone, marble, bricks, tiles and timber, as well as the lesser (but still essential) materials such as sand, lime and water. Some of these providers were themselves organised into trade groups, not fully recognised *arti*, but rather consortia, such as those that provided sand (*sabbiadori*), wholesale timber, and the furnace men (*fornaxieri*) who supplied bricks and roof tiles.

The three principal building guilds were also supported by a number of more specialised crafts, the chief of which were the *fabbri* (smiths), who provided metalwork of all kinds; the terrazzo layers; painters and decorators (*depentori*); other finishing crafts such as stone polishers (*lustradori*); *fenestrari*, who provided windows, and the famous *verieri* or *vetrai* of Murano, who provided the glass to go into these windows (figs 60, 61).

The Venetian building industry was organised in a manner little different from that of any other substantial late medieval city, although practices did vary somewhat from city to city. In Florence, for example, a 'rationalisation' process back in 1293 had resulted in the fusion of the guilds of masons and carpenters into a single entity, the Arte dei Maestri (fig. 64), whereas at Pisa during the fifteenth century the same two guilds joined together (partly as a result of greatly reduced numbers), only to part company again in 1477. The Siennese also adopted the Florentine approach in 1355, but there again the enforced merger lasted for only a few years; as a result of staged fragmentation, by 1489 there were three independent guilds once again on the Venetian pattern.[21] Nevertheless, it is doubtful whether any other Italian city had quite as many small, highly specialised guilds as Venice did; at their peak, there were around two hundred in all.

The natural subdivision of the construction industry into three principal groups had the advantage that each guild's statutes could be carefully tailored to their specific requirements, rather than being subsumed below an all-embracing (and inevitably more generalised) series of statutes, as was the case in Florence. Thus, the masons' statutes are much concerned with quality of stone, its provenance and identification, good practice at the quarry, and so on, whereas those of the master builders (*mureri*) lay considerable emphasis on the need for coordination and on the role of the master builder as the general manager of the building site. Some of the guilds, too, had specific concerns of their own that were sometimes reflected in clauses of their statutes; in the later fifteenth century the masons were much exercised by the large numbers of foreign members of their own *arte*, matters that affected the other two principal building crafts to a much lesser extent.[22]

FOREIGN MASTERS IN VENICE

It is a simple fact of record that much of the architectural glory of fifteenth-century Venice was built by men who were identified as foreigners. This rather sweeping term, however, requires more detailed analysis, since

59 Detail of the title page of the *mariegole* (statutes) of the guild of *mureri*, written and registered in 1271

forestieri working in Venice actually fell into three distinct categories, only one of which was truly 'foreign' (figs 52, 63, 65, 67–9).

First, craftsmen were drawn to the capital from both components of the Serenissima's own empire. From the Italian mainland to the west they came from the towns and villages of the Terraferma that stretched as far as Bergamo and Brescia, embracing most of the northern Po plain, as well as the hills and mountains of the Veronese, the Vicentino, the Marca Trevigiana and most of present-day Friuli. The second component, the empire *da mar*, was less significant in this context, and was chiefly important as a vital source of materials rather than of men, above all the stone from the quarries of Istria. Most of the few craftsmen from the empire *da mar* who worked in the capital also came from Istria and Dalmatia rather than the further possessions such as the Aegean islands or Crete. One of the more notable masters from the Dalmatian coast was Giorgio da Sebenico, about whom Deborah Howard has published important details.[23]

60 The *fenestrer* or window-maker, by Gaetano Zompini, an illustration for *Le arti che vanno per via*

62 The *terazer*, or terrazzo-layer, with his characteristic cranked rod for laying and levelling terrazzo, from an eighteenth-century watercolour by Giovanni Grevembroch

61 The Arti: the tools of the *terazer*'s trade, a sketch by Richard Norris, who visited Venice on the Grand Tour in 1769

63 A building site: detail from the thirteenth-century Canterbury Psalter

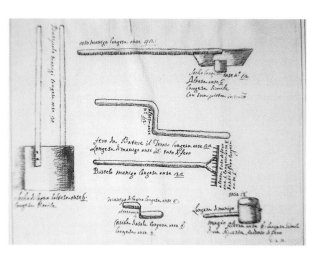

64 Detail of the tabernacle of the Arte dei Maestri di Pietra e Legname, Orsanmichele, Florence, by Nanni di Banco, *circa* 1408: relief panel showing masons and carpenters

The third category comprised real foreigners, that is, masters who came from other Italian states, the chief among them being the duchy of Milan (under the rule of the Visconti and then the Sforza), and from the Tuscany of the Medici. It is necessary, therefore, to note briefly the contributions made by each of these three components in turn.

The empire *da mar* is probably the simplest to analyse. From a survey of the surviving fifteenth-century records, it is clear that nearly all these migrant masters were stonemasons. Many came from the stone quarries of Istria itself, although we also find examples of masters from most of the chief settlements down the long Dalmatian coastline, from Cattaro (Kotor) in the south, via Trau (Trogir), Sebenico (Šibenik) and Zara (Zadar) to Fiume (Rijeka) and the towns of Istria, chiefly Rovigno, but also from Capodistria (Koper). There were also one or two migrants from the city state of Ragusa (Dubrovnik), which retained its independence and was never a Venetian subject.

A number of masters are simply identified in the records as 'Gruato', that is, from Croatia, with no further detail. But most were those who had made the short journey across the gulf from Istria, and some (including the numerous Gruato) were themselves closely bound up with the large-scale quarrying activities along the Istrian coast. Clans such as the well-recorded Taiamonte, the Sponza and the dal Vescovo all had quarrying interests, and all also had members who worked at one time or another as masons in the capital. There remain very few records of members of any crafts other than masons or quarrymen migrating to Venice from Dalmatia other than a handful of carpenters from Capodistria and Sebenico.[24]

From the Terraferma empire, however, the picture is rather more complex. The region itself varied considerably in character, from the extensive forested uplands of Cadore to the rich flatlands of the Po plain, scattered with its ancient, wealthy cities: Padua, Vicenza, Verona. From the eastern part of the Terraferma, broadly the present-day Friuli, the chief contribution made to the development of the capital was in the supply of timber, and of iron from Feltre. This large-scale commercial traffic was dispersed, and many traders in timber were based at Portogruaro, others at Treviso, both of which lay on the river routes by which timber was brought down to the lagoon from the upland forests. Closer to Venice were the many brickfields of Mestre and Padua (as well as those of Treviso), whence there was a good deal of traffic to the lagoon. A number of building masters from these nearer parts of the Terraferma also made their way to the city in search of employment, among them masons and *mureri* from both Padua and Chioggia.

Nevertheless, and apparently rather perversely, it is generally true to say that the further one travelled westwards across the great plain, the greater were the numbers of migrants to Venice; there are, however, clear reasons for this apparent logistical contradiction. Verona and Vicenza, for example, were (and still are) both marble-producing cities, each with their own tradition of skilled local stonemasonry, such that, for example,

65 Building walls: detail from the *Historie universelle* (late thirteenth century)

the fifteenth century, almost exclusively masons and sculptors, many of whom completed their professional lives in Venice. The origins of this plethora of local skill have been much debated, although undoubtedly the proximity of the great city of Milan, one of the largest in Europe, and, in particular, the requirements of its vast and uncompleted cathedral (fig. 66), formed the initial focus for the skills of these masters. Although earlier Lombard masters had also travelled widely, the notable expansion of Milan, as well as other important works in Lombardy, such as the Visconti castle in Pavia, gave plenty of opportunities, which were then further enhanced by the prospects of work in the Venetian territories, as well as Venice itself. Creative craftsmen such as Matteo Raverti first trod a path later followed by many others during the course of the century. Raverti had worked at Milan cathedral for some years (together with other masters from the Comasco) before moving to Venice around 1422, where he made an important contribution to Marin Contarini's new palace at Santa Sofia; he may have worked at San Marco in the same period. Raverti gathered around him at the Ca' d'Oro a number of other compatriots, all, like him, attracted to the opportunities of the maritime capital. It seems likely that, after the Venetian annexation of both Bergamo and Brescia, these expatriates decided that their own future lay with the still-expanding empire of the Serenissima rather than with the territorially reduced duchy of Milan. Throughout the 1430s and 1440s, too, tensions and a series of battles and peaces first with the Visconti and then the Sforza again may have persuaded expatriate Milanesi to stay in Venice rather than return, particularly after the 'grand alliance' of 1450 had brought Venice yet another prize – and rubbed still more salt into the wound of Milanese pride – in the city of Crema, once again at the expense of the Sforza.

The Bergamo masters came not from the city itself but from two valleys to the north, the Valle Brembana and the Val Seriana. The de' Grigi clan, for example, came to Venice from Alzano, in the lower Val Seriana, while Mauro Codussi came from Lenna, halfway up the Valle Brembana. When they arrived in Venice, however, most were simply identified as Bergamaschi, and they included two masons who worked at San Zaccaria, and several others; there were also a few masters in other trades: Antonio, Venturin and Bortolomio, for example, were *mureri*, while *maestro* Lorenzo was a carpenter.[26] The masters from the adjacent Milanese territory came from several locations. Some went to Venice directly from Milan itself, and among these outstanding figures were Antonio Abbondi (Scarpagnino) as well as signif-

masters such as Antonio Rizzo moved to the capital from Verona, as did lesser masons such as Piero d'Antonio and Zane Rizzo. Further west again was Brescia, another important producer of marble, and we find one or two examples of migrants, too, who made their journey thence to the lagunar capital.[25]

One region, however, stands out above all the rest for its remarkable concentration of skilled craftsmen: the Bergamasco and the adjacent lands of the Comasco. The former had become a Venetian possession in 1428, while Como and its own territory remained within the Duchy of Milan. Nevertheless, the cultural background of both cities was very similar. The lake shores of Como and Lugano and the valleys of the Bergamasco produced an extraordinary quantity of skilled masters in

66   Milan cathedral: detail of the exterior of the nave and crossing

icant secondary masters like Gasparin Rosso and Niccolò Romanello, both skilled stone-carvers who worked at the Ca' d'Oro in the 1420s.

The others came from the lakes, from Lugano and Como. The shores of the former were the birthplaces of Pietro Solari (Lombardo), from the village of Carona, and of Zuan (Giovanni) Buora, from Ostheno. There was also a further group of lesser figures from Carona, including Viellmo, Michele and Zan-Antonio, and from Campione, including *maestri* Zanin and Piero. From nearby Lake Como came the brothers Antonio and Paolo Bregno, as well as other families or clans, including the Frison, who worked at the Ca' d'Oro in the 1420s, and the Bello family, who were active at San Zaccaria in the 1450s.

The *maestri comacini*, as they were often collectively known, remained a unique phenomenon, the only clearly identifiable group of masters, who travelled in large numbers from their region of origin, and settled elsewhere. The etymology of their name has been disputed, although it is clear that it derives from Como or the Comasco, the *contado* attached to the city. Their prestige was considerable: having learned their basic skills in the quarries of their home villages, and refined them further on one or other of the many great projects in Milan, they were widely sought elsewhere. The *maestri comacini* were as well known in Tuscany as they were in Venice, and some travelled as far south as Rome, where they established their own expatriate confraternity. Similar groups were established in Lucca, Siena and Genoa.[27] In Venice, though, their group identity was less strongly defined. Like the native masters, they were required to register with the appropriate guild, that of the *taiapietra*, before they could practise their craft, and they were bound by its statutes. They were also required to pledge an oath of allegiance to the Republic.

Master masons (or others) who migrated from other regions of Italy to Venice in this period were comparatively rare. There is a handful of references to masons or sculptors, for example, from Florence, including the significant figure of Nanni di Bartolo, as well as a Niccolò Fiorentino and Zane di Martino da Fiesole, who assisted Pietro Lamberti on the tomb of Doge Tommaso Malipiero in the early 1420s. Lamberti himself was of Florentine origin, the son of Niccolò, who had also lived much of his life in Venice, where he was active from 1416 to 1451; he was to outlive his son, in fact, who died in 1435.[28]

Throughout the fifteenth century, therefore, there were many foreign masters working in Venice. Their services were frequently essential to augment the native masters and to provide sufficient numbers in an era of expanding population and considerable construction activity. Government intervention, however, was necessary on more than one occasion to protect the position of the native masters; in 1456, for example, the latter felt sufficiently threatened by the bringing in to the city of stone that had already been carved abroad that the Giustizia Vecchia was persuaded to impose a fine of 300 lire on any person importing finished stone. (This ban did not apply, of course, to stone brought across from Istria, since the peninsula was a Venetian possession.) And in 1469 the Giustizia decreed that any foreign master who wished to trade in stone or marble or establish a workshop had to be a permanent resident in the lands of the Republic.[29]

Although registration by foreign masters with the guild generally presented no difficulty, stringent conditions were at first imposed on those who wished to establish an independent workshop in the city, rather than remaining content to work on a day-wage basis, as many of them did. Those wishing to set up their

67 The title page of the statutes of the guild of stonemasons, 1517

68   The stonemason's yard: watercolour of a mason's yard at San Polo, dated 1545

own shop had to take up citizenship *de intus*, which was at first granted only after fifteen years' continuous residence, but which, by the later fourteenth century, became progressively easier to obtain. Indeed, by about 1400 simple proof of residency and guild registration was almost sufficient in itself, and if the master then married a native Venetian, citizenship became virtually automatic. Several foreign masters did, in fact, marry Venetian wives, including Matteo Raverti.[30]

Although the Republic itself thus broadly welcomed skilled foreign masters to enhance the prestige of the Serenissima, and to supplement local shortages of skilled labour, the native masters naturally had different priorities. While there was little concern regarding day workers, foreigners establishing new workshops posed a more direct threat to their own livelihoods, and the Venetian masters attempted to impose more restrictive practices onto the guild. Towards the end of the century, though, the masons' guild experienced a fairly serious crisis of numbers; on 12 October 1486 Antonio Rizzo, who was *proto* at the Palazzo Ducale, had to petition the Collegio directly to ensure that adequate numbers of foreign masters remained in the city to ensure progress on the site. As the Collegio recorded, 'Rizzo considers it necessary, so that the said masons remain in Venice to work on the Palace . . . that they are permitted to retain their own apprentices [*famulos*], and to keep their own workshops in this

city'. It was made clear, though, that this was a special dispensation, which would apply only until the palace was completed.[31]

Only a few years later, however, in 1491, the total number of native master masons had fallen to a mere forty (including the old and disabled), whereas the natives themselves stated that 'foreigners, that is, the Milanesi and those from alien lands, now number 126 in all, and they also have about 50 apprentices being trained'. The Venetian masons were understandably concerned that they now lacked the majority to control their own guild, and they succeeded in obtaining permission that the number of foreign masters eligible to vote should not exceed those of the natives. These relative numbers, and, in particular, the strikingly small number of Venetian masons, clearly demonstrate that the large group of important building projects being undertaken at this time – not only the Palazzo Ducale but also the Scuola Grande di San Marco, and that of San Giovanni Evangelista, and the churches and palaces being designed by Codussi and Lombardo – could simply not have been completed without this 'foreign' contribution, which then amounted to three-quarters of the total membership of the guild.[32]

This picture of a relatively small number of native masters compared with foreigners continued well into the following century. Certainly, the names of many of the most outstanding master masons and sculptors in the early sixteenth century are either those of 'real' for-

73

69 The mason at work: capital from the Piazzetta façade of the Palazzo Ducale (copy of fifteenth-century original)

eigners or masters from the Venetian Terraferma, among them the de' Grigi family, the Lombardo family workshop and Antonio Scarpagnino. Later again, we find the famous figures of Sansovino and Palladio, among others, augmenting the native skills.

THE FAMILY WORKSHOP

Although Venice was a great and wealthy city, it was not a metropolis of such a scale as to deny the development of networks among the masters of the building crafts. Indeed, by the last quarter of the century, when there were fewer than 200 qualified masons, it was feasible for a significant proportion of these men to know each other personally; they would also have been aware of the projects that the most prominent workshop heads were working on, and such matters must have been discussed regularly at the meetings of the guild. And sure enough, records confirm the existence of a number of such networks, of groups of men who worked together on several occasions on different projects, and who thus formed informal alliances; there were also sometimes more formal legal partnerships or companies. We should first, however, consider the individual shop, before making a few observations on these interconnecting networks.

The Venetian building workshop was essentially a family business, and this general statement holds true for all three of the principal construction guilds. Trades were usually continued in a linear fashion, from father to son and grandson, and this type of family 'company' (which was generally registered as such with the Giustizia Vecchia) was by far the most widespread arrangement. We find a simple father and son partnership, for example, in the case of Zane and Bartolomeo Bon, although since the latter was Zane's only son, the shop's character changed after Zane's death, when Bartolomeo took on Pantaleon di Paolo as his new partner. They also generally kept a couple of apprentices who were not family members. Bartolomeo himself had several daughters but no sons, and so the family firm effectively died with him. Other 'linear' workshops, though, proved more durable.[33]

Another notable family shop was that of Pietro Lombardo, with his two sons, Tullio and Antonio, both of whom became outstanding masters in their own right. The shop survived for a further generation, too, with Tullio's son Sante, later *proto* at the Scuola Grande di San Rocco. In families with larger numbers of sons, it was not uncommon for most, if not all, to pursue their father's career; thus, Zane di Martin Bello, a mason who worked at San Zaccaria in the years 1459–62, had four sons following in his footsteps, Iacomo, Matteo, Marin and Alvise. Similarly, the builder Bortolomio di Luciano was in business with his four sons, Andrea, Matteo, Marco and Alvise. And again, three brothers, Zane, Felipo and Andrea Pizolo, all worked together at the Ca' d'Oro in the 1420s.[34]

Nevertheless, the father to son 'dynastic' arrangement was not universal, and there are a number of other examples of families whose younger generations diverged into different careers. For example, Vettor Gambello, one of the sons of Antonio, who was *proto* at San Zaccaria, instead became a distinguished medallist and himself became a different kind of *proto* in charge of the government mint. Stefano Fasan, too, a mason at the Ca' d'Oro in the 1420s, had three sons, Zanin, Gasparin and Vettor, two of whom later pursued different careers – only Vettor stayed in the family craft.[35]

Continuity, though, remained the rule rather than the exception, and some of these family arrangements became large and complex. The Frison family, who migrated from Milan to work for Marin Contarini in the 1420s, numbered Frison himself, Martin di Vielmo, Zuan Frison, Piero and Gasparin di Frison di Vielmo, a confusing descriptive grouping (as recorded by Marin himself), which suggests cousins as well as sons in the same workshop. The Taiamonte family, too, originally from Istria, had several branches, two of which originated with Domenico, and continued down at least two further generations, with Domenico's two sons, Martino and Francesco, as well as their own two sons in turn, another Domenico and Luca, the last becoming one of the most prominent masters in the city. A further branch, perhaps cousins of this first group, was headed by Nicolò, who himself had two sons, Antonio (who lived at San Severo) and Martino, of San Trovaso.[36]

Another clan of masons and quarrymen with strong Istrian connections was the dal Vescovo family; the head of the company was Rigo (Federigo), who lived at Rovigno, and who had two sons, Lorenzo and Domenico, both in the same business. Lorenzo continued the tradition with his son Michelino, and Michelino's own sons in turn, Antonio and Domenico.

But the most complex and extensive of these clan groupings are the Gruato, although since the name denotes a place of origin – Croatia – as well as a 'family' name, we cannot define its precise consanguineous extent. There was a branch at San Felice in the capital, headed by Lunardo, and which continued the masons' craft down four generations, through Domenico, his son Francesco, grandson Lunardo and great-grandson Alvise. Francesco, too, had two sons, both of whom were masons, and one of them, Bartolomeo, produced two further generations of stoneworkers, Nicolò, and a grandson, Bartolomeo again.[37]

Although they can be studied more closely than the other two building crafts, the masons were not alone in evincing these patterns of family partnerships; the carpenters were equally well represented, partly, perhaps, a reflection of the typical working practices on site. Any substantial new building required a large workforce of carpenters – for a time – to install the upper floors and the massive timbers of the roof, and such groups were frequently formed by family partnerships. Piero Alegro, for example, who installed the roof of the Carità church in the 1440s, was assisted by his sons Zorzi and Marco; several decades later, a family company that included another Marco and Zorzi, sons of Alegreto di Damiano, was active in the 1490s at the Scuola Grande di San Marco. A third example is the Candio family, one branch of which seems to have consisted chiefly of carpenters, while another member, known simply as Candio, was sometime *proto* in the employment of the Provveditori al Sal. Master builders, too, followed the same general pattern. At Palazzo Giustinian in the later 1470s, much of the work was executed by the Da Torre family, Antonio, Bartolomio, Marco and Venturin. And most of the structure of the Carità church had been built by the partnership of Steffanino de' Pavari and his son Piero.[38]

Two further brief observations complete this sketch of the organisation of Venetian building workshops.

One is to note that a number of companies did not fall into the pattern of consanguinity: they were simply partnerships between (usually) two men who were not related. The other is that, in all three crafts, many masters were not members of a fixed company, but were employed as day workers (*zornalieri*), and who appear in the records simply as individuals.

Partnerships between unrelated masters were fairly small in number, although we know of a few; two masters who worked at San Zaccaria under Codussi (Bernardin and Manfredo) were unrelated, as far as we can tell, as were – perhaps – the other two pairs of masters who worked on different elements of the façade: Zuane and Mathio, and Agustin and Pasqualin. Nor was the Bortolomio who was Domenico Taiamonte's partner at the Scuola Grande di San Marco in 1437; but we know that Domenico had four daughters and no recorded sons, so it was for that reason that he went into partnership with another. At the same project in the late 1480s, Pietro Lombardo's formal partner was Zuan Buora, rather than his own two sons, although this probably reflects their youth and lack of experience in running a substantial workshop.[39]

The building materials industry was also largely in the hands of family companies or partnerships, some of them noble, others not. Two or three examples will suffice: the Busetto (Buxeto) family, consisting of three brothers, Bernardo, Nicolò and Michele, sons of Rigo, supplied stone for the Scuola Grande di San Marco in the 1480s; the Trevisan family supplied timber, both sawn beams and piles, for several major building projects, including the Scuola again; and the family of Bortolomio, Gasparin and Almoro da Pramaior all ran a timber supply company, and provided piles for the façade of the Ca' d'Oro in 1427.[40]

NETWORKS AND CONNECTIONS

We are able to piece together the careers of a handful of the leading masters of the fifteenth century, as well as those of a number of secondary craftsmen and suppliers. Many careers can be seen to overlap, through networks of contacts or of having clients in common. Indeed, one of the more striking ways in which these links can be traced is by looking at the secondary masters, figures whose careers shadowed those of their more illustrious contemporaries.

Such networks may be illustrated by examining the career of Bartolomeo Bon, the most outstanding master mason of the middle decades of the century. We find many links with other craftsmen that formed parallel biographies. There is no more striking example than the blacksmith Niccolò Luxe or Lusse, whose smithy was at Santa Maria Formosa. Luxe is first recorded contributing towards Marin Contarini's new palace at Santa Sofia in 1429, where Bon was chief mason. Luxe was engaged here intermittently until 1433, and provided virtually all the metalwork, including ties and straps for stonework, as well as locks and grilles for windows. In 1440 Luxe provided metalwork for the Corte Nova almshouses at the Misericordia, where again Bon carved some of the stonework, and where the carpenter Cristoforo Candio also worked. In the early 1440s Luxe once again provided metalwork for the tomb of Marco Morosini at the Madonna dell'Orto, itself once again largely the work of Bon, and where two other familiar names appear: Steffanino de' Pavari, the builder, and Cristoforo, the carpenter. Finally, in 1442–3 Luxe was employed by the Carità church, yet again following the carving of stone for the windows by Bartolomeo Bon; he remained involved there as late as 1452.[41]

The career of Pantaleon di Paolo also shadowed that of the younger Bon for some time before they established a more formal partnership. Pantaleon had also contributed to the stone-carving for Corte Nova, and he was employed both by the Scuola della Carità and by the adjacent church, the former in 1442 and the latter a decade later; his association with the church went back as far as 1426. But it was only in 1463 that Pantaleon and Bon were cited together as partners, engaged in uncompleted works at the Palazzo Ducale. Other, lesser masons' careers also overlapped those of both of these masters: Antonio Foscolo, for example, was engaged at both the Corte Nova and at the Ca' d'Oro, thus following Bon's own career for a time.[42]

In a slightly later period, similar connections can be found among most of the leading masters of the period. Zuan Buora, for example, worked at San Zaccaria under both Gambello and Codussi; later he worked in partnership with Pietro Lombardo at the Scuola Grande di San Marco, where Codussi completed the façade. Many more such links can be found in the chapters that follow.

CONTRACTS AND PROCEDURES

The smallest building projects were generally administered by a master builder or *murer*, who was responsible for the basic structure, and for coordinating the other crafts, chiefly that of the carpenters, and to a lesser extent the stonemasons. While the master builder had no training in the working of stone, he was generally responsible for the fixing of the limited quantities of stone that were required in such works; for example, in the construction of the Corte Nova almshouses for the Procurators, or for works of restoration or alteration. In such cases, he ordered the stone from one of the shops in the city; its use was generally confined to simple sections or slabs for door and window frames, for sills, gutters and perhaps cornices.

The *murer* was thus a coordinator as well as an all-round general contractor. On new projects he usually supervised piling operations, although this work was carried out by specialist gangs of pile-drivers, who remained something of a breed apart. But the *murer* still had to build his walls on top of these piles, so he had a close vested interest in their satisfactory installation. He also had to coordinate his own activities with those of the carpenter, whose contributions were required in stages, to install the upper floors and stairs, and, later, to fit the structure of the roof. Finally, the *murer* himself was again responsible for roof tiling and general finishing operations, including plastering, terrazzo flooring (always carried out by a specialist under his supervision), drain connections, and so on.[43]

On larger, more complex projects, the site organisational structure was naturally more intricate and hierarchical. There were a number of highly prestigious projects that consisted largely of carved stonework, and in such cases it was usual to appoint the chief master mason or sculptor as the contracted party, and agree an overall fee for the work in advance. Projects approached in this manner included the Molo window and the Porta della Carta, both at the Palazzo Ducale, as well as prestigious works of sculpture such as the ducal monuments by the Lombardo workshop, and (almost certainly) the Arsenale gate, although the accounts for the latter have not survived. In such works, the involvement of crafts other than that of the master sculptor-mason was fairly limited – chiefly the construction of simple support walls of brickwork – and was otherwise confined to what today we would call 'attendance' operations to assist the master mason.

The provision of stone for such works was usually the subject of a separate agreement; sometimes it was provided by the patron, on other occasions sums were given to the master in advance to go across to Istria and select and purchase stone from the quarries. Payment to the masters was generally made on a regular basis, at intervals, as the work progressed, usually by mutual prior agreement. Such prestigious works, though, were the exception rather than the rule, and most building projects of medium size required roughly equal contributions from each of the three chief building crafts. Again, though, the master builder took the coordinating role.

In all but the very largest and most prestigious projects, therefore, the master builder ran the site. Other than the general coordination of minor, specialised crafts (like terrazzo-laying) the only major operation outside his direct control was the installation of the roof structure. In several examples, the contracts to supply the timbers and to erect the roof were the subject of separate agreements made directly between the patron and the craftsman. This was the pattern, for example, at the Ca' d'Oro in the 1430s, at the Carità church in the 1440s, and again, later still, at San Zaccaria. The assembly of the roof was regarded as a substantial separate operation, quite distinct from the walls that the *mureri* had built to support it.[44]

The cost of the timber was often considerable, too, well beyond the means of the craftsmen to buy themselves in advance. It was thus usually ordered directly by the patron, following the specification of the master *marangono*. The assembly of the roof structure often required large numbers of manual labourers (*manovali*) as well as the carpenters themselves. While this opera-tion was in hand, too, no other works could be undertaken on site: it was not only impractical but highly dangerous. The only other craft that impinged on this process was that of the smith, who provided large quantities of nails, straps, ties, braces and other fittings to hold together the great trusses that formed the roof structure of most large new buildings.

Once the roof structure was complete, the master builder had to return to lay the roof finish, which almost always consisted of interlocking 'Roman' clay tiles. With the building now weatherproof, it was also possible to complete internal finishes, such as plastering to the walls, and the application of any decorative finishes, such as frescos or painted decoration to the ceiling structures.[45]

Only in the largest, most prestigious projects did the pattern of site organisation differ significantly from that sketched above; these were projects that employed a permanent salaried *proto*, and these will be the subject of later chapters.

70   Pile-driving, from an eighteenth-century watercolour by Giovanni
Grevembroch

Chapter Four

THE BUILDING INDUSTRY

Sources, Suppliers and Costs

Throughout the fifteenth century, much of the building supply industry was in the control of the nobility;
not by the Republic itself, but in a direct sense: many
nobles invested widely in the manufacture and supply
of building materials.

Most wealthy patrician clans had at least one branch
that counted the provision of construction materials
within their range of business activities. A selection of
'long' families (that is, the 'true original' nobility) who
were thus involved includes members of the Bembo,
Dolfin, Memmo and Morosini, as well as the most
prominent clan in this field, the Corner or Cornaro. A
glance at the 'short' families produces the equally illustrious names of the Barbarigo, Bernardo, Duodo,
Loredan, Pasqualigo and (here again the most prominent of the group) the Trevisan. Given the patchy
nature of surviving documentary evidence, we cannot
draw any broad conclusions as to the importance of
these activities within the clans' investment activity:
many records indicate an isolated deal, whereas elsewhere we find large-scale commercial enterprise.

The activities of the patriciate can be grouped into
three categories, corresponding to the three principal
crafts of the industry: the provision of timber for construction; the manufacture and supply of processed
goods, chiefly bricks and tiles; and the supply of high-
quality materials, that is, stone and marble. There was
little, if any, noble investment in the supply of humble
bulk materials such as sand and water, and only rarely

in the basic but essential lime for bricklaying and plastering. In this last category, one of very few records is
that of Marin Contarini, who owned kilns near Padua,
which supplied lime for his own new palace in the
1420s; and a second example, Marco di Polo Morosini,
who owned kilns in Istria.

STONE AND MARBLE

In the case of the noblest materials, marble and stone,
the involvement of the patriciate was less extensive than
we might expect; the overwhelming majority of stone
(in volumetric terms, certainly more than 90 per cent
of the total) came from Istria, and its transport across
the gulf was – like its winning and working – largely in
the hands of the masons and mason-dealers, both in the
city and at the quarries. The patriciate generally kept
at arm's length from these activities, and few owned
quarries themselves. Perhaps the return on the investment was too small to interest them; certainly, the distance would have meant leaving the quarry in the
hands of a member of the clan or a local manager.

The stone itself remained the essential building stone
of Venice, as it had in the fourteenth century, and
indeed was to remain in the following centuries.
Among the many references to Istrian stone in the
architectural treatises of the Renaissance, that of Alberti
was the first: 'Istria produces a Stone very like Marble,
but if touch'd either by Flame or Vapour, it immediately flies in Pieces, which indeed is said to be the Case
of all Stones . . . that they cannot endure Fire'.[1] Alberti

correctly attributed to the stone some of the characteristics of marble, although, as he probably knew, it is in fact a dense limestone. A century later, Sansovino made similar observations:

> A beautiful and marvellous thing is the real stone that is brought [to Venice] from Rovigno, and from Brioni, fortresses on the Dalmatian coast [in fact, on the west shores of Istria]; it is white in colour, and similar to marble, but firm and strong in character such that it endures for a very long time against the ice and the sun; from it can be made statues, which, when polished with felt like marble . . . have the appearance of marble.[2]

The quarries were all on the coast, but they fell into distinct groups, with different qualities of stone from each zone. The most important quarries, which produced not only the best quality but also the greatest quantities and the largest sizes of block, were at three locations: one was at Orsera, one a little further south, and the third was just south of Rovigno; all three were generically described as Rovigno stone. In many building contracts Rovigno stone is specified by name, as it was, for example, in that with Bon for the Porta della Carta in 1438. Stone of a secondary quality was obtained from Pola, 30 kilometres further south, and from the two Brioni islands, off the shore nearby. Brioni stone was yellowish and inferior to that of Rovigno. The third, and distinctly third-quality stone, was derived from Cittanova, north of Parenzo (Porec); it had poor frost resistance, and its use was generally confined to producing lime for mortar and plastering.[3] The statutes of the stonemasons' guild reflected their knowledge of these different qualities; for example, they forbade the use of different types of stone in one piece of work, and its place of origin had to be indicated, 'that is, from Pola, Parenzo or Rovigno or from any other place', thus identifying the three chief zones of production and grades of quality.[4]

Stone was not only ordered for a specific project, but for particular elements of work within that project. In large new building works, the *proto* or chief mason would usually go across to Rovigno to select, buy and arrange for the transport of the stone back to the city. He was almost always given cash in advance by his employer, since the sums involved were often considerable. Routine requirements, such as one, for example, for 100 feet (34.7 m) of simple steps, could be ordered in advance provided that the basic dimensions were established; large bedding slabs (*piere da leto*) for foundations could be ordered in a similar way. Small quantities for local refurbishment works could also often be bought direct from yards in the city. But for more complex or finished work, examination and selection at the quarry was essential.

As we would expect, the larger and more costly the building, the more stone was required, and hence more frequent visits across the gulf were necessary. San Zaccaria is the project about which we have the most detail, and it was also one of the costliest in its requirement for stone. Both Antonio Gambello and Mauro Codussi (*proti* in succession) visited Rovigno several times, while their seconds in command made still more frequent journeys. The indefatigable Venier, for example, was in Istria in 1459, 1460, 1461, 1463 and 1464, with further voyages in the 1470s. These visits were generally made in the summer, partly because the crossing was safer, but also because the quarrying season itself was the summer (as recommended by Vitruvius, Alberti and Sansovino), after which the stone could be properly conditioned before use.[5] Occasionally, masons were sent to work stone at the quarry itself, sometimes for a period of some months; again, we have the example of Venier in 1459 and 1476, and his colleague Marin di Zane in 1460.

Quarries were usually owned by groups or partnerships, many of them family companies. There were a number of large local clans in Istria, such as the Sponza, several members of which were involved with quarrying in different locations. The dal Vescovo clan was another, as was the Busetto or Buxeto family. Istria was such an old-established Venetian possession that there were many family ties across the gulf; the family of the well-known Luca Taiamonte, for example, was of Rovigno origin, and Luca himself, although long resident in the capital, owned land and property there; the Buxeto, too, had resident branches on both sides of the gulf.[6]

The process of bringing stone to the city was fairly simple. Since the quarries were on the coast, the blocks could be loaded directly into the cargo vessels. By law, all Istrian stone had to be brought to the capital before its onward distribution, either within the lagoons or to another city such as Ferrara or Bologna. The vessels used were *marani*, broad, long ships, lateen-rigged, and with either one or two masts. Their capacity was typically around 200 tonnes, and these sturdy vessels were also used to carry other bulk goods, such as grain or timber, around the northern Adriatic. On arrival in the city, it was sometimes necessary to transfer the stone to smaller vessels of shallower draft, in order to moor at the yard or building site.[7]

The involvement of the patriciate in this activity was not extensive. On the few occasions when stone was bought from the nobility, it seems to have already been in the city and readily available, perhaps surplus to requirements on another project. A rare example is the purchase of *lapidibus a lecto* (bedding slabs) from Paolo Bernardo in 1438 for the almshouses at Corte Nova in Cannaregio, and valued at 38 ducats.[8] More prominent are several occasions when stone was provided by the nobility for the prestigious reconstruction of San Zaccaria from 1458 onwards. In that year, Niccolò Bernardo provided 28 ducats' worth of stone in two deliveries, both again of bedding slabs; he also dealt in timber.[9]

In the autumn of the same year a large quantity of stone steps was bought from *ser* Paolo Barbo, payment being made by another nobleman, perhaps a partner, Emanuel Girardo. This stone, 102 feet (41.6 m) in length, was delivered to the site from Barbo's own house, again suggesting that he had stone left over from works to his own palace. In the following summer, Francesco di Giacomo Marcello provided 'Padua stone' (*trachite?*) valued at 60 lire.[10]

Such examples remain conspicuous by their rarity. More frequent, although still modest in scale, are records of the nobility providing marble and other rare stone for incorporation as special features in a new building. These pieces sometimes took the form of highly regarded Greek marbles or porphyry; sometimes they consisted of entire elements – capitals or columns – that were sold, often at high cost, for reuse. A few examples indicate the character of these dealings.

On 15 August 1443 the Scuola Grande della Carità bought a column and two slabs of marble from the Duodo family for their new *albergo*; they were delivered to the yard of Pantaleon (di Paolo?), at Santa Maria Zobenigo, to be worked further before delivery to the site.[11] On several occasions, marble was bought from the nobility for San Zaccaria, too. In 1459, for example, a sheet of marble worth 3 ducats was bought from Zuane Barbarigo; a few years later, the nunnery took delivery of marble columns that had been donated to them by Iacomo Barbarigo, Captain of the Gulf; and in 1464 another marble slab was offered free of charge by a 'zentilhomo da cha nadal'.[12]

Not surprisingly, the use of such slabs of rare marble was confined to the more grandiose projects. Towards the end of the fifteenth century, a great effort of construction activity by the Scuole Grandi provided scope for the incorporation of many such pieces into their ornate façades. At that of San Marco, for example, in 1491 Lunardo Vendramin sold a large quantity of Carrara marble, amounting to 263 feet (91.2 m) in length, which was to be sliced into panels; he also sold

small strips of *bardiglio*, the fine grey marble from Lucca in Tuscany.[13]

As discussed elsewhere, the recycling of stone and marble was a significant 'industry' in itself, and the classical ruins of Pola, Aquileia and elsewhere were all extensively 'quarried' (or perhaps we should say pillaged). Rare marbles were also almost certainly acquired by noble merchants on trading voyages to Greece and the Middle East: not only was the stone a useful ballast, but it could also be a profitable sideline.

Later, in the 1520s, the long process of building the Scuola Grande di San Rocco included the provision of two consignments of stone from noble suppliers, when Pietro Bon was *proto* in the early 1520s. In 1523 Francesco di Priuli was paid 15 ducats for serpentine, and four years later Carlo di Francesco Cappello, together with his partner Polo Loredan, sold two columns of Greek marble which had been ordered as much as three years earlier.[14] Finally, in 1528 the Procurators of San Marco, who were then building the Miani chapel at San Michele, under the supervision of Guglielmo de' Grigi, bought two sections of serpentine column, which were to be sliced into roundels and set into the stone pilasters of the chapel. They were bought from the Priuli *casada* for 8 ducats.[15]

A scattered picture emerges, therefore, of noble dabbling in this specialised trade, and it must have been a very minor sideline to their more important trading activities. But there was one small group of nobles whose position gave them greater opportunities, and these were high-ranking clerics. By definition they were all patricians, and both the patriarch of Grado and the Bishop of Torcello added the recycling of stone and marble to their more orthodox clerical activities.

In 1441, for example, the patriarch, Marco Condulmer, sold stone for the almshouses at Corte Nova in Cannaregio.[16] A little later, the Bishop of Torcello provided columns for two important projects, San Zaccaria and the great new west portal at Santi Giovanni e Paolo. Indeed, he contributed to San Zaccaria on two occasions in quick succession; on the first, a deal was struck with his agent, Zuane Gallo, and another interested party, Iacomo Morosino (acting for the monastery of San Ieronimo), for the provision of columns from the now-abandoned monastery of Sant'Andrea at Ammiana, within the bishop's see.[17] On the second occasion, stones were salvaged from another abandoned house in the northern lagoon, in this case a carefully unnamed monastery at Lio Mazor.[18] Our last example of such episcopal enterprise relates to the large columns of very fine Greek marble for the west doorway of Santi Giovanni e Paolo. These were to be supplied to

71 Torcello: aerial photograph of the present hamlet, with the cathedral, campanile and church of Santa Fosca

Bartolomeo Bon, who worked on the contract assisted by Luca Taiamonte and two others.[19] Since these last three deals all took place within a single year, 1456, it is highly likely, by simple extrapolation, that this was a widespread and lucrative activity, one that thrived despite government edicts and local bye-laws issued by the apparently ineffectual governor of Torcello, all of which forbade such despoliation (fig. 71).

This creative recycling of the lagunar heritage was not confined to the higher clergy, and there are several instances of humble *pievani* (parish priests) dabbling in the same field of business. That of Santa Maria Zobenigo, for example, sold columns and capitals to the Scuola della Carità in 1443,[20] and in 1460 San Zaccaria also bought marble from the priest of San Martino for 5 ducats.[21] To illustrate the point that the practice continued well into the sixteenth century, in 1528 a single marble column was supplied by the *pievan* and parish councillors of Santa Maria Formosa to the Procurators, to decorate the richly detailed Miani chapel. This was a shaft of 'marmoro zode griecho boletisini', 7 feet long and 1 foot in diameter (2.4 × 0.347 m). This highly prized piece cost 16 ducats and was to be cut down into four smaller colonnettes, 'per I do altarij minorij', to form pairs for each of the flanking altars.[22] In a similar manner, in 1536 the priest of Santa Maria Nova

sold eight marble columns to the Scuola Grande di San Rocco for a total of 55 ducats.[23]

Since all the monastic houses were administered by abbots or priors who were nobles, there was also a good deal of 'inter-monastic' trade in stones and marble. Both San Zaccaria and the Procurators who built the Miani chapel made deals with other monastic houses to supply them with marble. At the latter, two columns were bought from the prior of Sant'Elena, again in the busy year of 1528. Evidently particularly highly regarded, they were described as 'colone do comprade dal ditto monastero ... dj piera meschin dj piuj colorj atachade negre roze zalla et bianche molto bele' ('... with many different mixed colours including black, pink, yellow and white, very beautiful'). They were intended to flank the main portal of the chapel on the outside wall, and cost a surprisingly reasonable 14 ducats for the pair, each one being 6½ feet long and just under a foot in diameter (2.2 × 0.347 m).[24] And as a final example of this activity, the monastery of San Pietro Martire at Murano sold a single column of Greek marble to the Scuola Grande di San Rocco in 1526.[25]

BRICKS AND TILES

The production of bricks and tiles had been under the supervision of the Giustizia Vecchia since 1222.[26] This initial regulation was not a set of formal guild statutes but a code of good practice, which demanded, *inter alia*, that all such products should be soundly made, properly burnt and of the legally correct size; the kiln operators (*fornaxieri*) were themselves bound by statute a few years later, in 1229. The *fornaxieri's* active year initially ran from 1 May to the end of October, and in 1327 the masters were required to conduct at least five firings in this period, a number increased to six in 1350. The Republic itself frequently intervened in assisting towards the cost of building kilns to ensure regular supplies, and ease shortages. On several occasions – for example, in 1320, 1327 and 1393 – inducements were offered to build more kilns.[27]

From the earliest records there were both owners and masters in the industry, the latter responsible for the management of the works. In 1330, for example, the nobleman Niccolò Grimani owned two kilns and employed a master to operate them for him.[28] Other owners, though, were not absentee nobles, but rather owner-operators, also described as *paroni di fornaxe independenti*.

Many kilns remained in the city, producing bricks and tiles, and also lime for plaster and mortar. Although in 1292 the city's glassworks had all been transferred to

Murano to obviate the danger from fire, brick kilns seem to have been unaffected. In 1317, for example, kilns operated by one Niccolò stood at San Gregorio, and he was given permission to rebuild them in that year.[29] In the early fourteenth century there seem to have been serious shortages of bricks, since in 1320 the Maggior Consiglio offered 100 lire *di grossi* (1,000 ducats, a large sum of money) to any Venetian willing to build new furnaces.[30] And in the same year the Consiglio granted Giovanni di Simone Michiel of San Cassan the right to build a furnace at Tombello, near Mestre.[31] Only a few years later, the Consiglio gave the Giustizia Vecchia responsibility for the distribution of official moulds for bricks and tiles to all of the city's *fornaxieri*, to regulate their dimensions. Maximum selling prices were set at the same time.[32]

The purchase of timber to fire the kilns was controlled, and sources defined by the government. The wood had to come from Istria or Grado; the high-quality upland forests of the Friuli were forbidden for such humdrum purposes.[33] Occasionally, though, shortages of timber led to the derogation of these restrictions; in 1329, for example, Niccolò Grimani was permitted to broaden his field of acquisition.[34]

In 1350 an acute shortage of building materials led the Quarantia Civil (the justices responsible for the Terraferma) to issue a series of edicts to stimulate production. These shortages were a direct result of the appalling losses from the great plague of 1348, and the resultant acute lack of manpower in the city. All the kilns in the capital were sequestered by the government and were offered to auction to the highest new bidder, only one furnace being allowed to each applicant.[35] And in 1384 another acute shortage of timber (this time partly a result of the recent war with Genoa) drastically reduced production of bricks and tiles, such that the Quarantia decreed that all *fornaxieri* could acquire their own timber (with their own ships) from Istria, but only until September of that year.[36]

Nearly a decade later, in May 1393, the Senate recorded that there were then no kilns in Mestre, and that it had recently been necessary to obtain brick from Padua, which at this time was not yet a Venetian city. The Canale Salso, connecting Mestre to the lagoon, had been excavated in 1361, thus offering the facility of direct delivery by boat from the brickfields to the city's building sites. A government loan was now made available, of up to 2,000 lire *di piccoli*, to anyone wishing to build and operate new kilns in Mestre. The proposal was announced by public decree in Venice, Treviso and in Mestre itself.[37] This measure, combined with the new water access, was to prove decisive in Mestre's development as an important centre of production. The initial response, however, was slow, and only two applications had been made and approved by the following June, of 1394. So, as a further inducement, the loan facility was doubled to 4,000 lire.[38]

In 1418 violent storms struck the city and the Dogado. Among the casualties was the top of the campanile of San Marco, which was set alight by lightning. Another victim was Treviso (also a centre of brick production), which suffered so much damage that the Trevisani were allowed to buy bricks in Venice for their own use free of tax, until their own kilns were repaired.[39] A decade later again, the *fornaxieri* of Venice drafted a petition to the Provveditori di Comun, which was forwarded for determination by the Quarantia; it was debated on 14 June 1429. The furnace men lobbied for an increase in the maximum legal sale price of bricks but a reduction in that of lime. Their request was approved, together with another forbidding the *burchieri* (bargemen) of the city to accumulate stockpiles of bricks and tiles in their yards and warehouses; instead the materials had to be bought at the place of embarkation to the capital, that is, generally at Fusina or Marghera.

The price increase reflects inflationary tendencies in this period, and it was followed by a further proposal, by Niccolò Memmo, one of the Provveditori di Comun, to permit the Venetian *fornaxieri* to 'sell their bricks, tiles and lime as they wish, and subject to the same conditions as foreigners, who, in selling their own goods, are not subject to any fixed price'.[40] Memmo was unsuccessful at this attempted deregulation, and was defeated in the Senate by 78 votes to 43.

The controlled price of bricks now rose from 11 lire per thousand to 12 lire, and small bricks from L. 3.4.0. to L. 3.10.0. On the other hand, lime was reduced from 10 soldi per barrel to 8½ soldi. Later that year, too, the Giustizia Vecchia decreed that the provenance of all bricks had to be clearly stated by the vendor, on penalty of forfeiting the goods, as well as 'such financial penalty as the Giustizia may decide'.[41]

The Nobility and the Industry

The involvement of the nobility in the supply of both bricks and timber was far more important than their dealings in stone, and also more professionally organised. The many building programmes in Venice in the fifteenth century required the reliable, regular supply of exceptionally large quantities of bricks. New buildings such as San Michele, San Zaccaria and the Scuola Grande di San Marco, although faced with stone, all relied on a basic structure of brickwork onto which the cladding was fixed. Bricks were sometimes reclaimed from an earlier building on the same site, as was the case with Marin Contarini's new palace at Santa Sofia in the early 1420s. Reclamation was also perhaps still feasible on the abandoned monastic islands in the northern lagoon; stone was certainly still being pilfered here, despite official condemnation, and there is no reason to think that bricks were not recycled in the same way, although the rewards were lower. A third source, the classical Roman ruins at Altino on the nearby Terraferma, was probably exhausted by now, although in earlier periods Altino, too, had been a useful 'quarry'.[42]

In the fifteenth century, new bricks generally came from the adjacent Terraferma, most from Mestre, the rest from Padua and Treviso. Prohibitive transport costs generally made supplies from further afield uneconomic, although at times of shortage they were sometimes obtained from as far as Ferrara. Several Venetian noble clans were prominent in this field, particularly in the period from 1430 to the mid-1440s. Almost all the bricks for the upper storeys of the Ca' d'Oro, for example, were bought from *ser* Marco Bembo, most of them in regular deliveries of 3,000 at a time, equivalent to one fully laden barge load. Bembo owned a commercial brickworks of some size, since he was able to supply 60,000 at regular intervals over three months in the autumn of 1429.[43] In the same year, another nobleman, Antonio Venier, provided bricks for the almshouses at Corte Nova.[44]

A decade or so later, Andrea Polo and Iacomo Caroldo together supplied all the bricks for the new *albergo* at the Scuola della Carità, 38,000 in one series of deliveries alone; again, the two men ran a substantial commercial enterprise, which included providing roof tiles for the same project.[45] Towards the end of the century, a prominent noble family, the Loredan, provided large quantities of bricks for San Zaccaria, a project with which the clan was closely associated. In 1483 Lorenzo di Antonio supplied as many as 51,000 in the single month of July, and a further 25,000 in August. They were followed by a final consignment of 28,000 two years later.[46] Lorenzo's close involvement with the project will be discussed later; among his other roles he was the sponsor of Mauro Codussi as the new *proto* in 1483.[47] And early in the next century we find Polo Pasqualigo of Treviso, who, over a period of two weeks in 1507 provided 42,000 bricks for the Procurators, who were then restoring buildings in the estate of India Formenti.[48]

However, there was one noble *casada* that stands out above all the others in the extent of their activities in this field: the extremely wealthy Corner clan of San Samuele. Our first record of this substantial commercial enterprise seems to be that of 1428, when Zane di Francesco owned some brickworks at Sant'Elena, between Altino and Treviso, as well as further kilns at Isola di Cartura, beyond Padua towards Monselice.[49]

Zane Corner had two sons, Marco and Andrea. Around 1453 Andrea employed Bartolomeo Bon to begin building what was intended to be an imposing new palace on the Grand Canal at San Samuele; coincidentally, it was to be built on the site of former brick kilns. This palace, however, was never to proceed beyond the famous but fragmentary Ca' del Duca that we see today. Andrea and Marco were both deeply involved in the political plotting that followed the death of Doge Francesco Foscari in 1457. Donato Corner – from another branch of the clan – had attempted to obtain the ducal throne for his own father, Giacomo; Marco was implicated in the plot, and was involved in a second conspiracy when Bartolomeo Pisani tried to have Marco's brother Andrea elected to the Senate by fraudulent means. Andrea prudently fled the city, while Marco was banned from public office for ten years, and, as a result of this public disgrace, the site at San Samuele, with its barely begun palace, was confiscated by the Republic and given to the Sforza, dukes of Milan.[50]

Marco, however, made a rapid and spirited recovery from these setbacks; within five years he was trading again. He also fathered two of the most prominent Venetian figures of the later fifteenth century, Caterina, later to be queen of Cyprus, and Zorzi, widely believed to be the wealthiest man in the entire Republic. Marco had continued his father's interests in the construction industry, and supplied several of the most important projects in the city from 1439 until at least 1462. Of the three substantial projects of which we still have archival details, the first was the Corte Nova almshouses, for which he supplied up to around 100,000 bricks in 1439.[51]

The monastic church of the Carità, reconstructed in the 1440s, was also built almost entirely with Corner bricks. From July 1443 Marco supplied large, regular orders until the completion of both the nave and the chancel in 1452. The scale of his operations is apparent from the size and regularity of the shipments: from July to November 1443, for example, he provided 95,000 bricks in eight consignments, each of three or four barge loads, and deliveries of similar size continued until the summer of 1448. Corner signed a new contract in April 1451, guaranteeing to deliver 80,000 bricks in stages until the end of September, for the construction of the chancel. The monks negotiated a slightly better rate than usual for this order, L. 9.5.0. per thousand instead of the usual L. 11.0.0.[52] Finally, after 1462 (and Marco's temporary ban on trading),[53] he is also closely associated with San Zaccaria, where he delivered perhaps as many as 180,000 bricks in all.[54] Corner was clearly a manufacturer on a substantial scale, certainly the most prominent of the patricians who engaged in this field.

A final note provides evidence of another form of commercial ownership, that by the monastic houses. In 1418 there were extensive building works at San Pietro Martire on Murano; the bricks, 60,000 in all, were bought from the Friars Minor of San Francesco della Vigna in the city, at the usual commercial rate of 10 lire per thousand. The friars owned an extensive tract of land adjacent to the monastery, on the northern edge of the capital, within easy reach of Murano; they had constructed brick kilns on this land, perhaps originally for their own use, but which were also used on a commercial basis.[55]

The Costs of Bricks and Tiles

Fifteenth-century building accounts are always precise as to quantities and prices, usually because the patron paid for these goods directly. Much as the Venetian stonemason never had sufficient capital to pay for stone out of his own pocket, so, too, did the *murer* rely on his patron to purchase bricks for the works on his behalf. One of the best indications of availability and the condition of the industry is the purchase price of these essentials, which varied considerably over the course of the century. Bricks were described in one of three ways: *piere grandi* or simply *piere*, the standard full-size bricks; *piere piccole* and *piere da caminetij*. These last were small, special bricks, curved in shape, for the construction of chimneys. Most bricks fell into the first category, and their price varied from 8 to 14 lire per thousand. Bricks cheaper than this were probably reclaimed bricks or 'seconds'; in one example, at San Zaccaria, when *piere da tavolle* were required for hidden work in foundations, they cost only L. 7.10.0, at a time when the full market rate was 11 lire.[56]

The mid-fifteenth century was an era of comparative stability of both wages and the essentials of life; the variations in the costs of building materials therefore reflect local factors, chiefly availability and demand. Other than Mestre, Treviso and Padua, Ferrara is occasionally cited as a source, and more rarely still were bricks sourced from other centres of production, such as Camponogara (between Mestre and Padua) and Monselice.

Although on occasion there was a glut on the market such that these 'foreign' bricks could undercut the local products, more frequently there was a shortage in Venice as a result of high demand, so that it became necessary to import to meet it. An example of the first case was the purchase (in 1507) of bricks for almshouses at Santa Maria Nova when Treviso bricks were bought at only L. 8.5.0, compared with the usual price of 11 lire.[57] And in 1489 Paduan bricks for the Scuola di San Marco had cost only 9 lire compared again with the earlier, typical rate of 11–12 lire for local ones.[58] Usually, though, Ferrara, Padua and Treviso bricks were more expensive and were resorted to only in times of shortage. Such a time arose right at the end of the period of this study, when between 1531 and 1533–4 the price rose sharply from the very low level of 8 to 13 lire or even 14 lire in barely two years.[59]

Price variations were rarely as notable as this, though, and for nearly thirty years, from 1430 to 1460, almost all transactions fell within the range of L. 9.10.0 to L. 11.0.0. The occasional rises to higher levels can be attributed to serious flooding, which affected production in 1442 and 1444–5.[60] Bulk orders, too, were often negotiated to a more favourable rate;[61] at San Zaccaria in 1483, for example, when Lorenzo Loredan's close personal involvement with the project led to his supplying bricks at only 9 lire when the market rate was 11 lire.[62]

All new buildings also required roof tiles. They were produced in the same furnaces as bricks, and although most were locally produced, there were occasional consignments from elsewhere, from Padua, for example, in 1455, and Ferrara in 1477–8. Prices varied from 8 to 18 lire over the period 1430–60; no clear explanation is apparent, although because the scale of production was so much smaller (a new church like the Carità required well over 150,000 bricks but only 16,000 roof tiles), there were fewer economies of scale, and the market was more susceptible to fluctuations in demand. In general, the cost of tiles was about half as much again as that of bricks, reflecting the greater care required in all stages of production, from the selection of the clay to its formation in the mould, from firing to stacking and transporting; there were also losses due to breakage.[63]

TIMBER AND THE LESSER BUILDING MATERIALS

The city's demands for construction timber were considerable. Workers in timber fell into two groups, the *marangoni di nave* or ships' carpenters employed by the

Republic at the Arsenale, and the *marangoni di casa* or house carpenters. Later, in the sixteenth century, woodworkers were further subdivided into more specialised groups, among them the makers of picture frames and furniture. In practice, structural timber for building could be further divided into two basic types: unworked timber in the form of *tolpi* or stakes for driving piled foundations and for scaffolding, and worked (sawn or planed) timber for elements above ground, chiefly floors, staircases and roofs, as well as joinery for doors and windows.

The business interests of the nobility in the timber industry were broader and more numerous than the small number with interests in brickworks. Indeed, a fairly representative list of about sixty noble clans that provided building materials of all types between *circa* 1420 and 1520 reveals that half of these records, thirty in all, relate to the provision of construction timber, mostly carpentry but also *tolpi* for foundations.

We can suggest a few reasons why the patriciate was far more involved in the timber industry than in other aspects of construction activity. First, it may have been more profitable. Second, many noble families owned substantial estates in the upland forests of the Terraferma; in addition, there were Venetian nobles as governors of all the major timber-producing regions, based in towns such as Oderzo, Seraval, Udine, Feltre and Belluno. Third, to deal in timber it was not necessary to invest significant capital, such as that necessary for the kilns of large-scale brickworks. And finally, although not all new buildings required extensive use of stone, even the humblest row of cottages required significant quantities of timber for floors, roofs, doors and windows.

The nobility provided much of the timber for almost every new building project for which we have detailed records. Once again we find an illustrious roll-call from both 'old' and 'new' patrician clans: the Dolfin, Giustinian and Morosini among the former, the Barbarigo, Malipiero, Pasqualigo and Trevisan among the latter. As with the Corner clan's dominance in the supply of bricks, two families sprang to prominence in timber dealing, particularly in the period from 1440 to around 1470: the Trevisan and the ubiquitous figure of Costantin de' Briolo or Priuli.

The Trevisan were a large clan, although only certain branches of the *casada* were noble, the rest remaining *cittadini*. A branch based at Mazzorbo in the northern lagoon provided much of the timber for San Zaccaria after 1458; Bortolomio Trevisan provided hundreds of large piles to support the extremely heavy stone façade.[64] He was a dealer on a large, commercial scale.

Other members of the same clan were involved in construction projects at mid-century. Almoro, for example, supplied 'piuj legnamj' ('many timbers') for the roof of the chancel of the Carità church in 1465,[65] while Zaccaria di Pietro Trevisan supplied substantial beams for the reconstruction of Palazzo Giustinian at San Moisè in 1477.[66] At least one member of the family remained active in this field until well into the next century, when Domenego provided 3,000 piles for the Scuola Grande di San Marco in 1523.[67]

Although the provision of sawn, prepared timber was a different activity from the supply of piles, noble involvement in the former activity was also on a large, commercial scale. By far the most important dealer in the mid-fifteenth century was Costantin de' Briolo, whose dominant role parallels that of Marco Corner in supplying bricks. Costantin's family name is subject to an extraordinary variety of spellings (Broylio, Briolo, Priolo, etc.); he is probably the same Costantin de' Priuli (or Prioli) that Marin Sanudo identified as one of the city's 'huomeni famosi', the son of Lorenzo de' Priuli, and born, according to Sanudo, on 7 October 1420.[68]

In 1431, when Marin Contarini was building his new palace at Santa Sofia, he referred Niccolò Romanello, one of his most skilled stone-carvers, to the new Priuli *palazzo* on Rio dell'Osmarin (which still stands), where Romanello was to copy the detailing of the unusual corner window. The Priuli palace is described by Contarini as 'la chaza fo de ser Chostantin de priolij'. This Costantin was thus perhaps our own Costantin's grandfather and Lorenzo's father: Venetian Christian names were often reused not for sons, which was perhaps too confusing, but for alternate generations; Marin Contarini's own clan is an example: his father was Antonio, but his grandfather was another Marin.[69]

Our Costantin was active in the construction industry from the 1440s to the 1460s.[70] In the 1440s he provided a wide variety of timbers for the Carità church, including 'planks, boards and beams' (*palancule*, *tavole*, *travi*), and in the same period he supplied timber to the adjacent Scuola.[71] Later, in 1450–51, he again provided timber to complete the roof of the church's chancel. Costantin's yard may have been adjacent to his *palazzo*: in November 1443 a boatman was paid for transporting timber to the Scuola's *albergo* from 'cha da bruollo'.[72]

Costantin also provided timber for the Corte Nova almshouses in 1445, including floorboards and beams and rafters for the roofs.[73] And finally, like most of the major suppliers of the era, he was involved with the works at San Zaccaria, only a few minutes' walk from his own house. Timber for the new church came from many sources, including several patrician dealers – the Trevisan, Memmo and Morosini – and Costantin's contribution here took the form of a single large consignment, valued at 50 ducats, in March 1463.[74] More important suppliers to San Zaccaria were Almoro and Zusto Zuchato, who delivered 200 ducats' worth of timber in all, together with Zuanne Morosini, who in 1461–2 provided most of the timber to re-roof the old church.[75]

San Zaccaria took so long to complete that two generations were involved in the works. During Mauro Codussi's stewardship of the project after 1483, timber was sourced elsewhere; some roof timbers were provided by Andrea Mudaso,[76] while most of the remainder was delivered by Alvise Memmo and Benedetto da Pesaro, all three members of patrician dynasties.[77] Many other noble clans were also deeply involved in the timber trade. Andrea Pasqualigo, for example, delivered to the Scuola Grande di San Marco in the late 1480s, while later still, the same Scuola was supplied by both the Trevisan and Dolfin clans.[78]

The chief sources for piling timbers were the upland forests of the Cadore, whence the great logs were floated down the Piave and Tagliamento when they were in spring flood. Many new buildings have no records of piling operations, however, simply because, wherever possible, existing piles were reused. This was largely the case, for example, at the Ca' d'Oro in the 1420s, where only the façade required new piled foundations; and at the Carità church in the 1440s, where the new nave was squeezed between the existing monastic buildings and the campanile, which was also retained. Some decades later, at the Scuola Grande di San Marco, when the earlier building was destroyed by fire in 1485, the original foundations were again reused, a course of action that largely determined the dimensions and basic structure of the new building.

This is not at all surprising. Piling was costly and labour-intensive, and even in the dramatic case of the Scuola Grande di San Marco, there would have been little, if any, damage to the foundations, buried into the lagunar clay. But when an important project was begun *ex novo*, such as the new San Zaccaria, where a large, heavy stone façade was to rise where no such structure had risen before, then a veritable forest of massive new subterranean stakes was necessary. The Miani chapel at San Michele again required many piles, partly because the structure itself is particularly heavy, with extensive use of stone (and a stone domed roof), but also because of the precarious nature of its location, in the furthest corner of the island. Around 2,400 piles were necessary here to consolidate this small site, but even these proved inadequate, and Jacopo Sansovino was called in to effect strengthening works in 1560.[79]

The largest piling operation for which records have survived is that at San Zaccaria. The timbers were delivered in two stages, in 1458 and in 1462; the quantities indicate the impressive scale of these operations. In the first phase, nearly 4,200 piles were required, all of some size, while the operations of 1462 required a further 2,600. And to construct the timber decking (*zattaron*) on top of this forest, no fewer than 5,000 large planks were necessary, again all in 1462.[80]

Most piles were provided by specialised companies (*consorzi*) of dealers; they were subject to a duty or *dazio* on timber, payable to the Governador delle Intrade, and their activities were monitored by the Cinque Savii alla Mercanzia, the trading standards board. Many of the piles for Marin Contarini's new façade came from a family company based near Portogruaro, while the rest came from the company of Antonio and Zane del Amigo, who had a timber yard on the north shores of Cannaregio, and who dealt in both *tolpi* and in finished timber.[81] The piles for the Miani chapel were provided by Daniele Zonbolo, whose yard was at Murano, conveniently located for delivery to the site. Occasionally, sources other than the usual consortia were used, as was the case in 1457, for example, when extensive repairs were necessary to the quay in front of the Corte Nova alla Tana development, near the Arsenale. Here, the *tolpi* were sourced from the friars of San Giobbe, at the opposite end of the city; the quantity must have been considerable, since they cost 90 ducats, representing perhaps 4–5,000 in all.[82]

At the Ca' d'Oro, the piles bought from the del Amigo company cost 3 soldi apiece. The sizes of *tolpi* for piling were usually specified: 'small' (1 foot across), medium (1½ feet) or large, 2 feet across (0.347 m, 0.52 m and 0.694 m respectively). When Marin Contarini obtained such timbers from Pramaior, the smaller ones cost only 1 soldo apiece, whereas the largest were eight times as expensive, a reflection of the relative difficulty in obtaining such substantial timbers. Delivery charges were considerable, too: the Pramaior timber cost a further 40 percent on its purchase price in delivery and *dazio* charges before it arrived on site.[83]

At most large projects piles were costed by the hundred. At San Zaccaria, the medium-sized timbers varied from L. 8.10.0 to 13 lire per hundred, a significant range, since they were all ordered over only a four-year period; the very largest piles ranged from 17 to 20 lire per hundred. No doubt many factors played a part

72   Timber yards at Barbaria delle Tole, from Jacopo de' Barbari's woodcut of 1500

in these fluctuations, from the weather to their availability and demand in the city.[84]

Most of the timber yards were concentrated in one particular district, centred on the street known as Barbaria delle Tole, near Santi Giovanni e Paolo; *tole* is a corruption of *tavole*, that is, planks. It was the natural point of arrival into the city of the rafts of timber brought down the rivers and through the lagoon from the north. The larger commercial operations occupied long, narrow sites, with their workshops at the southern end, facing the street, and with yards and storage facilities behind them, stretching back to the lagoon shore, where the timbers were beached before seasoning. The yards were well established here by the early fourteenth century (figs 70, 72).[85]

The supply of construction timber from these yards depended very much on the nature of the project. The requirement for rough, sawn timber for San Zaccaria, for example, was limited to the *zattaron* for the foundations and for the unseen trusses in the roof. San Zaccaria was unique in Venice, however, in having stone vaulting throughout, whereas almost all other churches in the city had an open trussed timber roof, which, since it was exposed, had to be finished and decorated.

In general, the roofing of a large new building was approached as a substantial 'package' contract on its own. Since these carpenters had few resources, however, the patron usually negotiated a comprehensive all-in price for the timber itself, purchased directly from the yards in the Barbaria; such was the pattern, for example, at the Carità church and at San Zaccaria (fig. 73).[86]

Building Lime and Sand

Lime, a humble but essential material, was sold by the wooden barrel or *mastelo*, with a capacity of around 75 litres. Its production was largely in the hands of the manufacturers of bricks and tiles, both in the city and on the adjacent Terraferma. The provenance of lime is rarely recorded, although Padua was an important source, as was the northern coast of Istria, where the limestone was too poor to use directly in construction. Marin Contarini, for example, used lime from his own kilns near Padua in 1429, when building his new palace at Santa Sofia.[87]

Lime was generally characterised as 'white' or 'black'; the former was obtained from Padua and was derived from *scaglia*, a calcareous limestone, while the latter was generally obtained from Istria. The price of lime fluctuated considerably; in 1400 the typical price per barrel was 4 soldi, but by the time Contarini required supplies for his house, in the 1420s and 1430s, it had risen to 10 soldi on the open market, and he had to pay his own *fornaxier*, Bonaventura, 7 soldi even to cover his own costs.[88] A little later, in 1443, the Scuola della Carità paid between 6 and 8 soldi per barrel, while at the church next door the monks had paid only 5 soldi a few months earlier. More than ten years later, at San Zaccaria in 1458, prices varied from only 4 soldi up to 7½, again in the space of a few weeks; not surprisingly, we also see prices rising towards the end of the official season of production in October. The same general laws of fluctuation in supply and demand as we saw with bricks and tiles are again identifiable here. Here, too, we see the advantages of bulk buying as a way of keeping costs down: in 1460 San Zaccaria ordered very large consignments of lime, totalling 1,200 barrels, with well over half supplied at the highly competitive rate of 4 soldi. Here again, prices increased around the end of the century and beyond, such that at San Michele in the 1520 and the Scuola Grande di San Marco in 1534, the most typical price was now 7 or 8 soldi per barrel.[89]

Sand was equally humble, but equally essential to the building process. Its supply was in the hands of a small, specialised group of *sabioneri*, who had been recognised as an *arte* in their own right by the Giustizia Vecchia as early as 1280.[90] Sand for construction, and also for using as filters in the city's wells, was obtained from the Terraferma rivers, and was thus known as 'sabion de aqua dulci' (sand from sweet waters). It was transported in large barges known as *burchi* or *piati*. There were stringent controls over the maintenance and loading of these vessels to ensure that the sand was not contaminated with salt, that is, with lagunar water.

No foreigners were permitted to join the *arte*, and there was a brief period of apprenticeship before membership was allowed; apprentices were generally from ten to sixteen years old. Ownership of the *piati* rather resembled that of the *marani* used to transport stone across the gulf; some were single owners, or *cai di burchi*, while others grouped themselves into small companies, often with brother or fathers, to spread the costs of the investment between them.

On larger projects sand was delivered by the full barge load or even by a *burchio grande*. San Zaccaria's archive gives us some details of such operations: the sand was delivered by Zuan da Latisana, a small town on the Tagliamento, near Portogruaro. Zuan's sand, itself, however, was extracted from another river, the Brenta. Nearly sixty barge loads were required in all, at a cost of between 5 and 7 lire per load.[91] A little later, work at Palazzo Giustinian in July 1477 began with one consignment of sand from a *burchio grande*, followed by many lesser quantities from the smaller *burchi*, which had one-sixth of the capacity of a *burchio grande*.

Contracts, Wages and Methods of Payment

The Venetian patron in the fifteenth century had several ways of approaching the administration of a new construction contract, and we will now outline the forms of agreement that could be applied to such works, whether they were patronised by the state itself or by institutions such as the monastic houses or the Scuole Grandi.

THE EMPLOYMENT OF A *PROTOMAESTRO*

The essence of the role of a *protomaestro* or *proto* was that his post was permanent and salaried, and he was always paid directly by his commissioning client. The post frequently incorporated additional benefits, such as rent-free accommodation, but in the fifteenth century its adoption was confined to major government-sponsored or institutional projects. The *proto* was the coordinating, superintending master of the entire works, and was thus comparatively well paid, the other major advantage, of course, being security of employment and income for the duration – sometimes many years – of the project. Frequently, but not always, he was also the architect or chief designer of the work.

However, the small number of surviving examples of *proti* that we have reveal interesting differences in salaries. At San Zaccaria Antonio Gambello was paid 100 ducats a year when he took up his post in 1458, but his successor, Mauro Codussi, was paid only 80 ducats, the reduction being based on the premise that he would return to the Bergamasco every winter. Codussi also succeeded Pietro Lombardo at the Scuola Grande di San Marco in 1490, where he was initially paid only 5 ducats a month (60 ducats per annum), a salary that was increased a few months later to 6 ducats, still less than his income at San Zaccaria. On 25 October 1492, though, Codussi was suspended for his refusal to work for only 6 ducats a month; the disagreement was resolved, however, and he continued as

73 Bricklayers and roof carpenters on the scaffolding: detail of a fourteenth-century French miniature

proto until June 1495, when his permanent employment was considered completed.[92]

It is instructive to compare these salary levels to those paid by the Republic itself. The *proto* to the Provveditori al Sal was Niccolò Pain; in June 1486 his salary was increased to 90 ducats per year, which apparently brought it up to the level of that of his predecessor, Meneghin Bianco; Pain's earlier salary, though, is not stated. However, Pain's own successor, Bon the Bergamasco, was paid the same salary, 90 ducats, in 1495.[93]

Within the Palazzo Ducale itself, the remarkable career of Antonio Rizzo shows equally remarkable differences in remuneration; Rizzo had a far more successful career, at least in simple financial terms, than either Pain or Bon. As *proto dil palazzo* his initial salary in 1484 was 100 ducats; this was increased to 125 ducats in the summer of 1485, and then to no less than 200 ducats on 10 October 1491. This last was an exceptionally generous salary, partly the result of his persistent but successful lobbying of the Signoria, and partly a reflection of the importance attached by them to the completion of the Palazzo Ducale. After his disgrace, however, Rizzo's successor, Pietro Lombardo, saw his own salary reduced to Rizzo's former level – still a fairly good income – of 125 ducats per year.[94]

A review of government-paid salaries carried out by the Consiglio dei Dieci in 1495 also sheds some light on comparative incomes for one or two other masters then in the Republic's employment. The painters Giovanni Bellini and Alvise Vivarini, engaged in decorating the hall of the Maggior Consiglio with frescos, were both paid 60 ducats per year, while a lesser-known artist, Cristoforo da Parma, received 44 ducats, and Latantio da Rimini was given 48 ducats. On the same salary list – by way of further comparison – were Piero Sambo, *sorastante ai lidi* (chief surveyor of the sea defences), with 50 ducats, and Andrea Bonbozo, 'an accountant', with 60 ducats. To put these figures into context, an annual salary of 100 ducats was equivalent to around L. 2.10.0 (50 soldi) per day, about twice the daily rate of a craft master of medium rank and ability; an annual salary of about 50 ducats, therefore, approximately equated to a typical craft master's daily income, although again, the salaried man had the advantage of security of income, and fringe benefits as well.[95]

CONTRACTS: THE 'LUMP SUM' CONTRACT

Of the various forms of contract employed in this period, the 'lump sum' contract is the easiest to understand, but unfortunately is the least clear in what it tells us about the real level of remuneration that the masters received. A few examples indicate the nature of the work that was usually approached in this manner. Two of the most prominent and famous elements on the exterior of the Palazzo Ducale were contracted on this basis, the Molo window, carved by the dalle Masegne family in the years 1400–04 for an all-in sum of 1,900 ducats (fig. 74), and Bartolomeo Bon's Porta della Carta (1438 to *circa* 1443), for which the contract sum was 1,700 ducats. In between these dates, we can cite two examples from Marin Contarini's new palace: the carving and installation of the crenellation, again by the Bon workshop, for 210 ducats (fig. 75); and Zuan da Franza's decoration of the main façade for 60 ducats, both in the early 1430s. A little later again, in 1446, Piero Alegro contracted to install the new roof on the recently rebuilt Carità church for a basic 110 ducats, to which were added two further sums of 23 and 85 ducats, to total 218 ducats in all.

Still at the Carità church, two works of fitting-out were approached in the same way: Antonio Vivarini was to be paid 40 ducats for 'una anuncia', a depiction of the *Annunciation*, and he was to be given 200 ducats for the altarpiece. And finally, in 1489, at the Scuola Grande di San Marco, Pietro Lombardo and his associate Zuan Buora agreed to complete the façade to the *campo* (which was in fact finally completed by Codussi) for the considerable sum of 1,000 ducats.[96]

This group of examples indicates the range and nature of works that could be contracted in this manner, from a single work of art to a complex collection of operations to a façade, involving the carving and assembly of many elements of stonework: friezes, entablatures, statuary. It was the universal method of procurement for important 'freestanding' elements of a project, whether they were paintings, works of sculpture or architecture. In all such works the selection of the master was naturally of great importance; procurement in this manner generally meant that the patron intended to obtain high artistic standards in what was intended to be a prominent 'public' work.

In most cases, too, the patron knew the master in question already, since often he had completed work of a similar nature elsewhere in the city. Thus, the dalle Masegne brothers were well known for their work on the iconostasis at San Marco in the 1390s before they were appointed at the Palazzo Ducale; Bartolomeo Bon was equally well known for his work at Contarini's Ca' d'Oro before his employment on the Porta della Carta; and he had a long-established reputation as one of the finest stone-carvers in the city well before he was commissioned to design and carve the portals for the Madonna dell'Orto and Santi Giovanni e Paolo.[97]

74 Detail of the Molo window of the Palazzo Ducale by the dalle Masegne, built 1400–4

Since their work was the most prominent and prestigious, it is the stonemasons' contracts with which we are most familiar. Although not all such contracts were as all-embracing as those with the dalle Masegne and Bon, a number have features in common. By the time the contract itself was drafted and the price agreed, the master had produced a drawing which itself formed part of the agreement. Often, too, a date is stated by which the work was to be complete, and if so, there is usually a substantial fine in the contract for non-completion.[98]

These agreements were almost always used for main entrance portals, clearly defined works that were generally the most prominent feature of a façade. Bon's portal for the Madonna dell'Orto was contracted in this manner, and was the subject of a contract dated 21 June 1460, according to which he agreed to complete the entire work (again following an approved drawing) for 250 ducats. This form of agreement was used well into the following century; one of the last elements of work to be completed at the Miani chapel at San Michele, for example, was the subject of such a contract in 1533, when Guglielmo de' Grigi, who had

already build the rest of the chapel, now agreed to construct the last element, the stone cupola, for 350 ducats.[99]

Once the contract had been signed, records of the execution of the works (if they survive) usually consist simply of a list of staged payments to the master at intervals, with occasional agreements for supplementary payments if the work became more complex, or if the master could persuade the patron to part with a few more ducats. An agreement with Luca di Pietro in 1503 for a new internal doorway at the Scuola Grande di San Marco is typical: the portal was to be at the top of Mauro Codussi's imposing new staircase, and the doorway was to be 'like that into the albergo' (by Codussi himself). It was to be carved for 60 ducats; Luca was to be paid 'ten ducats immediately, and ten ducats more after 15 days, and so on from time to time . . . such that at the end of the work there still remain 20 ducats in the hands of the said *misser lo guardian*, to be paid on completion of the works'.[100]

Unfortunately, it is often unclear how long these works took to complete; and despite the threat of heavy fines, contracts were frequently completed months or

75 Detail of the outer corner of the façade of the Ca' d'Oro, by Zane and Bartolomeo Bon, subject to a contract drawn up by Marin Contarini on 20 April 1430

even years late. It is also unclear how many men were engaged on projects agreed on this basis, other than the master cited in the contract. There were always apprentices and assistants, about whom we have few, if any, data.

Such forms of contract were not confined to prestigious works of stone carving, and the same principle was adopted, for example, for the installation of a new floor or roof by the *marangoni*. At least two elements at the Scuola Grande di San Marco were contracted in

this way; first, *maestro* Griguol agreed to reuse the fire-damaged timbers to rebuild the *albergo* roof in 1488, for 25 ducats; and in the same year Zan Chandio and his partner Marin de Doimo agreed to install the new chapter hall floor for the all-in sum of 140 ducats ('or up to a maximum of 150 ducats'). The two men were given 79 ducats as an interim payment on 12 February 1490.[101] In a similar comprehensive manner again, Stefano de' Pavari and Cristofolo Candio (builder and carpenter respectively) contracted to build the whole of the Morosini chapel at the Madonna dell'Orto in 1442 for a fee of 410 ducats, excluding the stonework, which was to be the subject of a separate agreement with Bartolomeo Bon.[102]

Works contracted in this manner thus varied widely in their scope, size, character and complexity. At the lower end of the scale they shaded almost indistinguishably into what we might call the smaller 'elemental' contract.

SMALL ELEMENTAL OR 'UNIT' CONTRACTS

On almost all new projects there were many smaller, clearly identifiable pieces of work that could be contracted on a 'unit' basis. Once again the stone-carving craft offers the largest number of examples, since on most substantial buildings there were doorways, window surrounds, corbels, cornices and so on, all easy to identify and cost. If there was straightforward repetition involved, then a simple unit rate was generally agreed, multiplied by the total number of elements required. Thus, for example, Bartolomeo Bon provided two stone window surrounds for the Carità church at 25 ducats each, three further windows at 20 ducats each, ten corbel brackets at 10 lire apiece and three 'turrets' for the façade, at 20 ducats each (fig. 76). Many items of stonework could be approached in this manner, whether they were architectural elements such as windows or carved capitals, or pieces of pure sculpture: for the same building Bon carved two figures of saints for the façade for 25 ducats apiece.[103]

Similar examples abound at San Zaccaria a little later: Zuan Buora was paid 45 soldi in 1480 for each of a number of half-capitals that he carved; at the same project Bertuccio di Iacomo was paid a total of 200 ducats for carving six windows at 33 ducats apiece.[104] General builders, too, sometimes approached work in this manner. Thus *maestro* Steffanino, at the Carità, agreed to build the little cornice arches that we can still see today, for 8 soldi apiece in 1446, while much of the work of *maestro* Griguol at the Scuola Grande di San Marco was also approached in this way, including roofing the *albergo* and the installation of the staircase.[105]

It was often possible for other crafts to use the same approach. The making of timber windows, for example, was essentially a repetitive elemental exercise, and those for the Carità church were priced on this basis, as were (nearly a century later) the circular windows (*ochi*) at the Miani chapel in 1533, when Salvador da Muran agreed to make six of them, ready for building-in.

The rather miscellaneous contributions of black-smiths were again often approached in this way.

76 Window on the side wall of the Carità church, by Bartolomeo Bon, *circa* 1443

Although a good deal of routine ironwork, such as nails, ties and straps for stonework, was usually priced by weight, more complex, individually ordered elements such as locks and latches or *ferramenta* (grilles and screens) for windows or gates were priced by the piece. Such was the course adopted by Marin Contarini when Niccolò Luxe provided ironwork for the Ca' d'Oro in the 1430s.[106]

PAYMENT BASED ON LINEAR OR SQUARE MEASURE

Much of the stonework on important building projects was evaluated not on such a 'unit' basis but rather on the basis of the linear extent of the stone that was carved, again a method still in universal use today. The amount of stone that could be costed in this manner was extensive, ranging from simple large rectangular blocks for foundations and steps to quays, to door and window surrounds, and sometimes more complex elements such as cornices, vaulting ribs and string courses. This method was very simple to calculate, and relied solely on the knowledge of the mason evaluating how long it would take him to carve a certain length to the necessary profile, following an approved template or *sagoma*. The usual unit of length was the Venetian foot (347 mm), while simpler work was often priced by the *passo*, 5 feet (1.73 m). At the end of the work, particularly if it was extensive, the patron would usually commission another master to check the completed quantity and report back to him, so that the final account could be adjusted if necessary.

Simple bedding slabs for foundations (*piere da leto*) were fairly cheap, the chief cost being the purchase of the stone itself; little dressing was required, since these stones would not be visible in the finished building. Thus we find slabs for the foundations at Corte Nova alla Tana in 1457 priced at only 10 soldi per linear *passo*, whereas *schalini* or steps for the edge of a quay, for the same project, had to be worked to a proper finish, and instead cost 5 lire per *passo*, ten times as much. *Schalini* for the Scuola Grande di San Marco thirty years later cost twice as much again, L. 8.10.0 per passo; they may also have been considerably larger.[107]

More labour-intensive work was necessary on architectural elements such as cornice gutters. At the Scuola della Carità in 1443, simple *gorne* (gutters) cost a mere 5 soldi per foot before they were carved, but the cost of carving them (into the typical Gothic lozenge or dog-tooth pattern) increased their price fourfold, to 1 lira per foot. Simple door and window surrounds, such as those at the almshouses in the estate of India Formenti, cost much the same as uncarved gutters, around 6 to 9 soldi for window or door frames.[108]

On much more rich, complex façades such as that of San Zaccaria and the new Scuola Grande di San Marco, a similarly complex hierarchy of pricing was developed. At the former project, one of the first records, from 1458, details payment to Luca Taiamonte for three *schalini* (not steps, but the three lowermost plinths on the main façade) at the rate of 1 lira per foot. Much later, when a remarkable phase of creativity and productivity under Mauro Codussi in 1485 saw the upper façade completed, most work was dealt with on this basis; thus Meneghin carved *frixe* and *golla* at 3 lire per foot; Zuane and Mathio carved *pilastri di cantoni* (corner pilasters) for L. 3.2.0. per foot; the same pair also carved architraves and cornices (at 29 soldi per foot); *maestro* Vetor carved *grondalij* (gutters) for 3 soldi; and so on (fig. 77).[109]

A similarly complex pricing system was agreed a few years later at the Scuola Grande di San Marco, when in 1490 rates were agreed with Codussi and Domenego Moro for many elements on the façade. They included three rates for different profiles of cornices (at 12, 15 and 20 soldi per foot); a plinth at 10 soldi; the same rate for the *frixo negro* (a frieze of black marble); 12 soldi a foot for the bases of pilasters and 1 lira per foot for the pilasters themselves. Other elements were costed individually: large *mexole* (corbels) at $2\frac{1}{4}$ ducats each, smaller ones for windows at 4 lire apiece.[110] Other priced schedules cover almost every conceivable element of the façade that could be costed in this manner: jambs, thresholds, three further types of cornice, and so on (fig. 78).

There were other crafts, too, some of whose work was also essentially linear and repetitive. The carving of wood is an example; in 1429 at the Ca' d'Oro, a master Iacomelo carved an extensive amount of traditional rope mouldings to the edges of the main beams. All his work was priced on this basis, and amounted to some 900 feet in all.[111] A hundred years later, a broadly similar method was adopted at the Scuola Grande di San Marco where, in the early 1520s, Vettor da Feltre was engaged in the important task of carving the ceiling of the great chapter hall. The ceiling was to be coffered, richly carved and gilded, and Vettor was to be paid not on a linear basis but rather at the rate of 11 ducats per coffer; with a total of 147 coffers his total remuneration was to be the considerable sum of 1,617 ducats. By April 1535 Vettor had been paid a total of 1,360 ducats, so his task was by then approaching completion.[112]

The master builder or *murer* had responsibility for a wide range of coordinating tasks, from the laying of drains to the decoration of walls and the fixing of stonework. But his most fundamental role was naturally the building of the principal structural walls of brick; this work was also nearly always priced on the basis of an agreed rate per square *passo*.

One of our earliest fifteenth-century records is that of Marco d'Amadio, who was paid on this basis at the Ca' d'Oro in the 1420s, when Marin Contarini agreed a rate of L. 3.10.0 per *passo* with him. Maestro Christofalo (*sic*) was paid on the same basis at the Scuola della Carità in 1444, although the rate is not cited. Later again, there are other examples, such as that of the rebuilding of Palazzo Giustinian in 1481, when 300 *passi* of wall were constructed at a rate of only just over 1 lira per *passo*. It is not surprising to find that paving was priced in the same way as bricklaying; at Corte Nova in 1526, for example, four small courtyards were paved with bricks at the rate of 7 soldi per square *passo*.[113]

77 Detail of the central part of the façade of San Zaccaria, carved by several masters under Codussi's direction in the summer of 1485

DAY WORKERS OR *LAVORANTI*

Finally, we come to the craftsman who was paid on a daily basis, and we are able to define his income with precision. More craftsmen were paid on this basis than by any other method; they therefore formed an important 'pool' of skilled or semi-skilled labour throughout the industry.

We can now compare some of my earlier remarks on the Ca' d'Oro with a broader study of new buildings later in the century. In general, at the level of the senior masters, there was not a great deal of difference between the wages of the three principal crafts, and this holds true for many projects and over a long period. For example, Marco d'Amadio, who was Marin Contarini's first master builder at the Ca' d'Oro in 1425, was paid 2 lire (40 soldi) per day, while the equivalent master at the Carità church twenty-two years later received exactly the same wage. (This takes no account, of course, of any erosion in value through inflation.) None of the master builders at San Zaccaria was paid at this generous level, though; in 1458–9 their wage was typically 22–4 soldi, while even by 1485 it had risen

only to 28 soldi.[114] This probably reflects the different administrative structure, where the employment of a full-time *proto* effectively relieved the master builder of some responsibility and demoted him to a kind of 'sub-master': less authority thus reflected in a lower wage.

At the very bottom of the scale on site were the unqualified labourers, or *manovali*. They assisted in many operations in which considerable muscle was required, but little, if any, technical skill. As on all sites, such operations typically included hauling stocks of bricks and other materials to the place of work on the scaffold, assisting carpenters in raising roof timbers, unloading goods from delivery barges, and so on. At Contarini's house, few such men were employed, since a high proportion of the workforce consisted of skilled masters and their apprentices; the daily wage of labourers here seems to have ranged from 7 to 10 soldi. But the daily rates that they could command increased significantly in the following decades: already by 1426 *manovalij* at the Ospedale di San Barnaba were paid as much as 16 soldi a day, while later, at San Zaccaria, in 1458 a number of labourers were employed to help install the foundations, with daily rates of 14–17 soldi, nearly twice the rate that Contarini had paid thirty years earlier. Such levels were maintained throughout the long period of the construction of the church; nearly thirty years later we find *manovali* still receiving 14–16 soldi per day. A further thirty years on again, in the 1520s, the same wages were being paid at the Miani chapel.[115] The sharp rise in the later 1420s, therefore, established new, higher levels that were maintained thereafter for half a century or more. This undeniably reflects the considerable construction activity in this period, driving up the wages of this pool of essential labour.

Among the qualified craft guilds, that of the master *murer* is perhaps the most significant, since his coordinating role was essential on virtually every site in the city. One of our earliest records, relating to the hospital at San Barnaba in the 1390s, shows that even then the builders received a very reasonable rate of 29 soldi a day, while the master carpenter was paid 23 soldi and his day workers 18 soldi. Despite considerable variations in the early part of the century, the master *murer* was almost always comparatively well paid;[116] by the 1430s Marin Contarini had to pay even higher wages to his masters, first to Marco d'Amadio (40 soldi or 2 lire), and then to Cristofolo, the latter's wage reaching as much as 48 soldi a day. This last figure was unprecedented, and reflected Marin's urgency in completing the palace; at about the same time, the Procurators of San Marco, administering the estate of Giorgio Baseggio, paid their own builder only 32 soldi for works at the hospital on the Giudecca funded by this estate.[117]

A few years later, in the 1440s, though, the Scuola della Carità was paying their master builder a generous 42 soldi, while the carpenters received 31–6 soldi, a discrepancy that seems to reflect their perceived relative importance.[118] San Zaccaria remains the project about which we have the most detailed information; at the earlier stages of the works masters in the three crafts received similar remuneration, the masons typically on 18–26 soldi (depending on age and experience), and the builders from 22 to 24 soldi.[119] And at Palazzo Giustinian, twenty years later, a similar range can be identified; the senior master builder was given 24 soldi, the mason the same figure. The carpenter received a surprisingly higher 33 soldi for his contribution in rebuilding the roof, perhaps reflecting the difficult, dangerous nature of such work.[120]

It is useful to recall here the levels of salary paid to full-time *proti* in this period. Gambello's salary at San Zaccaria in 1458 was 100 ducats per year, which (based on a 240–50-day working year) equates to a daily equivalent of L. 2.12.0 (52 soldi), a figure that places him in a notably higher income bracket than that of

78 Detail of flank façade of the Scuola Grande di San Marco, carved by Domenego and Ieronimo Moro in the years 1489–90

his subordinates on site. And as we saw, other *proti* (notably Rizzo) managed to negotiate rates even higher than this.[121] At the Scuola di San Marco after 1485, Codussi was paid 6 ducats per month (31–7 soldi per day), which he considered insufficient, although since the work was by then approaching completion, it may also have reflected a lower perceived level of responsibility.[122]

We conclude with two projects from the early part of the following century, the Miani chapel and some works at the Scuola Grande di San Marco in the late

1520s. At the former, the master builder, Girardo, was paid 28 soldi a day, while his assistant was given 23 and their labourers a fairly generous 17 soldi; at the Scuola, by comparison, although the chief builder's wage was almost the same, 30 soldi, his own *manoalij* were paid an even more generous 20 soldi (1 lira) per day. Carpenters' wages were almost identical to those of the *mureri*.[123]

What conclusions can we draw from these incomes in the construction industry? There was no formal mechanism for controlling or regulating daily wages in this period; the market itself was the only regulator, and there was an almost infinite range of day rates possible, from the minimal 2 or 3 soldi paid to a new apprentice (who, of course, lived in with his master), up to the 2 lire a day or more that experienced masters could obtain. All were subject to individual negotiation and agreement, and were equally dependent on age and on the patron's own assessment of the skill and nature of the work itself.

Other than their comparative value, daily wage figures are, of course, of little worth without the other half of the equation: the costs of living and the pur-chasing power of that income. Nevertheless, these records suggest a fairly high degree of stability of income over a long period, despite some local fluctuations; a master builder in the 1390s could expect to take home around 30 soldi a day, and much the same in the 1440s, 1470s and even the 1530s. Despite the occasional peaks of as much as 40 soldi and troughs as low as 22, most examples over this long period are in the much narrower range of 28 to 34 soldi.

Much of the fifteenth century was an era of comparative stability of retail and food prices. Nevertheless, and although we still have insufficient detailed information as to the costs of the daily essentials, life was probably by no means excessively harsh for these craft masters. After all, they were living in one of the wealthiest cities in Europe, with a comparatively benevolent, stable government, and they were assisted, if necessary, by a network of social and charitable support, chiefly by the guilds themselves. In times of shortage, too, the Republic itself was wealthy enough to purchase grain from almost any source to keep the people fed, and often subsidised prices to ensure that needs were met.

79   The Porta della Carta, by Bartolomeo Bon and assistants, begun in 1438

Chapter Five

THE MASTER OF THE ANCIEN RÉGIME:
THE CAREER OF BARTOLOMEO BON

Bon's Early Work and the Ca' d'Oro

Bartolomeo Bon was the son of Zane, himself a stone-mason of some ability. He grew to become the most outstanding master stonemason-sculptor of his generation, one that saw the long, slow development of the indigenous Venetian Gothic style finally challenged and eventually superseded by a new vocabulary of design. Bon's career coincided precisely with this final rich flowering of Venetian *gotico fiorito*, and he was responsible, either solely or in collaboration with others, for a series of outstanding works, in most of which we can see fused the skills of architectural stone-masonry together with the integration of pure sculpted forms.

Bartolomeo's precise date of birth is not known. It is likely that he was born about 1404, and was at first the junior assistant of his father, who ran their small workshop usually with just a couple of apprentices or young assistants. Bartolomeo was outstandingly skilled, however, and was destined for far more creative work than the routine carving of Istrian stone for the typical elements of much late Gothic house-building work. This early skill was already clearly apparent in the well-head that he carved in 1427–8 for Marin Contarini's new palace at Santa Sofia (fig. 80), and which seems to have formed, if not exactly a traditional masterwork, then certainly a piece that Marin commissioned from him specifically as a demonstration of both his creative

skill and his ability in carving the difficult red marble of Verona.[1]

The early work of the two Bon has been discussed in great detail in an earlier book of mine on the subject of Marin Contarini's palace.[2] This was a unique project in a number of ways, not least in the extremely close involvement that Contarini maintained in its development, and his close attention to the detailed design of its many richly carved individual elements. Marin took the role here not merely of patron but that of project manager as well; his close concern with matters of style and design was probably as unparalleled in the city at the time as was his intention to make his new palace, in particular its façade, the richest and most ornate ever seen in Venice.

The particular case of the Ca' d'Oro and Contarini's role in its construction render it very difficult, therefore, to draw any wider conclusions as to the manner in which these last great Gothic palaces were more typically constructed. For example, Marin's employment not only of the Bon workshop but also of an important group of Milanese craftsmen under the overall supervision of the gifted Matteo Raverti indicates a characteristically fragmented, pluralist approach to the palace's overall design that again probably had few, if any, parallels elsewhere.[3]

The detailed design and the execution of the new palace were divided between these two teams of masters, with Contarini himself supervising both

80 The Ca' d'Oro: the wellhead by Bartolomeo Bon, 1427–8

81 The Ca' d'Oro: pendant tracery on the façade by Zane Bon, assisted by Bartolomeo Bon, 1427–8

groups' efforts. Raverti was given the responsibility of the design of the elaborate land gate, the external stair in the *cortile* and the elegant traceried *logge* to the first and second floors, on the Grand Canal façade; to the Bon workshop, on the other hand, Contarini delegated the detailed design of most of the rest of the façade, including the ground-floor loggia, the pendant-traceried windows (figs 81, 82) and the crowning crenellation. In fact, the remit of the Bon was much more generalised than that of Raverti, and while Matteo and his Milanesi confined their efforts to the above specific works, the two Bon were given a large variety of minor, miscellaneous works of carved stone, in addition to many elements of the façade, such that they really remained Contarini's principal masons for the palace.

The construction of the basic fabric of the palace itself, that is, its walls, floors and roof, was the responsibility of the general master builder, and Marin employed three different general building contractors in succession: first Marco d'Amadio, then a master Cristofolo and finally Antonio di Martini. The initial reason for this succession was that Marco died at a fairly early stage in the works; the construction of the upper parts of the palace that followed was itself a fragmented operation with little continuity for a single master to complete the whole fabric in one single process.[4]

Despite the highly eclectic nature of Marin's approach, in general terms the construction process was fairly typical of the time, and the role of Bartolomeo Bon here was no different in principle from that at the much less ornate church of the Carità in the 1440s.

By the later 1430s the Contarini house was complete, and, with its rich decoration of lapis lazuli and gold leaf, was the most remarkable façade to a private palace ever seen in the city. By now, too, its completion must have established or greatly enhanced several reputations in the city: that of Matteo Raverti, for example, in the elegant refinement of the two *logge* that he and Niccolò Romanello had carved for the palace; and Bartolomeo himself, of course, whose own contributions had included not only the fine wellhead, but also the remarkable pendant tracery to the upper floor windows, as well as many other, lesser elements. It may well have been the startling effect of those windows that suggested to the Venetian Signoria that Bon was the most appropriate master to employ on what was to be the most prestigious work of architectural masonry in the entire city: the new state entrance to the Palazzo Ducale itself, the Porta della Carta.[5]

82 The Ca' d'Oro: upper façade with the crowning crenellation, by Bartolomeo and Zane Bon, 1430–31; the upper loggia by Matteo Raverti

The Porta della Carta: Iconography in the Service of the Republic

With the completion of the great new Piazzetta wing of the Palazzo Ducale around 1438 (figs 83, 84), a narrow gap remained between its gleaming new stonework and the venerable patchwork-marble flank wall of the shrine of San Marco. Into this restricted opening, not much more than a slot, was to be inserted one of the great glories of Venetian Gothic: the Porta della Carta.

Documentary evidence for the construction of this elaborate gateway is sparse; nevertheless, the Porta is a pivotal work in several senses. First, it provided a physical link between the palace and the national shrine, a link overlaid with metaphoric and symbolic meaning; second, it marked the apogee of a unique architectural style; and third, it served as a symbolic representation of many of the characteristics of the Republic's perception of itself in this period of triumphant imperialism.[6]

As a physical form, it was the final link in a chain of construction activity that had begun a century earlier, in 1340, with the decision to rebuild the Molo wing of the palace; but in order to understand the reasoning behind the gate's design and appearance, we need to examine the more immediate historical context in which it was to be built. The Piazzetta wing of the Palazzo Ducale had been begun following the famously recorded decree of the Maggior Consiglio on 27 September 1422 that the old Ziani 'Palace of justice' was now so old and structurally unstable as to require complete demolition and reconstruction. The often-quoted decision bears repeating here: 'palacium nostrum deputatem ad jus reddendum ut evidenter apparet in dies minetur ruinam et tam ob necessitatem predictam quam pro providendo opportune quod dictum Palacium fabricetur et fiat in forma decora et convenienti, quod correspondeat solenissimo principio nostri Palacij novi'.[7] Work began on site in 1424, the design closely following that of the earlier Molo wing, and the fabric of the new Piazzetta wing must have been substantially complete before – although perhaps only just before – the decision to build the Porta della Carta.

The plane of the façade of the Piazzetta wing had already been established by the existing six-bay gable-end wall of the great hall of the Maggior Consiglio, and this plane had then been continued northwards to a point not far short of its abutment with the flank of San Marco. This new wing was clearly designed in order to maximise space: the old Ziani wing had housed some of the most senior and ancient magistra-cies of the Republic, but by now not only was it dangerously unstable but it was also far too small. The completed Piazzetta façade consists of eighteen bays, six formed by the pre-existing Maggior Consiglio gable wall, and a further twelve new bays; this total is one bay longer than the earlier Molo façade, a further indication of the desire to maximise space in the new wing.

Like that to the Molo, the Piazzetta façade is faced with deep colonnades on the two lowermost levels, and so when the Porta della Carta came to be built, not only was the available width very restricted, but its façade had to be set back several metres from the plane of the Piazzetta façade, otherwise some of the newly commissioned sculptural groups that terminate the north-west corner would already have had to be relocated or lost, including the exceptionally fine group of the *Judgement of Solomon* (fig. 86).[8] This sculpted group is usually accepted today as the work of Bon, and if it was completed around 1435, its successful conclusion would naturally lead the Signoria to continue Bon's association with the palace by approaching him to design the Porta della Carta. The iconography of these corner sculptures was carefully selected to balance and complete the themes established on the two earlier corners on the Molo façade; in particular, the dominant theme of Venice as the Republic of Justice that forms the principal iconographic image of the Piazzetta façade (fig. 85) was also to determine the iconography of the Porta itself.

The termination of the Piazzetta façade with these sculptural groups in this location indicates that the Signoria was aware that a gap would remain between this corner and that of San Marco, and therefore some form of entrance in this convenient location, immediately adjacent to the church, was intended from the outset; but we cannot know what form it had been intended to take originally – if its form had been debated at all – and it may have been intended to be purely functional. It was now to have a built structure, rather than simply remain a gap between two buildings, and the vaulted passageway that was to occupy this gap was probably begun in 1433, while the final stages of the construction of the Piazzetta wing were still in progress.

However, having decided, rather belatedly, it seems, that the outer face of this narrow gap would be filled by a new formal state entrance, the Signoria was faced with the fundamental difficulty of how to emphasise suitably this narrow portal, which not only stood between two monumental works of architecture, but which for much of the time would stand in the shadow, both figuratively and literally, of the great mass of the new Piazzetta wing.

83   The Palazzo Ducale: the Piazzetta façade, begun in 1424 and probably structurally complete by *circa* 1438

Faced with such difficulties, it was decided, perhaps inevitably, that only an elaborate, richly decorated screen would meet these challenges, and would at the same time be capable of incorporating the heavy symbolic and iconographic burden that the portal would have to bear. And it is indeed elaborate and richly decorated, although its original applied paint and gilding has long disappeared. In general aesthetic terms, though, its stylistic relationship with the regular rhythms and disciplined order of the adjacent palace façade is tenuous, its materials more varied, its vocabulary richer. Equally, too, of course, it has no stylistic connection with the rich marble veneers and Byzantine bas-reliefs of San Marco. Indeed, the Porta reads as a virtually independent work, and there was almost no attempt to form links between elements of its design and those on the Palazzo; even the chief horizontal features such as cornices and string courses do not align with those next to them. And in order to emphasise further its distinction and 'special' status the doorway of the Porta itself is square rather than a repetition or interpretation of the pointed arches of the palace's colonnades. The Porta must thus be evaluated on its own terms, as a sculpted screen, with specific ceremonial and iconographic functions.[9]

85 The Palazzo Ducale: the *Justice* roundel on the Piazzetta façade, *circa* 1430

A NOTE ON THE PREHISTORY OF THE PORTA DELLA CARTA

The only two surviving documents that refer directly to the Porta have been studied by scholars for decades. There is, however, a third contemporary record, which has received little attention and yet has an important bearing on the development of the Palazzo Ducale in this period. It consists of a long schedule of building works to be undertaken by a master builder named Steffanino, under the supervision and instruction of the Provveditori al Sal.[10] He was almost certainly the same Steffanino who was to work on the Morosini chapel at the Madonna dell'Orto in 1441–2, where he is recorded as Steffanino de' Pavan or de' Pavari,[11] and the same Steffanino (always in the diminutive) who worked at the Carità church after 1445.[12] A common link between all these projects is, of course, Bon himself, whose career was paralleled by that of Steffanino for a number of years after they both worked here at the Palazzo Ducale.

Steffanino's contract is dated 28 January 1438, about ten months earlier than the contract with Bon for the Porta della Carta itself. It embraced a number of disparate works in various locations in the complex of structures that then comprised the Palazzo Ducale,

among which (as well as the new Molo and Piazzetta wings) there still remained the old Ziani east wing along the Rio di Palazzo, where the ducal apartments were located. The contract was in the substantial sum of 850 ducats, and the work was extensive, although fairly straightforward in its nature.

Twenty-four different operations were listed, almost all of them concerned with vaulting in stone or roofing with *felze*.[13] There was also a small amount of simple wall-building. The operation that concerns us here, though, is the fourth on the list, 'l'andedo che se va de chorte su la piazza longo pie 55 large pie 15 voltarlo in 4 chroxere';[14] that is, Steffanino was to erect stone cross-vaults, four bays long, to cover the passageway connecting the *cortile* with the Piazzetta outside. This is the central section of the work that eventually became known as the Foscari Loggia or colonnade (fig. 87, 88), and which was finally terminated at its eastern end by the elaborate Arco Foscari. No walls are referred to in Steffanino's contract, so it appears that the basic structure was already in place, and required only the assembly of the vaults to render it complete. Indeed, work on the *andedo* (passage or route) had probably been begun as many as five years earlier, and Steffanino's

vaults were almost the last operations to complete here. The full extent of the *andedo* or *andito* that we see today has six bays, although the easternmost of these forms the base of the later Arco Foscari, while that at the western end forms the basic structure of the Porta della Carta, with four vaulted bays separating them. The Porta, of course, is no freestanding screen, but required considerable structural support behind it to render the whole work stable.

We have no detail of the progress of this work, and it seems highly unlikely that Steffanino's vaults were complete by the late autumn of 1438, when Bon signed his own contract with the Provveditori. Although the culmination of this axial route, the Arco Foscari, was not completed for a further two decades, it is clear that the fundamental decision to build a complete route into the heart of the palace dates from the very start of the process, and may even have formed an element in the decision as to the northernmost extent of the Piazzetta wing around 1424. The final stage in the development of this long, formal axial route was to be Rizzo's staircase, later known as the Scala dei Giganti.[15]

Steffanino was regarded as a master of skill and experience; the assembly of these (and many other) stone vaults was to be all his responsibility, although he could call upon the services of 'smiths or stonemasons or carpenters for the said works' as necessary. He would certainly have required extensive contributions from the last of these to form the vaults' centring. Steffanino was paid one-third of the sum in advance ('per sovenzion'), almost certainly to pay for the stone, one-third at the halfway point in his progress, and the balance on completion. If the extent of the works was to increase, he would naturally be paid more ('sia . . . pagado quelo el meritera'), whilst conversely, if the work was reduced, his fee would be scaled down appropriately ('se se fesse de mancho sia sfalchado quello mancho fosse fato'). He was provided with all necessary materials, including 'bricks, lime, sand, timber piles, and other *aparechiamenti*', all delivered to the most convenient location for the work (which was in several different parts of the palace, as well as the Foscari colonnade); the Signoria even provided Steffanino with a lock-up store on site where he could keep all his tools and materials, including *edifizij* (perhaps templates). It can be safely assumed that these measures would also minimise the disruption

86   The Palazzo Ducale: the outer corner adjacent to the Porta della Carta with the *Judgement of Solomon*, attributed to Bartolomeo Bon, but also to Pietro di Niccolò Lamberti, Nanni di Bartolo and Jacopo della Quercia

87   The Palazzo Ducale: the first-floor loggia of the Piazzetta wing, towards the Porta della Carta

to the Palazzo Ducale itself. Steffanino was also responsible for the removal of any demolition materials, which were to be dumped on the quay ready for removal in *piate* (flat-bottomed barges).

It is worth noting Steffanino's other tasks, in addition to the vaulting of the colonnade. Most of them were a direct result of a fundamental reappraisal of the security of the palace, and consist chiefly of work to the prisons and accommodation for the Signori di Notte, the nocturnal security police. Some were in the east wing, but most consisted of forming vaults in the ground floor of the Molo wing, near the Porta del Frumento. The east wing works consisted of the demolition and reconstruction of the palace's bakehouse, together with a vaulted stone roof to reduce the danger of fire spread; the bakery was located towards the north end of the Rio di Palazzo wing.

The contract then lists a long series of works to the prisons in the Molo wing, most of which were to survive in this new form for a very long time. All except one are cited by Sanudo in his codex of 1493, as well as his *Cronachetta* of 1530, and they can also be identified in a plan drawn by Zuan de' Piombi in the sixteenth century. They were only finally augmented towards the end of the same century when the new purpose-designed Palazzo dei Prigioni was built on the other side of the Rio di Palazzo by Antonio da Ponte.

BON AT THE PORTA DELLA CARTA

On 10 November 1438 Bartolomeo Bon signed a contract with the Provveditori al Sal for the 'porta granda da basso del palazzo a ladi la giexia di missier sam Marcho', the 'great gate . . . of the Palazzo by the side of the church of San Marco' (fig. 79). The Provveditori had been directed by the Signoria to fund the works, and the agreed fee was 1,700 ducats. The contract contained several important conditions, and the surviving document is bound into the ledgers of the Provveditori, who at the time were Tommaso Malipiero, Antonio Marcello, Paolo Vallaresso and Marco Moro.[16]

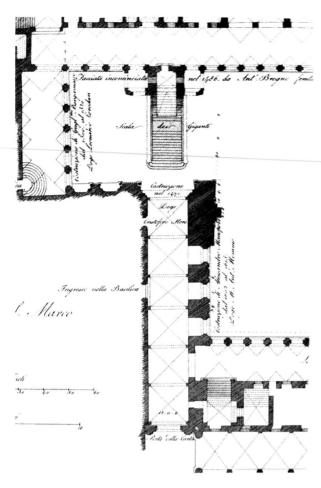

88 The Palazzo Ducale: plan of the Porta della Carta and the Foscari colonnade (from Cicognara, Diedo and Selva)

Much of the stone was to be provided by the Signoria, as well as marble for the foliage and cherubs that surmount the high-level arch. A significant amount of detail is covered by these 'pacti e chonvinzioni', as they are described, although by no means all of the work as completed is closely described. Bon's drawing had already been prepared to form the basis of the contract; it was certainly detailed enough to show the 'marmori di foiami di sovra dal volto' ('the marble wave decoration on the extrados of the arch'), and the 'puti nudi', which 'in between the said foliage decoration are to be fixed, as can be seen on the drawing'. Some of the other iconographic features were again to be carved in accordance with the approved design; specific mention is made of 'el sam Marcho in forma di liom, segondo la forma di uno disegno che per nuj e fato et a vuj in le vostre mani avemo consignado' ('the St Mark in the form of a lion, according to a drawing that was made for us, and which we have now consigned to your hands'). This may suggest that the *St Mark* was the subject of a larger, more detailed drawing, although a few lines later we read of 'una figura . . . di justizia secondo la continenzia del ditto disegno' ('a figure of Justice following the contents of the said drawing'), presumably the same one as that showing the lion. Since the figure of Justice is at the very top of the composition, the entire drawing must have been quite large and detailed, probably encompassing the entire elevation, as we would expect. Because the *Justice* was originally intended to be seen freestanding against the sky, Bon agreed that she should be carved completely in the round ('sia dopia si dentro chomo de fuora'), 'if the Provveditori so wished' (they did); it could then also be appreciated from the *logge* and *cortile* of the palace inside.

The chief elements cited in the contract are these: the doorway itself; the two prominent flanking buttresses, which at high level become pinnacles; the large panel containing the winged lion; the great window with its pair of twisted marble columns; the putti and foliage to the extrados of the arch; and the figure of Justice at the summit. The overall extent of Bon's remit was also specified: the Porta was to fill completely the gap between the wall of San Marco and that of the Piazzetta wing, and was to rise from the *bassamento* to the *Justice*. There is a further clause of a general nature, acknowledging 'all of the things that fall to our craft to be completed, and for which we are responsible'. Bon was not intending to carve the stone on site, but would work in his yard at San Marziale, and bring the completed elements to site for assembly.

There is, however, no specific mention of a number of prominent, even vital, elements of the completed work. Most notably, there is no reference to the four Virtues who occupy the flanking niches, and even the kneeling figure of Doge Francesco Foscari is not specifically mentioned, although the adjacent St Mark 'in forma di liom' clearly is. Nor is there reference to the prominent, deeply carved high-level tondo of St Mark as the Evangelist. Suggestions[17] that the iconography of these figures was finalised only later seem entirely plausible, and it was certainly feasible to design the work with niches for statuary, the precise iconography of which could be resolved later on. We have a parallel here in the case of dalle Masegne's great window on the Molo façade, carved forty years earlier. The contract is a notary's *atto* of 2 October 1400, and is drafted in terms very similar to those used in Bon's contract. In this earlier example the agreement again refers to a drawing, on parchment ('una carta membrana dessignatum'), which must have formed the contract document, since it indicated the overall size, shape and configuration of the window. There are further similarities with the Bon contract in that here, too, we have a large opening flanked by buttresses with niches into which statues were to be set, and crowned with pinnacles. Here again, although there is a specific reference to the 'figura sancti Marci in modo de leonis' (of Carrara marble), the remaining figure sculpture is simply indicated by the phrase 'figuris ymaginum tresdecim de petra bona pulera de cararia marmorea', thirteen figures of good quality Carrara marble, which were to be 'four and a half feet high', although the further, upper ones could be a maximum of 6 feet (2.26 m) tall. In other words, only the number of figures, their size and materials were specified at this stage, not the iconography of the images themselves.[18]

The Bon contract states that the work was to be complete within eighteen months, a difficult condition with which to comply, and on which I have also commented elsewhere.[19] The condition was certainly not met, as our second document clearly attests. This brief note is dated 17 April 1442, three-and-a-half years after the first contract, and is a *zetola* or aide-memoire, the essence (*tenor*) of which is that Bon was still well short of completion of the Porta, and he thereby promised to finish all that remained within a further twelve months, or face a daunting fine of 100 ducats.[20] Such a fine was equivalent to several months' work; Bon's father was also by now over 70, and may no longer have played a very active role in the workshop – he died in 1443. A great deal still remained to complete, including the tops of the flanking columns, and the three bas-relief angels that surround the upper tondo with the bust of the Evangelist. These were to be carved within three months; the tracery of the great window was to follow, and was to be complete two months later (figs 89, 90), together with 'le altre figure'. All other remaining carving was to be completed within a calendar year.[21]

In fact, very little above the bas-relief lion had yet been carved, and 'le altre figure' suggests that the four Virtues, too, were still incomplete. The final date of the completion of the Porta is not known. Nor, despite centuries of debate and speculation, is there yet a general consensus as to which of the figures of the Virtues was carved by whom.[22] What is certain, though, is that some of the figure sculpture is the work of others, rather than Bon, which goes some way towards explaining his inability to keep to the stipulated programme, since these 'subcontracted' works were to some extent beyond his direct control. Bartolomeo himself was extremely busy in this period, and from the

spring of the same year, 1442, he began a long, if intermittent relationship with the monastic church of the Carità;[23] a little later, he was also active at the Scuola Vecchia della Misericordia.[24]

The Porta della Carta still bears Bon's 'signature' (OPUS BARTOLOMEI), today in facsimile, on the architrave; the single name does not appear surprising in view of the age and imminent death of his father, and Bartolomeo may well have taken over the running of the *bottega* some years earlier. But it is also, of course, a reflection of Bartolomeo's status as the designer and chief master of the work, and of his reputation as the finest such master in the city.

ICONOGRAPHY AND SYMBOLISM

The *raison d'être* for the Porta della Carta was both practical and ceremonial. In practical terms it offered the only properly defined pedestrian entrance into the central *cortile* of the Palazzo Ducale from the great public spaces of Piazza and Piazzetta. Neither of the rebuilt Molo or Piazzetta wings had incorporated a ceremonial gate, and the only pre-existing land entrance was the Porta del Frumento, a spartan corridor in the centre of the Molo wing, between two groups of prisons. And in fact, other than the two elaborate central windows on the second floor (the effective *piano nobile*), both massive façades were entirely devoid of focal points or centralising features. These windows both had important iconographic roles; the Piazzetta window was set into the wing of the palace dedicated to the dispensation of justice, and its own iconography directly represented this pre-eminent role, one that was further extended by the Porta della Carta itself.

The location of the Porta was layered with symbolism, sandwiched as it was between the ducal chapel and national shrine on one side and the Palace of Justice on the other. Nevertheless, its awkward site and the late date of its commissioning and construction raise an important question. Why, only now, was the Porta introduced into the design of the palace at all? Or, to reverse the question, why was a grandiose formal entrance not worked into the design of one or other of the two rebuilt wings of the palace from the outset? Neither wing had incorporated a prominent formal entrance, where illustrious visitors might be received and ceremonial routes established. There were many state occasions when formal processions did take place (and there would be even more in the future) but no clear means of accommodating them. The answer to these questions may perhaps be sought in the way that the Serenissima regarded this citadel of power, and in the Republic's

89 The Porta della Carta: the great central window

90 The Porta della Carta: *St Mark*, 'in forma de leon', with the kneeling figure of Doge Francesco Foscari

own self-image in its relationship to the fabric of the city. The Venetian love of ceremonial is universally known and attested, as, for example, the endless visual re-creations of the famous meeting of Pope Alexander III and Emperor Barbarossa so clearly evince. But the proper location for such ceremonial was outdoors, not within the confines of the palace but in the Piazza, the Piazzetta and on the Molo. The Ascension Day *sposalizio*, the marriage of the doge to the sea, the various ducal *andate* (annual processional visits) to the churches and monasteries of the city, and later, the great pageants of the Redentore and Salute festivals: all of these took place outdoors, using the fabric of the city itself as their ceremonial backcloth, thereby identifying the festivals with the Venetian citizenry and, by extension, with the entire population of the Republic. The Molo, in particular, with Ziani's great monolithic columns, was a highly literal (as well as symbolic) gateway into the heart of the city, and was the location for the formal reception of almost all notable visitors to the capital.[25]

The Palazzo Ducale was different. It still bore vestiges of its ancient semi-fortified origins, while within it were concentrated all the supreme organs of state, administered by a closed oligarchy, self-perpetuating and self-defined, which had no need or desire to open its doors to the *minuto popolo*. This perception was modified later, it is true, but we can rightly regard the *serrata* (the closing of the Golden Book of patrician clans) of 1297 as the definitive attempt to define the patriciate permanently as a direct reflection of this hermetically sealed world, represented physically by the closed, finite form of the two new wings of the Palazzo Ducale.

Security was undoubtedly an important consideration, not from external aggression, the danger from which was considered negligible, but rather from within the city itself. The Baiamonte Tiepolo plot of 1310 must have brought home forcibly to the Signoria the potential vulnerability of the older Ziani wings of the palace, and it was surely no coincidence that when the new Molo wing was begun thirty years later, behind the light, airy stone colonnades along the Molo, at ground level at least, there was a stout, virtually solid wall, with only one narrow, easily defensible entrance. The design of the Piazzetta wing extended this principle, and the accommodation that lies behind this (again) almost solid wall consisted, significantly, of the offices for the palace guard, strategically located for rapid deployment if necessary, together with associated stables and prisons. Only at the much safer upper level was there a traceried loggia for the Signoria and Senate to assemble and observe events in the Piazzetta below. The Porta

91   The Porta della Carta: detail of the window tracery

della Carta may thus be considered as a literal after-thought, an acknowledgement that the heart of Republican power should indeed have a formal state entrance, a defensible one, to be sure, but one through which cardinals could be received and ambassadors dismissed. It was also, perhaps, a belated realisation that, far from being a physical representation of weakness, such an open gesture would enhance the prestige of the Most Serene Republic, both in the sense that it represented confidence in the stability and security of the Republic's institutions and in that it would offer a splendid opportunity for representations of symbolism and iconography at the very highest level.

The immediate political context also needs to be considered at this point. The reigning doge, and the Porta's effective sponsor, was Francesco Foscari, an ambitious, expansionist head of state, who had survived an assassination attempt a few years earlier. His reign in the 1430s had been characterised by intermittent warfare with the Visconti of Milan, but perhaps the most significant event in the period just prior to the construction of the Porta della Carta had been the Carmagnola affair. Carmagnola, the *condottiere* (mercenary captain) whose exploits in the years 1428–32 had brought the Republic crisis and political difficulties, had been tried in 1432; on 5 May he was found guilty of treason and was decapitated between Doge Ziani's columns in the Piazzetta. As the commander of the Republic's mainland forces in the struggles against Milan, Carmagnola had held a position at the very peak of military power, and his fall and condemnation

had a profound effect on the Signoria's self-image and in its confidence in its ability to select and control its military leaders. Nevertheless, the 1430s marked an overall success in Foscari's aggressive Terraferma policies, and the annexation of the Bergamasco in 1433 was to mark the greatest extent of the Republic's mainland empire. An era of political turbulence, therefore, was ultimately crowned with success, and there is little doubt that one of the purposes of the construction of the Porta della Carta was indeed triumphalist, reflecting the twin concepts of the increasing greatness of the Republic and the strength of its system of justice. And Foscari made equally sure that his own part in this era of expansion would always be associated with his reign by sponsoring the new state entrance to the palace.

The equation of Venice with justice is the crowning theme of the Porta's iconography. It is a triumphal arch dedicated to the Republic of Justice, under the direct protection of the Evangelist, whose shrine stood on the other side: it formed a physical bridge, therefore, between these two concepts of justice, terrestrial and divine (fig. 91).

The detailed iconography expands on this twofold role.[26] The overall programme is intended to be read from the bottom up towards the skyline and the crowning figure of Justice herself. The theme has already been introduced to us in the iconography of the Piazzetta wing, both by the roundel set into its façade and in the sculptural group of the *Judgement of Solomon* on the corner adjacent to the Porta, representing the concept of divine justice expressed on Earth. And the Justice capital immediately below the sculpted group reinforces the concept further with the figures of three great law-makers, Moses, Aristotle and the Roman emperor Trajan.

The four large figures in the niches flanking the Porta's entrance, representing the Cardinal Virtues, Pru-dence, Temperance and Fortitude, are joined here by Charity (fig. 92), since the fourth of these classical Virtues, Justice, was elevated to form the pinnacle of the entire work. The lower pair are Temperance (fig. 93) and Fortitude, with Prudence and Charity above them; Sansovino suggested, with good reason, that they were chosen to reflect the perceived virtues of Foscari himself ('Quattro figure poco minori del nat-urale dimonstranti le virtu nobili del Principe Foscari').[27] Although they were common enough images in the period, Foscari's own wishes surely played a role here, and his tomb in the Frari also has a trip-tych of three-quarter-length figures of the three 'theo-logical Virtues', Faith, Hope and Charity, in the panels below the image of the recumbent doge.[28] The physi-cal context of the Porta della Carta figures is, of course, very similar to that of such valedictory images.

The attribution of these four figures, all of white Carrara marble, has been debated for centuries. The cleaning of the Porta in 1979 permitted a much closer examination than had been possible for decades, although attributions are still by no means universally agreed. Prudence (top right) is generally agreed to be from a different hand than the other three, and was tra-ditionally attributed to 'a Tuscan master', although others have suggested Antonio Bregno. Temperance and Fortitude (lower left and right respectively) are both similar in style, and have been ascribed to Giorgio da Sebenico, but also to Bregno. Others have concluded that they are the work of Bon himself, although still others have proposed Niccolò Lamberti. Fortitude is the only one of the four to have been carved fully in the round. Both figures, but particularly Temperance, show distinct Tuscan traits, and the Siennese sculptor Jacopo della Quercia has been cited as a specific influ-ence on the works. Lastly, the figure of Charity (top left) has no clear stylistic provenance, and may again be the work of Bregno or from Bon's own shop.[29]

At the same level as the two upper figures is located the relief panel showing Doge Francesco Foscari kneel-ing in front of the winged lion. The present panel is a copy, carved by Luigi Ferrari in 1885 to replace that destroyed by Napoleon in 1797; the original work (of which only Foscari's head has survived, now in the Museo dell'Opera) must have been a fine, imposing piece; although it is difficult to gauge the accuracy of Ferrari's replacement, Forcellini's report in 1887 that it was 'as exact as possible at least in dimension and pose' suggests that its verisimilitude should be regarded with caution.[30] Nevertheless, with strong afternoon sunlight, the noble lion must have read as a very powerful image, proud and freestanding, holding the open book with the inscription 'Pax tibi marce evangelista meus' ('Peace to you, Mark, My Evangelist'). This is the Republican image, official and emblematic, although in 1438 it was, in fact, revolutionary. As far as we know, this was the first time that this now so familiar sculpted form had been publicly used on a building in the city; and the juxtaposition of Foscari's own image with that of the Republic's icon also broke new bounds, a direct adver-tisement of his patronage.

As an iconographic image, the winged lion had immense significance and had long been established on the Republic's coinage, always with the incumbent doge on the reverse side. It was undoubtedly as a direct result of the great impact of this composition at the Porta della Carta that a similar format was used twenty years later at the great gate of the Arsenale, the lion having the same orientation and a similar pose to that which we see here.[31] At the Arsenale, though, the lion stands alone and Doge Malipiero's sponsorship is con-fined to a carved inscription.

The Porta della Carta is thus an unequivocal statement of Foscari's direct patronage. It is generally acknowledged that the sculpted group was the work of Bon himself, as the chief master of the Porta as a whole;[32] Foscari was depicted with full ducal regalia, kneeling in front of the lion, not quite as a supplicant, but appropriately deferentially, as if to reinforce the impression that his policies and politics (highly contro-versial though many of them were) had always had the greater good of the Republic as their justification.

By contrast with the Marcian lion, the upper tondo with the bust of the Republic's patron shows Mark as a man rather than a quasi-mythical emblem: as the Evangelist, instrument for spreading God's word. In his left arm he holds the book into which it is said that he wrote the text of his Gospel, dictated to him by Peter. Bon is again almost certainly the author of the tondo, particularly since it was specifically cited in the document of 1442. Again, the work is boldly moulded, and the tondo containing the figure of St Mark again makes its appearance in Venice here for the first time. (There is an earlier tondo on the Piazzetta façade, of course, containing the figure of Justice, but it is quite different in style and iconography.) The Porta tondo is surrounded by the three angels also referred to in the

contract, figures again carved in fairly high relief, and one of which (on the left side) shows more refinement in execution than that on the right. This relief, together with the third one, on the top, is probably the work of Bon himself, that to the right probably from his workshop.

Further direct expressions of Foscari's patronage can be seen in the two *scudi* (family arms) on the flanking pinnacles. The arms themselves are each flanked by two putti; these are not stereotypical figures but robust small boys, and although they have been fitted with rudimentary wings, they are almost invisible from street level, such that the putti appear far more profane than divine. (The equally substantial putti on Foscari's own palace have rather more convincing wings.)[33]

The uppermost extrados of the arch is crowned by six more putti, three on each side, alternating with the characteristic luxuriant foliage decoration that is so typical of *gotico fiorito*, and of Bon's style in particular. These are clearly intended to represent angelic spirits, with their stumpy wings, but the carving is again so robust that they appear to be climbing the arch with considerable effort, a rather terrestrial denial of their attributes. These putti are almost certainly the work of Bon's workshop, and two or three are probably from his own hand. Here again, therefore, we see a lively, proto-Renaissance interpretation of traditional subjects that is characteristic of Bon's mature style, and can also be identified in several works from his later career.

Finally, the entire ensemble is crowned by Bartolomeo's own figure of Justice. Here she is doubly symbolic, not only representing the activities within the adjacent palace, but as a paradigm of Venice itself, the Republic of Justice. This double personification was itself taken from the earlier *Justice* tondo on the Piazzetta façade, carved between 1424 and 1436. In this earlier work, she is seated, crowned and holds aloft a large sword; she is also flanked by two lions.[34] Bon's figure is considerably larger and more dignified, although here again she is crowned and seated. Her right hand holds the sword but this time it is balanced (in both senses) by the scales of justice in her left hand: a rather less militant Justice (fig. 94), therefore, in whom the might of the sword of retribution is balanced by an emphasis on objective truth.[35] As noted above, the location of the figure has considerable significance; in the ancient world, the four Virtues themselves were prudence, temperance, fortitude and justice, all of equal

92　The Porta della Carta: sculpted figure of Charity, perhaps by Antonio Bregno, although also attributed to Bartolomeo Bon

importance, and it was essentially a Renaissance attitude – in fact, a re-reading of Plato – that raised justice
supreme above the others, since without justice civic
life was held to be of little value, even though the other
three Virtues may still be present.

According to John Pope-Hennessey, Bon's *Justice* was
in place by 1441, although, given the list of works that
still remained to be completed in April 1442, it seems
unusual to have had the *Justice* in place before lower,
more integral pieces such as the angels and the *St Mark*
tondo. The *Justice*, too, had been specified in the original contract of 1438: it clearly formed a vital, indeed
climactic element in the overall composition, very
probably at Foscari's specific request.[36]

Once completed, therefore, probably around 1443,
the Porta della Carta formed a superbly rich backdrop
for the ducal *andate* that took place on the great festive
days of the Venetian calendar, as we can clearly see in
Gentile Bellini's famous painting of the *Procession in the
Piazza* of 1496 (fig. 95). Its appearance was literally dazzling; the restoration of 1976–9[37] confirmed the painted
decoration and gilding that was originally applied to
the already rich collection of Carrara, Verona and *verde
antico* marble with which the Porta was constructed.
The niches containing the Virtues were decorated with
lapis lazuli, as was that of St Mark, while gilding was
applied to the canopies above the Virtues, the capital
below the figure of Justice at the summit, and to the
window tracery. Doge Foscari's coats of arms were also
painted, and there was further gilding to the robes of
the four Virtues.[38] In all, the work was a tour de force
of integrated architecture and sculpture.

After the publication of the aide-memoire in 1442, we
have no further detailed documentary records on the
palace for a further ten years. The next surviving record,
from 1453, sheds only a little light on progress on the
Arco Foscari, since it simply refers to some buttressing
or reinforcement to strengthen the south gable wall of
San Marco.[39] There is no mention of Bon here, since
the work was purely of a structural nature, and was
effected by a competent general builder; it was to be
carried out 'opposite the stairs by which one ascends
to the Appeal Court', where it was necessary to 'repair

93 The Porta della Carta: sculpted figure of Temperance, today
often attributed to Bartolomeo Bon, but also to Lamberti and
Antonio Bregno

liest construction of the palace by the Partecipazio doges, and are immensely thick. It seems likely, though, that concerns regarding the structural stability of some of these works led to the prolongation in the construction of the Arco Foscari, work on which was to continue for years after the death of its ducal sponsor.

We have one final document relating to Bon at the Palazzo Ducale; although the precise location is not stated, it is generally accepted as referring to the Foscari colonnade and arch. It dates from 1463, and is a *terminazione* (determination or decree) by the Senate, passed by 111 votes to 6, to order Bon and his partner to complete certain (unspecified) works.[40] Bon's partner was Pantaleon di Paolo, who had worked with him earlier, both at the Corte Nova almshouses and also at the Carità church.[41] Bartolomeo had entered into partnership with Pantaleon after the death of his father around 1442; it was an essential arrangement for the continuation of the Bon workshop since Bartolomeo himself had several daughters but no sons to train as apprentices.

The very late date of the 'ultimatum' makes it certain that the works referred to relate to the Foscari colonnade and arch rather than the Porta della Carta, which must have now been complete for some years. By its terms, Bon and Pantaleon had to complete the outstanding works or face a very heavy fine of 200 ducats, as well as their summary dismissal and replacement by others.

The text of the document, though, is difficult to interpret. The essence is that Bon had been overpaid for some stonework, and that he had to return to the palace to conclude other elements still incomplete, even after considerable pressure had been exerted by the Signoria. The work was 'to be extended in the direction of the Piazza and to gain access to the new chamber with ease'.[42] This access refers to the so-called Foscari stairs, now long disappeared, but which stood in the great central courtyard just to the south of the colonnade and led up to the halls of justice on the upper levels of the Piazzetta wing. The Senate not only demanded that Bon complete the work or he would be replaced by others (at his own cost), but, if he failed, the Provveditori al Sal were instructed not to employ him again, but rather they were 'to employ anyone else from whom we may hope for greater benefit to the Signoria'. Bon was thus threatened by a blacklist as well as termination of employment.

In the past, there have been other interpretations of the document, notably that of Zanotto,[43] who believed that Bon's chief task was the completion of the Piazzetta wing of the Palazzo; he suggested that its main

94   The Porta della Carta: the crowning figure of Justice, today usually attributed to Bon

and strengthen part of the exterior wall [of San Marco] to prevent . . . collapse', and possible damage or loss of some of the internal mosaics. It is not easy to identify these works today with precision, since the north wall of the Foscari colonnade is inextricably linked to the earlier south transept of the church, and in particular with the massive walls that enclose the Treasury. These walls are said originally to have formed part of the ear-

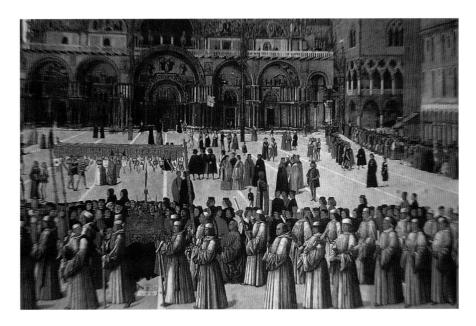

95 Gentile Bellini: *Procession in the Piazza*, 1496, Accademia, Venice. Detail showing the Porta della Carta just visible between San Marco and the Palazzo Ducale; it is depicted as being lavishly gilded

façade was not complete until 1463. Although this dating is no longer generally accepted, the suggestion that the Piazzetta wing was not yet fully complete has some merit. The period of construction, usually agreed as being from 1424 to the mid-1430s, is by no means long for such a monumental work, and internal decorations would certainly have continued for some years after the structural 'shell' was complete and weatherproof.

The document of 1463 thus almost certainly refers to the latter stages of the colonnade and/or the Arco Foscari at its termination, such that the most logical and comprehensible sequence of operations remains as follows: the fabric of the Piazzetta wing was largely complete by *circa* 1438; the basic structure of the colonnade was built in the period from 1433 to 1437–8, when Steffanino erected the vaults; the Porta della Carta was begun at the end of 1438 and was completed around 1443; decoration to the Foscari colonnade, however, continued and overlapped with the construction of the elaborate arch (fig. 96). It was interrupted, and perhaps significantly altered around 1453, when buttressing works were undertaken at the abutment with San Marco; work continued on the arch thereafter for many years, probably until the mid-1460s. By this time Bon himself was old (he died between 1464 and 1467), and the arch was finally completed, including some of its most prominent statuary, by Rizzo and Antonio Bregno.[44]

FOOTNOTE: BON'S ROLE AT THE PALAZZO DUCALE

Bon had already established a high reputation in the 1420s, and by the later 1430s he had certainly surpassed his father as a skilled and highly creative master, much of whose work falls into that rather elusive interface between architecture and 'pure' sculpture. Despite these undeniable skills, though, Bon was no master builder (nor, we may conjecture, would he have wanted to be), and in all his major recorded projects the construction of the basic fabric of the building remained the responsibility of others. The Palazzo Ducale was a special case only by virtue of its size and complexity, and the very long time span of its phased reconstruction, which was really completed only with the rebuilt east wing by Rizzo and then Pietro Lombardo in the early 1500s.

The palace itself had employed a *protomagister*, Pietro Baseggio, as early as the 1350s, and although Pietro may have been either a master mason or a builder, the importance of his role lay in his title, which placed him as the permanent head of the various craft masters under his overall control and coordination. The role of his contemporary, the quasi-legendary Filippo Calendario, often cited as the real architect or design master of the Molo wing, remains unclear; one of very few facts about Calendario is that he was executed in 1355 for his part in an infamous conspiracy lead by the doge, Marin Falier.[45]

97 Santa Maria della Carità as depicted in *Venice: Campo S. Vidal and Santa Maria della Carità (The Stonemasons' Yard)* by Canaletto, *circa* 1730

By Bon's era, unfortunately, the organisational picture is little clearer. Although he remained the sole master at the Porta della Carta, there is no evidence that Bon was the *proto* for the palace as a whole. In particular, his role in the construction of the Foscari colonnade and arch also remains unclear, despite suggestions that he did indeed have overall responsibility for the early stages of these protracted works. Certainly, at the Porta he was employed on the traditional basis of a master sculptor-mason, responsible for the design and execution of a particular piece of work. It was on a similar basis that he was employed on his next project, the reconstruction of the Carità church in the 1440s.

Santa Maria della Carità, 1440–1453

The Church was a prominent patron of architecture during the fifteenth century. Most parish foundations relied on the generosity of one or two leading patrician residents to fund major construction or restoration works. These residents often annexed parts of their parish church, or had extensions built onto it, for use as their own private chapels.

Surviving records of construction activity at the parochial level are meagre, however, and instead we need to turn to monasteries and nunneries for more detailed evidence of ecclesiastical patronage. Several religious houses completed ambitious reconstruction programmes in the early fifteenth century, the most remarkable of which are Santi Giovanni e Paolo and the Frari. These works, which had been begun several decades earlier, epitomised the same confident expansionism that had its lay equivalent in the numerous contemporary palace façades of the patriciate that lined the Grand Canal. The works at the Frari and Santi Giovanni e Paolo were replicated on a less monumental scale in several other churches, among them Santo Stefano, the Madonna dell'Orto and Santa Maria della Carità.

The Carità, although a good deal less monumental than the Frari, was by no means a poor foundation. The completed church, though traditional in style, was substantial and imposing, the chosen burial place of two doges, and was to be decorated with works by Antonio and Bartolomeo Vivarini and Donatello.

Today, if we leave the *campo* of Santo Stefano at its south-western end, rounding the church of San Vidal, we find ourselves in the precise location where Canaletto painted his famous *Stonemasons' Yard* in the late 1720s (fig. 97).[46] Unlike many of his *vedute*,

98 Santa Maria della Carità: engraving of the façade onto the *campo*, by Antonio Visentini, Venice, 1735

cation to San Salvador they soon returned to the Carità, where they remained and flourished. By around 1440 they felt sufficiently confident to instigate a complete reconstruction of the church. Their faith proved to be justified, and the church was completed in about a decade, funded solely by donations and legacies, at a cost of approximately 37,000 lire.

The building accounts were recorded in a modest little notebook, kept by Dom Agostin, one of the canons, and they begin, in his own words, thus: 'herein will be recorded to all who wish to examine them, by myself, dom. Agostin, all the expenses paid in connection with the new church of the Carità'. His little booklet, which can hardly be called a ledger, also contains lists of *elemosine*, charitable donations, over the same period.[49] Dom Agostin kept the accounts, but he was no accountant; he traced the construction process, too, but he was no architect.[50] Indeed, the project had no overall coordinating architect of any kind: it was essentially a 'builders' church', heir and successor of such earlier examples as Sant'Elena and roughly contemporary with Sant'Andrea della Zirada, San Giovanni in Bragora and San Gregorio.

Work began in 1441 with the driving of timber piles for foundations, although they were very few, indicating that most of the old foundations were reused; the site was also severely constrained from lateral expansion by the earlier campanile, which stood between the nave and the Grand Canal (fig. 99). Early hopes of saving the

however, this one has changed dramatically since he recorded it; today the Accademia bridge rises in front of us, while, on the far side of the Canalazzo, the monastic church of the Carità is today a rather sad sight. Now bereft of its campanile, much of the stonework, too, is gone, while the nineteenth-century conversion of the nave into the Accademia delle Belle Arti inflicted further alterations to both the exterior and interior of its remaining fabric (fig. 98).[47]

Nevertheless, it remains one of very few medieval churches for which detailed building accounts have survived, from which we can learn a good deal about how such churches were constructed. One of the oldest monastic foundations in Venice, the early history of the Carità is obscure, although it was rebuilt in 1120 and shortly afterwards housed a group of Augustinians from Ravenna. The church was reconsecrated in 1177 by Pope Alexander III during his famous visit to Venice to treat with Emperor Barbarossa, and it became enriched with donations and indulgences.[48] Immediately adjacent to the church was founded the Scuola della Carità, a little of the history of which will be touched upon later (fig. 100). By the end of the fourteenth century, the Scuola had built some fairly impressive accommodation of its own, with a façade that stood at right angles to that of the church, on the same *campo*.

In 1409 the prior, Francesco Cappello, introduced a new group, Augustinian canons from Lucca, to revive the house's then flagging fortunes. Despite a brief relo-

99 Santa Maria della Carità: detail from Jacopo de' Barbari, 1500, showing the campanile between the church and the Grand Canal

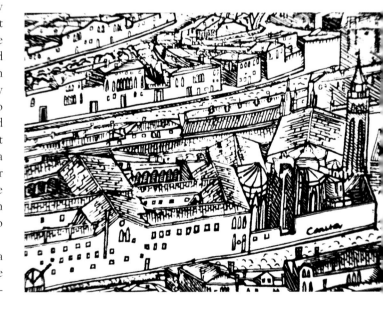

older porch, though, came to nothing and it was taken down in 1442.[51] In January 1442 stonework was squared and delivered to the site for the strip footings from which the nave walls were to rise.[52] By late winter the first consignments of bricks had begun to arrive, and we now meet the master builder responsible for this important stage of the works. His name was Piero, son of Steffanino, whom we met earlier at the Palazzo Ducale working on the prison vaults. Piero's men, probably six in two gangs of three, built a considerable extent of walling until the end of the following summer. When Piero left site in August for a year's absence elsewhere, his departure reflected the fact that work could not proceed further without the contributions of the master mason, that is, Bartolomeo Bon himself.[53]

As we saw earlier, Bon was the hub around which much of the major building activity in mid-fifteenth-century Venice revolved. Although his permanent workshop was small, his career not only defines the last stage of *gotico fiorito* as an indigenous style, but also reflects the beginnings of a new architectural order.[54] His complete œuvre effectively forms a definitive roll-call of these late Gothic masterpieces, from the Ca' d'Oro to the portals of the Madonna dell'Orto and Santi Giovanni e Paolo, from the Porta della Carta to the important, but fragmentary and elusive Ca' del Duca.[55]

Bon's house and workshop were still at San Marziale, as they had been when he worked for Contarini in the 1420s, and his association with the Carità was to extend over more than a decade, his shop supplying around three-quarters of all the stone for the church, both structural and decorative. Only towards the very end of works on site were small quantities provided by others, among them Bon's later partner Pantaleon.[56]

The Carità required a considerable amount of stone, despite the fact that it was essentially a brick structure with a timber roof. There were windows and door frames to be carved, pinnacles and statuary for the west façade, and the vaulting and capitals for the apses. Bon's first contribution was the carving of two windows for the façade in spring 1442, for which he was paid 50 ducats, and which were later followed by several others.[57]

It is useful to locate Bon's work at the Carità in the context of his career as a whole. Only a week before payment for these two windows, Bon had agreed to the aide-memoire from the Provveditori al Sal,[58] who, as we saw, had been exerting considerable pressure on him to complete the Porta della Carta. In the spring of 1442, when he became involved at the Carità, Bon still had much to complete for the Provveditori,[59] and it is

100   The Scuola Grande della Carità: relief panel of the Virgin with brethren of the Scuola, 1377

difficult to see how he imagined this conflict being resolved. We might have expected the Porta della Carta to have taken precedence over almost any other project in the city, since it represented the palace of government of the Republic itself; his ultimate patrons, the Signoria, could not have been more powerful and influential. Nevertheless, by no means did he concentrate exclusively on the completion of the Porta in the year or two after the Provveditori's ultimatum, despite the threat of a 100-ducat fine. Instead, in what almost seems like a calculated rebuff to the august patriciate, Bon began carving the church's new west portal, on which he worked for most of the summer and autumn of 1442, receiving 80 ducats payment in November, which included day wages for one or two assistants or *fanti*.[60] After November, however, he turned his attention elsewhere (almost certainly to the Porta della Carta), but he was back at the Carità again in January 1443 to carve the lancets for the façade,[61] and then turned immediately to the large central circular window or *ocio*, which, like the lancets, is now lost. This was completed in turn

101   Santa Maria della Carità: detail of nave window, by Bartolomeo Bon, *circa* 1443

by October 1443 at a further cost of 70 ducats.[62] The design of this 'eye' was modelled on that on the façade of the Madonna dell'Orto, a church with which Bon was very familiar. Both he and his father were members of the Scuola di San Cristofolo (Cristoforo) dei Mercanti, which met there, and his workshop was only ten minutes' walk away. These *oci* were characteristic features of late Venetian Gothic churches, and examples can also be seen at the Frari and a number of others.[63]

From the summer of 1443 notable progress was made by Piero's men on the church's flank walls and façade, building in Bon's stonework as the walls rose. No fewer than 105,000 bricks were delivered in this one season, almost all of them from the kilns of the wealthy Marco Corner. But by November Piero had to wait for more of Bon's stonework, and Piero Alegro, a carpenter, erected a high-level scaffold so that work could continue.[64] Bon's 'eye' was installed in November, and during the winter the three tall gables to the façade were erected by another bricklayer, master Bortolamio.[65]

During the winter Bon himself completed the bas-relief panel that was to be set above the entrance door,[66] while during the following spring and summer his workshop produced a further six windows, at 20 ducats apiece, for the rest of the nave (fig. 101). Since the nave walls could now be completed up to the level of the eaves, Bon then turned his attention elsewhere once

more, and for a full year we have no record of any work for the Carità.[67] It thus seems almost certain that this was not only the period in which the Porta della Carta was finally completed, but also the period in which Bon was working on the façade of the Scuola della Misericordia: see below.[68]

The winter of 1444–5 saw little progress on site, perhaps the result of the coincidence of an unpropitious season and a temporary shortage of funds. With the better weather of spring, the builders returned, led on this occasion not by Piero but his father Steffanino. It was to be a short season, though, chiefly spent completing the nave walls so that the installation of the massive timber roof beams could begin. Between July 1445 and September 1446 not a single brick was delivered, and the team of *mureri* was replaced by an equally numerous group of carpenters and labourers. In October 1444 the monastery had ordered a large quantity of timber (worth 200 ducats) from dealers based in the mountains at 'Cividal de Belum' (Belluno), the contract having been signed at the Balbi bank at Rialto.[69] In the following summer the order was concluded, with a consignment of a large number of planks for the roof covering, and *cantinelle* (laths), with which to decorate the soffit. Throughout 1446, therefore, attention was concentrated almost exclusively on the roof, and in anticipation of its completion, on 25 September the monks purchased 10,850 roof tiles from their usual supplier, Marco Corner.[70]

A few days later, on 1 October 1446, a contract was signed with Piero Alegro, who had already built the scaffold, and whose daunting task was to erect the imposing trusses that formed the framework of the roof, and which we can still see in place today. The work was to cost 110 ducats, and a week later, the great beams or *bordonali* were floated around to the site from the timber yards at Barbaria delle Tole. Hauling them in from the Grand Canal cost a further 40 lire in wages for the *fachini* (porters).[71]

As is often the case with carpenters' records, it is difficult to chart progress on the roof, and the simple lump-sum contract gives us no details of numbers of men or of Piero's method of working; all we know is that the last payment was made to him in February 1448, so the entire operation took him some sixteen months.[72]

Piero was dependent on one or two other crafts, however, one of which was the *fabbro*, the smith who provided straps, ties and thousands of nails to hold the roof structure together. Nearly all these supplies were provided by a familiar figure on the Venetian building site, Niccolò Luxe or Lusse, who was almost as ubiquitous as was the more renowned Bartolomeo Bon. Fifteen years earlier, Niccolò had performed a similar service for Marin Contarini when building his new palace at Santa Sofia;[73] a few years after his work for the Carità, Niccolò can be found at San Zaccaria, under the direction of Antonio Gambello, a site conveniently close to his foundry at Santa Maria Formosa.[74] For the monks at the Carità Niccolò provided a total of nearly 3,600 pounds of ironwork, for which he was paid 670 lire.

On 4 September 1445 Bon signed a new agreement with Dom Agostin's *frati* for carving two statues, of St Augustine and St Jerome, at 25 ducats apiece.[75] They were to be completed within a year and were to stand on the two outer corners of the façade; they were followed by several other pieces of high-level statuary. In the meantime Bon's workshop was carving the little stone modillions that support the blind brick arcades along the tops of the nave walls. Once these were compete, Steffanino could return and build the arcades themselves, which he did in the autumn of 1446 (fig. 102).[76]

Work on the roof continued until September 1447, tiling naturally being one of the last operations. Immediately thereafter, a master Lorenzo was paid for painting the laths that formed the decorative soffit to the roof, at a rate of 7 lire per hundred. In the same period, another carpenter, Niccolò, carved rope mouldings along the great principal beams of the roof.[77]

102 Santa Maria della Carità: detail of blind brick arches, built by master Steffanino in 1446

All the finishing touches to the exterior were provided by Bon's shop. In February 1447 his two figures of St Augustine and St Jerome were finally completed; yet again, therefore, Bon had failed to meet his deadline, the work having taken seventeen months instead of the stipulated twelve. But on 20 February they were hauled into place on the façade. Later, in August, he also carved the three stone aedicules that were to stand on top of the façade buttresses, and which Dom Agostin called *cambanilitij*, little bell-towers. They cost 20 ducats apiece; the fourth and last one followed a year or so later.[78] Bon's penultimate piece for the façade was the figure of God the Father, which was to stand on top of the large central gable; the contract was signed on 8 July, and the price was 30 ducats. We do not know how long it survived in this highly vulnerable location, however, and it was certainly gone by the late 1720s when Canaletto recorded the façade in detail.[79] Bartolomeo's final carvings for the façade were the characteristic *foiami* or wave decorations fixed to the sides of the gables. There were twenty-two pieces in all, and cost 1 ducat each; with these last elements in place, the church façade was now complete.

In spring 1448 the emphasis on site changed once more; now that the walls and roof were complete, it was time to render the entire structure fully weatherproof by glazing the windows; a master Bernardo was now commissioned to make stained-glass windows to fill Bon's stone frames.[80] He began with the west façade, for which he made three figures for the central *ocio*, as well as 'uno san iacomo e uno san zoane' (St James and St John) for the flanking lancets. These were special designs, but the rest of the nave windows were all identical, and were to be filled with pairs of saints. Bernardo made the first of these, St Augustine, for around 9 ducats, but, rather surprisingly, the canons turned to a different master for the next one, which was made by a master Mafio (Matteo). Since it was also slightly more expensive than Bernardo's, however, they returned to him for the remainder, about a dozen windows in all, including figures of St Anthony and St Luke, which were delivered to site two or three at a time. They kept him in work until spring 1450, although Bernardo was to return a few years later, in 1454, to make the windows for the chancel.[81]

From September 1448 to spring 1450 there was another long hiatus in the work on site, the only exception being Bon's west portal; in July 1449 Dom Agostin finally closed his books on this work, the latter stages of which had cost 150 ducats. Immediately afterwards, the portal sculpture was painted by Ercole del Fiore; the door frame itself followed in the spring of 1450, although the imposing doors themselves were not hung until two years later again.[82]

The construction of the chancel was not funded by the canons from charitable donations, but by the governing board of the adjacent Scuola, which donated 1,200 ducats over a period of sixteen years. It also paid for the new altarpiece, painted by Bartolomeo Vivarini.[83] In March 1450 the *banca* had voted an initial 500 ducats so that work could begin, and almost immediately Steffanino returned to site once more. With Bernardo's windows also now fitted, Steffanino was able to plaster the internal walls. Later in the same spring we find deliveries of *tulpi* (stakes) for the foundations of the apsidal chapels. Structurally, the chancel was a virtually separate entity from the body of the church; not only did it require new foundations, but it was also to be vaulted in stone, in contrast to the open timber roof of the nave. Piling continued throughout the summer, and from June stone blocks were set onto the *zattaron* to form the bases for the enclosing walls. In the spring of 1451, however, Steffanino was replaced by a new master, Mapheo, and our chronicler, Dom Agostin, placed an order for no fewer than 80,000 bricks, delivered between April and September.[84]

In the meantime Bartolomeo Bon's long association with the church was not yet concluded, and his yard was now engaged in carving pilasters, bases, capitals and *archivolti* (vaulting ribs) for the chancel, all of which work seems to have been completed by July 1451, when Agostin recorded a total expenditure of 212 ducats on all these items together.[85]

Despite the order for so many bricks, the builders did not return until spring 1452, when the necessary sand and lime were also ordered so that the walls could begin to rise. During this further hiatus, though, across the city in Bon's yard, Bartolomeo had now been joined in partnership by Pantaleon, who completed the remaining capitals, but also worked on several of the tall lancet windows for the apsidal chapels. On 24 March 1452 Agostin records a payment of 192 ducats to the Bon shop for six such windows, and additional sums paid direct to Pantaleon for a further five.[86]

A week or so later Mapheo finally began erecting the chancel walls. He had a number of assistants, perhaps as many as twelve, so progress was very rapid; Corner's initial 80,000 bricks were followed by an additional 20,000 in May and further smaller deliveries throughout the summer. In September, Niccolò Luxe provided ironwork for building-in the windows, and by the autumn men were required to install Bon's vaulting ribs. This operation, too, was completed with some speed before the worst of the winter weather. Already, by November, some of the roof timbers were being hauled into place, and by December work had already begun in fixing the 5,000 roof tiles that Agostin had recently bought. Mapheo was finally paid off in March, by which time the chancel structure was effectively complete, although Bon still had one or two finishing touches to add inside, including two carved emblems of the Carità and nine little figures or statuettes, which were supported on brackets on the chancel walls.[87]

Although the chancel still lacked windows, most of 1453 was devoted to the building of a new sacristy, and with Mapheo now gone, the master builder was a new man again, Zoane, who built the sacristy walls between May and early autumn. The doorway connecting the sacristy with the chancel was carved by Pantaleon and was installed in September. In the following spring it was decorated with a figure of the Virgin and Child, the work of a *maestro* Donato, then living in Padua, and better known to us today as Donatello.[88]

We have no records of expenditure in 1455, although Bernardo must have been completing the chancel windows, since in 1456 Agostin noted a general settling-up with him in the sum of nearly 100 ducats. A little earlier the monastery had been given a generous donation of 200 ducats by the adjacent Scuola for a new altarpiece, which was commissioned from Antonio of Murano, the renowned Antonio Vivarini; the master later persuaded the canons that his efforts were worth more than the 180 ducats that he had originally contracted with them, although they also had to find money for an elaborate frame at a cost of a further 32 ducats.[89]

The Scuola continued to fund works in the chancel for a number of years. Among them were further embellishments to the altar, and in 1464 the Scuola paid for the marble paving to the chancel. Finally, in November of the same year, a master Marin, *pictor*, was paid 3 ducats and 16 lire for decorating the choir; this probably consisted of the frescoed surfaces of the vaults, some of which can still be seen today.

The construction of the church over twelve years or so was in many ways a fairly straightforward project, largely guided and coordinated by the master builder, but with significant contributions from the Bon workshop, and by the carpenters who installed the roof. The stonework that Bon and Pantaleon provided was a characteristic mixture of routine architectural elements such as cornices, some rather more skilled items such as the window surrounds and the aedicules, and finally a few elements of figurative sculpture, such as those for the main façade. The likely organisation of the yard and the execution of these works is also easy to imagine; the former elements would have been carved by apprentices or 'juniors'; the more intermediate works probably by a combination of one or other of the masters together with a reasonably experienced assistant; and finally, the figurative works, much of which were almost certainly carved by the master himself, perhaps with some assistance, again, on the less demanding elements, from his apprentices.

Some Brief Notes on Other Works and Attributions from the 1440s

There are several other works often attributed to Bartolomeo Bon, most of them dating from the period from the later 1430s to around 1450, some with considerably more unanimity – and justification – than others. Among these attributions are the main west portal of Santo Stefano, the remodelling of the Scuola Vecchia della Misericordia in the 1440s, and some works of pure sculpture at the Frari.

The splendid west porch of Santo Stefano (fig. 103) is often given to Bon simply on the basis that he was the most prominent exponent of mature *gotico fiorito* in this period, and the portal is nothing if not *fiorito*. Lorenzetti, Franzoi and di Stefano have all attributed the work to Bon, although there is no documentary evidence. Wolters has dated the work to the 1430s, which would make it contemporaneous with, or slightly earlier than, the Porta della Carta. It is certainly a highly expressive work, particularly the exuberant crowning wave decoration, although the door surround is more typical of the period, and has much in

103 Santo Stefano: detail of the west portal, *circa* 1430s, perhaps by Bartolomeo Bon

common, for example, with the main, side portal of San Polo. Lorenzetti also attributed to Bon the figure of St Paul above the doorway of the latter.[90]

A more substantially architectural work was the major remodelling of the Scuola Vecchia della Misericordia after 1441 (fig. 104). The Scuola itself was first built in the years after 1327, when the adjacent abbey of Santa Maria in Valverde agreed to allow it to construct a new meeting hall on land adjacent to the monastic church. In 1412 the Scuola was permitted to construct its *albergo*, which stands on the north side of the main chapter hall, on land formerly occupied by part of the monastic cloister. In 1431

104 The Scuola Vecchia della Misericordia: pendant traceried window on the façade, rebuilt after 1441

corners of the façade are also similar to those that Bon carved for the Carità church in 1447.[91]

There are several works of figurative sculpture sometimes attributed to Bartolomeo. Among them are the figure of St Francis on the main west portal of the Frari; the portal of the Emiliani chapel at the same church; and the relief group of the Virgin and Child with two angels on the portal of San Marco (to the Emiliani chapel), once again at the Frari (fig. 105). The last of these three, however, is sometimes attributed to the dalle Masegne, while the San Marco portal has also been attributed to Niccolò Lamberti and Jacopo della Quercia, as well, of course, as to Bon himself.[92]

105 The Frari: north portal, sometimes attributed to Bartolomeo Bon

the building was enlarged, since it was by then too small for the membership. The decision to rebuild the façade followed this extension, and was made on 6 August 1441. It was necessary to demolish the chapel of Santa Cristina in order to do so, and the façade was rebuilt over the next three or four years; the work exerted even more pressure on Bon during this busy period, because he was still completing the Porta della Carta and providing stone for the Carità church. Bon's new façade for the Misericordia is sadly bereft of its most prominent original feature, the fine relief panel of the Virgin and Child (fig. 106) with members of the confraternity, now in the Victoria and Albert Museum in London; its former location is clearly identifiable on the façade today. Of the features that remain, though, the two flanking windows, with their pendant tracery, are clearly modelled on those at the Ca' d'Oro, carved by Bartolomeo and his father in 1427. The two little aedicules that crown the outer

106 The Scuola Vecchia della Misericordia: relief sculpture of the Virgin and Child with members of the Scuola, by Bartolomeo Bon, *circa* 1445

The Later Work of Bartolomeo Bon

A CHAPEL AND TWO PORTICOES

Bon's professional career provides us with an exemplary collection of projects that demonstrate clearly the range and character of the work that the master produced over four decades. If his precise role and status appear rather ambivalent and elusive to us today, this is partly because he was active in an era that was beginning to experience important change; active at the very end of a long period that, despite important stylistic developments, had itself been essentially evolutionary; and during which, in terms of the purely practical aspects of the craft of the sculptor-stonemason, and in methods of building construction, very little had changed. Simultaneously both the city's finest stonemason as well as a master in the complex art of integrating architectural masonry and figurative sculpture, Bon remained also essentially a craftsman, in a city of masters in dozens of specialist crafts.

On a different level, though, Bon was a local man, living for many years in the same house in the parish of San Marziale, with his yard adjacent. One of the most striking features of Bon's career is the location of many of his known and attributed works. With the outstanding exceptions of the Porta della Carta (*sui generis* in so many ways), the Ca' del Duca and the Carità church, all the rest of his known œuvre is located in the northern part of the city, in an arc from the Madonna dell'Orto to Santi Giovanni e Paolo. Within this compact zone are located the Ca' d'Oro, the Scuola Vecchia della Misericordia, the Corte Nova almshouses, the Scuola Grande di San Marco, and, of course, the two churches at the eastern and western ends.

This concentration is certainly no coincidence. The Bon workshop, easily accessible from all these sites, was undoubtedly regarded as one of the most important in the city, and it was natural enough both for patrons to approach a master whose shop was close at hand and equally for Bartolomeo to accept such commissions. The Bon family also had a lifelong association with the church of the Madonna dell'Orto, and its adjacent Scuola di San Cristofolo (Cristoforo), both of which were only a few minutes' walk away. Indeed, so close was Bartolomeo's identification with the church that, in 1443, when he was first commissioned by the Carità (on the other side of the city) he was identified as 'Bortolamio da lorto', rather than 'da San Marziale', his home parish, the correct and almost universal means of identification of the time.[93]

The original dedication of the Madonna dell'Orto had been to San Cristofolo, and the Scuola of that name, which met in a hall on one side of the church *campo*, housed the trade guild of the Mercanti, of which Zane and Bartolomeo were both members. Their association with the church thus preceded, by many years, Zane's request, in 1442 – when he wrote his will – to be buried in the portico. The construction of the church had been begun in 1365 by Fra Marco Tiberio from Parma, founder and general of the monastic order known as the Umiliati. Construction, however, took a considerable time, and it is likely that the first church was considerably shorter than the present one, although the original nave survives largely intact (figs 107, 108).

The fortunes of the establishment changed abruptly in 1377, though, with the discovery of a miracle-working image of the Virgin in the adjacent orchard. It was introduced into the church by the Mercanti,

108   The Scuola di San Cristofolo dei Mercanti at the Madonna dell'Orto. Both Zane and Bartolomeo Bon were members of the Scuola, which was rebuilt in 1570, to a design sometimes attributed to Palladio

who thenceforth, together with the Umiliati, began to administer the many offerings that flowed from supplicants. Slowly, too, the church's dedication changed, such that it became known as the Madonna as well as (or instead of) San Cristofolo. Severe structural problems, however, began to develop at the east end of the church (probably the result of subsidence or inadequate foundations), and between 1377 and 1399 much of the chancel deteriorated such that it was in danger of collapse. In 1399 the Maggior Consiglio made the rare gesture of a 200-ducat donation for rebuilding, which also incorporated some prudent buttressing to the nave walls.[94]

Zane Bon wrote his will on 25 March 1442. He made a number of fairly modest bequests, as well as leaving the more substantial sum of 100 ducats to his widow. He asked to be buried inside the church portico, with his tomb raised two or three steps up from the floor: 'unam sepultura ab introitum portam principalis s. maria ab orto . . . cum gradibus duobus ul tertius de lapidibus viris'.[95]

Sadly, there is no record that these wishes were carried out, although only three weeks after Zane's will was signed, on 17 April a contract was drafted by the church for a project with which Bartolomeo was to be closely involved. This was an agreement with two other familiar figures, Steffanino the builder, and Cristoforo Candio, the carpenter, for the construction of a chapel dedicated to the memory of the nobleman Marco di Girolamo Morosini. It was to be the first such chapel at the church.[96]

Morosini had written his own will a year earlier, on 24 April 1441, according to the terms of which 'there was to be constructed immediately my own *archa* [sepulcher] to be set within the right-hand wall of the church . . . and here is to be placed my body'. There was also to be erected an altarpiece 'et altrij adornamentij', for all of which he had left the substantial sum of 'up to 1,000 ducats', to be disbursed by his executors, the Procurators of San Marco *de citra*.[97]

The general specification for the chapel was described in the contract with Steffanino. As we often find in this period, the building masters were referred elsewhere for guidance as to the detailed design; in this case, the chapel was to be the same height and width as the chapel of the Lando family, which had been built recently at San Pietro in Castello, while the depth was to follow that 'at San Francesco della Vigna', although the document does not identify which particular element of that church: perhaps the chancel. (San Francesco was rebuilt in the sixteenth century by Sansovino and Palladio.)

The names of both Candio and Steffanino are, of course, familiar to us already. Candio was active at about the same time on the almshouses at the nearby Corte Nova, while we have just seen the close working relationship between Steffanino and Bon at the Carità church.

At the Morosini chapel, the work of Steffanino and Candio was a collaboration; for 410 ducats they were to build the whole structure of the chapel between them, only the carved stonework being excluded from their remit; this was to be provided by the Bon workshop. The fabric was essentially complete by the summer of 1443, and in August Steffanino was paid for decorating the inside walls and for transporting some of Bon's stone. The latter's contract dates from 18 May 1442, and Bon was given 100 ducats in advance to buy the necessary stone.[98] His father Zane received several payments from May 1442 until the following summer of 1443.[99] On 5 June 1443 two noblemen, Filippo Correr and Vettor Barbaro, who had stood surety for the 100 ducats' advance to Bon, were relieved of this obligation since the work was now effectively concluded. At this point in the brief records, too, we find yet another familiar name, Niccolò Luxe the smith, who provided metalwork for four windows.

We have little detail of the Bon contribution, although it must have included the archway that links the chapel with the body of the church as well as window surrounds and sills. Immediately after the chapel was complete, Bartolomeo was asked to carve the altar, and on 6 June 1443, the day after the first surety was discharged, Correr stood surety again, alone this time, for a further 76 ducats so that Bon could proceed with the altar. Although Zane Bon's name is also cited, he had only a few more weeks to live, and payments were made solely to Bartolomeo, who worked on the altar until 6 February 1445, by which time approximately 160 ducats had been spent in all. The final finishing touch to the chapel was the altarpiece, painted by 'Johannis pictor', who was paid a total of 70 ducats in instalments until 1445.[100]

Fifteen years later, with his father now long dead, Bartolomeo received a new commission at the Madonna dell'Orto, one of his last. The later work of Bartolomeo is less well documented than, for example, at the Carità church, and for this reason the project is of considerable importance. Not only is it a late, mature work in which we can see further stylistic developments, but the new portal for the church was contemporaneous with another similar commission, that for the great west portal of Santi Giovanni e Paolo; we thus have a unique opportunity to compare two works identical in function but different in many detailed aspects of their design.

In spring 1460 Bartolomeo submitted a design for the portal at the Madonna dell'Orto, facing the *campo* and the canal (fig. 109). His direct patron was not the church itself, but the adjacent Scuola di San Cristofolo dei Mercanti. The doorway was to be surmounted by a statue of St Christopher, the church's original dedicatee and patron of the Scuola. The contracted price for the whole ensemble was 250 ducats and the portal was to be completed within fifteen months of the signing of the contract, which took place on 21 June 1460; the signatories to the contract were Bon himself and Giacomo Arnoldi, then *rettore* or governor of the Scuola. Although not a direct party to the contract, the Umiliati were expected to contribute half of the cost of the works.[101]

As was often the case, Bon's preliminary drawing was not followed precisely, since, as well as the crowning figure of St Christopher (fig. 110) there was also to be

110   The Madonna dell'Orto: sculpted figure of St Christopher by Bartolomeo Bon

109   The Madonna dell'Orto: portico by Bartolomeo Bon, begun 1460, completed *circa* 1483

a figure of the Virgin and Child set into the lunette above the doorway; this figure was almost certainly never executed. The contract also refers to other figurative works ('gli altri intaglj chomo sta el ditto disegno'), which are not identified, but which must have included the outer flanking figures of the Virgin and the Angel of the Annunciation, if they were indeed part of the initial iconography.

Bon was also faced with a fairly typically heavy fine, of 50 ducats, if he did not complete the work within the contract period. Even in the context of his time, however, in which works frequently took twice the specified period to complete, some kind of record was established here at the Madonna dell'Orto, since it was to be no less than twenty-three years before the entire portal was assembled in place; by this time even Bartolomeo himself had died. One of the fundamental reasons for this extraordinarily protracted delay was the fact that, in 1462, two years after the contract, the canons of San Giorgio in Alga, a small islet in the lagoon, took over from the Umiliati, following enquiries into the (mis)conduct of the latter order. The canons soon made it clear that they did not consider themselves bound by legal agreements entered into by their predecessors, and this new policy is illustrated by the fact that work on the portal, extremely intermittent though it was, continued to be funded by the Scuola (di San Cristofolo) dei Mercanti and not the monastery.

Accounts of expenditure were kept by the Scuola, beginning on 23 July 1460;[102] at the time, the Scuola was funding not only the new church portal but various other works at the still-incomplete church, including the chancel and sacristy. Bon was given 50 ducats to purchase stone, and there are a number of further payments in 1461 and 1462, interspersed with costs for other operations, including chancel windows and 3,000 new roof tiles. After summer 1462, though, work on the portal came to a complete halt for four years. At some date between 1464 and 1467 Bartolomeo died, and it was only on 11 May 1466 that the two flanking marble columns ('and other things') were delivered to the site. And a further nine years were to pass before the Scuola recorded a payment to Maria, Bartolomeo's widow, who was still living in the family house, 'for porters who carried the stone for the church portal from the *bottega* of the said [Maria] to the church'. Even now, though, the portico was not yet complete, since we then read that six years later again, on 15 October 1481, the two principal columns for the doorway were now finally raised and fixed in position.

The extent of work that Bartolomeo had completed by the time of his death has long been debated, particularly since the finished portal consists of a mixture of purely late *gotico fiorito* elements together with others of distinctly Renaissance appearance. Wolters has recently suggested that the work was executed in two or three distinct phases, the first comprising the inner surround to the doorway itself (which is purely Gothic), followed by the outer columns and then finally by the crowning arch with its wave decoration. This appears highly plausible; certainly, not all of the stone carving was complete when Bon died, and as late as the spring of 1482 a master Zuane di Jacopo was paid for the crowning wave decoration to the extrados of the outer arch. In fact, the very last record dates from 1 March 1483 (twenty-three years after Bon's contract), when Jacopo, the father of Zuane, was paid for the assembly of the final elements, including running lead to locate the iron cramps for the stonework and for an unnamed painter to 'depenzer et adornare el baston de s. Christofolo'.[103]

Despite the extraordinarily protracted time scale, Bon's contribution must have been considerable. By October 1461 he had already been paid a total of 225 ducats, indicating that most of the stone was already carved; the principal works still outstanding, as the records confirm, were simply the acquisition of the two large columns, the completion of the wave decoration, and the final assembly of the whole on site. This could not have taken place until the columns were available, and it seems feasible that it was the difficulty in obtaining these columns that drew the process to a halt in 1462. Such a hiatus would not be at all surprising; substantial marble columns were highly prized, were expensive, and were often recycled from elsewhere. It is revealing to note that no costs attached to their eventual acquisition; they were thus almost certainly a gift from another source.[104] These conclusions – particularly the value of payments made – indicate that, far from being an unfinished work of Bon's (much of which is therefore the work of others), in fact almost all of the portal was carved by him, with the main exception of the high-level wave-decoration, itself fairly routine work of the period.

The completed portal is a richly detailed work, principally *gotico fiorito* in style, but with Renaissance elements incorporated, notably the fluted semicircular arch in the lunette, reminiscent of Codussi's slightly later façade at San Michele of *circa* 1470 (fig. 111). The attribution of the three sculpted figures, however, still gives rise to debate. The crowning *St Christopher* is almost always (correctly) attributed to Bon himself, and it bears the same general relationship to the portal as his figure of Justice at the Porta della Carta. The figure is specifically cited in the original contract, and we would expect such elements to be carved by the contracting master personally, rather than 'subcontracting' them to others. Written attributions to Bon go back at least as far as Francesco Sansovino (1580),[105] and there is little contradictory attribution. The two flanking figures, though, have been subject to more debate. They were cited only in general terms in the contract, but we have no record of any other named master responsible for their execution. To the left of the lunette is the Angel of the Annunciation, with the Virgin on the right. Recent claims, based solely on stylistic evidence, have concluded that the Angel is the work of Rizzo, while the Virgin is said to have been carved by Niccolò di Giovanni Fiorentino. However, there is no supporting documentation;[106] two other figures of the *Annunciation* (now in the Victoria and Albert Museum, London) are

111 The Madonna dell'Orto: detail of portico, with one of the
capitals

sometimes accepted as the work of Bon, and there is
thus some justification for the suggestion that they were
intended for the portal but never installed, and were
instead replaced by the present figures.[107]

Other than the figure sculptures, the most striking
features of the portal are the central lunette and the
crowning four-centred arch, with its foliage. The lunette
is occupied not by a bas-relief group, as we might
expect, but by a superb large, plain slab of porphyry,
very rare and of considerable value. Was this slab, as
Wolters has suggested, the *pietra* (in the singular) that
lay in the workshop until Maria, Bon's widow, finally
had it consigned to the site in 1475? In any event, the
design of the lunette alone clearly indicates that Bon
was willing and able to adopt Renaissance elements
in his later work, such as the Ca' del Duca,[108] as
further examination of his second church portal also
demonstrates.

The Portal at Santi Giovanni e Paolo

For centuries, the stately, monumental and imposing
west doorway of the great friary church of Santi Giovanni e Paolo had no known author; it was only in 1961
that Gallo identified it as the work of Bartolomeo Bon,
thus providing us with this invaluable comparison with
the Madonna dell'Orto (figs 112, 114, 115). The doorway
was not the result of generous private legacies, as had
often been assumed, but was instead the result of the
industria of the *religiosi predicatori* (the preacher-friars)
themselves. It was traditionally dated to 1458, and this
date is also confirmed in the documents published by
Gallo; a record dated 10 April records the purchase of
eight large marble columns, bought at a cost of 148 lire
and 16 soldi.[109] They were obtained from Torcello,
almost certainly salvaged from classical remains or abandoned early Christian churches, and were delivered to
the site on 5 September of the following year; in fact,
as we can see, only six of the eight were to be used in
the portal. Bon's first recorded involvement dates from
24 April 1459, by which date, though, he had already
been working on the portal for some time, since he had
been paid a total of 403 lire; this represents as much as
a full year's work. In the same period, too, two other
masters, Antonio and Marino, had been carving *retorcu-
los* (rope mouldings) for the flanking pilasters, while
another master again, Jacobo, had been working on
column bases. Bon therefore had a small team of fairly
experienced masons to assist him in this monumental
work, and they had probably all begun working at about
the time that the columns had been purchased, in the
spring of 1458. By November 1459 a further record
notes that the monastery had paid out 285 lire for additional expenses on the portal since August of that year.

Bon's own direct involvement with the work seems
to have concluded with a payment on 2 February 1460,
when he was given 186 lire; it was described as his
'salary', which implies that he had been employed and
paid on a regular basis for the duration of the works
rather than being paid for individual elements, or on
the basis of an original 'lump sum' contract. In a way
this seems appropriate, given his age, skill and enormous
experience; he must by now have been regarded as the
'grand old man' of Venetian architectural sculpture, precisely the kind of greatly skilled master to whom the
overall management and coordination of such an
important work could be entrusted. But perhaps by
now his age was beginning to limit some of his physical abilities; some work still remained to be completed
in early 1460, and nearly two years later again, three
other masons were brought onto the site and worked
on the stone from November 1462 until February 1463.

112 Santi Giovanni e Paolo: upper part of the great west portal, begun by Bon in 1458, completed *circa* 1463

113 Santi Giovanni e Paolo: detail of portico, showing two of the capitals; the relief decoration to the frieze was probably completed after Bon's death

114 Santi Giovanni e Paolo: central bay of the portico with its Gothic arch

115 Santi Giovanni e Paolo: detail of portico, with rich carving to the extrados

These were indeed the final finishing touches, however, and the masons, Domenico Fiorentino, Luca and Lorenzo, were all carving the fine relief work on the friezes.[110] This relief work has a rather Lombard character, although executed, at least in part, by a master from Florence.

It is clear, therefore, that most of the great west portal was indeed the work of Bartolomeo. The delicate carving to the friezes (fig. 113) was executed by others after his death, and although we cannot be certain whether or not this work fell within his original design control, Bon was certainly receptive to new influences of this nature, as the Ca' del Duca also demonstrates with great clarity; it was certainly Bon himself who established the basic configuration of the great flanking columns, which are set in pairs, a relationship that not only echoes some of the arrangements at San Marco but also reflects classical precedents. In 1457, for example, work had also begun on the great new gate,

the *porta magna*, at the Arsenale, and although its architect remains unknown, the arch was modelled closely on the Roman arch at Pola, and, like it, is flanked by paired classical columns.[111]

The west portal of Santi Giovanni e Paolo is nevertheless basically an ornate, late example of *gotico fiorito*, with its pointed central arch and its rich rope mouldings in Istrian stone and *rosso di Verona*. What the portal demonstrates, though, is that it was quite possible for elements of the two styles to coexist happily: a Gothic arch below which is a refined neo-classical frieze, rich foliage capitals with rope mouldings and classical cornices, the entire ensemble forming a richly integrated whole.

The portal itself is more powerfully monumental than that at the Madonna dell'Orto, its scale reflecting that of the great church behind it. In that sense, therefore, both portals in their different ways harmonise with their contexts. The façade of the Madonna dell'Orto is a particularly refined and elegant example of late Venetian Gothic, with its large traceried windows and uniquely galleried arcades to the tops of the side wings; in this context Bon's own refined portal fits perfectly. The west façade of Santi Giovanni e Paolo presents a more difficult composition to analyse, since it was never completed in the manner then intended, that is, with stone cladding to the lower part of the entire façade, up to the level of the top of Bon's portal. We should also note that in the same year of 1458 Antonio Gambello had begun the façade of San Zaccaria, which was itself to be richly clad with stonework; indeed, the portal at Santi Giovanni e Paolo is still sometimes ascribed to Gambello, despite documentary evidence attributing the work to Bon. This is not, of course, to deny that there may have been influences from Gambello on Bartolomeo, although it is equally clear that Bon himself retained an open mind regarding new stylistic influences, as a brief reference to his last important (and most elusive) work will make clear.

THE CA' DEL DUCA: AN ELUSIVE SWAN-SONG

In this sketch of Bon's career, I have concentrated on those projects that are definitively attributed, and at least partially covered by contractual and other building records. The last of these projects, however, is in many ways the most fascinating and yet elusive of all of his works: the fragmentary palace on the Grand Canal near San Samuele today still known as the Ca' del Duca.

Although strictly outside the scope of the present study, since it is a private commission, it remains stylistically a crucial work of the period of transition, and hence justifies some observations.[112]

The original patron of this famous palace was Andrea Corner, who began the necessary new foundations in 1457. In the same year, however, Andrea had been tried and found guilty of corruption; shortly afterwards he fled to exile in Cyprus. The drawings, particularly that for the revolutionary façade, then passed to Andrea's brother Marco, although it is clear that very little other than groundworks and some foundations could have been achieved on site prior to Andrea's fall from grace.

Two or three years later, in 1460, Antonio Guidobono, who was the ambassador in Venice of Galeazzo Maria Sforza, duke of Milan, completed negotiations for the purchase of the barely begun palace in exchange for a house at San Polo already in the duke's possession. In December Guidobono wrote to Sforza from Venice, and suggested that the duke should send his own architect, Filarete, to Venice to examine the drawings that had already been prepared by Bon, and to prepare a *modello* for the duke showing the completed proposal.[113] A few weeks later Sforza issued a safe-conduct pass to Benedetto Ferrini, who then also travelled to Venice. On his arrival, however, Bon famously refused to give him access to his own drawings for the palace; Ferrini remained in Venice for six months, and despite Bon's refusal, was able to furnish Sforza not only with a basic description of Bon's proposed façade, but also some proposals of his own as to how the palace should be completed. Bon's own scheme was based on a long façade with two flanking towers, with facings of marble in diamond pattern to the lowermost storey, and with a central waterfront loggia or *riva* supported by huge columns of marble. Apart from these details of design, extremely important though they are, the other remarkable feature of the new palace was to be its size: the façade was to have been immense, certainly the largest private palace ever seen in the city, and, at around 166 feet long, was on the same kind of scale as the Palazzo Ducale itself. As to the detailed aspect of its design, the use of a very broad, essentially tripartite plan and façade, and particularly the incorporation of flanking towers (*torreselle*), represented the revival of much earlier Venetian-Byzantine forms, such as those on the Ziani Ducal Palace and on the now much-restored Fondaco dei Turchi, where the outermost bays are extended upwards by one storey to form corner towers. Defensive in their distant origin, these towers had already lost any such function by the thirteenth century, so that their purpose thereafter remained almost solely aesthetic. The reference to diamond-pattern rustication, though, is by no means a historic reference, but rather a revolutionary feature of unclear provenance.[114]

On 26 January 1461 Ferrini wrote again to Sforza, via the latter's secretary, Giovanni Simonetta. Doubtlessly offended by Bon's uncooperative attitude, Ferrini remarks that although 'Andrea Corner had a very generous spirit because he began a magnificent and stupendous undertaking', nevertheless, 'as you can see from the drawing, the result turned out badly, as he was ill-advised by his own engineers'. A few weeks later, on 7 March, Sforza replied to Guidobono in Venice that he had now received 'models' (probably drawings) of the house from Ferrini, and he was therefore able to understand and modify the design to reflect his own wishes; these were that the house should be 'in the modern style, and in the way in which we build here in our territory [Milan]'. Crucially, though, he adds that 'the façade on the Grand Canal will be in the Venetian style', despite the 'ill advice' of Corner's 'engineers'. Guidobono wrote to Sforza again only two days later, commenting that

> you intend to do the façade in the Venetian manner and then the house in the modern and Lombard style. I do not doubt that Your Excellency will indeed give them a better form than the Venetian one; nevertheless the Venetians like their own style and manner better. I believe that it will cost more because some foundations will need to be extended and changed.

These foundations had thus clearly been installed on the basis of a façade *alla veneziana*, that is, with a tripartite form based on the grandiose Venetian–Byzantine configuration initiated by Bon.

Work was not to proceed very much further on this great project. On 14 July 1461 Ferrini was told to return to Milan; although it has been suggested that work continued on site in his absence for a further year or two, there is no documentary evidence, and it seems more likely that the project was abandoned fairly soon afterwards. By 1465 Sforza's financial circumstances had become so difficult that he was forced to pawn his jewellery to pay debts incurred in Venice (on the palace?) and certainly no work took place after his death in 1466.[115]

We are left, therefore, with this famously elusive fragment, a massively rusticated quoin at the angle of the Grand Canal and the Rio del Duca (fig. 116), with two great embedded columns, one at the canal angle and the other forming the termination of the *torresella* at the other end; we also have the diamond rustication between the two columns and down the flank façade to the canal, together with some impressive courses of rusticated rectangular stonework forming a plinth or basement from which the huge façade was intended to rise. Despite considerable further recent research and attributions, many uncertainties still surround this fragment: is the section that we see today precisely that which had been completed by Bon prior to Sforza's purchase? Or did Ferrini undertake further work in 1461? And what is the source for the extraordinary diamond rustication?

The source usually cited as the 'hidden' influence (or even the hidden architect) behind this façade is Filarete (Antonio Averlino); Filarete was also in the service of Sforza, and had been in Venice in spring 1458; we have a letter from him, dated 10 April, advising that he was leaving the city with a drawing showing how the duke's house was to be built. We do not know the contents of that drawing; it may perhaps have been a copy of Bon's own proposal, although this seems unlikely given the latter's hostility towards publication of his proposals. Perhaps it was Filarete's own initial sketch; most importantly, though, we do have the famous illustration from his treatise of a design for a palace 'in a marshy place',[116] which does have much in common with the design that Bon was so reluctant to hand over

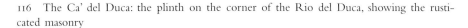

116   The Ca' del Duca: the plinth on the corner of the Rio del Duca, showing the rusticated masonry

117 Filarete: design for a palace in a marshy place from the *Trattato*

to Sforza's emissary (fig. 117). Filarete's drawing shows a long, imposing façade, which is in effect a Renaissance reworking of the Venetian-Byzantine *palazzo-fontego*, complete with corner 'turrets' (here modernised to form light, open *logge*) and a spacious central *riva*, as well as a typically open central first-floor loggia. Another characteristically Venetian detail is the fanciful crowning crenellation. Of even more particular interest is the fact that Filarete emphasises the more solid appearance of the two outer bays not only by their modern *torreselle*, but by a different pattern of fenestration on the ground floor to these two bays, and by the use of diamond rustication on the ground floor below the sills of the windows, again, only on these two bays.

Filarete was in the service of Sforza, and wrote the *Trattato* between around 1460 and 1464, although it was not published until the nineteenth century.[117] Nevertheless, it seems certain that the design for the palace 'in a marshy place' derives from this period in Venice of around 1458, and that Filarete's many illustrations, which would ultimately all be bound together into the treatise, were known individually by cognoscenti at the time. Although it was clear that a good deal of stylistic compromise would be necessary in order to reconcile the palace design (probably under Filarete's influence) with Sforza's own wishes, therefore, it is certain that it had been begun by Bon, including the great columns, the rustication and the intended *torreselle*. Since these elements (together with the foundations that such a traditional Venetian tripartite arrangement clearly inferred) already stood, the Sforza version was perforce destined

to be essentially a compromise between a 'Venetian though revolutionary' façade and a Milanese plan and interior.

If we accept that this unique fragment is the work of Bon, influenced by Filarete, how can we locate it in the context of Bon's own late style? It is clear from the portal of Santi Giovanni e Paolo that Bon was receptive to modern and different design approaches, as, for example in the use of paired classical columns (and in the scalloped surround to the lunette at the Madonna dell'Orto), and so there is no reason to suppose that he was not capable of rising to the challenge of a powerful, wealthy and influential client such as Corner, and develop a truly monumental palace façade; his contemporary work at Santi Giovanni e Paolo was also grandiose and monumental in scale. And, like the church portal, the façade of the Ca' del Duca is a hybrid, a fusion of traditional Venetian motifs with more revolutionary elements. Indeed, had the project been completed along the principles stated by Sforza, the final result would also have been a stylistic hybrid, a fusion of Venetian façade composition with Lombard fenestration.

Footnote

The working career of Bartolomeo Bon covered the period from around 1420 to the mid-1460s. In some ways Bon was a unique figure, a master skilled in a number of overlapping fields: in architectural stonemasonry, in skilful but essentially traditional *gotico fiorito* decoration, in the integration of purely sculpted forms within a strong architectural framework; and as a 'pure' figure sculptor. Despite his still fairly traditional position in the organisational structure of the Venetian construction industry and its systems of patronage and commissioning, Bon was nevertheless considerably more than simply a proficient and gifted master carver in these various fields. He was also a creative artist, who was by no means confined to *gotico fiorito*, and who, in the later 1450s and 1460s, was clearly aware of the stylistic changes that were afoot beyond Venice.

The general perception of his social and cultural role in Venetian society almost certainly remained that of the skilled craftsman. Several aspects of his œuvre, however, suggest that appreciation of his skills was beginning to reflect a more progressive attitude on the part of his patrons. The extremely prominent 'signature' on the (almost purely Gothic) Porta della Carta is also noteworthy in this respect: the fact that the Signoria happily conceded such pride of place in recognition of the 'sole master' seems to be unprecedented in state-sponsored works in this period. Later, too, his clear ability to assimilate Renaissance elements into his work indicates a sensibility considerably more receptive and alert than that of many (if not most) of his contemporaries. The last few years of his career marked a period of stylistic transition, in which we can recognise the slow absorption of these new influences into the long-established Venetian aesthetic tradition.

118 The Arsenale: the main water gate and (left) the stone Porta Magna of 1460

Chapter Six

INTERMEZZO:
STYLISTIC TRANSITION

The Porta Magna at the Arsenale

The Venetian Arsenale was one of the most impressive military complexes in Europe, the key to the defence of the Serenissima and to the extensive network of trading routes on which the Republic depended for its wealth. It was naturally imbued with great symbolic importance, overlaid onto its practical role as the heart of a mercantile and military empire.

Towards the end of the fifteenth century, Marin Sanudo described the Arsenale as 'truly one of the finest things that may be seen [in the city] . . . it has a circumference of xx *stadij* and is located in the parish of San Martino, with magnificent walls all around; and here are constructed continuously the great galleys for the *viazij*, and light galleys for the navy (figs 118–20)'.[1]

A century later, Sansovino made much the same observations, but was even more emphatic as to the might and vital role of this great strategic nucleus:

> But the base and foundation of the greatness of this republic of ours, and the honour of all Italy, and to put it even better, and with greater accuracy, of the whole of Christendom, is the place called the Arsenale . . . One enters through a very beautiful old gateway, built in a noble style of architecture in the reign of Pasquale Malipiero in the year 1457, with a great lion of marble at the top, above which is positioned on the frontispiece a figure of Santa Giustina, carved in the round, all in marble, and larger than

life-size, carved by the hand of Hieronimo Campagna, Veronese, and below, on the portal, is written 'Leon de Molino, Marco Contareno, Al. Capello; I Duce inclito Pascali Maripetro'. And on the right side in the squares below the columns: 'Christi Incarnatione MCCCCLX'.[2]

The great gate of the Arsenale remains a seminal building in the architectural history of Venice, the first surviving fully Renaissance structure in the city (fig. 121). It owes its existence to two events: the brief but important reign of Doge Pasquale Malipiero (1457–62) and to the capture of Constantinople by the Turks, a few years earlier, in 1453. The latter provoked considerable concern in Venice as to the condition of the Republic's own military capabilities, a concern that was exacerbated by the decision of the Ottoman sultan to begin construction of a great new arsenal in the newly conquered former capital of the Eastern Empire. A year or two later, in 1455, the Venetians responded to this potential new threat by beginning a programme of works at their own extensive Arsenale. The coordination of these works was the responsibility of Leone da Molin and Jacopo Barbarigo, the first two newly appointed – and initially temporary – Provveditori of the Arsenale.[3]

One of the first of a series of improvements was the modernisation of the Arsenale Vecchio, the original nucleus of the complex. The large sheds that lined

119 The Arsenale: fifteenth-century shipbuilding sheds on the west side of the Darsena Vecchia, the original nucleus of the naval base

both sides of this basin were rebuilt; those on the west side have survived today, although now roofless. Attention also turned to the Arsenale Nuovo, the much larger basin to the east, and particularly its southern flank, the zone adjacent to the *corderie*, the ropeworks. These new buildings were probably supervised by Pietro Bon, the *prothomagister Arsenatus*. A number of new sheds, covering both wet and dry docks ('voltij di terra, voltj d'acqua') were built in the winter of 1457–8, and the whole operation was largely complete by 1460.[4]

The new land gate was also completed by 1460, but to understand its significance we need first to turn to the character of Doge Malipiero, who had been elected at the age of 72 on 30 October 1457. Although it was to be brief, Malipiero's reign was quite different in its nature from the record thirty-four-year reign of his immediate predecessor, Francesco Foscari. Despite the ominous events in the Balkans, Malipiero's guiding principles were the maintenance of peace and stability, characteristics identified in the writings of his nephew, Domenico, in his *Annali veneti*.[5] Elsewhere, Pasquale was described as a 'homo in vero de grande intellecto e de sumo saper e dotrina'.[6] His reign, therefore, to some extent marked a reaffirmation of one aspect of the 'myth of Venice', 'peace as a condition for strength and stability', as Ennio Concina has put it. In 1460, when the Porta Magna was complete, Malipiero was described by a contemporary as 'totus moderatus, totus quietus, totus pacificus'; his period in office, therefore,

was essentially an interlude of tranquillity after Foscari's long, often turbulent reign.[7]

Not only was there peace abroad, but in general, too, harmony within the Republic itself. Equally important, and crucial to the construction of the Porta Magna, was the fact of an intellectually enlightened head of state, patron of this different cultural atmosphere. In 1460 Malipiero established a second *cathedra* (chair of study) at the Scuola of the Chancellery of San Marco, to reinforce 'studia humanitatis'; one of the two weekly lectures was to be on the subjects of 'arte oratoria aut in historia', on classical lines.[8] Sansovino claimed that his reign saw the introduction into Venice of an invention that was to transform Western culture in a matter of a few decades: the printing press. Although Sansovino erred here, the general association of Malipiero's reign with enlightened cultural advancement is appropriate enough, and printing did flourish and expand rapidly in the period after the reign of

120 The Arsenale: entrance to the bakery (1473), where provisions for the navy were produced

facing page 121 The Arsenale: the Porta Magna, completed in 1460

VICTORIÆ · NAVALIS · MONIMENTVM
· M D L XXI ·

his equally enlightened successor, Cristoforo Moro. In sum, his reign gave a considerable boost both to humanist thought and to the developing view of Venice as 'the new Rome'.[9]

The Arsenale gateway has often been attributed to Antonio Gambello, although no documentary evidence supports the claim. At the time of the gate's construction Gambello was *proto* to San Zaccaria, where he was employed on a regular, salaried basis. His known architectural œuvre is so small, though, that it is impossible to link him to the Porta stylistically, and it is certainly quite different in character from his work at San Zaccaria.[10]

There is, though, a connection between Gambello and Doge Malipiero that perhaps forms a tenuous link between the *proto* and the Porta. The medal struck to commemorate Malipiero's reign was analogous to that made for his predecessor, Foscari, which had perhaps been designed by Antonio Gambello, and was made by his son Vettor, a medallist who was himself the *proto* or supervising officer at the Zecca (mint). The Malipiero medal, which Concina has suggested probably originated from a proposal by Pietro Barbo, was inspired by the classical Roman medals of Marcus Aurelius. The theme of *renovatio imperii* forms the dominant element of Malipiero's reign, and it is thus natural that a doge who exploited such an imperial theme in his own celebratory coinage should adopt it equally enthusiastically at the new Arsenale gateway. Contemporary references to him in this imperial vein are numerous: Candiano Bollani, for example, in his *elogio* given to Doge Cristoforo Moro (his successor) in 1462 refers to Malipiero as 'tu caput, tu dux, tu imperator', although this last title was by no means an official ducal honorific. In a similar manner, Francesco Capodilista ingeniously (and somewhat sycophantically) interpreted the genealogy of his surname as a derivation from 'ala imperii', the wings of the imperial eagle.[11]

The architectural lineage of the Arsenale gate is clear. Its ancestors lie not in Trajan's Forum in Rome, but closer, and well within Venice's own traditional sphere of influence: the city of Pola, across the gulf in Istria, where a sturdy classical Roman arch, known as the Arch of the Sergii, and dating from around 30 BC, can still be seen today. When we examine this classical model, its singular and striking appropriateness for the Venetian Arsenale is immediately apparent. Although Malipiero's was essentially a reign of peace, the Arsenale itself remained the symbol of Venetian naval power; what more appropriate metaphor could be found than a triumphal arch, symbol of military victory, of dominion, of the conquest of foreign foes? At this

level, the new gateway would send a clear, unequivocal message across the Mediterranean to the newly installed sultan in Constantinople.

But – and here lies its real importance – almost nowhere else in Italy, not even in Rome or Florence, had this triumphant classical motif yet been given new life after having lain dormant for so many centuries. Venice as the new Rome: this is perhaps the finest single example of this complex conceit rendered material. How could the concept be more appropriately expressed than here, at the entrance to the Arsenale, bulwark of the west, bastion of Christianity against the 'infidel' usurper in the east (fig. 122)?

It is likely that Gambello himself had visited Pola in his governmental capacity as surveyor of defences, since Pola was a significant naval base itself; but since the Porta Magna cannot be attributed to him with certainty, it is useful to make one or two other observations as to its possible author and the immediate cultural context in which it was built. We know, for example, that Fra Giocondo went to Pola in this period, as, later, did Giovanni Maria Falconetto, who made at least one study of the Roman arch there; others may well have made the same journey both before and after these two.[12] Another possible candidate, advanced by Concina, is Filarete (Antonio Averlino). Among the links in this suggested chain are the fact that Doge Malipiero was a close personal friend of Francesco Sforza, duke of Milan. In 1459 Galeazzo Maria and Filippo Maria, his two sons, were both in Venice, and on at least one occasion dined with Malipiero; Filarete himself had also been in Venice in the previous year. This was the period in which Sforza's own arrangements for his palace in Venice were being significantly altered, and the house at San Polo was instead replaced by the acquisition of the fragment of the palace that Bartolomeo Bon had begun for Andrea Corner at San Samuele.[13]

Several aspects of Filarete's architectural approach suggest at least an influence over the design of the Arsenale gate; his taste for rich trabeation is one of them, as is his penchant for fine Greek marble. More substantially, he had already had experience in the 'rediscovery' and adaptation of the classical triumphal arch in 1454, when he designed just such an arch – temporary, in this case – for Sforza to celebrate the Peace of Lodi.[14] Two further specific links are suggested by Concina: one is Filarete's practice of affixing stone balls onto parapets, as evinced by illustrations in his *Trattato*, while the same work also illustrates his use of paired classical columns standing forward of a screen wall. The Arsenale gate originally had three stone balls

122   The Arsenale: the Porta Magna, detail of the central arch: the winged Victories were added after the Battle of Lepanto in 1571

on the attic storey and a further two on the principal cornice of the main order; only the last two remain today.[15]

A further contemporary comparison is also of interest. As we have just seen, at precisely the same time that the Porta Magna was being built, not far away at Santi Giovanni e Paolo Bartolomeo Bon was working on the monumental new west portal to the great Dominican church. Bon's work is more than a little transitional in its general style, partly, no doubt, because it is attached to a quintessentially Gothic church; but the outer framing of the portal is formed by two pairs of prominent, freestanding columns in front of the portal itself, with bold architraves and a richly carved frieze. Clearly, the introduction and use of such motifs had already taken root among more than one of the leading masters of the city, since there is no evidence to link Bon directly with the Porta Magna. Colonna's *Hypnerotomachia Poliphili* also illustrates a portal with paired columns.[16]

The final potential influence is the famous triumphal arch at the Castel Nuovo in Naples, the first stage of which was built in the years 1453–8, and is often attrib-

uted to a Dalmatian, Onofrio di Giordano; several other masters, though, contributed towards its refined decoration. The lowest order of this rich, complex work once again has pairs of columns standing forward of the arch itself, although here they are fluted, with Corinthian capitals. In this they resemble the classical arch at Pola, but not the Porta Magna, whose columns are not fluted, and are surmounted by refined, but essentially Byzantine (and recycled) capitals. Cultural links between Venice and Naples were not particularly close in this period, however, and it seems likely that Onofrio had taken as his own exemplar either the Pola arch itself or perhaps some other classical survivor in Naples or Rome. Nevertheless, Venetian travellers may well have brought back to the city reports of this startling new work.[17]

The Porta Magna at the Arsenale was in essence a fairly simple composition, although it was rendered more complex later by the addition of further triumphal accretions. It has a single large portal, flanked by the paired columns discussed above, and the arch is surmounted by a small attic storey. The four columns, of Greek *cipollino* marble, are the most prominent fea-

145

123   The Arsenale: the Porta Magna: detail showing the winged lion

tures, although their Byzantine capitals are perhaps of the eleventh or twelfth century. It is almost certain that both columns and capitals were salvaged from some earlier structure, perhaps in the Venetians' own lagoon. All the rest of the gate, though, is of new Istrian stone, with the sole exception of a narrow band of pink Verona *broccatello* on the architrave.

The construction of the arch can be dated to the period between January 1458 and the end of May 1460. It replaced an earlier land gate that was probably fortified, and which would have formed an integral part of the enclosing walls of the Arsenale. On the trabeation we can read the salient details of its patronage; on one side the inscription of the incumbent doge (*I Duce inclito Pascali Maripetro*) (fig. 124), and on the other the names of the three Provveditori of the Arsenale, *Leo[ne]de Molino, Marco Contareno, Al[bano]Capello*. Patricia Fortini Brown has recently remarked on the dates of construction carved into the plinths of the principal order; that on the right side gives the date in conventional terms (*XI INCAR[NATIONE] MCCCCLX*) but that on the left plinth records the date in relation to the mythical date of the foundation of Venice itself in AD 421:

AB URBE CON[DITA]M[ILESIM]O XXX.V.IIIIo.; that is, 1,039 years after the city's own establishment.[18] The recording of the date in this manner was intended to reinforce the great antiquity of the Republic and the implication that it would last for an equally long time in the future. The little carved putto in the keystone is also significant, since it represents *Abbondanza*, and is another reference to Malipiero's patronage – the same figure can be seen on his tomb monument in Santi Giovanni e Paolo.[19]

Above the main storey of the arch is a much lower attic; it is framed by very squat pilasters and surmounted by a rich, but very fussily moulded tympanum, with a scallop shell in the centre. Like the main order below, the tympanum was also originally capped by three stone balls – the Filaretian touch – which are still visible in Matteo Pagan's view of the city in 1559; in 1578, though, after the Battle of Lepanto, they were replaced by two flanking urns and the crowning figure of S. Giustina. The dominant feature of this order, though, is the massive Venetian lion, holding the open book in his paws (fig. 123). In general, it resembles that carved by Bon for the Porta della Carta around 1440, although

146

124 The Arsenale: the Porta Magna: detail showing the twin columns and entablature with the inscription of Doge Pasquale Malipiero

the sculptor of the Arsenale lion remains unknown. Its orientation is the same, however, with the lion facing the left, although here there is no kneeling doge, and the lion completely fills his allotted space. Indeed, he appears somewhat over-sized for it, since the tail extends well beyond the stone frame.

In essence, the iconographic programme of the Porta Magna should be read from the base upwards to the crowning pediment, much like the more complex iconography of the Porta della Carta. In the latter case, the programme's climax is the crowning figure of Justice, whereas at the Porta Magna the sequence is simpler; the original programme terminated with the scallop shell set into the tympanum, the shell itself representing Venus, or rather, Venice as Venus, the goddess born from the seas.[20]

On completion in 1460, the Arsenale gate did not yet have a clearly defined place in the urban fabric of

125   The Arsenale: the Porta Magna: one of the stone lions at the bases of the columns

the city, since initially it was simply a more grandiose replacement for the earlier land gate. Intended to form a prominent Renaissance urban statement, it was only in the years after its completion that a fitting setting was devised for it. By 1463 military campaigns had become a serious drain on the coffers of the Republic, damping down the spirit of costly urban *renovatio*, but in 1467 the Senate decided that the setting of the gleaming new gate should be enhanced; eleven houses were purchased from the parish of San Martino with the intention of demolishing them to form a new public square. The plot eventually cleared was to measure 34 *passi* by 9 (around 57 metres by 15) and although its longer axis ran across the front of the gate rather than orthogonal to it, it did provide a generous space for formal events, such as the visits of the doge to the Arsenale, accompanied by his substantial retinue. That the process was intended to enhance the dignity of the gate (and the city as a whole) is evinced by the justification for the Senate's decision: 'ad ornamentum ac utilitatem non tantum ipsius domus, sed etiam istius civitatis'.[21]

It was fully appreciated, therefore, that once completed the gate's immediate context required appropriate spatial dignity; the Collegio ratified the intention a few months later, referring to the 'dignitas operis', and the intention to provide 'una platea ante hostium ipsius arsenatus, per pulchrum et honorificium, ut in pulcherimo sit prospectu sicuti operas dignitas exiget'.[22]

It may be useful here to sketch the later history of the gate in order to distinguish between the original structure and its later accretions. The first important alterations were a result of the naval victory of Lepanto over the Turks, which took place on S. Giustina's Day, 7 October 1571. To enhance further the glorious image of the gate, therefore, two winged Victories were added to the spandrels above the arch itself, although in truth they are large and rather awkwardly formed to wedge into the available space. It is also significant to note that the arch's classical predecessor at Pola also has winged Victories in the spandrels, following the usual Roman formula, although they are considerably smaller and surprisingly delicate for such a robust context. (We may wonder why the Arsenale arch was not built with its Victories from the outset; but it was not built to celebrate a specific victory, and it was clearly felt more appropriate to wait until such an event occurred.) A few years later again, in 1578 the arch was crowned by Girolamo Campagna's large statue of S. Giustina herself, a further allusion to Lepanto.[23]

Later still, the complex terrace was added in front of the structure itself; it was formed in 1682, with its attendant figures of mythological gods and goddesses. Finally, and in celebration of yet another military triumph, this time the reconquest of the Morea by Francesco Morosini in 1689, the flanking lions were added (fig. 125). The two largest ones, closest to the entrance, were brought back from the Piraeus by Morosini as booty.[24]

The practical function of the arch as originally built was simple and straightforward. It formed the only pedestrian point of access into the whole complex of the Arsenale, even after the great sixteenth-century expansions. Immediately adjacent, of course, is the water entrance; enlarged on at least two occasions to take account of the increased size of shipping, the water gate remains inherently militaristic and traditional in appearance. Built of brick and crowned with crenella-tions, it forms a point of emphasis along the general enclosing walls of the great naval base.

The land gate is quite different. Smaller, much richer in appearance, and all built of gleaming white stone, its impact is achieved not by its scale but by its strong contrast with the whole of the remainder of the Arsenale complex. This was the entrance through which the thousands of *arsenalotti* poured every day, and through which illustrious visitors were ushered on their carefully supervised guided tours.[25] On its completion the arch must have made a striking impression on Malipiero's contemporaries. Its psychological importance, though, was also to be validated shortly afterwards; Doge Malipiero himself was buried on 7 May 1462, and he was succeeded by Cristoforo Moro. Within months Venice was to be at war with the Turks.

126 San Michele in Isola: façade to the lagoon, by Mauro Codussi, begun in 1469

Chapter Seven

THE ERA OF CODUSSI

San Michele in Isola and the Campanile of San Pietro in Castello

Mauro Codussi was born in the village of Lenna or Lentina near Bergamo around 1440. Our earliest documented record is his appointment in Venice in 1469 to design the new church of San Michele in Isola, for the monastic order known as the Camaldolesi.

He was trained as a stonemason, one of the large number of skilled masons from that region who migrated to Venice in the fifteenth century. He probably worked for the Camaldolesi at Classe, near Ravenna, before his appointment at San Michele, and he visited Ravenna later, in 1477 and 1478. These visits, together with the evidence of his built work in Venice, strongly suggest a knowledge of the work of Alberti at the Malatesta church of San Francesco in nearby Rimini (1447–60). His understanding of the classical heritage can be inferred from his known visits to Verona and to Pola in Istria, to select and buy stone; in both cities there were notable classical remains: the Roman arena, amphitheatre and arch at Pola and the extensive Roman survivors at Verona, including the imposing arena.[1]

Work at San Michele (fig. 126) may have begun in 1468, but the surviving records start in the following year, and our knowledge of the construction of this remarkable church is based chiefly on surviving correspondence between the abbot, Pietro Donà (or Donato), who was then living at Classe, and his deputy in Venice, Pietro Delfin (or Dolfin), who supervised the

construction works. The Albertian link is further strengthened by our knowledge that both Donà and Delfin were aware of his influential treatise, *De re aedificatoria*, and may have owned copies; both men were outstanding scholars and intellectuals in the humanist spirit.

San Michele remains an extraordinary work, remarkably mature for a master who was still probably only in his mid- to late twenties when it was begun, and – as far as we are aware – whose first major commission this was. Its design represents a sophisticated synthesis of elements both evolutionary and revolutionary, and it is really necessary to consider the two principal elements, the façade and the body of the church itself, individually. Whilst we can only speculate as to the extent of Codussi's youthful travels and the knowledge gained thereby, the façade of San Michele marks both the recognition of a powerful local tradition in façade design and an appreciation – clearly gained from elsewhere – as to how this tradition could be radically reappraised.[2]

The reinterpretation of tradition can be identified in the tripartite form of the façade, with the taller central section representing the nave and the lower flanking bays cladding the two side aisles (figs 127, 128); the trilobate form echoes those on a number of slightly earlier and roughly contemporary late Gothic churches such as San Giovanni in Bragora, while the radiused form of the dominant central pediment recalls those rich examples on San Marco itself. Even the two tall lancets that light the aisles can be seen as a 'translation'

127   San Michele in Isola: detail of the upper part of the façade

1464, where the sarcophagus has a frieze decorated in beautiful Roman lettering. Many possible sources, therefore, can be traced in the façade of San Michele in Isola, although every one – directly or indirectly – can be traced back to Alberti.

The language of the detailing of the façade is clearly of the Renaissance; despite Codussi's reinterpretation of the composition of the traditional Venetian Gothic façade, therefore, traditional detailing has been cast aside in favour of the new language. The decision to clad the entire façade with dazzling white Istrian stone also marks a radical departure from tradition in the city. The very prominence of the site had a direct bearing on this decision: there would have been little point in cladding the façade with costly stone if it could not be appreciated as a composition in its entirety; Palladio was to take an identical stance a century later in the façades of San Giorgio Maggiore and the Redentore.

128   San Michele in Isola: the west doorway

129   Detail of the façade of Palazzo Rucellai, Florence, by Leon Battista Alberti, 1446–51

of the traditional Gothic lancets of many earlier churches in the city into the new language. This composition, though, also recalls the façade of Alberti's San Francesco in Rimini, not as we see it today, incomplete, but in the design on the medal made by Matteo de' Pasti, showing how it was intended to complete the upper façade. That Codussi had travelled more extensively than the above notes suggest can also perhaps be inferred from the shallow rustication applied to the church façade, which is reminiscent of the work of Bernardo Rossellini for Pope Pius II at Pienza, and particularly the Palazzo Piccolomini; Alberti's own façade for Giovanni Rucellai in Florence (begun *circa* 1453) also incorporates flat, refined rustication (fig. 129). Yet another influence might be that of Luciano Laurana, who (like Codussi) incorporated Roman lettering on the façade of the courtyard in the ducal palace at Urbino in 1465;[3] once again, though, we find a further source for this element in Alberti's sepulchre for Giovanni Rucellai at San Pancrazio in Florence, begun in

130 San Pietro in Castello: the campanile, 1482–4

Michele already marked him as an outstanding master, quite different in his intellectual rigour from his contemporaries.

His second Venetian commission, from 1482, further reinforces these remarkable characteristics: this was the restoration and completion of the campanile for the cathedral of San Pietro in Castello.[5] The existing tower itself had been completed only recently (1463–74), but had apparently been badly damaged by lightning. His patron here was the patriarch, Maffeo Girardi, whom Codussi already knew from San Michele, and the fundamental decision to clad the tower entirely in Istrian stone was a further landmark in Venetian architecture. It was to be the first and only bell-tower in the city to be finished entirely in this manner (figs 130, 131, 133); even the great campanile of San Marco itself comprised a plain brick shaft, with stone detailing confined to the bell-chamber and the capping. As noteworthy as this decision, though, was the vocabulary that Mauro used: simple, powerful and 'Roman' in its boldness, it was a statement that transformed the traditional campanile into a new monumental element in the city's fabric.

Shortly after the work to the bell-tower was begun, Codussi was chosen to succeed the deceased Antonio Gambello as *proto* for the completion of the monastic church of San Zaccaria; he had clearly established himself in the city by now as a master of outstanding creative skill and originality. The design and construction of San Zaccaria was a long, complex matter, though, and it was to be more than thirty years between Gambello's original appointment and the final completion of the last stages by Codussi in the later 1480s.

Generous funding, of course, also had to be made available, but San Michele was patronised by a number of remarkably wealthy and enlightened Venetian patrician dynasties.[4]

The interior of the church offers a rather different mixture of traditional elements and radical new approaches (fig. 132). The plan is basilical, with the nave flanked by two narrow side aisles, and with an apsidal east end, very much in the monastic tradition, although the detailing of the colonnades is highly inventive; Mauro reinterpreted the classical orders here in a remarkably creative manner. His characteristic approach to the design of church interiors is also already manifest, and was to be refined further in the later, more centrally planned churches of Santa Maria Formosa and San Giovanni Grisostomo: the overriding qualities in all cases are clarity of form, precision of detailing and the restrained, disciplined use of ornamentation. The refinement and sensitivity of Codussi's work at San

131 San Pietro in Castello: detail from Jacopo de' Barbari's woodcut of 1500 showing the earlier, Gothic church and Codussi's new campanile

facing page 132 San Michele: interior of the nave

133   San Pietro in Castello: the campanile

Codussi and His Clients: Patterns of Patronage

In a number of senses, Mauro Codussi has a claim to being identified as the first true architect of the Venetian Renaissance. For example, he was not primarily a sculptor-mason like the older Bartolomeo Bon; instead, his career developed from that of a skilled master stonemason to become, in more than one sense, his own master. While Pietro Lombardo's greatest abilities were in the field of pure sculpture and of sculpted and decorated architectonic forms, Codussi's were the gift of understanding, organising and manipulating three-dimensional spaces, of creating spatial hierarchies. Mauro also developed the discipline to differentiate logically between the essential elements of structure, the skeleton of vaults, ribs and columns, and the non-structural planar surfaces or other, purely decorative elements. He developed a logically applied vocabulary of structural and non-structural elements that was unique in Venice at this time, and had far more in common with the rational, mathematical philosophies of Alberti and Brunelleschi than with the work of any of his Venetian contemporaries. Codussi's decorative finishes are rarely applied to planar surfaces; the façade of the Scuola di San Marco is perhaps the only exception, but had already been begun by another – Pietro Lombardo. In almost all cases, his decorative elements fuse with or grow from the structural form itself: the upper façade of San Zaccaria, for example, or (even more clearly) the internal spatial hierarchies of Santa Maria Formosa. His vocabulary, frequently inventive or even wilful (see the capitals at San Michele), is nevertheless clear and incisive.

During his working lifetime, Codussi was given titles almost as varied as were possible in the vocabulary of his day: 'taiapiera'; 'maestro' (unspecified); 'proto' (at San Zaccaria and the Scuola Grande di San Marco); 'lapicidia et murario' (at San Pietro in Castello); a simple 'murario' at Santa Maria Formosa, where he was clearly nothing of the kind; 'magistri Mori lapicide' (again at Santa Maria Formosa); and finally, after his death in 1504, as an 'architect'.

It could be argued, of course, that these various titles simply reflected a flexibility of terminology and vocabulary that was typical of the age, that such titles were bandied about more or less indiscriminately, and that we should thus read little significance into them. This would be a serious error. There was nothing 'flexible', for example, about the title of *proto*, nor was there in the use of the names of the three principal construction crafts; all three related to legally registered guilds, together with compulsory membership of one or other of them, and with adherence to their statutes and codes of conduct. The above terms were used by his patrons, we must not forget, not by Codussi himself, and they reflected their own perceptions of his role in these various projects. He was called a *murer*, for example, at Santa Maria Formosa, probably because he was to be responsible for the complete reconstruction of the church, which naturally involved a great deal of wall-building and general construction. And where (as here) he was given specific authority over other crafts, the contracts almost always identify this responsibility.

There are three fundamental levels on which we can evaluate Codussi's contribution to the Venetian Renaissance. The first is his creative skill and stylistic vocabulary, particularly in the manipulation of internal spaces (in his churches) and in the development of the façades of Venetian palaces. This stylistic development has been analysed admirably by others, first by Angelini, and then by Puppi, Olivato Puppi and John McAndrew; there is thus little point in adding further to these perceptive analyses. The second level is his role in the construction process and the organisation of the building site, much of which is discussed later. The third, though, first discussed by Puppi and Olivato Puppi, is the extremely significant matter of Codussi's relationship with his patrons and the nature of those patrons themselves.

Mauro Codussi numbered among his patrons, over the period from the start of San Michele in 1469 to his death in 1504, many of the most prominent and influential clients in the city. Most of his commissions were obtained by personal contacts, through a network of influential individuals, many of whom knew each other very well. Although he did undertake work for institutions, notably the two Scuole Grandi, nevertheless his two most prominent fields of activity – where his own skills developed in two quite different directions – were private palaces and churches. In both typologies the personal contact remained of considerable importance. Private palaces naturally almost always had a single, individual client, while churches, on the other hand, generally selected their architects by the institution of a commissioning board or *banca*, again small in numbers, and where personal contacts were easy to establish and cultivate.

Codussi's most important project in terms of these networks of patronage was his first work in Venice: San Michele. The abbot in the later 1460s was Maffeo Gerardo or Girardi, who was later to achieve the highest ecclesiastical office in the Republic, the patriarchate, and who provides us with the first of these links of patronage. Girardi was a highly educated man of great culture and knowledge, as were almost all the abbots of this important house. He continued the patronage of building works begun by his predecessor, Paolo Venier (who had built the 'chiostro piccolo'), by ordering the construction of the church's fine new campanile in 1456. Twelve years later, just as work was about to begin on the new church, he was elected (at the insistence of the Senate) to the patriarchate, based at San Pietro in Castello, although he was by no means lost to our network.[6]

Girardi was replaced as abbot at San Michele at the end of 1468 by Pietro Donà, again a man of formidable intellect, and who was equally determined to continue building the new church. Financial difficulties in getting the project under way, however, together with the opposition of some of the monks, impeded progress, as did Donà's many visits to Ravenna, where the Camaldolesi had recovered their monastery at Classe, and with which Donà was also closely involved.

As a result of these commitments at Ravenna, Donà left a locum in Venice, Pietro Delfin. Delfin had been born in 1438, and was another humanist and intellectual, very much in the same mould as Donà; he became the chief driving force behind the rebuilding works. He also maintained a close correspondence with Donà in Classe, in which the skills of Codussi were highly praised. With Delfin's unflagging enthusiasm, the new church was sufficiently far advanced by the autumn of 1477 to be inaugurated, a ceremony at which Donà himself was also present.[7]

Pietro di Vettor Delfin was an outstanding figure of his era. The inscription on his memorial tablet on the right side of the church at San Michele (erected in 1525) describes him as 'viro sanctimonia, eloquestia, Ac omni humanitate praedicto, cum Religionem per v & xl annos integerrine rexisset' ('noble, pious, eloquent, with all of his expected humanity and compassion, who ruled and protected this religious house for forty-five years'). He was indeed a man of many skills: humanist, scholar, chronicler, religious philosopher. Sansovino, in his *Venetia*, notes the titles and subject matter of some of his more important works; they included 'un volume di sentenze di santi Padri. Lib. 4 d'Epistolle. Diverse Orationi. Un Dialogo contra fra Hieronimo Savonarola. Diverse argomenti sopra l'Orazione di Cicerone. Et una Cronica delle cose Venete, molto particolare & distinta, la quale si legge a penna' ('a volume of the sayings of the Holy Fathers; four books of Epistles; various orations; a dialogue with Fra Geronimo Savonarola; various debates on the orations of Cicero; and a history of Venetian events, very notable and important, which can be read in manuscript'). A catholic output indeed.[8]

Marin Sanudo, the diarist, was also a close friend of Delfin; the list in his own *Cronachetta* of 1530, summarising those noble houses of the Republic that were by that time extinct, was, he says, obtained from Delfin's own researches, adding that Delfin's chronicle, the '*Cronaca delle cose venete*' (or *Annalum venetorum*) was then in the hands of Marc-Antonio Loredan.[9]

In 1479, with the church well on the way to completion, Pietro Donà died, and Delfin was unanimously elected as his successor. Less than two years later again, however, on 10 December 1480, Delfin himself was elected general of the order, and moved to Camaldoli, in the Apennines east of Florence, where the mother house was sited. He remained there, although he did make occasional visits back to Venice, certainly in 1481. His monument, again in the church at San Michele, duly records his ultimate accolade as 'Priori Sacrae Eremi Camalduli, Ac eiusdem Ordinis Generali . . .'. For Codussi, therefore, both Donà and Delfin were highly influential humanist patrons, and there can be little doubt that his own reputation grew steadily while the church was under construction.

During the latter stages of construction a further important group of noble patrons became closely involved with the completion of the project. The first was Marco Bertuccio Zorzi, who in 1475 donated 100 ducats towards the establishment of a chapel on the right side of the chancel, and this was completed within two years.[10] Zorzi was to turn to Codussi again a few years later, in his capacity as a private property owner, when he asked him to remodel his own substantial palace at San Severo around 1480. The next important patrons at San Michele were Tommaso and Bernardo Loredan, who gave 180 ducats in 1481 towards the church's completion;[11] another branch of the same clan was to be the most important benefactor of all in the furtherance of Mauro's career.

In the following year, 1482, Girolamo Donà gave 100 ducats to pay for the paving of the chancel,[12] and in 1500 Pietro di Lorenzo Donà, a relative of the former abbot (who had died in 1479), left a handsome legacy of 1,500 ducats, with which to endow the chapel to the left of the chancel.[13] The Cappella della Croce (in the left aisle) was patronised by Pietro Priuli, Procurator of San Marco, and finally, there was Andrea di Niccolò Loredan, a very wealthy patrician, who effectively became the principal patron of the whole project. Loredan also paid for the construction of the dome, all clad with lead, which stood over the crossing, as well as the chancel. Andrea di Niccolò was to make two further significant appearances in Codussi's later career, before his untimely death in 1513 at Creazzo, during the crisis of the League of Cambrai.[14] This group of noble Venetian clans – Donà, Loredan, Zorzi, Delfin – collectively formed perhaps the most influential gathering of patrons in the Republic; with men of this wealth and intellectual stature behind him, Codussi's career could hardly fail to flourish.

Further commissions were indeed to flow towards Mauro from this august gathering of the patrons of San Michele. At about the same time that Codussi was approached by Zorzi to redesign his palazzo, in 1482 the patriarch, Maffeo Girardi, now based at San Pietro, but still closely involved with the completion of San Michele, decided to complete the cladding of the campanile of the cathedral. As we saw, the commission was awarded to Codussi.[15]

Girardi's own career was a notable one, and did not terminate at the patriarchate; his monument, at San Pietro, also recorded his election to Rome as a cardinal. Sanudo relates that he died in 1492, at a very great age, on a journey from Rome back to Venice. Girardi also patronised building works elsewhere: in 1488, a few years before his death, he laid the foundation stone for the rebuilding of the ancient parish church of Santa Margherita; he also founded the Augustinian nunnery of Santi Rocco e Margherita, near the Campo Santo Stefano, in the same year.

In the year after he began the campanile of San Pietro, Codussi was appointed *proto* at San Zaccaria, to replace the deceased Gambello. By now his reputation was well established, but extremely significant are the names of the two men who witnessed and sponsored his employment at the nunnery: Pietro di Lorenzo Donà and Lorenzo di Antonio Loredan, both of whom had been closely involved with San Michele.[16]

We now trace Codussi's career a further eight years forward; on 15 November 1491 he was commissioned to design the important new parish church of Santa Maria Formosa (fig. 134). The result was to be his most complex, refined church interior, a superb spatial composition representing a master at the peak of his abilities. On this occasion three men were appointed to form a *banca* to supervise fund-raising and to monitor progress on the works; they were Paolo Trevisan, honoured with the title of *cavaliere*, Antonio Grimani, and (once again) Pietro di Lorenzo Donà.[17] The last of these three men therefore emerges as Codussi's most important patron to date, first at San Michele, then at San Zaccaria, and finally here at Santa Maria Formosa. The other two names, though, are also significant. Antonio Grimani had already had an exceptionally long, chequered, indeed extraordinary career. He was an extremely wealthy merchant, who had built up an

awesome reputation for shrewd international commerce; he was born (according to the sometimes unreliable Sanudo) in 1434, and most of the first half of his career had been spent in accumulating wealth through trade. In November 1491 he had been appointed to the *banca* for the rebuilding of Santa Maria Formosa, and three years later, in 1494, he was elected Procurator of San Marco *de citra*, an indication, perhaps, of his rather belated political ambitions. Five years later again, he was a surprising choice as Captain General of the Sea, despite his comprehensive lack of maritime experience. He was in command of the Venetian fleet in the confused and confusing debacles against the Turks later identified as the Battle of Zonchio, during which muddled commands had led to significant Venetian losses. Stripped of his command (and the Procuracy), Grimani was exiled to the obscure Dalmatian island of Cherso; after a few months of banishment, he fled to Rome, where his son was a cardinal, and thence eventually returned to Venice. He was rehabilitated with

134   Santa Maria Formosa: general view of the interior, completed *circa* 1504

extraordinary rapidity and was re-elected as a Procurator (*de supra* this time) in December 1510. His rehabilitation reached its apotheosis barely six months later again, when on 7 July 1521 he was elected to the throne of San Marco itself, to become the oldest doge in Venetian history at the age of 87. Needless to say, his reign was brief (and ineffectual), and he died on 7 May 1523, to be buried in the now lost church of San Antonio di Castello.[18] Codussi's patrons were certainly men of character and distinction.

Paolo Trevisan, the last of the three members of the Santa Maria Formosa *banca*, was probably the same Trevisan who was a member of the Senate when the new clock tower in the Piazza was debated; his name is one of the links between the tower and Codussi, its probable architect.

Mauro Codussi is associated with three remarkable palaces in Venice, the first of which, the Zorzi, was noted above (fig. 135). The second was designed either for Marco Lando or for his father Pietro, who had married into the Corner clan in 1471. We have no direct personal links between the Lando and Mauro's earlier group of patrons from San Michele, and there is no contemporary documentary evidence to link Mauro conclusively with the *palazzo*, although the attribution is almost universally accepted.[19] We are on much firmer ground with the third, the magnificent Palazzo Loredan (later Vendramin Calergi) on the Grand Canal at San Marcuola. The palace was commissioned by Andrea di Niccolò Loredan, who had been one of Mauro's earliest patrons at San Michele in the 1470s. The new palace was begun *circa* 1502, although it was not completed until 1509, three or four years after Codussi's death. The façade, today always attributed to Mauro, represents his later work at its most magnificent, monumental and self-confident. It was the most imposing palace in the entire city when it was completed, and still remains one of the very finest today (fig. 136).[20]

Like Grimani, Loredan also had an illustrious, not to say colourful, career after his early patronage at San Michele. Head of the Consiglio dei Dieci, he then became Luogotenente (regional governor) of the Friuli in 1507. His refusal to accept the post of Provveditore Generale for the region resulted in six months imprisonment, although his military abilities were considered too valuable to be wasted, and in 1513 he was given the vital post of Provveditore Generale at Vicenza during the Cambrai crisis. It was this posting that led to his death; immediately after the battle with the Spaniards at Schio (which led to a Venetian retreat), Loredan was captured and was assassinated on 7 October 1513.[21] He left no sons, but

some interest in the *palazzo* passed to his cousin Alvise and his son Andrea. When Loredan's body was returned to Venice, it was taken, appropriately, to San Michele, where he was commemorated in the chapel that he had funded, and which Codussi had built. His memorial has a rather verbose inscription, which reads in part, 'ANDRE. LAU. NICOL. F. CUIUS ANIMI VIRTUTES . . . AETERNITATIS MEMOR ANNUA PECUNIA MONACHIS PIE LEGATA, MAGNIFICAQ. TESTUDINE HUIC TEMPLO ADDIT . . .' ('Andrea, son of Nicolò Loredan, whose valorous soul . . . bequeathed in his eternal memory annual funds to the pious monks [and] added the magnificent cupola to this temple . . .').

What conclusions can we draw from these brief biographical notes on some of Codussi's powerful and colourful patrons? One is that they were all men with individual power of patronage and direct influence, rather than being simply members of the oligarchy that ruled the Republic. They had the wealth, intellect and ambition to influence directly the built form of their own capital city, and they chose the most creative master in Venice to help them to achieve those aims. It was Mauro's power of creativity, of spatial inventiveness, and also of the practical organisation of the site, that made him the preferred master of his generation to these wealthy patrons; it was his ability to translate individual wishes into built three-dimensional form, on a truly monumental scale if necessary – as at Palazzo Loredan – that made Codussi the pre-eminent architect of the early Venetian Renaissance, the first man who fused the skills of the traditional master mason, the organisational abilities of the *proto* and the creative genius of the modern architect.

A Note on Pietro Lombardo and his Patrons: A Multi-Facetted Master

It is instructive to conduct a similar exercise, albeit perhaps rather superficially, on the patrons of Codussi's great contemporary, Pietro Lombardo. Pietro's career had some important differences of emphasis from that of Mauro, and these differences, too, are reflected in somewhat different patterns of patronage. First, and most obviously, his initial reputation was established as a sculptor rather than an architect, and in the commissioning of works of sculpture, individual patronage is usually paramount. Nonetheless, we do find a broader variety both in the pattern of patronage of Pietro Lombardo and in the range and character of his patrons themselves.

135   Palazzo Zorzi: façade detail, by Mauro Codussi, begun *circa* 1480 for Marco Bertuccio Zorzi

136 Palazzo Loredan (later Vendramin Calergi): detail of the façade, begun by Mauro Codussi for Andrea Loredan in 1502, and completed by *circa* 1508

Lombardo's role in the early Venetian Renaissance is in some respects more difficult for us to evaluate today than is that of Codussi. There is – or appears to be – a clarity in Codussi's intellectual development that seems to make his work more 'in tune' with the structural clarity and honesty of the present-day heirs of the Modern Movement. Lombardo was perhaps a more complex master: certainly his œuvre was broader, and he was an extraordinarily skilled master in three distinct – albeit somewhat overlapping – fields: pure figure sculpture; applied or architectonic decoration; and in the creation of major works of architecture.

His three famous ducal monuments, those of Pasquale Malipiero, Pietro Mocenigo and Niccolò Marcello, were – despite their very public nature – all direct family commissions, not state-sponsored works.[22] Malipiero was, as we have seen, an enlightened Renaissance head of state, an intellectual and a 'man of moderation'. His funeral monument represents a characteristic Venetian compromise incorporating the traditional Gothic canopy together with an outer 'Florentine' frame, with pilasters, architrave and a semicircular head, the overall design of which is closely related to Pietro's portal at San Giobbe.

Pietro's first important architectural work was, in fact, at San Giobbe, where his patron was also a man of formidable intellect, Cristoforo Moro, who was to be Malipiero's immediate successor as doge: both men and both works had a good deal in common. Moro himself was a senator when he first met Bernardino of Siena, the Franciscan preacher who arrived in Venice in 1443, and settled at San Giobbe. The two men became close friends; Bernardino died at L'Aquila in 1444; only six years later, he was canonised by Pope Nicholas v. As a result of this close association with both Bernardino and San Giobbe, Moro later funded the construction of the chancel of the church to a design by Pietro Lombardo. Moro was also sometime ambassador to Rome; in 1462 he was elected doge and invested further funds in the church. When he died in 1471, he left the considerable sum of 10,000 ducats for the completion of San Giobbe, and he was buried in the chancel. Pietro's work at the chancel was preceded by the new portal (circa 1471), but the chancel itself, with its cupola, was probably not completed until 1493.[23]

The church portal is a highly refined work, strongly Florentine in inspiration, and with much in common with the outer framing of the Malipiero monument. Once this work was complete, it must have been fairly clear to Moro that his continuing to employ Pietro on larger, more purely architectural elements of the church

was likely to result in more innovation, on an accordingly larger scale. Although there is no documentary evidence, it seems highly likely that Pietro did visit Florence; the San Giobbe portal also has strong links to Desiderio da Settignano's Marsuppini monument in Santa Croce, and further Florentine links were to follow in the church cupola.

Pietro's chancel arch was probably the next element to be carved. It is an imposing, if rather heavy Renaissance work, with richly decorated relief work to the pilasters and richly moulded profiles to the arch itself. The chancel has a square plan, surmounted by the cupola on pendentives. The cupola itself is strongly influenced by Brunelleschi; there is a remarkable clarity and purity to the design, which makes it appear much more purely Florentine than the richness that we associate with Pietro's later work at the Miracoli and the Scuola di San Marco. Indeed, it exhibits the logic and structural clarity that are today more often associated with Codussi. Despite some significant difficulties in establishing its precise dating, the cupola probably dates from the early 1470s, and was perhaps the first example of this form seen in Venice. (Codussi's San Michele was roughly contemporary but we cannot tell which was built first.) The San Giobbe cupola is Florentine even to the detail of the roundels in the pendentives, probably carved by Pietro himself. The cupola itself is a precise hemisphere, and this form became very influential in Venice: Lombardo himself used it again at the Miracoli, and Codussi did elsewhere, at Santa Maria Formosa, for example. McAndrew has suggested that the aesthetic inspiration for the cupola may have come from the intellectual (and well-travelled) Moro rather than from Pietro himself.[24]

Pietro's architectural *capolavoro* is the church of Santa Maria dei Miracoli. The patrons of the church's construction were a wealthy citizen family, the Amadi, originally from Lucca in Tuscany, and whose family seat stood only metres away from the church site. It was on the Amadi family's land that the famous image of the *Virgin* was found, an image that, it was claimed, worked numerous miracles. The Amadi's legal ownership of this image was confirmed by the Collegio in 1480, and this definition led to the family sponsoring the construction of the Miracoli church to house the image.[25] The two men principally responsible for the work were Francesco and Amato Amadi, both sons of Angelo; this initial patronage was continued by Francesco's son Alvise, and his nephew, another Angelo. Francesco himself was a noted poet and man of letters, with an extensive library. The Amadi, although 'mere' citizens, also played an important role in the government of the

Republic in this period; Francesco's other son Agostino was secretary to the Consiglio dei Dieci, while Agostino's son Pietro became secretary to the Senate. Permission to construct the church was obtained by Alvise and Angelo from the patriarch, Maffeo Girardi, who, as we have seen, was also one of Mauro Codussi's early patrons. Among the other major benefactors of the Miracoli church were Francesco di Alvise Diedo, Francesco Zeno, Marc'Antonio Soranzo and Marco di Niccolò Soranzo; Marco's father Niccolò was one of the Procurators of San Marco. Among these patrons perhaps the most notable was Francesco Diedo (1433–1484), an important humanist scholar, who wrote a highly regarded life of St Roch (San Rocco). He was also appointed to a number of important embassies, to Austria, Savoy, Milan and Rome.[26]

The offerings made towards the construction were many and generous; the foundation stone was laid on 8 December 1480 by Patriarch Girardi, and it was largely complete within six years. In 1487 the adjacent nunnery was also complete, and twelve Franciscan nuns ('poor Clares' from Santa Chiara at Murano) were installed to administer the church; the two buildings were linked by a high-level bridge (later lost). On 30 December 1489 the venerated painting of the Virgin was put in place over the high altar.[27]

The Miracoli is Pietro's tour de force: not only a masterpiece of ingenious planning on a highly restricted site, it is also a triumph of the integration of architecture and refined sculpted decoration. Concina has suggested that the overall design of the church may have been based on the form of the paleo-Christian sarcophagus, examples of which could be seen at Ravenna and elsewhere. There is no doubt that, at the Miracoli, Pietro was patronised by an influential group of humanists, very similar to the group that patronised Codussi at San Michele. There is no doubt, either, that on its completion the church attracted high praise from many, Venetian and visitors alike. Marin Sanudo, in his description of the city in 1493, described it as 'una bellissima chiesa, torniata di marmi, lavorata all'anticha'.[28]

Two important mid-career works were the modernisation of the Scuola Grande di San Giovanni Evangelista, including the entrance screen in the *campo*, and the works at the Scuola Grande di San Marco, described in detail in chapter Nine. As noted elsewhere, working for the Scuole Grandi was often a perilous matter for many masons and architects in this era: there was the constant rotation of office-holders and lack of continuity of administrative policy; there were frequently major reappraisals of artistic direction; and there were often financial crises to impede progress. With

such erratic patterns of patronage, it seems likely that personal connections and influence had only a limited value, since although a master might find an immediate rapport with one Guardian Grande, the latter would be replaced, often within months, by another who might have quite different priorities and networks of influence. Pietro's work at the Scuola Grande di San Giovanni Evangelista took place in the late 1470s and was complete by 1481; a full thirty years later, in 1514, Pietro was elected *gastaldo* of the Scuola, but he was now an old man, and died shortly afterwards.[29] It seems unlikely, therefore, that, with such an extraordinary time lapse, there was any direct patronal connection between the two events. And in the case of the Scuola Grande di San Marco (as we will see later) Pietro's employment there terminated in November 1490, extremely abruptly, in less than happy circumstances.[30]

The two works that characterise Lombardo's architectural œuvre most clearly are probably the Miracoli church and his work at the Scuola Grande di San Giovanni Evangelista. Superficially very different in their form, they are united in that they both establish a strong sense of place where it did not exist before. They do this by two entirely different means: in the case of the Miracoli church, the building itself creates the space by its dominant presence and its precise, compact form. It creates around it a series of minor local 'settings': the tiny *campo* at the front, the view of the flank wall onto the canal from the adjacent bridge; the composition from the bridge and even smaller *campiello* at the rear; and the view from the *campo* of Santa Maria Nova (broader now that the church itself is demolished), as well as the slightly further view from the Ponte del Piovan.

The Miracoli is perceived as an object in space, completely freestanding, which is an almost unique experience among the hundred or so churches in Venice. The Scuola Grande di San Giovanni Evangelista creates its effect by being precisely the opposite: the creation of an identity by means of the ordering of a space between two buildings, and the imposition of a series of constructs to define the extent and character of that space. Formerly a broad but fairly anonymous *campiello* between the flank wall of the church of San Giovanni and the long, mostly *gotico fiorito* façade of the Scuola, the space was, in fact, a fairly busy public right of way, as it remains today. It could not therefore be brought into the legal ownership or control of either the Scuola or the adjacent parish church. Pietro first defined and compartmentalised this space, dividing it into two zones, one significantly larger (longer) than the other. They were separated by the 'invention' of the screen wall, which serves two or three functions simultaneously. It defines the two spaces; it provides a grand, richly detailed triumphal arch announcing the Scuola's presence, complete with inscription and symbols; and it maintains the public right of way by the generous portal in the centre. The smaller entrance space thereby created and defined was given architectonic order by means of a discipline of pilasters, cornices and architraves. Each flank wall, on either side of the central screen, is divided into three equal bays by means of pilasters, bases and capitals, with horizontal definition formed by string courses and cornices. The larger *campiello* beyond the screen was barely affected, but the sense of arrival and 'ownership' by the Scuola of the courtyard in front of the screen – the parvis – was complete. And the larger *campiello* was also given definition by the screen at one end, while being enclosed at the other end by the entrance to the Scuola and the continuation of the pedestrian route via the *sottoportego* and Corte Vitalba beyond it. Proceeding down the fairly nondescript Calle del Magazen today, it is gratifying to observe the evident signs of amazement when a tourist suddenly comes upon Pietro's magnificent stage-set screen: it still has precisely the visual effect that was originally intended. The same sense of richness, of theatre, of the creation of sumptuous 'events' in the city's fabric is equally apparent in the façade of the Scuola Grande di San Marco, discussed in detail in a later chapter. Although the element of surprise is perhaps not quite the same, there is no doubt today of the lasting impact of this opulent work, comprehensively cleaned and restored in the years 2003–5.

One of Pietro's last important works was the decoration of the Badoer-Giustinian chapel at San Francesco della Vigna. Funding for the chapel was left in the will of Girolamo di Giacomo Badoer, which was written in 1494; in this will, he initially left funds for a marble altar in the chapel. A year or so later, on 1 July 1495, a codicil was added, clarifying his desires in further detail. The complex relief decoration took several years to complete, and the final assembly incorporates the work not only of Pietro, but of his sons Tullio and Antonio as well. It was completed in 1509; two years later Pietro retired from his post of *proto* at the Palazzo Ducale, so it seems likely that his health was perhaps already beginning to deteriorate.[31]

Even in the case of the Badoer chapel, we can again identify Pietro's creation of a specific sense of place, surrounded, in this case, by a series of superbly executed relief panels. A previously fairly anonymous side chapel is thereby transformed into a highly particular enclosure, now 'owned' (both legally and spatially) by a specific Venetian family.

In summary, therefore, Pietro's professional career was thus significantly more varied in character than that of Codussi; since a large part of his œuvre consists of works of pure sculpture, with individual patrons, the pattern of patronage is rather more diffuse, with less evidence of the tightly interwoven matrix of personal links that characterised that of Codussi. We may conclude that Pietro's most significant patrons were probably Pasquale Malipiero and Cristoforo Moro: both were important intellectual figures, and both made influential marks on the city in terms of their patronage of Pietro at a comparatively early stage in his career. Moro, in particular, clearly wished to make an intellectual statement by his employment of Lombardo, and although he did not live to see the work at San Giobbe complete, Pietro's Malipiero monument and the San Giobbe portal must have given him a clear idea of the style that his heirs might have expected to see.

Chapter Eight

SAN ZACCARIA

THE CHURCH OF SAN ZACCARIA is one of the most important buildings of early Renaissance Venice. It is remarkable in several respects: first, the plan of the church is highly unusual, and is unique in the city; second, the church is exceptionally richly built, with extensive use of stone and marble; third, the long period of its construction spans the era of transition from the late Venetian Gothic to the Renaissance; and finally, in the manner of its construction we can examine and understand some of the significant developments in the role of the architect in this era. Begun by Antonio Gambello in 1458, the church was only finally completed by Mauro Codussi more than thirty years later.

History

San Zaccaria was a monastic house of considerable antiquity. According to legend, the church was established by St Magnus, Bishop of Oderzo, in the seventh century, but it was rebuilt in 811 during the reign of Doge Angelo Partecipazio. It was completed in 829, the last year of the reign of his son and successor, Giustiniano. These were momentous years for the emergent Republic; in 810 the seat of government of the lagunar confederation had been transferred from Malamocco to Rivo Alto, where it was to remain for the next thousand years. And in the year that San Zaccaria was completed, the body of St Mark himself was brought to the lagoon's new capital, where the first chapel in his honour was then begun.

The reconstruction of San Zaccaria by the Partecipazio doges incorporated a newly established Benedictine nunnery, to which was donated, by Leo v, the Eastern emperor, the body of Zacharias, father of John the Baptist. Zacharias was highly venerated, and the church's future as a place of pilgrimage and a centre of offerings and patronage was assured. Legend also relates that the abbess of the new foundation, Agostina Morosini, presented the doge, Pietro Tradonico (r. 836–64), with the very first ducal cap or *corno* of gold, encrusted with jewels. The *corno* became a symbol of the dogeship for the whole life of the Serenissima, and an essential element in the coronation rite. The earliest stages in the history of San Zaccaria, therefore, were closely identified with the establishment of the Republic itself, and the nunnery continued to be patronised by both doges and emperors; eight of the Republic's earliest doges chose to be buried here.[1]

The first small, basilical church was considerably enlarged in the tenth century. From this period dates the present crypt, one of the oldest surviving structures in the city, and similar to that of San Marco, with a central nave flanked by two colonnades, side aisles and a low, vaulted ceiling. The church was badly damaged by fire in 1105 and a further programme of restoration took place in the years 1172–4, in the reign of the indefatigable Sebastiano Ziani. This resulted in an essentially new church, still basically basilical, but with its plan modified to form a Latin cross, and with the stilted arches typical of the period. Across the façade was a

137   San Zaccaria: the portal of the main façade, perhaps by Zuan (Giovanni) Buora

colonnade in which the tombs and monuments of the early doges were located. According to Paoletti, the church had three aisles 'divided by two parallel rows of columns . . . the capitals of which . . . until 1595 could still be seen in place' in the old church. They apparently took the form of eagles, and were to inspire the unusual capitals carved by Giovanni (Zuan) Buora for the new church in the 1480s. Francesco Sansovino, writing in 1580, explained that 'in gratitude to the said Leo [Leo v, Eastern emperor], the doge had capitals for the columns carved in the form of the Imperial eagle, which can still be seen in the old church'.[2] The nunnery was already richly endowed by Ziani's time, and became the most highly favoured in the city for the daughters of the nobility; it also remained under the direct patronage of the doge, who visited in procession every Easter Sunday. One of the most ancient ceremonies of the city, this *andata* took place every year until the fall of the Republic in 1797.

By the early fifteenth century, San Zaccaria had assumed a late Gothic appearance, with a series of modernisations that resulted in the loss of most of the earlier Byzantine structure. The eastern end was rebuilt in 1440, and survives today as the chapel of San Tarasio, with its central polygonal chancel and two smaller side apses.[3] In 1442 frescos were painted on the vaults of the chancel by Andrea del Castagno and Francesco da Faenza; these paintings have also survived, and depict God the Father, Saints and Apostles. Thirteen years later, in 1455, a contract was drafted with two master wood-carvers (*intaiadori*), Marco and Francesco Cozzi, to carve choirstalls for the church. Marco was the finest wood-carver of the day, and his work can also be seen at the Scuola della Carità, where he carved the rich, coffered ceiling of the *sala capitolare* around 1484, and again at the Frari, where he completed the magnificent choirstalls in 1468. The stalls for San Zaccaria were to be modelled on those at Sant'Elena and Santi Giovanni e Paolo, and – no doubt as a result of commitments elsewhere – they took the workshop no less than nine years to complete; an inscription records that they were put in place in 1464.

In the same period, though, the structural stability of the church gave rise to concern in the nunnery.[4] The abbess brought this concern to the attention of both the incumbent doge, Francesco Foscari, and to the pope, Callixtus III; her plea for aid was successful, since not only were a number of works undertaken to the existing church, but it was also decided to embark on the unusual course of constructing a completely new, larger church not in place of the old, but immediately alongside it, and structurally contiguous with it.

The New Project

The new church was to stand just to the north, and was to incorporate parts of the newly strengthened existing fabric, such that the north aisle of the old church was to become the south aisle of the new one. Work on this complex project, including the imposing new church itself, was to continue for much of the remainder of the century, and the completed work forms a remarkable example of the stylistic transition from Gothic to Renaissance integrated into a single structure. The detailed design was also to incorporate some highly inventive and original work, some from the hands of Gambello and his masons, some from those of Codussi.

The basic plan of the church is unusual in several respects (fig. 138). The length of the site, between the *campo* and the monastic buildings at the rear, is com-

138 San Zaccaria: plan of the new church, with the converted old church to the south (from Cicognara, Diedo and Selva)

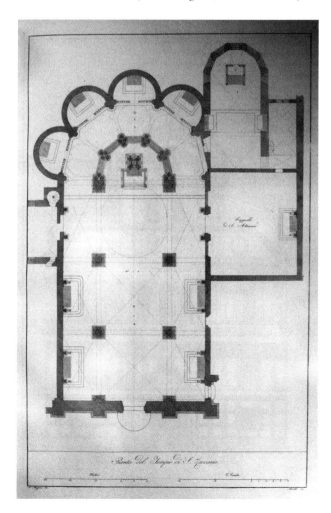

paratively short, and so the nave, while very high and spacious, is only three bays long (figs 139, 140). These three bays, though, are very generous, such that the nave space is virtually contiguous with those of the side aisles. The most unusual feature is the polygonal chancel and, behind it, the ambulatory with its four radiating chapels. The polygonal chancel focuses all attention on the high altar, with the venerated remains of the patron below it. The ambulatory is unique in Venice: but the form is widespread in France, since it enabled pilgrims to circulate around the patronal shrine below the altar, and it was also used for processions by the monks and nuns of the order. The plan of the vast, imposing mother church at Cluny also had a similar plan (on a much larger scale), which itself derived from the famous schematic plan of St Gall, dating from 811–27. There was a further impressive example of such a form much closer at hand, at the Santo in Padua, where the remains of the highly venerated St Anthony were the object of huge numbers of pilgrims every year. This last was probably the immediate inspiration for the use of this plan-form here.[5]

The church has survived virtually unchanged since its completion by Codussi around 1490. Much of our information regarding its construction is kept in a large, highly detailed account-book, recording expenditure from 1458 to 1466 and from 1472 to 1489. With the exception of this six-year lacuna, the accounts were carefully and accurately maintained, the entire operation – on paper, at least – seemingly run in an efficient and professional manner.[6]

Antonio Gambello was appointed *protomaestro* of the project in May 1458. The use of the title has great significance since, as far as we know, the appointment of a *proto* at San Zaccaria was the first time that the title was used on projects other than those instigated by the Republic: the venerable and ancient nunnery of San Zaccaria was to be reconstructed in style, and Gambello was to design and build it for them. He was appointed on the basis of an annual salary of 100 ducats, beginning on 15 May 1458. As we have seen, this was a generous allowance, and Gambello was also given the use of a house on the *campo* adjacent to the site, a benefit that did not have a large monetary value (rents were low in this period), but which was extremely convenient, and ensured not only that Gambello could virtually supervise progress from his bedroom window, but that he was always on hand when summoned by his patrons to discuss costs and progress. Although not formally notarised, the contract was apparently renewed regularly until February 1466, when a new notarised agreement was drafted.[7]

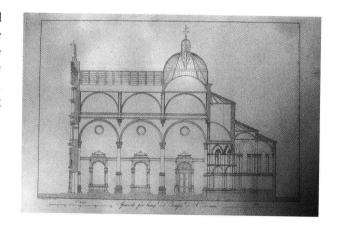

139 San Zaccaria: long section of the new church, showing the short but very tall three-bay nave, and the eastern apse chapels (from Cicognara, Diedo and Selva)

Gambello's role therefore combined that of the designer of the new church with that of the superintending master of its construction, what today we call the contract manager. His terms of employment were closely modelled on those of the government's own *proti*, and his design responsibility is confirmed very early in the records, since in the same spring of 1458 Gambello was paid for the construction of a model of the proposed church. It was made of timber, and was completed by 1 May, just before his contract of employment was signed.[8] He was responsible for all of the

140 San Zaccaria: detail from Jacopo de' Barbari's woodcut of 1500, with the *campo* paved with brick and stone, and the monastic buildings to the south of the church

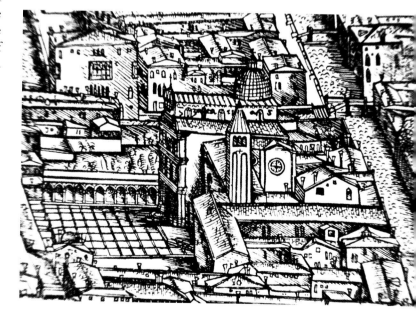

general coordination on site, for the ordering and payment for materials, and for integrating all the specialist crafts under his overall control.

The building accounts were supervised by the abbess, Marina Donato (or Donà), and the prioress, Agnesina Giustinian. The abbess also appointed two treasurers or *massari*, Maria Barbarigo and Elena Malipiero, to keep the books on a daily basis; overseeing the works, too, was Zane Benedetto, the *gastaldo general* or chief warden of the nunnery. There was also a full project board or *banca* which could be convened to discuss major aspects of the design or of policy. We also have several records of the nunnery's dealings with the bank of Niccolò Bernardo at Rialto.[9] In all, therefore, the project was set up in a highly professional manner; the contrast with the extremely modest way in which Dom Agostin recorded expenses on the new church of the Carità a decade or so earlier – complete with mathematical errors – could hardly be more marked. Needless to say, there are no glaring accounting mistakes in the San Zaccaria documents, at least in these early years.

The accounts begin with a list of the names of the residents of the nunnery, and the initial donations made by each of them towards the building of the new church. There were thirty-eight nuns in all, and these first contributions totalled 255 ducats, a useful if modest start to the fund-raising effort. As we see from their family names, including those noted above, these nuns represented many of the most distinguished and wealthiest clans of the Venetian patriciate.[10]

Gambello's model has an important place in the history of the development of the architect, because it seems to be the earliest written record of such a model that has survived in Venice. The masters who made it were two joiners, Niccolò and Alegreto, assisted by two apprentices, Francesco and Andrea. In addition, a boatman had to be paid to deliver the timber to the site itself, where the model was apparently made.[11] As discussed earlier (pp. 61–4), the model was called for by the nunnery as a means of expressing in three-dimensional form what the completed church was to look like, particularly the complex spatial arrangement proposed for the chancel and the eastern apses, where it was proposed to construct an ambulatory with radiating chapels in the French manner.

This model was retained as the basic design reference guide for eight years, until July 1466, when it was found necessary to make a new one; the cost of this second model, 140 lire, was slightly higher than the first, although what the relationship was between the two we can really only guess. Certainly the making of a second model after construction was fairly well

advanced on site suggests either a major element of redesigning or possibly a more detailed model to explain certain specific elements of the church: perhaps, for example, Gambello's proposal for the completion of the façade, which at this stage had progressed only as far as the top of the west doorway.[12]

Building Operations

The long, complex building operations can be divided into some six fairly distinct stages; distinct, that is, on the ground, but far less clear from a simple chronological reading of the building accounts. Particularly difficult to disentangle are the accounts for the first few years when work was simultaneously being executed in the building of the new church and in extensive alterations to the old one. Nevertheless, we can broadly divide the project into the following phases:

First, work to the old church, chiefly in the period 1458–63. This was structurally complete by 1462; fitting out and decoration then followed.

Second, the first stage of building the new church. These operations included extensive new foundations; the purchase of large quantities of stone; the employment of many masons to work it; and the construction of much of the basic structural brickwork of the new church. This stage was complete by around 1466, although in fact there was little progress after 1463. This may indicate, *inter alia*, some changes in the design and may in turn have resulted in the call for the second model in 1466.

Third, there was a long period of work, chiefly by the stonemasons, from 1473 until the death of Gambello in 1481. Numbers varied from only one or two stonemasons up to a large group of about twelve. Gambello himself was abroad on government business during some of this period.

Fourth, there followed a hiatus of about eighteen months after Gambello's death, until the appointment of Codussi as his successor, during which time progress continued at a very modest level, with only two masons on site, Venier and Zuan de Betin.

Fifth, the appointment of Codussi on 12 June 1483 was reflected in an almost immediate increase in activity on site, which was continued until the autumn of 1487. In this period the church was completed, vaulted and roofed.

Finally, in 1488 the new sacristy was constructed, and in the period to 1490 several works of fitting-out took place within the new church, including decorations and the commissioning of paintings.

The fabric of the old brick Gothic church was drastically modified in the period after 1458 to provide several distinct forms of accommodation (figs 141, 142). Its north aisle was effectively to be 'lost' in its transformation into the south aisle of the new church. The existing nave and chancel, though, were subdivided by inserting transverse walls in two locations, thereby dividing the church into three parts. The easternmost section became the present chapel of San Tarasio, the central section (which is almost square on plan) became the nuns' choir, and the western part became the new *parlatorio*, with a grain store above. The nuns' choir was re-dedicated in 1595, since which date it has also been known as the chapel of Sant'Atanasio.[13]

The *parlatorio* was to be reached by a new doorway directly onto the *campo*, so that visitors could be received there without having to enter any part of the convent itself. A little further south, a large new double doorway from the *campo* gave direct access to the granary, which was located on the upper floor to offer protection from damp and rodents. The new doorway was completed by December 1458, and was carved by a mason called Bertuzi (Bertuccio) di Iacomo; in fact, Bertuzi was responsible for nearly all the alterations to the old façade onto the *campo*.[14] He required various items of metalwork to hold his stone in place, and here we meet once again one of the most familiar figures in the construction industry in Venice in the mid-fifteenth century, Niccolò Luxe, the blacksmith, whose smithy was at nearby Santa Maria Formosa.[15]

It is difficult to gauge progress on the old church, although the façade alterations were probably completed during the winter of 1458–9; in January 1459, for example, a master builder from Padua, Zuane Pavan, was paid for cutting the special bricks for the blind arcading along the top of the façade.[16] Special bricks like these were usually cut on site, and there is a similar record of 'piere taiade' (cut bricks) at the Carità church in 1444 and 1446.[17] Considerable further work took place on the old church between spring 1459 and the end of 1461. This was undoubtedly assisted by the Senate voting in February 1461 the sum of 1,000 ducats to assist the progress of the project. By the end of the year the old church was ready to receive a new roof, and on 15 December a number of large beams or *bordonali* were ordered. In the following spring, two distinct operations were in progress: one was the roofing of the old church, followed by the fixing of new tiles; the other was the carving, by a master called Gasparin, of six small capitals for the iconostasis. He was

141 San Zaccaria: the old church: detail of the façade, altered in the years 1458–62

probably the Gasparin Rosso who had worked on Contarini's palace in the late 1420s, where he also carved capitals for the *cortile* windows; he was clearly considered something of a specialist in this field.[18]

Installation of the new roof was a major operation, and the principal structure consisted of twenty very large beams, each 24 feet (8.3 m) long, together with twenty-five smaller ones, as well as twenty *chiavi* (tie-beams).[19] Work did not begin until May 1462, but was to continue until well into the following spring.[20] Hundreds of timber planks were also necessary to form a deck on top of the roof trusses, and once again Niccolò Luxe provided all the necessary ties, straps and nails.[21] The roofing was under the control of a *maestro* Polo, whose fee was 29 ducats; he also agreed to forego the customary wine allowance ('e senza vin'). His small army of assistants during the autumn of 1462 included nine masters and twelve labourers, such that progress was very rapid indeed. Following ancient, time-honoured custom, the completion of the roof was celebrated with a *festa* on 30 October, when 2 ducats were spent by the nunnery on 'le torte [pastries or sweetmeats] facte per el coverto de la ghiexia'. The roof tiles were delivered and fixed in three consignments, in November, December and March 1463.[22]

The restored old church was now basically weatherproof, and the nuns could bring it into use while the long years of construction of the new church continued on the other side of the new dividing wall. There were still internal finishes to complete, though, and

Antonio da Bergamo was paid for painting and gilding the cross-vaults, the 'fields' of which were painted blue, with more gilding to the bosses at the intersection of the vaulting ribs. Another painter, Zorzi Bagnuol, was responsible for decorating the new chapel of San Tarasio, including figures of the prophets and of St Zacharias, while gilding was also applied to the cross-vaults and capitals here (fig. 143); further works of beautification to the new nuns' choir included the carving and decorating of the choirstalls.[23] In late 1463 and early 1464 several other activities were continuing, among them the supply and fitting of the new circular windows ('ochj') that we can still see today on the façade of the old church.[24]

The choirstalls, however, ordered from the Cozzi brothers back in 1455, were the most expensive fittings in these newly refurbished parts of the complex. The agreed rate had been 10 ducats per stall; since there were to be forty-nine stalls in all, the total final bill was 490 ducats, in the region of 3,000 lire. The nuns had a very clear idea of the design of the stalls that they wanted. They were to be based on those at Sant'Elena, but were to have a row of 'blind arches' along the top, modelled on the (now lost) stalls at Santi Giovanni e Paolo. By contrast, the foliage carvings, which run up from the arms to these canopies, were to be modelled on those at Santa Fosca, 'although better if possible'. The request for surmounting hoods was in addition to the agreed design, and cost a further 100 ducats; the stalls still had to be decorated as well, and Andrea da Muran was paid a further 40 ducats again to apply the rich gilding and azure painting, work that was finally completed in April 1465.[25]

THE NEW CHURCH

We must now retrace our steps back to the late spring of 1458 and the beginnings of the construction of the new San Zaccaria, which was to rise adjacent to the old (fig. 144). Wherever possible, it was customary in Venice to reuse existing piled foundations, as we saw at Contarini's new palace in the 1420s, and at the Carità church.[26] At San Zaccaria, however, there were no pre-existing foundations to reuse for the new church, so this frugal approach was not possible. Gambello's first major task, therefore, was to organise this vital stage in the project. Orders for the very first *tolpi* (stakes for piling) had been placed as early as March 1458, a few weeks before Antonio's official appointment, and a large series of consignments followed until August.

The new church was intended to be an impressive structure, incorporating a great deal of stonework; since

143 San Zaccaria: the old church: frescoed vaults in the chapel of San Tarasio by Andrea del Castagno and Francesco da Faenza, 1442

Istrian stone is very much heavier than brick, this meant that the new foundations had to be particularly robust; this, in turn, meant exceptionally large quantities of timber piles. The first consignment consisted of no fewer than 1,000 small piles, 1,700 larger ones and around 1,200 of unspecified size. They were bought from three different sources, one of whom was Bortolomio Trevisan of Mazzorbo, in the northern lagoon near Torcello; Trevisan supplied structural timber for the church again in 1462.[27]

Many of the larger piles – which were mature tree-trunks, 2 feet (0.694 m) across – were destined to support the massive load of the new façade.[28] Although ultimately the upper façade was to be completed by Codussi, Gambello, too, had planned a rich, elaborate façade from the outset, incorporating a great deal of stonework, as we can infer from the small section that was constructed to his design.

Progress in driving the piles was rapid; by June a master called Guidoto was already beginning to fix the first of the large planks that formed the *zattaron* or deck on top of this subterranean forest of stakes, and from which the walls themselves would rise.[29] Pile-driving required a substantial workforce, the muscle of *manovali* as well as the skill of the masters themselves; in May, for example, the site team consisted of two or three masters and a labour gang that rose to as many as twenty-eight men; in June, numbers peaked at thirty-two.[30] There were still fifteen men at work until the

142 San Zaccaria; the relationship between the old church and the stone façade of the new one; the campanile (thirteenth century) is one of the oldest in the city

144 San Zaccaria: façade of the new church, begun by Antonio Gambello and completed by Mauro Codussi

end of August. The labourers were all paid a flat rate of 14 soldi per day, not an unreasonable wage, while the masters received 26–8 soldi, again a good level of pay. In the same period a number of barge loads of *tera da savon* were delivered to site; this was a type of marly clay, originally used in making soap (hence the name), but which was also used for making mortar for stonework in foundations.[31]

Gambello supervised these operations personally. His pay, although generous in principle, was erratic in nature: 2 ducats at the end of May, 20 in early June, 14 in early September, and a further 14 ducats at the end of the same month. He received only one more payment in that year, the next being just 5 ducats in two instalments in the following March.[32] He may have also been in receipt of a more regular income from the government in his capacity as advisor on fortifications; it is difficult, otherwise, not to imagine the nunnery's highly irregular payments as being other than extremely inconvenient. They had considerable expenses else-where in this period, too, and there were heavy costs associated with the foundations. The piles alone had cost 100 ducats and the wage bill to the site labour force was around 20–30 ducats a month.

By August the piling was effectively complete. The next stage of the works, though, required considerable quantities of a different material entirely: the large rec-tangular blocks of Istrian stone known as *piere da leto*, 'bedding slabs'. Payments for stone had already begun at the time of Antonio's appointment; on 28 July the nunnery paid the banker Niccolò Bernardo for the balance of money due to Simon de Vatie, who provided 485 blocks of stone for the foundations, delivered in two stages. Other consignments came from different suppliers at intervals between May and August, amount-ing in all to some 600 tonnes. All of it comprised simple, squared blocks of ashlar, accurately dimensioned but not dressed to a fine finish, since they would not be seen in the completed work.

There was also considerable activity by the *mureri* in this period, as records of deliveries of their own crucial materials indicate: 1,250 barrels of lime over the summer and autumn, as well as ten barge loads of building sand delivered in July alone. The familiar figure of Marco Corner provided no fewer than 100,000 bricks in 1458–9,[33] and 170,000 during the second stage of building the structural walls in 1462–3.[34]

Stonemasons

From the late summer of 1458 there were further con-signments of stone, bought from the nobleman Emanuel Girardo. The first mason to carve finished stone was Luca Taiamonte, a prominent figure on the Venetian sites in this period, and son of another mason called Francesco. Our first record of Luca is at the Corte Nova almshouses around 1440,[35] although there he was engaged in routine carving for door and window sur-rounds. He probably also worked with Bartolomeo Bon on the west portal of Santi Giovanni e Paolo in 1459 and (again with Bon) at the Madonna dell'Orto in 1473. Luca was born *circa* 1410, and so was around the same age as Bon, perhaps a little younger. His father had a partnership with his uncle Martino for a time, while Luca himself owned vineyards at Rovigno, across the gulf; he was also engaged in dealing in stone from Istria, whence his family originally came.[36]

Luca is first recorded on 21 May 1458, when he agreed to carve the stylobate for the imposing new façade onto the *campo* (fig. 146, 147). The contract was based on a fee per linear *passo* of stone carved, and Luca thereafter worked on the three receding courses of stone that we see today at the base of the façade. He was given an advance of 40 ducats to buy stone, paid through the account of the banker Niccolò Bernardo once again, and the work took him until the follow-ing spring; Luca had also prepared a *mostra*, that is, a *sagoma*, a template based on Gambello's model but to a much larger scale. He had also helped to complete one or two elements on the refurbished façade of the old church, including a dentil course around one of the doorways.[37]

Bertuzio di Iacomo was the other prominent mason in this early period of the works. On 11 October 1458 a contract was drawn up by which he agreed to carve six windows for a total fee of 200 ducats. As was so often the case in this period, too, they were to be mod-elled on some already completed elsewhere: 'four of them to be of the same height and width and to the same design as those at the church of the Carità . . . and two to be of the same design or type as those on the said church, facing the ferry [i.e., the Grand Canal]. Four are to be completed by the end of next March [1459] and the other two by the end of the May following.'[38]

Bertuzio was given 30 ducats in advance by the nunnery's banker, Niccolò Bernardo; five of the six windows are those to the ambulatory screen at the east end of the choir (fig. 145). A glance at these windows indicates that they are almost identical to the surviving windows on the flank walls of the Carità, carved by Bartolomeo Bon in 1443–4. Both sets have paired lancets with trefoil heads, and a small quatrefoil in a stone circle at the top.

145　San Zaccaria: the nave, towards the high altar

ern lagoon that were now depopulated and were eventually to be almost abandoned, as their waterways slowly silted up and the spread of malaria became more acute. These columns had cost the nunnery as much as 160 ducats, half payable to the agent and the other half to Iacomo Morosini on behalf of the monastery of San Girolamo, which also had an interest in the ruins at Ammiana.[39]

Only two months later, a second collection of ten columns was acquired, again from the Bishop of Torcello, for a further 125 ducats. At least some were complete with their bases and capitals, and they had come from another abandoned monastery, described only as the 'church of San . . . at Lio Mazor', the name carefully left unidentified.[40] As we have seen, despite government condemnation, such reuse was so widespread that eventually almost all Torcello's own monastic houses were to meet a similar fate; no trace of any of them survives above ground today.[41]

These two sets of columns are those that we now see around the ambulatory behind the high altar, all of *cipollino* marble. There are twenty-two in all, placed in four groups of four in the main colonnade and two groups of three where they abut the main piers of the chancel arch. The bases of all of them are the same, so those that had arrived without bases were clearly given new ones to match. The capitals, though, vary in design, and some are the result of the rather eclectic creativity of Zuan Buora.[42]

The acquisition of these columns corresponds to the period when Bertuzi was carving the upper order of ambulatory windows, and there was clearly a close connection between these two processes. Stylistically the two superimposed orders offer us a fine example of the 'marriage of styles', between what is clearly a Renaissance lower order, with semicircular arches, and a Gothic upper order, an openwork arcade modelled on the Carità windows. The juxtaposition may perhaps appear surprising to stylistic purists, at least partly because it is chronologically 'inverted', with the older style built above the newer one. We should remember, however, that there was a long period of 'overlap' in Venice from around 1470 to the end of the century when there was a quite peaceful coexistence between the two styles.

Despite much conjecture over the centuries, no simple explanation has been forthcoming; one possibility is that Gambello had built the lower order in the new style, but that it had not been well received by the nunnery, which then requested a return to more traditional Gothic forms for the upper order. The overall architectonic form, that is, the facetted chancel, open

In September 1458 the nunnery purchased twelve marble columns, bought from Zuane Galo, the factor or agent of the Bishop of Torcello; the columns had come from the former monastery of Sant'Andrea at Ammiana, not far from Torcello. Ammiana was one of a number of formerly well-settled islands in the north-

146   San Zaccaria: the socle and the lower part of the west façade, designed by Gambello and executed by Luca Taiamonte in 1458–9

147   San Zaccaria: detail of one of the two relief panels set into the first order of the façade, showing figures of prophets

colonnaded ambulatory and radiating chapels, was itself quintessentially French, and if the abbess (or anyone else) had ever seen this arrangement first-hand, then they would probably have seen the impressive late Romanesque example of the Santo at Padua. The reused *cipollino* columns of the lower order are surmounted by a highly inventive collection of capitals, which again may have been too 'advanced' for their tastes. Nevertheless, to our own broader, more pragmatic tastes, the combination of styles is remarkably successful.

At the end of 1458 Gambello assembled a small team of masons to work as day workers; they included Venier, Zuane Bello, and Iacomo and Matteo, Zuane's two sons. The masters received 26 soldi a day, young Matteo only 18 soldi.[43] Venier was to have a very long association with the church, and already seems to have acted as superintending master over the others, since in 1459 and 1460 he went to Istria to select and buy stone on Antonio's behalf. Venier was at San Zaccaria continuously until July 1461, when there was a break in his contract until 1463; in June 1463 and in March 1464 he again went to Rovigno (for a month on the second occasion) and it is clear that by now Venier had become Gambello's second in command, taking charge when he was away on government business. When site records begin again in 1473 after a six-year gap, we find Venier active almost continuously for a further eight years. With such a wealth of accumulated experience it is not surprising to find that he was to run the site himself for a time after Gambello's death, until a replacement could be found.[44]

Gambello himself, too, played an active role in the selection and purchase of stone in these first few years. His first journey to Rovigno had been in June 1459, followed by a second in January 1460; on this occasion he was given 80 ducats by the Bernardo bank to buy new stocks.[45]

The purchase of reclaimed marble from the Bishop of Torcello was representative of widespread semi-clandestine activity. A smaller scale example is the purchase of marble, in April 1460, from the parish priest of San Martino; a year later, slabs of decorative marble were acquired from Iacomo Barbarigo, Captain of the Gulf, apparently as a gift, Gambello having only to pay for the cost of transport. Antonio himself made four more visits to Istria between December 1460 and January 1462, again leaving his trusted deputy Venier in place on site.[46] Sometimes, though, masons were sent to Rovigno to work the stone at the quarry before bringing it over to the capital. In 1460 Martino de Zuane spent 103 days there, receiving a daily wage of 26 soldi; in the following year he was there again for a further 119 days, and this time he was not alone – with him on the quay on 26 July was Donado, apprentice of another site master, Laziero.[47]

Throughout the latter part of 1460 Gambello kept a sizeable team of masons busy, not only those noted above, but also Zorzi from Carona (Pietro Lombardo's home village), Alvise de Zuane and Zuane Cavozo; there was also a Vetor di Antonio. (This last may possibly have been Gambello's son, although his birth date is usually given as *circa* 1455.) Good progress was made, chiefly on the lower part of the façade and on the chancel. The number of masons often reached eight, but was never fewer than three or four.

During 1462 attention was primarily concentrated on the old church, particularly the roof and the costly choirstalls.[48] Thereafter, progress continued on the new church at much the same rate until the spring of 1464, after which there is a six-year gap in the accounts.[49]

Among the little knowledge that we have of this lost period is the making of the new model in 1466.[50] The first phase of building works is summarised in these accounts under the names of the two *gastaldi* who were in their posts in this period. Expenditure under Iacomo da Cha Gellin or Gebellini (1465–73) totalled 262 lire *di grossi*, and under his successor Antonio Foscolo was a further 121 lire *di grossi*.[51] This combined total was equivalent to 3,830 ducats or around 23,000 lire *di piccoli*. There were still many years' work ahead, though, before a total cost could be estimated. A useful comparison can be made with the Carità church reconstruction, which had reached a final cost of around 38,000 *lire di piccoli* on completion in 1452, and with the total cost of Marin Contarini's new palace at Santa Sofia, which was about the same as San Zaccaria's costs to date.[52] When finally completed around 1490, however, San Zaccaria was to have cost considerably more than either of these two works, perhaps three times the construction costs of the Carità church.

The period after our records begin again in 1473 with *gastaldo* Foscolo saw considerable variation in the extent of progress on site. Much of 1474, for example, was a very active period, with the numbers of masons varying from eight to as many as fourteen; thereafter, though, from Christmas 1474 right through to the spring of 1476, there were only two masons in regular employment, Venier and his partner Laziero.[53] The meagre records of the period give us little detail, though; in particular, we have no precise information on the exceptionally fine and unusual plinths to the great nave columns. The lowermost sections, the panelled bases, seem to be the work of Gambello himself, but above them stand extraordinary scroll-like plinths, from which rise tall octagonal pedestals. Crowning these pedestals themselves are further richly carved 'bases', from which the columns themselves finally rise (fig. 148). The whole grandiose composition is unique, and not all can be directly attributed to Gambello with certainty. The equally fine capitals that crown the columns are the work of the elusive (but imaginative) Zuan Buora, and the bases may be his as well.

Fortunately, we have one precise series of records from 1476. In May Buora began carving the capitals for the nave columns, assisted by a partner known as Luca da Isola. Their rates of pay (they were paid on a day-work basis) were very good, reflecting the highly skilled nature of the work, and Luca sometimes received as much as 2 lire (40 soldi) a day. The carving took them from May to the end of the summer, and the capitals justify detailed inspection, since they are as unique as the bases. They are broadly Corinthian in form, but have an imperial eagle with outspread wings on each of the four principal faces. As we saw earlier, the imperial image refers to the patronage of the church by the Eastern emperor, and reflects the design of the earlier capitals formerly in the old church. In this way the imperial connection was maintained, although Buora's capitals are by no means Byzantine in character. Rather, they are truly Roman in inspiration, a reflection perhaps of the concept of Venice herself as the new Rome. Domenico Duca (or Doxe), another skilled master who had worked on site in 1460, also now returned to carve capitals, some in conjunction with Luca; for a time they

148 San Zaccaria: detail of one of the bases of the great nave columns

worked on half a capital each. At least some of the nave capitals were already complete by early July, when it took no fewer than twelve 'porters' to manoeuvre them into position on top of the columns.[54]

In April 1477 Gambello was called away on one of his tours of duty overseas for the government. The nunnery was extremely concerned about the effect that his absence would have on both the quality of work on site and progress generally; new agreements ('pati e convention') were therefore drawn up with him on 12 April. Antonio was henceforth obliged to leave a sound experienced deputy in his place if he went away, someone who 'fully understands the design in order to make the stonework profiles for the masons, so that they may lose no time'. Gambello would receive no salary while he was away, nor did he retain the right to his apartment on the *campo*. His contract would thus be 'frozen' until his return, although the agreement also stipulated that it would be kept ready for a period of up to ten years, so that it could immediately be 'reactivated' on his return to the city.[55]

Antonio's locum is not specifically named in the agreement, and there were four masons on site on his departure (Vetor, Laziero, Venier and Domenego Moro), together with six *mureri*. In the event, and despite the nuns' concerns, productivity did reduce significantly, such that by early 1478 Venier was the only mason left in the yard. For more than four years, to November 1482, Venier was paid a regular but very low wage of 10 *soldi* per day; on such a modest retainer he must have been engaged in only the most routine of tasks, and it is clear that virtually no important progress – at least on stonework – was made in this long period.[56]

In the early summer of 1479 one of the giant monolithic nave columns was obtained; it was delivered by Domenico, son of Rigo dal Vescovo of Rovigno, who had supplied bulk stone to the site back in 1460.[57] And later that year, we find another unusual supplier of materials, the Bishop of Brescia; a record dated 12 November notes that the bishop, Domenico de Domenicis, had donated twelve large marble columns to the church at some time in the recent past, together with some smaller ones. They may have been a gift, but it was a gift with conditions, since the *quid pro quo* was that the bishop was to be offered one of the apsidal chapels 'in which to put the tomb for himself and his relatives'. The record continues: 'Since the nuns left the choice [of chapel] to him, he decided to choose the second chapel on the right, as one enters, above which there is to be a sculpted image of San Zaccaria'. The agreement was honoured, as we can still see today by the inscription dated 12 November 1477. His columns

149   San Zaccaria: relief panel on one of the bases of the ambulatory columns

150   San Zaccaria: detail of the junction of the bases of the nave colonnade and that to the ambulatory

cannot be identified with certainty, although it seems likely that they were located around these apses. The case offers a good example of what such contributions could hopefully purchase in the next life in exchange for material benefits in this one (fig. 149, 150).[58]

Work on the main internal structure continued into 1480. In spring there was a sharp increase in numbers once more, as Venier, who again had worked alone for some months, was now joined by Laziero, Ziane da Bergamo and Zuan Buora. Once again, too, we find Buora engaged in the skilful carving of capitals, this time the unusual smaller ones to the ambulatory. Among other works, he carved ten half-capitals here for 45 soldi apiece. The intention now seems to have been to progress the colonnades to both naves and ambulatory reasonably quickly, and then to continue the walls above them so that the roof could be begun. In the summer of 1480, too, a large number of bricks were delivered to the site and a team of five *mureri* was engaged in building up the walls.[59]

Antonio Gambello died during the winter of 1480–81, certainly before the end of February. He left a large family: his widow and four sons (Marco, Vetor, Ruzier and Briamonte), as well as two daughters, Orsa and Elena. Vetor seems to have been the eldest, and, together with both Briamonte and Ruzier, had begun to train as a mason, although Vetor's later career took a different course and he became a distinguished medallist and *proto* of the government mint. Antonio had not died wealthy, not surprisingly, given the demands of his family, and in September 1481 the Collegio voted a small pension for his widow to help her through the next few years, 'until an alternative provision can be made', that is, presumably until her sons were able to support her. The pension (1 ducat per month, or L.1.6.4.0) was by no means large, but was perhaps enough to feed her children, and it was paid from the funds of the Provveditori al Sal.[60] The pension reflected Gambello's role as government inspector of fortifications and was not connected to his role as *proto* at San Zaccaria.

During 1480 the number of craftsmen on site had steadily reduced again, from a total of around ten masons and builders in April to only two active masons (Zuane da Bergamo and Venier) by June. Work was to continue at this desultory level for a full year; from March 1481 to February 1482 the only men regularly on site were Venier and Zuan de Valentin – sometimes Venier was entirely alone. What is equally notable is that Venier was again engaged on simple tasks, and we have the unmistakable picture of the site virtually at a standstill again until Gambello's successor could be appointed.[61]

Venier and Zuan must have continued the work as defined by Gambello before he died, and the design of the unusual second order of the façade may be the result of this caesura in the office of *protomaestro*. Certainly, the design of the blind arcade, with its niches and scallop-shell heads, is not the confident work of Codussi (unlike that directly above it), nor does it evolve logically from Gambello's rich, squared panelling below it. Nevertheless, some of the other work executed under Gambello's supervision (especially the internal capitals and bases) incorporated considerable invention and quirky creativity, and we might ascribe these blind arches to Venier's interpretation of Gambello's own intentions.[62]

There was another reason for the limited progress after Antonio's death, and that was the prosaic one of a shortage of stone. On 16 November 1481 the nunnery paid a dealer called Dorigo de Roman 230 lire for delivering 288 *miera* (around 135 tonnes) of stone from Istria to the site; in the same shipment there was another of the giant monolithic columns for the nave, itself weighing around 9.5 tonnes. The porters or *facchini* who manoeuvred the stone from the barge (*piata*) moored on the Riva degli Schiavoni nearby were rewarded with a barrel of wine as well as cash.[63] The following spring, *maestro* Vetor spent a week working the surface of the column to obtain an appropriate finish.[64] Despite this long period on site without a superintending *proto*, work did proceed on some elements of the Gambello design. Laziero, for example, continued carving the stone ribs of one of the main vaults in the spring of 1483.[65]

Mauro Codussi, the New proto, 1483–90

It is not clear what Venier was engaged on in this period, although his work must have been based on whatever details had been left to him by Gambello: there was as yet no other model. Venier also spent some time at the Scuola Grande di San Marco, perhaps because there was simply not enough to keep him fully employed here; after many years' service under Gambello, though, he followed his master to the grave in 1483. The great nave columns were, of course, a further element in Gambello's long-approved scheme, and at least two others were already in place on site when it arrived. The general configuration of the nave, therefore, with its three large, spacious bays, essentially formed the heart of the Gambello design.[66]

But on 12 June 1483 the history of San Zaccaria changed profoundly, with the appointment as *proto* of the most creative master of the early Venetian Renaissance, Mauro Codussi. The brief entry in the building accounts summarises the essential terms of his contract; the abbess at this time was Lucia Donà and the contract was witnessed by two stewardesses (*camerlenghe*), Sammaritana Marcello and Camilla da Mula, as well as two noblemen, Piero di Lorenzo Donà and Lorenzo di Antonio Loredan. The names of the noblemen are, of course, very familiar: Piero had already known Codussi at San Michele in the early 1470s. He was also related to the abbot at San Michele, another Piero Donà, the tireless patron of the new church and Codussi's personal mentor. Piero di Lorenzo was also a generous patron at San Michele, and funded the church's left lateral chapel; when he died he also left the generous sum of 1,500 ducats towards the monastery. The Loredan, too, were intimately connected with San Michele and patronage of Codussi; Antonio was also related to Andrea di Niccolò Loredan, another patron of the church, and who funded the construction of the chancel. Twenty years later, around 1500, Andrea was to commission Codussi to design his magnificent new palace on the Grand Canal at San Marcuola.[67]

Soon after Codussi's appointment, in July there began a long series of deliveries of bricks to the site, a clear indication that progress had now restarted in earnest. Previously, almost all of the bricks for the church had been provided by Marco Corner, but this time a series of consignments, around 50,000 in all (over only three weeks), were instead supplied by Lorenzo Loredan. (They were also provided at a discount, 9 lire per thousand instead of the current market price of 10 lire.)[68]

Under the guidance of these two enlightened noble patrons, the nunnery (and the abbess in particular) was well aware of the significance of the appointment of Codussi, a master of very different reputation from the rather esoteric but essentially late Gothic style of Gambello. Codussi was a man of the future, in the sense that his own style, while still maturing, was essentially progressive and humanist, as all of Venice could already see at San Michele, whose white Istrian stone façade gleamed across the lagoon. Codussi's vision would shortly be confirmed again in his elegant, refined detailing for the palace of Marco Zorzi, very close to San Zaccaria, at San Severo. San Zaccaria's noble, 'imperial' façade is Mauro's most prominent contribution to the completion of the church, while his incorporation of a dome also has symbolic significance, with its echoes of San Marco as well as San Michele.[69]

Codussi's agreement with the nunnery stipulated a salary of 80 ducats per year; it was accepted that he would return to his home village of Lenna every winter, where he would usually stay for two or three months. In effect, therefore, his salary was equivalent to Gambello's 100 ducats for a full year. He was also explicitly required to coordinate all the other trades on site, and was to be in overall charge of both masons and builders.[70] Not surprisingly, Codussi's appointment immediately led to a renewed vigour in progress on site. From a mere two or three craftsmen in May and June, numbers increased to nine or ten masters and a roughly equal number of *lavoranti* in July and August, a remarkable burst of summer activity to make up for two years of little progress. Loredan's brick deliveries were an essential element in this new phase of activity.[71]

During the six years that Codussi worked at San Zaccaria, he gathered around him several important secondary masters. The chief was Zuan Buora, whom, of course, he had inherited from Gambello. Buora was head of his own workshop, with a partner, Manfredo di Paolo da Bissone, and was later to work at the Scuola Grande di San Marco in 1489 as the partner of Pietro Lombardo.[72] Also important contributors were a mason called Corradino, who had worked with Codussi at both San Michele and San Pietro di Castello, and Mauro's own brother Bernardo, a rather elusive figure who completed some of Codussi's projects (such as Santa Maria Formosa) after his death.[73]

Codussi's great challenge was to complete a church largely designed by another, and which was already well advanced on site. Although his contribution to the magnificent façade – most of it, in fact – is clearly identifiable, his relationship with Gambello's nave interior is more difficult to analyse. Two or three of the great nave columns and their capitals were already in place, as were the flanking walls and the double colonnade to the ambulatory. The remainder of the nave, though, including its ceiling and roof, was still an open shell, and the vaulting to the side aisles had not yet been begun.[74] Nevertheless, work began again immediately; Loredan's bricks were required to complete the upper parts of the nave walls, and on 24 July 1483, still only a few weeks after Mauro's appointment, Felipo di Marco from Orsera and Zian de Martin from Rovigno were paid for more stone ribs 'to go above the existing work in the *sepurchio*', that is, the chancel where the titular saint was to be buried.[75]

At the same time the façade to the *campo* had not been forgotten, although the upper orders had been languishing as a plain brick wall for some years. Zuan

Buora worked on a new frieze for the main portal in July, assisted by Domenico Moro and Zorzi Gruato. Buora's frieze has not survived, however, and the present one is plain. The portal is a rather unusual element in the façade as a whole; lacking the strength and vigour of Codussi's work at the higher levels, it is a lighter, more decorative element, more Florentine or Lombard in character than Codussian (fig. 137). The richer parts seem to be the work of Domenico Duca, who returned after an absence of six years to carve the 'confeterie' (decorative relief panels) to the portal and its surround. The pilasters, in particular, are richly carved in the manner of Pietro Lombardo, while the segmental pediment is also rather thin and refined compared to the powerful screen that rises above it. It seems likely that Duca himself designed the portal before Codussi had fully taken control of the design of the rest of the façade.[76]

During the same autumn we find a direct link between Codussi and Lombardo, the two greatest figures of the early Venetian Renaissance; on 23 September Mauro bought 8 ducats' worth of 'black Verona marble' from Lombardo, probably for some elements inside the church. Lombardo was working at Santa Maria dei Miracoli at this time, where this stone was used, so it was probably surplus to his own needs. A week later Codussi himself went to Verona to take delivery of more marble.[77] He also made a number of visits to Istria, and his brother, too, was sent over more than once. Mauro was in Rovigno in December 1483; a little earlier he had sent Zuan Betin and Felipo di Marco across the gulf, and in the following April we read that Zuan, together with Bernardo Codussi, had spent most of the winter there, not only buying stone but working it at the quarry.[78] Traffic across the gulf was particularly busy in this period, and Mauro himself went again in the winter of 1486–7, breaking his usual habit of returning home to the Valle Brembana; he was there again in August 1487.[79]

On 24 January 1485 Codussi's contract with the nunnery had been renewed on the same basis as the original one, but on condition that he begin work again immediately, on that same day. It is clear that the nunnery wished to maintain the new impetus on site, and although Mauro did begin immediately, he still seems to have found time to return to the Bergamasco for a short period; by 1 March, though, he was already back in the capital. Between April and August he was in Istria once more, selecting and supervising the cutting of yet more stone.[80]

The summer of 1485 saw remarkable progress on the façade, partly a result of the delivery of these large quantities of stone (fig. 151–3). To this end, Mauro engaged a number of masons at the same time to carve different elements of this rich, complex screen. They consisted chiefly of three pairs of masons: Zuane and Mathio, who carved pilasters for the outer corners ('i pilastri dj cantonj') as well as the 'architravo e la cornixe'; Agustin and Pasqualin, who carved five windows (probably those to the third order); and Manfredo and Bernardin, who worked on twenty of the small Corinthian capitals. Finally, there was Meneghin, who carved 'le frixe e golla' (friezes and throatings, or cyma mouldings): a high degree of specialisation and rationalisation, therefore, to speed up the process. The many bricks delivered in the summer of 1485 (around 45,000) were perhaps for the backing wall to the uppermost part of the façade and the vaults. At the eastern end of the church, too, by December Jacopo della Costa was being paid for completion of the chancel roof.[81]

In the following year, the emphasis seems to have shifted once again to the building itself behind the new façade, and the works that remained on the façade thereafter were decorative rather than structural. On 19 August another milestone was reached, with the completion of the main central vaults; a few weeks later, the nunnery organised a celebratory meal for the masters on site, 'un disnar ala maistranza per far el colmo'. It was a fairly modest *disnar*, however, since the cost was entered at only around 2 lire.[82] In the same period, Zane and Mateo were carving the volutes for the three radiused sections at the very top of the façade; small pieces of more luxurious marble still remained to be inserted into the façade, and in November 1487 Mauro bought a piece of porphyry, followed by twelve more about a year later, for setting into the high-level frieze.[83]

Back inside the chancel, though, considerable work was still necessary to complete the interiors of the chapels; some of the cornices and vaulting ribs were carved by Corradino, Mauro's old companion, who was joined by Antonio da Brioni, from Istria, who carved 26 passi (130 feet; 45.1 m) of these cornices in the spring of 1487. Other masons helped, including Vetor and his apprentice son, and a mason called Perin.[84] Other interior operations included the inserting of iron ties to strengthen the nave colonnades; some of these ties run longitudinally down the arcades, with others laterally at high level; this time the ironwork was not supplied by Niccolò Luxe, who must surely have died by now, but by Zuan de Vielmo, of San Luca. The fixing of the high-level circular windows (*ochj*) also took place in the same period.[85]

151 San Zaccaria: detail of the second order of the façade, probably designed by Gambello, but completed after his death in 1481

152 San Zaccaria: detail of the fourth and fifth orders of the façade; all of the façade above the second order is the work of Codussi, much of it carved in 1484–5

153 San Zaccaria: the crowning pediment to the main façade (*circa* 1485), a more powerful reworking of that at San Michele

The crowning cupola was one of the last elements to be completed. It is supported on a timber framework that raises the cupola considerably higher than the low, vaulted inner dome, which is very much like the inspirational models at San Marco. This cupola was constructed in the summer of 1489, and was clad on the outside with expensive sheet lead, which had cost some 190 ducats (1,200 lire) to purchase.[86] In the same summer, one of our very last records notes that Jacopo de'Vechi had been paid 3½ ducats 'to paint the prophets around the church', in fresco; a few weeks later a master Antonio was also paid, this time for prophets on the ambulatory walls, for a further 2 ducats.[87]

Finally, to complete the entire complex, the sacristy, too, was rebuilt in 1488–9, although work on the conventual buildings to the south and east of the church was to continue for some decades. Some other structure had already stood on the site, just north of the new north aisle, since twenty-eight boats full of *ruinazij* (demolition material) were removed in the spring of 1487. The present sacristy is a later reconstruction again,

rebuilt in 1562 on the same site as the Codussian structure. Codussi's sacristy required new foundations and 1,410 piles were delivered and then driven into the Venetian clay by Stefano di Zorzi in the spring of 1488; foundation slabs followed in May. The walls were built fairly rapidly immediately thereafter, mostly between April and the end of October. On 16 October 10,000 new roof tiles were purchased, some for the church itself, the remainder for the sacristy.[88]

At some time shortly before 1500, too, the single-storey wing along the north side of the *campo* was built, with its round-arched colonnade (fig. 154). Depicted in de' Barbari's view of that year, it has been much altered since, but originally consisted of a simple elegant 'cloister', which may well have been built to a design by Codussi, and which provided a weatherproof, covered link from the church to the gateway into the *campo* to the west.[89]

154　San Zaccaria: the cloister on the north side of the *campo* was originally an open colonnade, built shortly before 1500, and visible on Jacopo de' Barbari's woodcut of 1500

155　San Zaccaria: details of columns and capitals to the ambulatory; the columns were acquired in 1460 from a former monastery at Ammiana

Mauro Codussi's contributions towards the completion of San Zaccaria were twofold: the design and construction of the high-level work within the body of the church (the nave cornices, the vaults, the apsidal chapels and the cupola); and most of the imposing façade, that is, all the orders above the row of blind arches. In the former elements we can see clearly his rigorous and sharply defined detailing already matured. The use of stonework is purely structural and is confined to the main skeleton or framework, clarifying both its form and function. The stone for these elements is not the almost universal white Istrian limestone, but rather the so-called *piera negra*, the 'black stone' of Verona. It is in fact dark grey, and thus forms a dramatic contrast with the plain white stucco of the walls, spandrels and vaults (figs 155–7). This precise, disciplined articulation is decidedly un-Venetian, and we have to look towards Tuscany to find the source of Codussi's inspiration. This was surely the use of fine grey *pietra serena* in Florence and its surrounding towns in the early Tuscan Renaissance, above all, of course, in the work of Brunelleschi at the Ospedale degli Innocenti, at San Lorenzo and at the Pazzi chapel. The coffered ceiling at San Michele also has echoes of Brunelleschi at San Lorenzo.[90]

The façade of San Zaccaria, though, evinces a different aspect of Codussi's developing character. Powerful, strongly moulded in a highly theatrical manner, it is a remarkable development from the revolutionary, and yet still rather flat, refined façade of San Michele. San Zaccaria repeats the three basic elements from the earlier church, which in turn logically represent the three component spaces of the church behind: nave and aisles, in both cases terminated with two flanking quadrants and a crowning central semicircular tympanum. Here, though, the effect is of a triumphal arch rather than simply a façade, with the complex rhythms of the two lower orders giving way at the top to a massively moulded crown, its sculpted figures silhouetted against the sky. The orientation is such that afternoon sunlight emphasises further these dramatic plastic qualities.

The impression of a triumphal arch is by no means a superficial one. San Zaccaria was one of the most important religious houses in Venice. Patronised by popes and doges down the centuries, there was hardly a noble clan in the Republic without some close connection with the church: some were buried here; many sent their daughters here; many made generous endowments to the nunnery.

156   San Zaccaria: details of columns and capitals to the ambulatory

157   San Zaccaria: vaulting to the nave by Mauro Codussi, completed in 1486

The only churches of comparable stature in the city were the two great preaching houses of the Franciscans and Dominicans.

This triumphal and confident self-expression fitted well with the city's self-image in this period. The degree to which it was now acceptable to incorporate within the façade of a church such literally triumphant classical imagery is difficult to establish; but this great screen, rising majestically over its modest *campo*, can hardly fail to invoke an image of self-confidence, order and power.

A Tale of Two Churches: The Carità and San Zaccaria

The histories of the construction of these two churches differ widely in many respects, despite the fact that they were both built in the same city within a few years of each other. In fact, their construction history epitomises a number of the important changes that were taking place in Venice in this period: stylistic changes; changes in the design and management of the construction

process; and changes, too, of levels of expenditure and hence in the degree of the elaboration of finishes between the two buildings.

The Carità was not an unusual church, and the approach to its construction was essentially traditional, both in aesthetic terms and in the manner of its building. It can be safely and comfortably located within the established Venetian Gothic tradition; largely built of brick, its roof was of timber, with its structure exposed, as Venetian church roofs nearly always were (only a few were vaulted with stone); and the use of structural stonework was confined to the vaults of the chancel and its flanking chapels. Most of the architectural features, though, were of stone, and again can be fitted within the characteristic local tradition. Details such as the high level blind arcades, the circular west window, the 'tabernacles' (aedicules) on the corners of the top of the façade all derive from earlier examples, and were in turn followed by others in the next couple of decades. If we examine the exteriors of San Giovanni in Bragora, San Gregorio, Santo Stefano, Sant'Andrea della Zirada, the Madonna dell'Orto, and even the grandest of them all, the Frari and Santi Giovanni e

Paolo, all built or completed in the first half of the fifteenth century, we find common threads and elements throughout the group.

Nevertheless, some aspects of the Carità's exterior reveal the lack of an overall coordinating master: the (now lost) asymmetrically located lancets on the façade, for example, and the three unusual, tall gables, indicate a less than fully controlled design discipline. It was essentially a 'builder's church' or even a 'pattern book' church, consisting of the bringing together of elements that had all been used elsewhere in the city, and of their assembly in this particular manner in this location. Contractually, the monastery relied on the expertise and traditional skills of a local firm of master builders, Piero and his father Steffanino, who distributed day wages to the men under their supervision.

At San Zaccaria we find many strong contrasts in the organisation of the building process. From the outset, this was to be a highly prestigious project, well funded and well organised, a church that would have few peers anywhere in the city. Gambello himself was appointed with full design responsibility as well as overall responsibility for the management of the construction process. It was to be a very costly church, incorporating a number of highly unusual and inventive elements, including the bases and capitals of the great nave columns. But with the appointment of Codussi, the nunnery signalled its intention to complete the church in a wholeheartedly modern manner, and Mauro himself completed the façade in a triumphant, confident style. On its completion, it must have been as much a subject of discussion as his dazzling façade at San Michele had been a generation earlier. Francesco Sansovino, writing a full century later, still found it worthy of great praise: 'It is imposing, and rich with the most beautiful and finest marbles, with a finely composed and ornate façade at the front'.[91]

Chapter Nine

THE SCUOLA GRANDE DI SAN MARCO:
LOMBARDO AND CODUSSI

THE HISTORY OF THE Scuola Grande di San Marco brings together the biographies of the two most important masters of the later fifteenth century in Venice: Pietro Lombardo and Mauro Codussi, who were, in turn, responsible for this remarkable building. In essence, therefore, we find a similar situation to that at San Zaccaria, where a work initially designed and begun by one master – in that case Antonio Gambello – was also completed by another; the first master at San Marco was Pietro Lombardo, but here, too, the project was to be completed by Codussi.

The Scuola Grande di San Marco boasted a unique status among the city's Scuole Grandi since it was dedicated to the patron saint of the Republic himself; its members always regarded it as superior to the others, although technically all were of equal standing. For the same reason, too, the Scuola made a particular effort to express this perceived pre-eminence by lavish patronage of the arts, particularly painting and architecture; almost all the great figures in these fields in the later fifteenth century were members of the Scuola, including the painters Bartolomeo Vivarini and Gentile and Giovanni Bellini. Among the architects, masons and sculptors who were members were Bartolomeo Bon the Bergamasco, Giorgio Spavento and Antonio Scarpagnino.[1] Like the other original Scuole Grandi, that of San Marco was established elsewhere, and it first met at the lost church of Santa Croce, where it had been founded in 1260. We know nothing of the appearance of this first hall.[2]

The early fifteenth century saw important building programmes undertaken at the Scuole Grandi, which paralleled the notable activity in the private sector, and in the completion of the great monastic houses. In July 1437 negotiations took place between the Scuola Grande di San Marco and the Dominican friary of Santi Giovanni e Paolo for a plot of land immediately adjacent to the west façade of the great church; on 3 July the Consiglio dei Dieci approved the terms of the lease.[3] It was a fine site, more prominent and dignified than those of the rival Scuole of San Giovanni Evangelista or the Misericordia, although it did resemble that of the Scuola della Carità, which stood on the *campo* of the Carità church, with its façade facing the Grand Canal. In particular, though, the status of Santi Giovanni e Paolo as the ducal 'pantheon' ensured that the new Scuola would form a prominent backcloth for many ceremonial occasions in the Republic's future.

The façade of the new Scuola, like those of the Carità and the Misericordia, was again to be built at right angles to that of the adjacent church, facing the spacious *campo*, while on the west side it was bounded by the busy Rio dei Mendicanti. At the north end, though, the city's limits were considerably smaller than they are today and the extensive reclamations of the Fondamente Nuove were still decades into the future. The Scuola's plot thus extended as far as the shore of the lagoon, and a loggia was later built at this north end, with a quay for mooring (fig. 159). Finally, on the

159 The Scuola Grande di San Marco: detail from Jacopo de'
Barbari's woodcut of 1500, showing the Scuola, the *campo* and
the church of Santi Giovanni e Paolo. The north end of the
Scuola then faced the open lagoon

east side, the new Scuola was bounded by the existing
cloister of the monastery.[4]

On 22 July 1437, a week before the lease was signed,
the Scuola commissioned two masons, Domenico Taiamonte and Bartolamio Lanzo, to provide 350 feet of
'scalini', that is, rectangular slabs of stone, to form the
foundations for the new Scuola.[5] A week later, two
master builders were also appointed, Mafio and Stefano
da Cremona, and a master carpenter, Alvise Guasta.[6]
The construction process was to be organised in the
traditional manner, although the later history of the
Scuola was to illustrate a rather different approach to
procurement.

On 29 July the lease was signed.[7] Barely a week later
Bartolomeo Bon was asked to carve a large portal, 9
feet (3.1 m) high and 6 feet 3 inches (2.1 m) in width.
It was to be completed by the end of September, and
since it was priced at an agreed rate of 1¼ ducats per

foot, it must have been fairly straightforward, repetitive
work. The timescale, too, was very short.[8] Indeed, the
most striking aspect of the Scuola on its new site was
the extraordinary rapidity of its construction: barely
eight months after commencement, on St Mark's Day,
25 April 1438, the new building was dedicated by the
members of the confraternity.[9] Even allowing for the
fact that materials from some existing structures on
the site were reused, and for the fact that few, if any, of
the internal decorations were yet in place, it was still a
remarkable achievement.

At the time, too, it was considered a prodigious
accomplishment. Marcantonio Erizzo records that

> on the xxv of April 1438 they began to inhabit the
> building of the Scuola dei Battuti of m. san Marcho,
> which was built anew by the contributions of the
> *fradelli* at SS Zuanne Polo, and before that it had been
> at Santa Croce . . . And on that day there was a great
> celebration and triumph, and they were accompanied
> by all the other Scuole di Battudi, and all of the Frati
> came laden with countless Reliquaries . . . And the
> construction of the said house, and scuola, from the
> driving of the foundations to the completion and
> roofing was all executed within 7 months and 11
> days.[10]

Much of the money was donated by the *fradelli*, while
a good deal of the remainder was raised by dues levied
on the increased membership which had been granted
by the Dieci, and which drew in a further 1,160
ducats.[11]

Given the great rapidity of construction, the fabric
itself must have been little more than a large, simple
shell; there was insufficient time for the carving of
much decorative stonework, nor had there been much
time to develop the detailed design of the façade. This
first hall was based closely on existing halls elsewhere,
which were used as patterns; particularly relevant was
the Scuola della Misericordia, not far away, which was
also being modernised in this period, and with which
Bartolomeo Bon's workshop is also associated.[12] The
structure of the San Marco hall probably consisted of a
large rectangular envelope, with a row of columns in
the lower hall supporting the floor of the first floor
chapter hall or *sala capitolare*. One of few more elaborate elements was the relief panel of St Mark blessing
the *confratelli*, and which was to be reused in the reconstruction of 1487. The author of the panel is not
known, although it is often attributed to Bon; its original location has also been the matter of debate. Unusually, a record of 1470 describes its location as being on
the inner face of the façade, rather than on the exte-

rior;[13] it seems highly likely that one or two difficulties of coordination arose during the extraordinarily rapid construction programme, and this may explain the (possibly temporary) location. The panel was certainly relocated on the new façade after 1485. The interior of the Scuola was decorated and elaborated as funds became available, although the fabric itself was complete by 1445.[14] The ceiling of the chapter hall was decorated between 1440 and 1442, and that of the *albergo*, the smaller meeting room, followed in 1443, as did the staircase.[15]

Contemporary accounts by visitors to the city confirm the richness of the Scuola's decoration. Felix Fabri, for example, recorded that it was 'pretiossisimam, auru ab intus vestitam'.[16] Again, though, this impression was probably (initially, at least) chiefly confined to some elements of the interior, since it is inconceivable that an elaborate façade could have been completed in so short a period. The altar was commissioned in 1445, although the interior itself was still not finished thirteen years later, when the Scuola asked the Consiglio dei Dieci to permit thirty new members (with their enrolment fees) so that the *adornamento* could be completed.[17] This *adornamento* continued slowly throughout the 1460s; by 1466 two paintings for the chapter hall were completed, and the *capitolo* decided to commission a further number, 'between three and five' to complete the cycle. Both Jacopo and Gentile Bellini were appointed to paint their contributions, the former with two pictures, one of which was *Christ Among Thieves* for the *albergo*. Gentile was also to paint two, one showing Pharaoh's armies drowning in the Red Sea, and the other Moses and his people in the desert. Other works were commissioned a little later from Bartolomeo Vivarini, Lazzaro Bastiani and Giovanni Bellini. By around 1483 or 1484, therefore, the interior of the Scuola housed a magnificent assembly of *instorie* or cycles of narrative paintings by the city's finest masters. None was to survive.[18]

On 1 April 1485, just before Easter, the Scuola Grande di San Marco was destroyed by fire (fig. 160). The disaster is described in Malipiero's *Annali*, written a few years later:

> . . . on the evening of Holy Thursday, the *fradelli* of the Scuola di San Marco, gathering in their hall to go to Sant'Antonio, left [the hall] but also left alight the candles on the altar; and the wind blew open one of the windows on the west side, such that its

160   The Scuola Grande di San Marco: eastern part of the façade (from Cicognara, Diedo and Selva)

curtain passed over the candles and was set ablaze; and it burned the altar and the roof above, so that within four hours all was burned; and it was but a little way from also setting afire the church of San Zuan Polo; and later, with the aid of the Signoria and the *fratelli* it was rebuilt greater than it had been before . . .[19]

The Senate met two weeks after the disaster, on 16 April, and in an unprecedented gesture voted a large sum in reconstruction aid, in two distinct forms. The first was an immediate credit of 2,000 ducats, to be drawn from the account of the Camerlenghi, the city treasurers; the second was a longer-term credit, consisting of 100 ducats per month over a period of two years, giving a combined total of 4,400 ducats.[20] This remarkable (and remarkably generous) response was the only time in the history of any of the Scuole Grandi that the government granted direct financial assistance, a reflection not only of the magnitude of the disaster

but also of the unique importance of this Scuola in the eyes of the Republic. Four days after the funds had been voted, the Dieci further assisted the financing of the reconstruction by permitting the Scuola to enlarge its membership again, with 100 new *fratelli*, a concession that was reiterated two years later, when a further 100 were permitted.[21]

Reconstruction

The surviving archive of the Scuola is extensive, and contains more than forty documents enabling us to trace at least some of the reconstruction process. However, there is no surviving comprehensive building account ledger, so that the picture, while rich in certain details, remains fragmented.[22] On the same day that the Senate made its financial commitment, the Scuola itself also decided to hire 'protj over maistrj' ('proti or rather masters') to examine the wreckage of the burnt-out structure and identify elements that might be salvaged for reuse.[23] From later evidence, we know that two important pieces of sculpture were pulled from the devastation: the relief panel noted above and the figure of Charity, also attributed to Bon, and which stands today over the main portal.

It is unclear whether it was feasible to salvage any other stonework, although some of the great timber beams from the *albergo* were far from completely destroyed; three years later, master Griguol the builder was asked to attempt to clean them down and re-fix them.[24] Large, square baulks of oak or larch are often very durable in fires, when frequently only the outermost layer is carbonised, leaving the 'heart' largely intact. It was also feasible to reuse the foundations, which must have been little damaged, if at all, by the fire; the retention of this buried forest of stakes saved considerable time and money. It is difficult to imagine, though, that much of the façade could have been saved (fig. 161). The *albergo* was the furthest part of the Scuola from the fire's source, and had been less seriously damaged; since only the *albergo*'s timbers are mentioned for salvage, the roof and floor of the great chapter hall, seat of the blaze, must have been too badly damaged. In such circumstances, too, the façade was probably dangerously unstable, as at least one record suggests.[25]

All these first decisions were taken with great rapidity. On 20 April, too, the same day that the Dieci had permitted increased membership, the Scuola appointed five building commissioners (*provveditori sopra la fabbrica*) from their own membership, to supervise, record and manage the funds for reconstruction.[26] They were charged with 'determining the needs of the said building, with the minimum of expense, and as sparingly . . . as is prudently feasible'. The Guardian Grande, Tomaso Bragadin, was to be responsible for the disbursement of funds; clear, accurate accounts were to be kept. There followed some small payments to Zorzi Grando, a builder, for timber, probably for shoring and making-safe the ruins of the Scuola, since the main entrance to the monastic cloister of Santi Giovanni e Paolo was immediately adjacent, and many members of the public would pass directly in front of the façade to reach the adjacent bridge.[27]

That seems however, to have been the first, last and only construction activity on the site for more than two years. Despite the impressively efficient setting up of funds and appointments, the site remained deserted until August 1487, the only relevant activity being the reaffirmation of the lease agreement with the friary, which was re-drafted in August 1486.[28] It closely resembled its predecessor, except that the length of the chapter hall and the *androne* below it was to be increased slightly (by 5 feet; 1.73 m), and the Scuola was now permitted to append a new chapel at the far, north end if they wished, at some date in the future. The width of the great hall was not changed, nor was the location of the *albergo* on the east side, abutting the monastery.

The lack of progress on site seems to have resulted from the failure of the Senate to honour its commitment to fund the works, rather than any lack of enthusiasm on the part of the Scuola itself. Only in March 1488 did the Senate make available 1,400 ducats, in belated recognition of the sums voted in principle three years earlier.[29] The Camerlenghi simply did not have the funds to transfer to the Scuola, since they were reliant on the Signoria; at this time the Republic was at war with Ferrara and the papacy, a costly campaign that drained the exchequer at the Palazzo Ducale, and, indeed, resulted in sharp reductions of expenditure on site there, too.

Nevertheless, the Scuola must have accumulated some funds from fees paid by new members, first in spring 1485 and again in June 1487 (fig. 162).[30] On 7 August 1487 the Scuola finally appointed Griguol de Antonio, from Padua, as their master builder. His appointment was confirmed by Domenego de Piero, the Guardian Grande, who was also one of the *provveditori* for the works.[31] The document described very clearly the extent of Griguol's responsibilities: not only was he responsible for 'building all of the walls necessary for the said fabric', but also for fixing in place

162   The Scuola Grande di San Marco: eastern part of the façade, with the abutment to the church of Santi Giovanni e Paolo

all of the stonework, doors, windows, vaults, pilasters, cornices, architraves, both below and above, marble cladding where necessary, plastered and decorated and 'beautifying' [*belizando*] within and without, and all of the other works that are the *murer's* responsibility, and *eziam* to make the covering of timber planks . . . [the roof decking].

For the walls he was to be paid at the rate of one third of a ducat (approximately L.2.1.0) for each square *passo* of wall. Griguol was to build all the flank wall to the Rio dei Medicanti in 'piere taiade', which were to be plastered and polished to a fine smooth finish ('fregade . . . per modo le sia benisimo'), for which operation he was to receive 25 ducats.[32]

Griguol was therefore employed as the traditional all-round master builder. He had some responsibility for coordinating the operations of the carpenters, although the installation of major structural elements such as the roof was here (as always) the subject of a separate contract made directly between the patron and the company of *marangoni*.

Unfortunately, there is a further gap in our records at this point, until January 1488; in the meantime the Scuola had attempted to boost its funds further by calling in outstanding debts. On 13 January Griguol was subject to a new agreement, which casts light on the design process for the new chapter hall and the *androne* below it. The Guardian Grande, Domenego de Piero, wrote that

> for the greater beauty and strength of the said building, [Griguol] is to erect two rows of columns below the floor beams [*travadura*] of the said scuola, five in each row, making ten in all, as well as four half-columns which will stand against the [end] walls, two at each end, and for which work we are in agreement on this day with maistro griguol de Antonio, our *murer*, who is to form the foundations for the said columns, sufficient and strong enough for the said [purpose] . . . for their manufacture he is to have 20 ducats for each of the said columns.[33]

Although the record is admirably clear in indicating the way in which the structure was to be set out, with its double colonnade, it is unusual in that the 'manifatura' of the columns was Griguol's responsibility and not that of a master mason who, it seems, had not yet been appointed. Certainly Griguol was responsible for forming the new foundations and for the erection of the colonnade itself. Stone-carving, though, was beyond the remit (and the training) of the master *murer*, unless he was also qualified as a mason. There are some

curious anomalies in the building of the new Scuola, and it was to be a further fifteenth months before the stone for these vital elements, the ground-floor columns, was itself acquired.

Five days after commissioning Griguol, the Scuola ordered a great quantity of timber from a nobleman, Andrea di Paolo Pasqualigo, for most of the structure of the first floor. Among these timbers were six great *bordonali*, massive beams, each one 9 *passi* (45 Venetian feet (15.6 m)) long, 'precisely, and no shorter', all of good quality larch, and measuring 1½ feet (0.52 m) in breadth (*in bancha*) and 1¼ feet (0.433 m) *in contillo*, in depth; they cost 12 ducats apiece. The destination of these great baulks is easy to establish, as we can see today: they were to form the two 'spines' of the first-floor structure, resting on the two colonnades, and forming continuous beams or architraves down the whole length of the imposing lower hall.[34]

A great deal more timber was necessary to complete the first floor: 'questi tuttj di supra contenuti che sono per la prima travadura de dicta scuola'. These consignments included a further 100 *bordonali* most of which (ninety in all) were to form the cross-beams that spanned between the outside walls and the two 'spine beams'. Nor was this the last of the timber ordered from Andrea; another list schedules further supplies required on site before the following Christmas, of 1488. These consisted of two batches of forty-eight more *bordonali*, half of them 5½ *passi* long (27½ feet (9.5 m)), and the rest 12 feet (4.1 m) long 'precisely'; the order also contained 150 *reme*, smaller, squared sections usually cut from larger *bordonali*, and used to form the secondary structure of a roof.

With this impressive amount of timber ordered, the Scuola could now appoint a master carpenter to assemble both the first floor and then, later, the roof of the main halls. On 12 March, therefore, Zuan Candio and his partner, Marin de Doimo, were appointed to erect 'all of the *bordonali* onto the two rows of columns'. They also had to complete the floor of the chapter hall, which was to be 'all of larch, with its soffit coffered, with the *cantinelle* of the type that will be provided. And [they are to] make a cornice one foot wide which joins together the *bordonali* [i.e., to form wall-plates] all around [the perimeter of] the wall'.[35] Later, the same two masters were responsible for installing the roof: 'Item they are to build the roof with its two pitches, together with its *cadene* [ties] . . . *colomelj* [posts] *et bragierj* [brackets]'; they were to be paid in all, for the first floor and the roof, the sum of 140 gold ducats, although the Scuola gave itself the discretion of increasing this to 150 ducats, if most of the *provveditori* wished to do so ('a conscientia de dictj proveditori over dj la mazor parte di loro'). Payment was to be made weekly, and if the two did not fulfil their obligations, the Scuola would replace them with others and they would be contra-charged.[36]

On the same day that this contract was signed (and notarised) the Dieci made a further concession to help fund the works by agreeing to the suspension of the Scuola's charitable distribution of bread, wine and *minestra* to the indigent, the money thus saved being diverted into the building works. With the benefit of hindsight, we may regard this as one of the first small steps down the path towards self-glorification at the expense of the charitable functions of the Scuole Grandi that was later so vociferously criticised by Alessandro Caravia in his *Sogno* of 1541.[37]

Three months after the contract with Candio was drafted, on 12 June, we find evidence of the condition of the other, smaller element of the Scuola, the *albergo*. Griguol and his assistant, Damian, were to build the ceiling and then the roof, wherever possible using beams salvaged from the fire-damaged hall, repaired, cleaned-up and refaced. The roof was to have iron ties, and there was to be a small staircase up into the roof space; the whole operation was to be completed for 25 ducats.[38] Progress on site, however, seems to have been rather disorganised. While Candio and Marin may have been working the timbers for the first-floor structure, there was still no sign of the stone colonnade onto which the floor was to be assembled; it was only in the following spring, in April 1489, that the Scuola finally acquired the necessary stone.

A week later, on 1 May, we finally meet Pietro Lombardo, with his partner, Zuan Buora, who were now paid 100 ducats for the urgent purchase of the necessary materials. The two men were either 'to go, or send [someone] immediately to Istria, to transport the stone for the needs of the said scuola . . . and to complete the work which they have begun. And to continue the works with haste. And this work is to take place in as brief a time as possible.' There is the usual provision, too, that Pietro may be replaced if he fails to respond with due diligence.[39]

Why had the Scuola left it for so long before proceeding with this vital element of the reconstruction? There is no clear answer from the documentation, although it is significant that Pietro was already in the employment of the Scuola before May 1489 and had begun (but not completed) some work for them already: possibly, we may speculate, the plinths for these columns, which are carved with fine relief work. However, two-and-a-half months after this urgent

instruction, the Giustizia Vecchia ordered Pietro to deliver the stone immediately, that is, within one further month, since it had still not made its way to the site.[40]

Although we have no record of when Pietro had first started work for the Scuola, he had certainly been appointed as the senior mason, as we would expect of a master of his skill and reputation. He had just completed the church of Santa Maria dei Miracoli, only a few minutes away, and the church was formally dedicated on 30 December in the same year, by the patriarch (and patron of Codussi), Cardinal Maffeo Girardi. The recent completion of this dazzlingly skilful work must have given the Scuola a very clear idea of the richness and refinement of Pietro's technical style and design capabilities; such richness and refinement were now to be employed on the façade of the new Scuola.[41]

The completion of the internal ground-floor colonnades was by far the most urgent task that Pietro faced in the summer and autumn of 1489, assisted by his two sons and the talented Buora. We must note, though, that Pietro was not given the title or role of *proto*; this goes some way towards explaining the fragmented and badly coordinated start that had been made on site. By November, though, work had advanced sufficiently far on the main structure for attention to be concentrated on the façade. Lombardo and Buora, both still described as 'taiapiera conpagnj sopra el lavor de la fabricha dela ditta schuola' ('stonemasons and partners in charge of the work on the fabric'), were now to carve some of the stone for this façade, for which they had produced a *disegno*; this was possibly a model, but was more likely a paper drawing. The record is extremely important since it establishes Pietro as the master responsible for the overall design of the façade, although the text is not entirely unambiguous.[42]

The contract refers to Pietro's obligation to 'complete the said works', although some important elements had not yet been started (figs 163–5). They included the 'sam marcho grando che va de sora in forma de lion chon le do figure che mancha che vano ne la zima', that is, the large Marcian lion and the two statues in their niches on the flanks of the uppermost gable. These were separate works, although Lombardo and his *compagni* were to complete all the remaining elements to the façade, the design principles of which had already been agreed. These included an 'instoria granda' (narrative bas-relief) that was to be located 'between the two windows', although this panel was never actually installed. Pietro, Zuan and their assistants were to finish some of the work by the end of the following January, and the rest by the end of February or face the usual enormous fine, which in this case was to

163 The Scuola Grande di San Marco: detail of pedestal to one of the columns in the ground-floor hall, by Pietro Lombardo's shop, 1489

be levied by a reduction in the agreed value of the work from 1,100 to 1,000 ducats, a sum that did not include the carving of the *instoria*. Pietro and Zuan agreed to these terms, although since the latter was illiterate, his commitment was pledged by another mason, Michele da Stefano.

One reading of this document is as a requirement to complete before the end of February 1491; in fact, it states that certain elements must be complete 'per tuto el mexe de zener prosimo che vien', that is, January 1490, and the rest by 'el seguente mexe de febraro', 'the following month of February', again of 1490. This gave Pietro only three months to complete the works, and this implies an enormous effort on his part, given that the sum involved (and thus the extent of work) was considerable. It certainly took longer; we have already seen examples of unrealistic deadlines being set by demanding patrons, usually accompanied by the threat

of extremely heavy fines, which hardly ever seem to have been enforced. Perhaps the threat alone was perceived as a sufficient inducement, since the levying of such onerous fines would certainly have ruined the masters concerned. It is almost certain, therefore, that these works drifted on into the latter part of 1490; they were sufficiently far advanced by 7 November for Mauro Codussi and Antonio Rizzo to be called on to adjudicate on them.

This document is the only source for the attribution of the design of the façade to Lombardo, although this vital information is partly undermined by all the matters to which the contract does not refer, which are as important as those which it does identify. The fact that the *instoria granda* was never executed reflects further prevarication on the part of the *banca* of the Scuola, not at all an unusual occurrence, as we will see again shortly. The Marcian lion was to be the subject of a separate contract, and we cannot tell whether Pietro himself was to carve it or whether it was to be 'subcontracted'. The two figures of soldiers missing from the façade were still missing in 1500, and were an exceptionally late contribution; the other statues on the skyline are also not mentioned in Pietro's contract because they, like the figure of Charity, had been salvaged from the earlier building. It is difficult to be sure, but it appears that a considerable part of the lower façade itself was already complete by November 1489, when this contract was signed. The figure sculptures had to be the very last elements to be added; the Marcian lion and the other pieces could not have been fixed in place until not only the underlying brick wall was constructed, but also the sheathing of the façade with sheets of marble; this cladding could not be fixed after the statuary.[43]

At the same time, masonry work was proceeding elsewhere, with a different team of masters. This was the stonework for the long flank façade along the Rio dei Mendicanti, and was carved by Domenego and Ieronimo Moro, almost certainly under the overall supervision of Lombardo. They had begun on 19 July 1489 and continued until the conclusion of the work on 1 April 1490.[44] This flank façade is in marked contrast to the rich, ornate façade to the *campo*; it consists of two superimposed orders of twelve bays, ten of which correspond to the length of the great halls inside, the *androne* and the upper chapter hall. Since the internal structure is divided into only six bays by the twin colonnades, however, there is no direct structural relationship between this six-bay interior and the serene rhythm of the ten-bay exterior. This may again be attributed to the fact that the Scuola had appointed no

164   The Scuola Grande di San Marco: main portal

165   The Scuola Grande di San Marco: detail of the main portal, with Bartolomeo Bon's figure of Charity and his relief panel of St Mark with members
of the Scuola, both salvaged from the earlier structure

proto to coordinate and rationalise the structure; it may
also reflect a desire to present a refined façade to the
world regardless of the internal arrangements; and it
may even have resulted from the necessity to reuse the
existing foundations of the earlier building on the site.
From the exterior, it does not matter, and the canal
façade may be judged on its own merits; it is only
inside the halls that one becomes aware that the
windows have no logical relationship with the bay
spacing of the colonnades.

This flank façade is subdivided by a complex cornice
at first-floor level, and a similar one at the roofline; each
bay is divided from its neighbours by an elegant, rather
Codussian pilaster, with a bas-relief disc set into the
centre. Each bay, too, is lit by a single round-arched
window with a fluted extrados and fluted capitals. The
design cannot be the work of Codussi, since his
employment at the Scuola had not yet begun, and it
must therefore be that of Lombardo. It has a cousin in
the long side wall of his own Miracoli church, which

again flanks a canal, although the church is far more richly clad with slabs of marble. The ordered rhythms of both works are clearly related, and represent Lombardo's style at its most structured and disciplined. Unlike those at the Miracoli, though, the two superimposed orders here do reflect the two storeys of the interior (figs 166, 167).

Domenego and Ieronimo worked prodigiously on this extensive but highly repetitive stonework for eight months, during which time they produced 226 feet of frieze, 227½ feet (78.9 m) of cornice, thirty-four bases for pilasters, ten pilasters, ten capitals and 131½ feet (45.6 m) of *frixo negro* (the frieze of 'black' Verona marble). They were sidetracked for a day or so, however, to fix the 'san marcho' onto the main façade, which was in place by April 1490. For all this effort, the original contract sum had been 195 ducats, of which Ieronimo was to receive 151 and Domenego a mere 44 ducats, indicating that the latter was very much the junior contributor, although he was described as Ieronimo's *compagno* or partner. In the event, a re-measuring exercise on completion of the works brought a revised fee of 1,283 lire, or approximately 207 ducats.[45] The canal façade was therefore largely complete by the spring of 1490; that to the *campo* was a far more complex matter, as we will see in a moment.

In February 1490, just before the settling-up with the two masons, the work of the carpenters, Zuan Candio and Marin de Doimo, had also been completed, and here, too, it was measured and re-evaluated. On 12 February an entire committee of fellow masters and experts presented their report to the *provveditori* of the Scuola. There were six of them, all carpenters, and their conclusion was that Zuan and Marin should be paid 75 ducats now, on account (the text is altered from 79 ducats), and the balance of 41 ducats payable on completion; it is also clear from their report that the first floor was now in place, together with at least part of the roof of the chapter hall.[46]

But the spring and summer of 1490 were a period of crisis, or at least of serious difficulty in the finances of the Scuola. On 3 May, for example, it was decided to roof the chapter hall with traditional clay tiles instead of lead sheet, which was more prestigious but far more expensive. Later into the summer, on 25 July, the *banca* recorded that it was faced with vast outgoings on the building works; the claimed 'hundreds of ducats a week on timber alone' is surely an exaggeration, unless it refers to moneys long overdue to Andrea Pasqualigo. Nevertheless, the *banca* requested postponement of the repayment of a 1,000-ducat debt to the adjacent friary, which was agreed.[47]

If the summer saw financial difficulties, the autumn witnessed a crisis of a different nature. On 7 November it was decided to assess the work that had been completed to date by Lombardo, Buora and Bartolomeo, the son of Domenico Duca. The assessment was to be undertaken by Antonio Rizzo, *proto* at the Palazzo Ducale, and Codussi, 'Moro da San Zacharia'. The two were charged with evaluating 'all that had been done in excess of the contracted design' ('de piui del desegnio suo marchado') and similarly all that had been omitted from the approved scheme, 'quelo aveseno manchado del marchado e del desegno'.[48]

There follows one of those tantalising lacunae that are such a prevalent feature of the building accounts of the period. The report of Rizzo and Codussi is lost, and we have no direct indications as to its contents. Nevertheless, the results of its publication were dramatic: henceforth, the name of Pietro Lombardo is never recorded again in the documents of the rebuilding of the Scuola, and he was promptly replaced by Mauro Codussi, who was given the formal title of *protomaistro*. Debate has continued to the present day as to the reasons for Pietro's abrupt dismissal – or perhaps his resignation – and his replacement by the master who, at a simple level, might be thought to be his greatest rival. Equally intensive has been the debate as to the respective contributions of the two masters towards the completion of the Scuola's extraordinary façade.

The facts of Codussi's appointment are easy enough to establish. From an account of December 1491, Mauro had begun service as *proto* at about the same time as he was commissioned to evaluate Lombardo's work, probably (and probably significantly) just beforehand. From November 1490 to March 1491 he had been paid 5 ducats per month; after this 'trial period' he negotiated an increase to 6 ducats, or 72 ducats per year.[49] The fact that only at this very late stage had the Scuola decided to appoint a master with the title and powers of a *proto* confirms that their earlier, traditional system of appointments had proved unsatisfactory; and so they belatedly decided to try the system in force at the Palazzo Ducale and San Zaccaria. Codussi had therefore been brought in to manage the construction process to completion, and, in particular, to complete the rich, complex façade. He had already proved adept at such late-stage operations by his triumphant conclusion to the façade of San Zaccaria after the death of Gambello, and the members of the *banca* were undoubtedly hoping that he would bring the same skills to work for them.

Funding remained a problem, however. In January 1491 the Scuola had once again approached the Con-

above 166 The Scuola
Grande di San Marco: the
façade to the Rio dei
Mendicanti, designed by
Pietro Lombardo and
carved by Domenego and
Ieronimo Moro in
1489–90

left 167 Santa Maria dei
Miracoli: façade to the
Rio dei Miracoli, by
Pietro Lombardo, 1481–8

siglio dei Dieci with a further request to suspend charitable distribution to continue to fund the works; on this occasion it was agreed to suspend their obligation to distribute bread and wine for five years.[50]

Codussi remained in the Scuola's employment on the same salaried basis until June 1495. On several occasions he went to Istria to buy stone, including twice in 1492, in March and again in May. But he also maintained his old pattern of returning to his homeland, the Valle Brembana near Bergamo, for the winter; he was certainly there, for example, in the winter of 1491–2.[51] But in the following autumn of 1492, on 25 October, Codussi was relieved of his post at the Scuola, because he would no longer accept his salary, which was still 6 ducats a month. The decision to suspend him was taken by Zuan Trevisan, the painter Gentile Bellini (then Guardian da Matin) and Vetor Ziliol, the deacon, although the whole *banca* had been in agreement with the decision.[52] Mauro almost certainly took advantage of this suspension (which turned out to be only temporary) by once again returning to the Bergamasco. He was back in the city in the following spring, however, and was reinstated as *proto*; by 11 April he was once again on his way to Istria to buy more stone.

The façade was not the only part of the Scuola being progressed in this period, and on 8 February 1493 it was decided to proceed with paving the lower hall or *androne*; the work was to be carried out by Zuan de Mafio, from Parenzo in Istria. The paving was to be in a chequered pattern, with alternating squares of 'piere rosse e negre', all of them to be 1 foot (0.347 m) square in the central 'nave' of the hall, between the two rows of columns, but $1\frac{1}{4}$ feet (0.433 m) square down the two side 'aisles', an interesting optical refinement; the agreement was witnessed by Codussi himself.[53]

At the end of the year 1493 Griguol, the long-serving master *murer*, submitted his schedule listing the works that he had executed over the previous six-and-a-half years. The work had certainly been extensive, amounting, *inter alia*, to a total of 1,138 square *passi* of brick walling, that is, more than 28,000 square feet (3,400 square metres) in Venetian measure, a prodigious effort indeed. His work also included most of the brick walls that support the richly carved gables on the front façade, which rise considerably higher than the roof behind them. By now, nearly all of the structural brickwork for the entire Scuola had been completed, with the exception of the tops of these façade gables.[54]

As early as the summer of 1492 attention had begun to shift towards the internal decoration of the great halls. Gentile Bellini, the Guardian da Matin, had offered to paint a group of pictures for the first-floor

168 The Scuola Grande di San Marco: detail of the portal to the staircase, by Mauro Codussi, before 1495

albergo, in cooperation with his brother Giovanni. The first painting to be executed was to be a huge canvas that would fill the entire wall opposite the doorway, above the *banca*. Gentile had been 'inspiradi da inspiration divina piui presto che umana', an inspiration more urgent and divine than earthly, and the work was to be executed partly as a memorial to his father, Jacopo. The brothers proposed that they would paint the canvas for only 50 ducats for each of them, but it was to be many years before the first painting of the San Marco cycle was completed: the *St Mark Preaching in Alexandria*, today in the Accademia, was finally commissioned only twelve years later, on 1 May 1504.[55]

In 1494 Codussi's attention transferred from the façade to the staircase that was to link the lower great hall with the chapter hall and the *albergo* on the first floor. We have very little documentary detail of this influential work, which was later to be surpassed in richness by Codussi's own elaboration of the same basic design for the rival Scuola Grande di San Giovanni Evangelista (figs 168, 169). The principle of the San Marco stair, though, seems to pre-date its construction by some time. It was already specified as a double-branch staircase in the memorandum of agreement of 1486 with the adjacent friary, just prior to the start of building works. It was to be designed 'ascendum ex una parte, et descendum ex alia'; in other words, it was to consist of two long flights that would begin near the two ends of the lower great hall, and rise to meet in the middle at the top landing.[56] Its location down the

169   The Scuola Grande di San Giovanni Evangelista: Codussi's staircase, *circa* 1498

east flank of the Scuola meant that it was necessary to lease an additional narrow strip of land from Santi Giovanni e Paolo. It seems, therefore, that its basic layout was not Codussi's own original idea, since he was only appointed four years later, although he may had been consulted over its design.[57] Such a stair was unusual, but not entirely without precedent in the city, while its practical layout was well suited to the highly restricted site. (A similar double-branched stair, in this case external, could be seen at the Fabbriche Vecchie at Rialto, where it rose in the Campo di Rialto Novo, giving access to first-floor stores and offices.)[58]

The Scuola's staircase was to have two widely spaced entrances from the ground-floor *androne*, one close to the front façade and the other near the back corner. We should recall that, when it was built, the rear façade of the Scuola still faced the open lagoon, with a quay immediately outside; if the Scuola was approached by water from the north, therefore, this northern end of the grand stair was well positioned for access to the first floor.

The account of Griguol's work in December 1493 makes it clear that the stair's supporting wall was already constructed, and the structure as a whole was completed very shortly afterwards; Codussi's stonework must surely have been complete before his own final dismissal in May 1495. By the time of Griguol's departure from the site in October of the same year, the two ground-floor portals were in place, but not that to the top landing. The staircase itself was demolished in 1815, but was reconstructed after 1945, using some of the original material. The original portals, however, do remain;[59] all are fine, rich works in Codussi's characteristic style.

The staircase was highly regarded from an early date; in 1581 Sansovino drew attention to the 'due scale commode e ricche'.[60] Later, Tommaso Temanza, the architect and critic, writing in the 1760s, gives us a rare detailed description:

One reaches the upper hall by spacious diverging stairways, with landings at the bottom, halfway up, and at the top. The stairs are arranged, one confronting the other, and meet in a common landing at the top, from which one can enter the upper hall through a magnificent archway.

Temanza was also aware of the spatial subtleties of the axial progression:

since the arch at the bottom . . . is low and pinched, on account of a little room above the landing there, whereas the arch at the top is high and wide,

Martino [sic] invented a clever adjustment at the second landing . . . by using a thin cornice . . . above the low arch [of the first run of stairs], and setting a blind arch above it, matched by three more on the other sides, the four all together bound the pendentives on which [he put] a little dome . . .[61]

On 7 June 1495, with the stairs complete, the *banca* met to discuss Codussi's position. Only a week earlier, the Guardian Grande had reported that 'un texoro' ('a fortune') had been spent on the works so far, and two months later, on 1 August, the scale of the Scuola's cash-flow difficulties became dramatically apparent, when the *banca* stated baldly that 'we find ourselves at present without any money, and in great need and laden with debts'.[62] A further two months later, the position had not improved, and 100 ducats of investment were withdrawn from the Camera degli Imprestiti as a short-term measure.[63]

It is hardly surprising, therefore, that on 7 June it was decided by a narrow majority of the *banca* (seven votes to six) that Codussi's contract should now be terminated.[64] Their opening statement is significant, because it confirms their perception of his role:

Having been provided for the construction of our *schuola* from time to time a salaried master [*chapo salariato*] in order to conduct the works towards their greatest possible perfection, and according to the circumstances of these works, the said salary has been increased or decreased, at present the said work is found to be at an end, such that the expense of the said salary is no longer necessary, [as all that remains] to be completed are certain works of decoration that will be undertaken by the hands of various masters who will be paid solely for their [own] craftsmanship . . . it is hereby proposed by the *spettabel messer* Alvixe Charlo, *vardian grando* of the *schuola* of *miser* San Marcho . . . that the expense and monthly and annual salary of *maistro* Moro is to be terminated, and from this day hence there will be neither salary nor obligations save that from time to time he may work . . . for the said *schuola* [in which case] he will be paid for his skills in the usual manner . . .[65]

Later that year a second general reckoning was undertaken with Griguol, the master builder. There was some dispute as to the extent and value of these works, though, and an undated document from about this period lists many operations that Griguol had carried out, with prices against them. This was perhaps the contentious list, and we have another, more definitive one, from 29 October 1495, recording that three 'arbitrators' had been brought in to resolve Griguol's rightful entitlement. These three men were Giorgio Magno, Giorgio Spavento (since 1486 *proto* for the Procurators of San Marco) and Pasqualin Donato, all described as *murari*, and who were to 'cognoscendum, Arbitrandum, arbitramentandum, amicabiliter componendum extimandum, Laudandum, Condemnandum et Absolvendum', which excessively florid Latin simply meant that they were to measure and evaluate the extensive work that Griguol had executed.

To summarise their conclusions, the three *savii* stated that he was due a final sum of 57 ducats and 18 soldi in settlement. Over this long period Griguol had coordinated all the lesser crafts, organised deliveries of all necessary materials and fixed stonework carved by the master masons.[66] He had also built 11 *passi* of foundations below the *albergo*; he had fixed four square windows; delivered and fixed all of the stone to the north façade, facing the lagoon, together with its three aedicules; delivered the stone for the front façade; executed various works in the porter's lodge; formed the centring of all the arches; fitted four doorways on the ground floor and one on the first (to the *albergo*); and finally, and not unimportantly, he had laid the sewer, paved the toilets and provided and fixed the communal timber bench with its row of openings, for this same sanitary accommodation.[67]

In addition to this impressive list of works, however, there was a further schedule that he had not completed, and in some cases had barely begun. Still left incomplete were the plastering and decorating of the wall surfaces ('above and below, inside and out'), including that to the 'sala da basso' (the *androne*), which the Scuola would have completed by others at Griguol's expense if he did not proceed with it. More importantly, there remained to be fixed 'doors and large windows'; specifically mentioned is the 'portal grando che son [*sic*] sul pacto de la scalla', that is, Codussi's portal at the head of the staircase, which gave access to the great chapter hall, as well as the windows to the staircase's flank wall.[68]

We have few building records after this date, although internal decoration continued well into the new century. In August 1496 the construction of the Cappella della Pace began, but was to continue in a desultory manner for more than twenty years.[69] In 1491 the manufacture of the benches for the Scuola was first mooted, but progress was again extremely slow; it was to be a further eleven years before Nicolò di Marco was commissioned, in May 1502, to carve the first bench, at the rate of 5½ ducats for each place. Later, in September, he was approached again to carve the

remainder, but at the reduced rate of 3 ducats per place, but the work was apparently never completed.[70]

Since the first great cycle of paintings had perished in the fire of 1485, it was also necessary to commission a new cycle from the leading masters of the day, many of whom were members of the Scuola, including the two Bellini. Gentile had died just before finishing the great new painting for the *albergo*, but it was completed by his brother Giovanni.[71] In the same period, Piero and Biaxio da Faenza were making decorative panels for the ceiling of the same hall.[72] Some years later, Giovanni Bellini was asked to paint 'una historia de missier S Marco', to be located above the *albergo* doorway, opposite the earlier picture. A few weeks later, though, the Guardian Grande, Vetor Ziliol, noted that the confraternity was still in acute need of funds, and was owed 1,000 ducats, which, when received, should be spent on the altar and chapel of the chapter hall.[73] The very last major work to the fabric of the Scuola itself was the ceiling of the same hall. In July 1519 a design was finally selected following a competition, and the contract was awarded to Vetor da Feltre. A timber model presented by Vetor had formed the basis of his selection, and he was to carve the ceiling, with 147 coffered panels, at an agreed rate of 11 ducats per panel; the ceiling has survived, although it was damaged by a bomb in 1917.[74]

The Façade

The Scuola's façade remains one of the most remarkable in Venice, and has attracted high praise from a very early date. Canon Casola, that peripatetic connoisseur, described it in 1494, when it was barely (and perhaps not even) complete, as 'richa e bella de marmori e di auro'; much later, Francesco Sansovino wrote that the façade was 'tutta incrostata di marmi finissimi con assai bella struttura'.[75]

These and many other laudations concentrated on the richness of the façade's finish; but this richness has often resulted in its being appreciated purely as a decorative screen, a counterpoint to the Gothic monumentality of the adjacent church, and as a backcloth to festivities in the *campo* itself, rather than as the outward manifestation of a very substantial building. In this it reflects something of the theatricality of Pietro Lombardo's style, as well, of course, as his sculptural and technical strengths.

Despite their similar plans, none of the other original Scuole Grandi today projects their two component elements (*albergo* and *sala capitolare*) onto their public façades. The *albergo* at the Carità is so much smaller and so subservient to the façade of the main hall (later rebuilt by Massari in 1760) that it reads merely as an anonymous link between the Scuola and the adjacent church. At the Misericordia, the *albergo* wing is around the back and not visible to the public at all; while at San Giovanni Evangelista the unusual shape of the site resulted in the two halls being placed end to end rather than at right angles to each other. Only here at the Scuola Grande di San Marco (and considerably later at San Rocco) do we see a façade on which are projected these two very different volumes.

At the Scuola Grande di San Marco they are both treated in a similar manner, so that it requires more than a passing glance to appreciate that the three equal bays of the east side represent the smaller *albergo* wing, while the three taller bays to the left, with their ascending arrangement of gables, represent the great chapter hall behind. In the overall composition of their façades, Lombardo seems to have been more comfortable at the Miracoli church, where the clean, precise volume of the new church, with space all around it, could be clearly understood for what it was: a single, barrel-vaulted, aisle-less internal space.[76]

The two wings at San Marco are differentiated in a number of ways, particularly in the treatment of the two entrance portals. The *albergo* element is also more disciplined and restrained, with the exception of the two famous false perspective panels on the lower order. On the ground floor there is a central portico, flanked by these two panels (fig. 171), while on the first floor two large single lights in the outer bays each flank a solid central bay, in the middle of which is a prominent, patriotic lion in a rich tondo. On the skyline are three equal semicircular gables. The whole ensemble is richly detailed, with all the wall surfaces clad with sheets of marble; the articulation consists of fielded Corinthian pilasters to the lower order and fluted pilasters to the first, while the two orders are divided by an exceptionally rich and complex combined frieze, architrave and string course (fig. 177). The gables are capped by urns flanked by acanthus leaves, while the large first-floor windows are also framed with rich surrounds, with bas-relief pilasters and triangular pediments (fig. 170).

The same general vocabulary is employed in the more prominent left section of the façade, although with many differences of detail. Instead of three equal bays, here the bays are unequal, and the two flanking sections frame a central bay that is considerably wider. This bay is dominated by the large ornate portal, with its two freestanding columns, and a deeply moulded canopy projects above the first-floor cornice. The inner

170   The Scuola Grande di San Marco: first-floor window, detail (after recent cleaning)

portal is also richly carved, larger and more prominent than that to the east wing, with a large keystone in the form of a cherub or putto (fig. 172). Flanking the portal is the other pair of relief panels by Tullio Lombardo. The first-floor fenestration repeats the principle of the eastern wing, but here the central panel (where the *instoria* was to go) is blank, faced with plain marble panels. The whole ensemble is crowned by a positive crescendo of gables, the outer pair with statues in niches, the central one highest of all, with the lion of St Mark standing on a prominent cantilevered pedestal. The array of statuary is crowned by the figure of St Mark on the uppermost central gable (figs 158, 173).[77]

Most of the debate over this extraordinary façade has centred on the relative contributions of the two successive masters, Lombardo and Codussi. The overall

208

171   The Scuola Grande di San Marco: the east doorway

172 The Scuola Grande di San Marco; detail showing the keystone to the arch of the main portal

façade alludes to the apostle's shrine in other ways, too, in its sheathing of rich panels of marble, and in the complex composition of the main central gable, with its detached columns. Other elements on the first floor generally attributed to Codussi are the windows to the *albergo* as well as the pair that light the chapter hall. If this attribution is correct, then Codussi was effectively responsible for most of the first floor, although he was still strongly constrained by the complexities of the work of Lombardo directly below, and also presumably by the desire of the Scuola to have the façade completed in a consistently rich manner.[78]

The façade is thus composed of two unequal elements, both of which are symmetrically arranged within themselves. The larger element is focused on the tall, elaborately detailed portal. Bon's relief panel is mounted inside the boldly sculpted form of the projecting gable, itself supported by freestanding columns of marble standing on pairs of superimposed pedestals. When inspected closely, however, this whole composition is something of a hybrid assemblage. The relief panels and the figure of Charity were salvaged from the earlier building, while the two columns, with their very short shafts and tall complex bases and plinths, are themselves also 'recycled' elements from another, earlier structure. Although there were recent precedents in Venice for such tall plinths (and comparatively short columns), such as the equally inventive examples at San Zaccaria, it was clearly something of a test of ingenuity to assemble these truncated shafts to form part of a suitably imposing overall composition.[79]

ICONOGRAPHY

The dedication, function and social role of the Scuola determined all the main elements in the façade's rich iconography. Dedication to the Republic's patron saint took precedence over all other imagery, and, as at the Porta della Carta, he is represented here in more than one manifestation. In his role as patron of the Serenissima Mark is represented by the large figure of the winged lion, high in the centre of the west part of the façade, directly over the entrance portal (fig. 174). He carries the open book with its inscription, all of which imagery forms the official universal symbol of the Republic itself. (We need to record here that the present carving is a nineteenth-century replacement, with reversed orientation; the original orientation, facing left, was the same as that on the Porta della Carta and the Arsenale gate.) Within the main portal, St Mark appears in his more specific role, as patron of this particular Scuola, in the relief panel showing him bless-

design, and the detailing of the lowermost order, is the work of Pietro and his sons (as well as Buora), so that Codussi's contribution was effectively confined to the completion of the first floor and the uppermost features. There is little about the façade that is strongly Codussian, and much that is strongly Lombardesque, although among those few features that do appear markedly Codussian are the strong fluted Corinthian pilasters to the first floor and the second entablature, which is more architectonic and disciplined than the lower one. Also attributable to Codussi are the semicircular gables, familiar features in his œuvre from both San Michele and San Zaccaria, but which could just as easily have been inspired by the façade of San Marco itself, also dedicated to the Republic's patron. Here at the Scuola they are more intricate and less bold than the great crowning gable at San Zaccaria, although they are, of course, rising from a richer, more fussily detailed façade that was in essence the work of Lombardo; such a treatment was clearly more appropriate here. The

173 The Scuola Grande di San Marco: upper part of the western section of the façade, by Mauro Codussi. The arrangement of semicircular gables has echoes not only of San Michele and San Zaccaria but of San Marco itself

174 The Scuola Grande di San Marco: the winged lion on the west part of the façade, after the restoration of 2004–5

175 The Scuola Grande di San Marco: lion tondo on the eastern part of the façade

defender of the faith of the Scuola (and, by extension, the Republic), representing the *amor proximi* of the Evangelist, as we might say, as opposed to the winged lion elsewhere on the façade, which represents the spiritual defence of the same institutions, that is, the *amor dei*.[81]

The patron appears in human form, too, in several locations on the façade. Not only is he naturally the central figure in the relief panel over the main doorway, but is also represented in the two ground-floor bas-reliefs on the eastern part of the façade, usually attributed to Pietro's son Tullio. These illusionistic panels represent Mark healing the Alexandrian cobbler Anianus (fig. 176), and the Baptism of Anianus. Following our analysis of the symbolism of the two representations of the leonine form, both divine and terrestrial, we can draw a parallel interpretation in the case of these two bas-reliefs, as Sohm has perceptively observed. They again symbolise the two

ing the *confratelli*, a theme adopted elsewhere (for example, at San Giovanni Evangelista), with the appropriate patron in a similar composition. This format was well established, and had been used at the Carità as early as 1345, and at the Misericordia in the same period.[80]

In yet another manifestation, the patron is represented by the two stone lions flanking the main portal, and forming the focal points of the two false perspective relief panels. Not strictly Marcian, such an arrangement – less three-dimensionally fictive, however – can also be seen at the Arsenale, where a traditional martial motif was revived in a highly appropriate context. At the Scuola, though, they are – equally appropriately – rather less martial, more restrained and dignified. The final leonine form is the powerfully modelled tondo on the right side of the façade, in the very centre of the *albergo* wing, and carved by Viellmo (Guglielmo) da Carona in 1495, almost certainly as part of Codussi's overall composition (fig. 175). The precedent was perhaps Bon's tondo at the Porta della Carta, although there Mark is in human form, as the Evangelist.

None of these last three lions, the two flanking the portal and that in the tondo, is of the Marcian winged type, but instead are naturalistic beasts; in medieval iconography, the lion is also associated with the Resurrection, and thus draws attention to the quasi-ecclesiastical nature of the Scuola, particularly the great chapter hall, in which masses were conducted. The patronal link is clear enough, however, and we can also regard them as practical, physical versions of the

176 The Scuola Grande di San Marco: detail of one of the relief panels by Tullio Lombardo: *St Mark Healing the Cobbler Anianus*, 1489–90

177   The Scuola Grande di San Marco: detail of the east doorway and frieze, after the restoration of 2004–5

facets of the guiding principles of the Scuola. First, practical material assistance (*amor proximi*) is offered by Mark healing Anianus, whose hand had been injured while working at his craft. In the second panel we see the reception of the cobbler into the Church by his conversion and baptism by Mark, the representation of *amor dei*.

There are a number of curious aspects to these relief panels, the most prominent of which is the relationship between the carved figures and the illusionistic perspective of their fictive context. In both cases, the figures are crowded into one lower corner of the panel and appear quite out of scale with the much larger fictive frame behind them. Given the widespread recycling of materials in Venice in this period (reused columns, capitals and so on), it is highly tempting to conclude that this was some kind of ad hoc composition, an attempt to reconcile elements apparently ill-coordinated with each other. At the time, these panels seem to have been unique in the city, and thus probably represent something of an experiment on Tullio's part. His work at the Arca (shrine) of the Santo in Padua (1500–05 and 1520–25) shows that he was later to develop the format in a very much more refined manner. At the Scuola, therefore, perhaps the board was happy to indulge Tullio with this rather daring experimentation to further its image as a source of enlightened patronage.[82]

The relocation of the salvaged figure of Charity directly above the entrance represents not only the physical continuity of the Scuola itself (reborn, phoenix-like and thus 'resurrected' from its own ashes), but also the continuity of its essential functions, one of which, again, the practising of *amor proximi*, is represented by Charity, its prominence emphasising this vital role.[83]

The façade incorporates other pictorial representations, some of which have precise iconographic significance. Among the most prominent are the six relief panels on the plinths to the entrance portal, now badly weathered. The three to the left of the doorway represent the Passion of Christ; in the first we see three putti about to sacrifice a lamb, while in the second an altar can be discerned, with the flame prepared on top of it. In the third panel four putti (perhaps representing the evangelists) remove the container of the flame at the end of the rite (fig. 178). The three panels on the right side are less clear, although one interpretation is the triumph of humility over greed and avarice, an appropriate theme for a confraternity in which all members were theoretically equal, and worked towards a common good.[84]

213

178　The Scuola Grande di San Marco: detail showing the relief panel on the plinth of the main portal

The portal itself is flanked by two richly carved pilasters. On the top of one is the figure of a pelican, another symbol of charity, while on the top of the other is a phoenix, again representing the rise of the Scuola itself from its own ruins; St Mark, too, was associated with miracles such as the raising of the dead. Finally, above the two imposts of the porch are two large stone figures of saints. They have been identified as St Peter Martyr and St Dominic, the latter a natural association with the adjacent Dominican friary of Santi Giovanni e Paolo. St Peter Martyr was also a Dominican, and there was a chapel dedicated to him in the adjacent church.[85]

Conclusory Note

The rebuilding of the Scuola took about a decade, and it is useful to relate the period of its reconstruction to the careers of the principal masters involved. Pietro Lombardo had begun Santa Maria dei Miracoli four years earlier, and the church was largely completed at the time of his appointment at the Scuola in 1489. His monument to Doge Pasquale Malipiero in the adjacent church of Santi Giovanni e Paolo had been carved some years previously, although that to Pietro Mocenigo was more recent, completed around 1481. His third ducal monument, that to Niccolò Marcello, may have barely been finished by the time that the Scuola began its rebuilding programme.[86] But it was certainly the successful completion of the Miracoli, Lombardo's most substantial work of architecture to date, that had led to his appointment here.

The Scuola's second master, Codussi, had long completed his own first dazzling work in Venice, San Michele, while his equally startling gleaming white campanile for San Pietro in Castello was itself being constructed during the first stages of work at the Scuola.[87] More influential and relevant here, though, was San Zaccaria, where Mauro had replaced the deceased Gambello in 1483, embarking on the last stage of an important but difficult and sensitive project. It was the confident way in which he tackled this task that eventually led to his replacing Lombardo at the Scuola Grande di San Marco in 1490 – by which time San Zaccaria itself was virtually complete – and where he was to remain until 1495.[88]

What conclusions can be drawn as to the overall philosophy of the Scuola towards the design and construction process? The master builder, Griguol, was in post on 7 August 1487, and the master carpenter, Zuan Candio, on 12 March 1488. But there is no record of stonemasons until the apparently urgent appearance of Pietro on 1 May 1489. Griguol was thus the general master builder, responsible for his own craftsmen and the coordination of others.[89]

So much all falls within the traditional organisation of the site, as we have seen on many projects since Marin Contarini's Ca' d'Oro in the 1420s.[90] Despite the size and scale of the new Scuola, Griguol was no *proto* and it seems, therefore, that Lombardo was brought in as a sort of quasi-*proto*, and certainly as designer of the façade. Nevertheless, his role remains ambivalent and elusive. He is documented as definitively involved with the Scuola only for eighteen months, from April 1489, when stone was hurriedly acquired for the columns to the lower hall, until November 1490, when he was apparently abruptly dismissed. In the record of this arbitration, Lombardo is cited in the preamble as *proto*, not alone but collectively, with his 'compagnj' Zuan Buora and Bartolomeo di Domenico. Clearly, all three could not have been *proti* of the fabric, since the whole point of the title of *proto* is as chief master, senior to all the others, and there is no other evidence (such as monthly salaries) to indicate that any of them were. The overall impression of a general uncertainty of approach by the Scuola towards Pietro is heightened when we read, in the text of this same arbitration document, that these three men are referred to not as *proti* but simply as *taiapiera*.[91]

Over these and the following decades almost all the Scuole Grandi were to have difficult, often turbulent relationships with their *proti* or architects. The history of the construction of the Scuola Grande di San Rocco was to become perhaps the most notorious *cause célèbre* in this respect, and was the grand project for which Alessandro Caravia reserved his most splenetic remarks concerning the relative priorities given to charity on one hand and self-glorification on the other;[92] but the chronicle of the Scuola Grande della Misericordia, too, particularly the role of Sansovino in that sad, protracted saga, charts a course of such grandiose, ambitious planning, ineffective budgeting, vacillation and downright unprofessional conduct as to make one wonder why any reasonably successful master would want to have anything to do with such unreliable and inconsistent clients.[93] And this observation leads us back to the fundamental difficulties that affected – indeed, afflicted – all the reconstruction projects of the Scuole Grandi until the middle of the next century. Their constitutions were consciously modelled on that of the Republic itself, and, as we know, the Republic abhorred individual concentration of power, almost all decisions being made by committees large or small.

The Scuole Grandi, too, had their *banche*, their *provveditori sopra la fabbrica*, their Guardian Grande; as Francesco Sansovino remarked when his *Venetia, città nobilissima* was published in 1581, each one was almost a republic in miniature.[94] Their fundamental difficulty, though, was that every twelve months most of the senior decision-makers were replaced by others, in an annual exercise of 'musical *banche*'. Continuity and consistency of policy were therefore extremely difficult, if not impossible, to achieve. In May 1489, for example, when Pietro Lombardo was given 100 ducats to acquire stone for the *androne*, the Guardian Grande was Niccolò Rizzo; a year later, when the crisis over Lombardo's work broke, there was a new Guardian Grande, Alvise de' Dardani, who, with his *banca*, seems to have had quite different ideas as to whether or not Lombardo was indeed following the approved *desegnio*.

When this dispute did arise, the Scuola turned for guidance to the two most prominent masters in the city, other than Lombardo himself; and it does seem that they finally learned an important lesson from the termination of Pietro's contract. Although the Scuola continued to have the benefit and continuity of the highly experienced Griguol (who remained on site for eight years), he was a 'mere' builder, unsuitable to be awarded the role of *proto*. Indeed, when Codussi was appointed, it was the first time in the Scuola's history that they were to employ a permanent, salaried *proto*, providing guaranteed supervision and continuity.[95]

Chapter Ten

THE PALAZZO DUCALE AFTER 1483:
RIZZO AND LOMBARDO

Much of the architectural history of Venice in the late fifteenth and early sixteenth centuries was defined by acts of God, which were far more influential – indeed, pivotal – in the redevelopment of the city than were any conscious long-term policies on the part of the Signoria or the Council of Ten. Venice was indeed transformed by stages into a great imperial capital, but it is salutary to remind ourselves of the underlying reasons for some of the more important transformations of the Renaissance. Although occasional earthquakes inflicted significant damage (in our period, notably those of 1425 and 1512), and from time to time a disastrous flood ruined the stocks of the merchants of Rialto, the one calamity that filled the Signoria and the citizens themselves with far more dread than these was fire.[1]

Both of the nerve centres of the city were devastated by fire on at least one occasion. At Rialto the conflagration of 1505 razed the Fondaco dei Tedeschi to the ground, resulting in its urgent and extremely rapid reconstruction.[2] Nine years later, there was to be a far greater disaster, at the end of which barely a building still stood on the entire island of Rialto except the Palazzo dei Camerlenghi and the little church of San Giacometto.[3] At San Marco there had been fires at the Palazzo Ducale in 1474 and 1479, but neither was as serious as that which concerns us here, which was to result in the first fully Renaissance element at the palace, the rebuilt east wing of Antonio Rizzo.[4]

On the morning of 14 September 1483 the sacristan of the little private chapel of the doge extinguished the candles after morning mass, and left the chapel empty for the rest of the day. At about five o'clock, one of the candles, which had not been fully extinguished, fell over and thus began the conflagration. It spread to the ducal audience chamber and thence to the Sala del Mappamondo; eventually the whole of the northern part of the east wing onto the Rio di Palazzo, including the ducal apartments, was destroyed. The southern parts of this wing were not damaged, though, since they were separated from the northern section by a small *cortile*, which the fire did not cross.[5]

The indefatigable Marin Sanudo provides us with a contemporary footnote:

> The following morning the doge went to live in Ca' Duodo, which is on the other side of the *rio*, opposite the Palazzo del Doge, and a wooden bridge, covered, and closed at the sides with windows, was built from the upper gallery of Ca' Duodo. By the bridge one could go from the Camera del Doge [in the palace] to the house where he was staying. The Collegio gathered in the aforesaid camera to hold audience. To *ser* Alvise and Tomà Duodo the Signoria agreed to pay 100 ducats a year as rent for the house.[6]

The losses were therefore restricted to the northernmost of the three blocks that had occupied the eastern

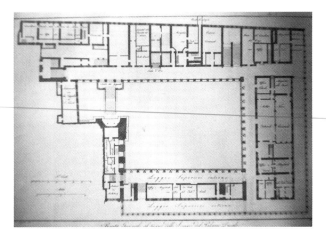

180　The Palazzo Ducale: plan at the level of the first-floor *logge* (from Cicognara, Diedo and Selva)

edge of the site since the time of Doge Ziani in the 1170s. This block had a private staircase, connecting the ducal apartments directly with San Marco, giving secure access for services. The block had extended south for rather less than half of the total length of this east wing. At its southern end was the small *cortile* noted above, and south again was the block containing the hall of the Senate on the upper floor. Further south again there was a small inlet of water or *cavanna*, and then finally the massive back wall of the Molo wing, rebuilt after 1340, and within which was the great hall of the Maggior Consiglio (fig. 180).

The final decision on the reconstruction of the ducal apartment block was taken by the Senate; it was the Senate, too, that directly appointed its architect, Antonio Rizzo. However, it was the Serenissima Signoria, the highest council of all, that issued instructions to the Provveditori al Sal to fund and supervise the recon-

181　The Palazzo Ducale: detail plan of the ducal apartments (from Cicognara, Diedo and Selva)

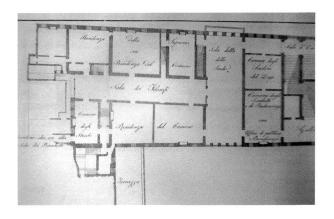

struction. First, though, a debate had to be held as to the nature and extent of the new works.

As was also to be the case with the disastrous fires in the latter part of the sixteenth century (in 1574 and 1577), the debate was lively, with widely divergent views and philosophies expressed by the Senators. The fire had taken place at a singularly unfortunate time in respect of funding large-scale, expensive public works. The Republic was deeply involved in the War of Ferrara, and faced a formidable alliance of Ercole d'Este (duke of Ferrara), the marquis of Mantua, the Florentines and the Milanesi, the last under the rule of Ludovico Sforza. In the event, the war was of fairly brief duration, and a peace was signed in the following summer of 1484, according to the terms of which Venice increased its Terraferma empire still further by the acquisition of Rovigo and the Polesine at the expense of the Este. Nevertheless, the immediate aftermath of the fire seemed an unpropitious time for acts of urban grandeur, as contemporary records of these debates attest.

The majority in the Palazzo Ducale favoured a fairly modest reconstruction. As Sanudo again recorded,

> it was decided in *pregadi* [the Senate] on the [date missing] to build the palazzo on three storeys so that it would look most beautiful, and that the funding shall come from the *oficio dil sal*; other members of the Collegio wanted only to rebuild the said palace as it was before, spending only 6,000 ducats, but ser Niccolò Trevisan, who was Savio da Terraferma, was of the opinion that the Signoria should buy the houses on the other side of the *rio*, and there build the palace and habitation of the doge, and the palace on this side would then be altered to provide public offices and not the private accommodation of the doge; but this opinion was not admitted (fig. 181).[7]

Domenico Malipiero records the debate in very similar terms: 'the majority did not wish to spend more than 6,000 ducats on repairs because of the *stretezza* ["tightness"] of the times; but later it was resolved to build completely anew'.[8]

It was six more months before an important decision was made regarding the money for the project, but on 8 March 1484 the Signoria made the Provveditori al Sal responsible in principle for funding and supervision of the works.[9] A couple of months later, it was conclusively decided not to pursue the more ambitious proposal of Trevisan, but instead to rehouse the earlier elements of accommodation on the same site, on three storeys instead of the previous two, to provide more space. Proposals were also invited as to the form and appearance of the new block; we have no details as to the originators of these 'models', which may not have been physical models, but perhaps design ideas or preliminary drawings.[10] We now come to the crucial appointment of Antonio Rizzo, who was in his new post by the early summer of 1484, although the Republic's choice of Rizzo has seemed to many later writers more than a little unusual in view of his career up to that date.

Antonio Rizzo

As John McAndrew has observed,[11] 1484 was not only a difficult year in financial terms in which to embark on a major new construction project, it was also far from ideal in the architectural history of the city. There was no single outstanding master architect, no experienced *proto* to whom this most prestigious of projects could be more or less automatically given. The two most notable masters in the city were neither – for different reasons – ideally suited. Mauro Codussi had completed the new church at San Michele a few years earlier, but was still comparatively young; he was also unable to give the palace his undivided attention. In August 1482 he had signed a contract with the patriarch for the completion of the campanile of the cathedral of San Pietro in Castello;[12] and on 12 June 1483, only three months before the fire, he had been appointed *proto* to San Zaccaria. Codussi thus had as many commitments as he could deal with, while the Signoria needed a full-time *proto* to devote his energies to the new wing. Mauro's work in Venice to date had also been daringly innovative and he was unlikely to have found universal acceptance among the gerontocracy of the Senate. It is stimulating to imagine, however, what might have resulted had Mauro been appointed instead of Rizzo.[13]

The other outstanding master was Pietro Lombardo. He had been in the city for a few years longer than Codussi and at around 50 was also at least five years older. He had completed San Giobbe in the early 1470s, and by 1474 had established a flourishing workshop. He had also carved the official monuments to two deceased doges, Pasquale Malipiero and Niccolò Marcello; more recently still, he had carved the highly praised monument to Pietro Mocenigo, completed probably in 1481.[14] Nevertheless, the character of these works gives us an indication why he was probably also considered unsuitable to become *proto*: other than San Giobbe (begun by another, possibly Gambello), they were all works of sculpture rather than architecture. His own

masterpiece, Santa Maria dei Miracoli (fig. 182), had been begun in 1481, but its completion was still some years in the future; the project must also have taken up a great deal of his time. This lack of substantial architectural experience appears to be the chief reason for passing him by in favour of Rizzo, who, however, was himself equally inexperienced. (There is a certain irony, of course, in the choice of Rizzo rather than Lombardo, as the later history of the palace will reveal.)

Rizzo had been born in Verona around 1440, but his career in Venice began about 1465.[15] His involvement at the Palazzo Ducale coincides with the deaths of both Bartolomeo Bon (*circa* 1464 or a little later) and Bon's partner, Pantaleon di Paolo, in 1465. Bon and Pantaleon had had a long association with the palace, and, in particular, with the Foscari colonnade and loggia, with which Rizzo, too, was also to be associated.

Prior to 1484 Rizzo was, like Lombardo, regarded primarily as a sculptor, certainly not an experienced *proto*; indeed, there are no confirmed architectural attributions to him before his appointment at the Palazzo Ducale. His first important works in Venice are the three altars in San Marco dedicated to San Giacomo, San Polo and San Clemente, completed in 1469. A little later, Rizzo carved the two famous statues of *Adam* and *Eve* for the niches on the Arco Foscari. Again, these are small, freestanding works of sculpture, and there is no indication that Rizzo had a larger involvement in the design of the arch as a whole.[16] From the mid-1470s to his appointment as *proto*, however, Rizzo's sculptural output was prolific. One of his most outstanding works is the tomb of Niccolò Tron, the insignificance of whose brief reign (1471–3) is belied by Rizzo's superb funerary monument in the Frari, made in the years 1476–80.

To mitigate – indirectly – this serious flaw in his candidacy, we know that Rizzo had distinguished himself in the service of the Republic. On 9 January 1484, a few months after the fire, the chief Provveditore al Sal, Domenego Trevisan, was instructed by the Signoria to take testimonies from various people regarding Rizzo's actions at the siege of Scutari, a town in Albania where in 1478 the Republic had attempted to hold out against the Turkish invaders.[17] This was the second time that Scutari had been besieged, the first being in 1473, when the attackers were successfully repulsed. Five years later the Venetians were surrounded again, and this time the citadel was eventually lost. Rizzo distinguished himself during this second siege, as the testimony of two Franciscan friars (Fra Alvise di Niccolò and Fra Zuanne di Zorzi) makes clear: 'Rizzo was at the second siege, where he was seen continuously doing his patriotic

duty in all of the *batarie*, and the said *maestro* Antonio was seen at the bombards, making stone balls and whatever was necessary'. Rizzo himself testified that he had been a 'taiapiera da bombarda' during the term of Alvixe Querini, the Conte or governor; revealingly, too, Domenego Trevisan testified that Rizzo had been a 'salaried stonemason of San Marco', in other words, he had already been in the service of the Republic back in the capital on a regular basis.[18]

Rizzo was injured in the siege ('wounded on more than one occasion', as Trevisan records), and on 12 February it was decided that he should receive a modest war pension 'in recognition of having deported himself faithfully'. He was to be given 'together with his sons, one ducat per month from this office, every month, for their provisions, which will continue for twenty years . . . beginning on 17 January just passed', that is, of 1484.[19] It seems likely that this recognition of honourable service had some bearing on Rizzo's appointment to the post, for which he was less than ideally suited.[20]

Rizzo was appointed shortly after the decision in May 1484 to reconstruct the palace on the original site. We have no precise date, but he was given a new title, *proto dil* palazzo, and a salary of 100 ducats per year, the same income that Gambello had received at San Zaccaria.[21] Sadly, we have no detailed accounts of the reconstruction works; ironically again, they were destroyed in yet another later fire at the palace. Our knowledge of progress is thus very sketchy, and effectively confined to a series of *terminazioni* and other decisions by the Signoria regarding expenditure on the project. One such early decision was the Signoria's decree, on 10 February 1485, regarding medium-term funding. The *terminazione* ordered that, of the 900 ducats allocated every month from the Provveditori's coffers to pay for repairs to the *lidi* and the sea defences, 500 ducats were now to be diverted to help pay for the rebuilding works.[22]

Nearly a year later, the matter of the doge's own temporary accommodation required attention. Doge Giovanni Mocenigo had died on 4 November 1485, but his successor, Marco Barbarigo, had a very large family that could not all be accommodated within the Duodo house across the canal. The Provveditori were therefore instructed to locate a larger house, which they found at Santa Maria Zobenigo, which was then rented out by the Commissioners of the estate of Ca' Dandolo to the nobleman Lorenzo Venier, for 70 ducats per year. The 'reverend monsignor' Venier was primate of San Marco, but he confirmed that he was patriotically 'content to concede the said house for the use of the prince'.[23]

We have some indications on progress at the palace. Much later, Sansovino was to claim that it was during Marco Barbarigo's brief reign (he died on 14 August 1486, to be succeeded by his brother) that the façade of the new wing was begun: 'fece fabricar la faccia del Palazzo Ducale, che guarda sopra la Scala scoperta di marmo', that is, the façade above the Scala dei Giganti.[24] Contemporary records, however, reveal that the picture is not as straightforward as that.

THE SCALA DEI GIGANTI

On 11 November 1485, only a week before the coronation of the new doge, Marco Barbarigo, the Maggior Consiglio had voted on some significant alterations to the ritual of the investiture of the new Serene Prince; it was this decision that led to the construction of Rizzo's new staircase, which was built specifically to form a platform for the new rituals.

The Maggior Consiglio's decree explains the reasons for these revisions:

> The principal insignia of our most Serene Doge is the ducal cap [*corno*]; to give it due recognition, he should receive it publicly and solemnly, rather than in a hidden manner, without any further ceremony, as has been the custom until now . . . It was therefore proposed that when the future Prince and his successors are elected, and they accept the standard of San Marco at the altar, and the doge will be brought through the Piazza and into the palace, he will ascend these stairs to accept the oath of fealty, immediately after which the veil will be placed on the head of the doge by the most junior councillor and the ducal *corno* will be placed by the most senior councillor, saying these words: 'Accipe coronam Ducatus Venetiarum'.[25]

A manuscript in the Correr Museum from the same year records that the new doge was crowned at the top of a flight of stairs ('et insta lordene decreto in la sua electione in sopra la scala del ditto palazzo aceptado . . . la sua promissione'),[26] where the veil was placed by Zuanne da Lezze and the *corno* by Piero Memo, exactly as prescribed by the new *terminazione*.

However, it was clearly impossible to have constructed a permanent new stair in the mere eight days between the decree and Barbarigo's coronation, and even a temporary one would have been difficult. It is probable, therefore, that the old external stair (long since lost) in the south-east corner of the main *cortile*, which gave direct access into the Maggior Consiglio,

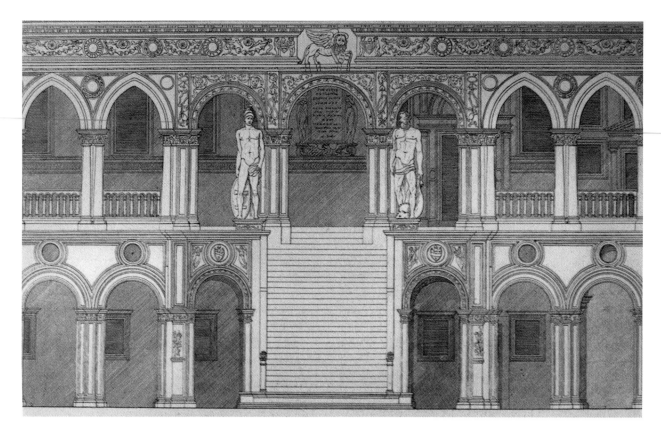

183   The Scala dei Giganti: detail of elevation towards the Foscari colonnade (Cicognara, Diedo and Selva)

was used for the purpose until Rizzo's new stair was completed. Marin Sanudo confirms that the rite took place 'at the top of the stone staircase' in his chronicle of 1493.[27] Barbarigo himself, however, was to sit on the ducal throne for only a few months, until August 1486, so there was still insufficient time to complete the new stair in time for the coronation of his brother and successor, Agostin. Although begun in 1484, therefore, the date of completion of Rizzo's stair remains unknown. By the time that Sanudo wrote his chronicle in 1493 there had not yet been another ducal coronation since that of Agostin Barbarigo; in the following year, though, another contemporary account from Canon Pietro Casola records that 'a new flight of steps was [still] being built, a stupendous and costly work' (fig. 183).[28] This was indeed Rizzo's new stair, and it must have been virtually complete by then, since Casola saw the doge, Agostin Barbarigo, standing at the head of the stairs, 'and he then went into the palace, to his own apartments'. It was in use, therefore, not yet for ducal coronations, but certainly for other state occasions.[29] And by the time of the coronation of Barbarigo's own successor, Leonardo Loredan, in 1501, it had been completed for some time.[30]

Function and Symbolism

The principal ceremonial axis into the Palazzo Ducale was already in existence by the 1460s, with the completion of the Foscari loggia and arch. This axis had its origins in the Piazzetta outside, with Bon's Porta della Carta, and the purpose of the Foscari loggia was to draw visitors into the heart of the palace, not simply in the practical sense, by providing a sheltered route, but also in a symbolic sense. The loggia and arch 'point' directly towards the ducal apartments, and the audience chamber that would be the goal for important visitors.[31]

The Scala combines several functions related to, and forming a continuation of, those of the Porta della Carta. The whole composition, therefore, the Porta, the colonnade, arch and stair, needs to be considered as an ensemble, as the collective embodiment of the developing concepts of the Republic and its head of state. Triumphal arch, axis and stairs: three of the most powerful elements in our spatial vocabulary. As we have seen, the Porta itself embodies the symbolism of the Republic as the seat of justice together with its link with the patron, Mark, and the parallel concept of

184　The Foscari colonnade, towards the Scala dei Giganti

divine justice. We then have the axis, the spacious colonnade, drawing us into the nucleus of power (fig. 184). Finally, framed in the last bay of the Arco Foscari, we have a violent contrast between darkness and light, and before us, almost precisely on axis, we see the staircase, bringing in the third dimension, that of height, into what so far has been a horizontal progression. Progressing down this route today, one is impressed by the boldness and drama of this spatial sequence; the final vista, particularly in afternoon sunlight, is quite literally dazzling, as we see the stairs breaking forward from the gleaming white stone mass of the *rio* wing behind. It does not take a great deal of imagination to recreate the splendid scene of the ducal coronation, with the crowd of dignitaries below, straining their eyes upwards towards the ritual (figs 179, 185).

This was almost an apotheosis, the crowning of the Serene Prince against the backdrop of the great new palace, the balcony almost an altar, and the whole spectacle forming a powerful development of the iconographic and symbolic role of the doge in relation to the people of the Republic.[32]

The detail of the Scala is rich and complex, incorporating a good deal of carefully chosen imagery. This imagery is essentially imperial, a reflection of the perception of the Republic as it had developed over the previous eighty years: no longer an aquatic empire based on Mediterranean trade, the Republic was one of the principal territorial powers of Italy, and hence could more closely identify itself with the territorial empire of ancient Rome. This classical empire had itself been based on land, on armies, on terrestrial

223

185   The Scala dei Giganti: detail at the top of the stair, flanked by Sansovino's two 'giants' (in fact Mercury and Neptune), 1566

power and communications, in contrast with Venice's traditional empire, whose own imagery essentially revolved around ships, and isolated rocky fortresses scattered over the eastern Mediterranean. And so here, on the Scala, we see the full range of classical symbols of empire: figures of winged victories, shields, helmets, Roman tunics; and although there are also less militaristic classical references – cornucopia, vases, candelabra – there are also the most overt, direct Roman references found anywhere in Venice up to this time: SPQR (*Senatus Populusque Romanus*, the Senate and People of Rome) coupled with the modernised SPQV (*Senatus Populusque Venetus*), for example, an unequivocal evocation of the Republic as descendant of ancient Rome.

A great deal of this overt Roman imperial symbolism reflects the personal *imprimatur* of Barbarigo himself. Along with the direct – even flagrant – appropriation of the 'SPQR', there are other, more personalised abbreviations: ABDV, for example, *Agustinus Barbadico Dux Venetiarum*; and, more tellingly still, the same 'ABDV' but this time with 'FF' (*fieri fecit*) added to it: 'Agostin Barbarigo, doge of Venice, had this work constructed'. Taken collectively, these motifs, symbols and abbrevia-

tions push still further the limits of personalisation (as well as classicisation) of the ducal office as they had been developed earlier by Francesco Foscari. Rather like Foscari, Barbarigo was arrogant and ambitious, and his rise to the throne of San Marco can only be described as meteoric. He was elected a Procurator of San Marco on 27 November 1485, within days of his brother's election to the ducal throne. Only nine months later, immediately on the death of Marco, he was elected doge.

The affixes on the Scala dei Giganti are no mere statements of record ('This work was erected during the reign of . . .'), but were intended to reflect directly the power and prestige of a man who technically was still considered *primus inter pares* among the Venetian nobility (fig. 186). Despite his princely pomposity, however, Barbarigo did not lack apologists during his reign; after the nominal Venetian victory at Fornovo (July 1495), during which far more Venetian troops were lost than French, Marin Sanudo ingratiatingly entitled him 'the new Augustus', while the poet Ventura di Malgate matched this hyperbole with 'prince of my new Rome'.[33]

Barbarigo's later career, though, offers a salutary lesson in the use and abuse of power; by the time of

186 The Scala dei Giganti: detail showing the arms of the Barbarigo and winged Victories in the spandrels

his death in 1501 he had become intensely unpopular. As usual, an inquest was held to investigate his conduct during his term of office; when the results were made known, Sanudo rapidly acknowledged his own errors of judgement: in his diary entry for 15 December 1501 he refers to the oration of the inquisitor Antonio Loredan, who denounced the 'tante horende, abominabile et spaventose manzarie et extorsion dil doxe morto, vendition di justitia, robamenti de le nostre camere et di nostri subditi' ('so much dreadful, abominable and fearful corruption and extortion by the former doge, the sale of judgements, the stealing [of funds] from our own chambers and from our own subjects'). There was a great deal more in the same vein, in a speech that lasted four hours, all of it listened to in respectful silence.[34]

Construction

The plan of the Scala, as is well known, is not precisely orthogonal to the façade of the Palazzo, since this would have prevented a precise alignment with the Arco Foscari below. Instead, the plan is skewed slightly towards the south, so that the bottom of the Scala is precisely in the centre of the arch. The refined way in which this is achieved is a triumph of the resolution of the organic with the formal.[35]

The stair rises in a single straight flight, with one half landing, the lower flight having fourteen treads, the upper thirteen; the spacious top balcony extends to left

and right to occupy three bays of the first-floor loggia of the *rio* wing of the palace. Such a freestanding stair is very unusual in Venetian architecture, where external stairs traditionally rise against one wall of a building, and are supported by an arcade on the outer face. Almost all stairs in private palaces were of this type, as were those earlier stairs (now lost) in the courtyard of the Palazzo Ducale. A perspective drawing by Jacopo Bellini (British Museum, London) is remarkably similar in its general configuration to the Scala dei Giganti, and may have been used by Rizzo in designing the present stair (fig. 187).

The construction materials are also particularly rich, notably the cladding to the outer flank walls, which are finished with grey, white and pink *breccia* (Brescia) marble; the lesenes are of Carrara marble, while the risers of the steps are decorated with complex niello decoration with a black impasto. Some elements may even have been gilded, such as the bas-reliefs of the lesenes (fig. 188).

There is almost no documentary evidence on the execution of the Scala. A record from 10 April 1489, concerning a specification for work to be carved by Zorzi Gruato, and which certainly relates to a rich, refined staircase, may refer to Rizzo's stairs, although recent opinions differ sharply. Its dating is approximately correct, and if it is not, in fact, for this stair then its location cannot be identified today.[36]

187 Drawing of a staircase by Jacopo Bellini, perhaps the model for the Scala dei Giganti

188   The Scala dei Giganti: detail showing relief decoration to one of the supporting columns

Evidence of Rizzo's progress on the new wing is also sparse, although a few documents shed light on one or two aspects of this important project. On 12 October 1486 the Collegio debated a *supplicatione* made by Rizzo regarding the employment of Lombard masons at the palace. The statutes of the masons' guild then forbade foreign masters working in the city the full privileges of setting up their own workshops, and they were only allowed to work on a day-wage basis. Rizzo, who in the plea is described as 'ingenioso opifice . . . Architectore Palatij', was concerned that this discriminatory statute was denying him the masters necessary to expedite progress, and he urged the Collegio to waive it. His plea was successful, with the result that Lombard masters were now permitted to run their own shops, and, perhaps more importantly, could train their own apprentices for the future: 'ipsi lapicide tenere possint famulos'. This dispensation, however, was intended solely to expedite works on the palace itself ('usque quo perfinita erit fabricha Palatij') rather than serving a broader purpose in opening the Venetian labour market to others.[37]

A year later the Signoria expressed concern at the apparent lack of careful control over expenditure, not simply on the east wing, but also in 'voltj, botege e palazzo e preson'. They issued a decree on 22 November 1487 that the *proto* could not consent to any 'agreement, contract or invoice' ('acordo, marcado over poliza') without first agreeing the extent and cost of the work in the company of three 'or at least two' of the Provveditori al Sal, who were to 'diligently examine, together with the *proto*, and any other expert who may be called, the costs of . . . both goods and of craftsmanship'.[38] The *poliza* (bill or invoice) had to be countersigned by the Provveditori and by the *proto* himself. A daunting fine of 100 ducats was to be levied on those who failed to follow this procedure. Whether it was, in fact, diligently followed seems very doubtful, as we will see below.

Four years later again, Rizzo succeeded in negotiating a salary rise for himself. He had now been *proto* at the palace for seven years, although his original remuneration of 100 ducats had already been increased once, to a generous 125 ducats. In October 1491, however, he launched a heartfelt plea to the Provveditori, claiming that he could not continue at such a level ('el non puol viver ni far dote a la sua vechieza ni a la fameia sua'), and further, that he had had to close his own workshop, since the demands at the palace were such that he had neither the time nor the energy to maintain it; but that, had he been able to do so, his income would have been three times that which he was currently receiving from the Republic. In order that he could continue at the palace 'cum buon cuor et animo' ('with a good heart and spirit') it was unanimously agreed by the Provveditori that his salary should be raised to 200 ducats, an extraordinarily generous salary, considerably higher than that awarded to his successors.[39]

The Signoria, though, remained constantly concerned about the costs of the works. The Dieci, meeting on 16 December 1495, recorded that in the three years to that date a total of just over 1,386 lire *di grossi* had been spent on the reconstruction, that is, 13,860 ducats or around 86,000 lire *di piccoli*. A ceiling was now put on future outgoings, which were not to exceed 100 ducats per month or 1,200 over a year, without the express advance authorisation of the Dieci. All of those concerned were bound by this decree: the Provveditori, the secretaries of the *soprastanti* (supervisors) and, of course, the *proto* himself.[40]

This new cost ceiling represented barely a quarter of the expenses that had been incurred over the previous three years, and was a dramatic indication of the level of reduction now considered necessary. In the following spring, both Domenico Malipiero and Marin Sanudo noted the results of this marked reduction in expenditure; in both cases they attributed the reduced activity to the costs of the current war with Naples. Interestingly, too, although both diarists also refer to the start of the construction of the Torre dell'Orologio in June 1486, neither of them suggests that the cost of the tower itself might have diverted funds from the Palazzo. Nevertheless, Sanudo bluntly records that 'la fabrica dil palazzo, per queste guerre era alquanto suspesa', 'because of the wars, work on the Palazzo is effectively suspended'.[41]

Only a week later, the Dieci met again. They now decreed the elimination of several posts and salaries formerly paid by the Provveditori al Sal, and also revoked some posts that had been revived since 1489. The record of their meeting is particularly valuable since it indicates the number of men employed at the time on the Palazzo Ducale. The Provveditori had formerly had a wages budget of 60 ducats per month, from which seven men had been paid; numbers were now to be reduced to just four masons, Alvise de Domenego, Bertuzio, Zuan da Spalato and Michiel Naranza. None was highly paid; Zuan had the highest wage at 24 soldi per day, and all were paid weekly in arrears, on a Saturday.[42] Elsewhere in the palace at the same time, decorations were continuing in the great hall of the Maggior Consiglio. Among those employed (with their salaries) were Giovanni Bellini (5 ducats per month), Alvise Vivarini (5 ducats), Cristoforo da Parma (3 ducats) and four other painters, as well as two shared apprentices.

Yet another effort at tightening up disbursement procedures began only a few weeks later, in March 1496, when the Senate confirmed that the measures theoretically instigated by the Provveditori back in November 1487 – but perhaps never followed – were now to be reintroduced. Henceforth two appointees were to be made from the Provveditori to review and confirm all expenses. It was perhaps as a result of these new fiscal disciplines that Rizzo's fate was to be so dramatically decided.[43]

Antonio Rizzo's remarkable and highly successful career as *proto* of the Palazzo Ducale was to end abruptly. On 5 April 1498 the news broke publicly: he had been investigated and found guilty of the embezzlement of large sums of money destined for the works. Marin Sanudo's diary entry for that date records the scandalous news in rather breathless terms:

> Francesco Foscari and Hironimo Capelo, appointed to examine the accounts . . . had found that mo. Antonio Rizo, *taiapiera*, the master in charge of the construction of the Palazzo for the last 13 years, at a salary of 200 ducats a year, had taken more than 10,000 ducats by recording [in the accounts] more than had actually been spent . . . up to now 97,000 ducats have been spent on the Palace, an incredible sum, but a good part of which has been stolen . . .[44]

As the story is related by Marin's contemporary, Domenico Malipiero, Rizzo, realising that his activities had been discovered, sold his house and fled to Ancona and thence to Foligno, although in the meantime he had been summoned to appear before the Dieci. It is generally believed that he died there shortly afterwards. According to Malipiero, once the news of his death was confirmed, 'everything of his that was found, was sold'.

Pietro Lombardo at the Palazzo Ducale after 1498

By the time of Rizzo's precipitate departure, much had been achieved at the new east wing. Most of the main fabric of this northern section, including the ducal apartments, was probably complete, so that Lombardo's attention was chiefly concentrated on the interior, including a number of very fine fireplaces, which have survived today.[45]

Pietro Lombardo took over the practical running of the site immediately after Rizzo's flight. He was already his deputy, and took over the *de facto* post of *proto* on 6 May, about a month after Rizzo had left,[46] although the appointment was not formally confirmed until the following spring. On 9 March 1499 the Senate decreed that 'since Maistro Antonio Rizo has absented himself from the city . . . it was necessary to provide for the running of the said works, Maistro Piero Lombardo was nominated and substituted . . . who, with great diligence and study has attended to the works since 6 May last'.

Pietro offered to give up his own workshop to attend exclusively to the palace, although he seems to have no more done so in practice than did the other *maestri* in such posts: Giorgio Spavento, for example, who was *proto* to the Procurators of San Marco. Pietro's salary was not as high as the maximum awarded to Rizzo, and was reduced to 120 ducats per year. He was, however, eligible for bonuses or rises if appropriate, on an ad hoc basis. A couple of weeks later, on 21 March, his appointment was ratified by the Dieci, who also confirmed his salary.[47]

Some light is shed on Pietro's responsibilities by an instruction issued by the Signoria on 7 March 1499, a few days before the Senate confirmation of his appointment. The Signoria instructed the Provveditori al Sal to obtain a valuation of repair works in the great hall of the Maggior Consiglio by Giorgio Spavento.[48] Spavento, as *proto* of the Procurators, had responsibility for the maintenance and repair of the buildings around the Piazza and Piazzetta. He had evidently carried out some propping of one corner of the hall, which had 'threatened collapse', as well as 'many other works beyond his normal duties' ('molti altri lavori de piu del suo incanto'). A dispute had arisen over the value of these works, and Rizzo had failed to agree with the three *stimadori* appointed to assess the work. With Rizzo now gone, on 19 July the Signoria confirmed that a new valuation was to be undertaken.[49]

Pietro remained *proto* at the Palazzo Ducale until 1511; he died four years later. The southern part of the new wing (figs 189–92) was structurally complete by 1503, when part of it was roofed with lead, and thereafter he must have been chiefly concerned with internal finishes and fittings. Lombardo and Spavento seem to have worked, if not together then closely parallel in this period. In 1503, for example, Lombardo had been charged with the restoration of the 'palazo vechio', that is, the Molo and Piazzetta wings. These works included some roofing, since the roof was leaking and required four *miera* (4,000 lbs) of lead to repair it;[50] this was

189   The Palazzo Ducale: east wing: the façade to the *cortile*

190   The Palazzo Ducale: east wing: detail of *cortile* façade

191   The Palazzo Ducale: façade towards the Rio di Palazzo

192   The Palazzo Ducale: detail of the façade to the Rio di Palazzo

beyond his normal duties. Four years later again, it was Spavento who was responsible for the construction of the little chapel of San Niccolò, which still stands today next to the eastern apses of San Marco.[51]

The ill-defined extent of the remit of the two masters is rendered even less clear by further records from 1507–8. These works were all within the Palazzo Ducale itself, and included the restoration of benches and windows in the hall of the Maggior Consiglio and works to the audience chamber of the Capi del Consiglio dei Dieci, the Cancelleria and the Pregadi (Senate), areas that we would have expected to have fallen within Pietro's remit.

In 1507 repairs to the prisons were deemed essential: 'it is considered of great importance that the cells and torture chamber are to be strong and secure' ('considerata la grandissima importantia de j cameroti di la Camera del tormento che siano forti e securi'). This work, like most of these other operations, had been begun on the direct instructions of the Dieci, who had assumed more direct power over any building works that had any bearing at all on the security of the state.

We have few references to Lombardo himself in these last few years. Perhaps his age was beginning to render his contributions less effective, and he was about 70 by 1505; this is also perhaps why Spavento was becoming more involved in the east wing. Nevertheless, Pietro remained salaried *proto* until 1511, his enormous skills and experience still perhaps allowing him to make some contribution well into his seventies.

Chapter Eleven

THE TORRE DELL'OROLOGIO:
THE TRIUMPH OF *CIVITAS*

THE CONSTRUCTION OF THE TORRE DELL'OROLOGIO on the north side of the Piazza San Marco was one of the most significant works of improvement in the city centre in the late fifteenth century, combining, as it did, practical value, civic splendour and urban improvement in a single work. It was one of the very few such works within the scope of the present volume (the Arsenale gate is another) that was not the result of a necessary response to a natural disaster, like the fires in the Palazzo Ducale and at the Fondaco dei Tedeschi. Nor was it the replacement of an old, worn-out structure, serving essentially the same function as its predecessor, as, for example, the Molo and Piazzetta wings of the Palazzo Ducale, or the rebuilding of the Procuratie Vecchie. Rather, it was a totally new element in the city's form, a conscious attempt to raise the civic – as opposed to the spiritual or political – status of the heart of the empire.[1]

The relationship between the Piazza and the commercial nucleus of Rialto has always been an important one, and the physical link, the rather randomly jointed collection of streets known as the Mercerie, has been the chief commercial axis of the city since these twin hubs came into existence. Sanudo described the Mercerie (at the time the Torre was being constructed) as 'lined with shops on both sides . . . Here is all the merchandise you can think of, and whatever you ask for is there'. The southernmost of these streets, today called the Merceria dell'Orologio, forms a straight line from

the little *campo* of San Zulian to the north side of the Piazza, very close to the façade of San Marco itself. This Merceria formerly crossed a narrow canal, the Rio di San Basso, which ran parallel to the north side of the Piazza, and which was reclaimed in stages, becoming in turn first the Piscina San Basso, and eventually the present Calle Larga San Marco. The Merceria itself reached the Piazza through an archway, wider than the others, in the long arcade of the original Procuratie Vecchie, the two–storey Byzantine block that occupied the north side of the Piazza.

The Procuratie contained a single storey of accommodation above this ground–floor colonnade, and it continued eastwards a little beyond the present clock tower, as far as a short, narrow alley, the Calle del Pellegrin. It was into this almost endless range of simple, repetitive stilted Byzantine arches that the Torre dell' Orologio was to be inserted.

Despite the modest existing arrangement of a simple archway where the Merceria entered the Piazza, the site had considerable urban and symbolic importance: the point at which the chief commercial artery met the Piazza of the patronal saint, and where quotidian trade gave way to civic and national dignity: an ideal location, therefore, for a civic focus such as the clock tower, which could combine a practical function with the *gravitas* necessary so close to the patronal shrine.

The site faces the façade of San Marco at a fairly acute angle; but from further afield it terminates the

194 San Marco: the Sant'Alipio portal

vista from the Molo and Doge Ziani's columns, where illustrious visitors would be received as they disembarked. On arrival, therefore, the Torre would read as a beacon of *civitas*, with its strong vertical emphasis; the richness of its design, too, would provide a powerful contrast to the simple, functional red–brick shaft of the campanile of San Marco. The arch at the base of the new Torre would form a gateway (a *bocca* or 'mouth') into the teeming commercial heart of the city beyond; from the other direction, that is, proceeding south down the Merceria, the arch frames the great spaces of the Piazza and Piazzetta, with San Marco to the left and the Molo and its columns further beyond. Yet further still could be seen the masts and spars of the fleets moored in the Bacino, from which the Republic's wealth and power derived.

Civic clocks were still fairly rare in this period. In 1410 a small clock had been installed at Rialto, and mechanical clocks themselves had been developed in the late thirteenth century; there was a public clock on the north end of the main façade of San Marco, known as that of Sant'Alipio, as is the north portico (fig. 194). It had been installed in 1384, and was therefore already a century old by the late fifteenth century. The Signoria thus decided – initially, at least – to replace it with a new one, more modern and sophisticated, and doubtlessly more reliable, too. A degree of local rivalry may have had a bearing on this decision: in nearby Padua, now a subject city, a clock had been mounted on the civic tower as early as 1344, the work of Iacopo

Dondi, and it was said to have been the first such civic clock erected in Italy (fig. 195). It had been remade in the years 1427–37 by Giovanni delle Caldiere, and now proudly adorned the tower of Padua's own Piazza della Signoria, surrounded by civic structures. Delle Caldiere's new clock was a complex device, showing not only the hours and days but also the sun, the signs of the zodiac, the phases of the moon and the planets. It still stands today, although directly below it now is Giovanni Maria Falconetto's classical portal, added in 1532. The elaboration and sophistication of this device can hardly have escaped the attentions of the Signoria, and it seems almost inescapable that once the decision had been made, it should seek to emulate the Paduan example.

Construction of the Clock and the Tower

We have a good deal of documentation on the making of the clock and its installation; what we do not have is evidence of the identity of the architect of the tower. Today the design is frequently attributed to Codussi, although on general stylistic grounds rather than more substantial evidence, and it must have been a collaborative effort, since the clock's physical requirements were so specific.

Nevertheless, one important, and overlooked, aspect of the project should be identified at the outset: in 1493 the government decided to approach a master to design and build a new clock, not – at this stage – to be housed within a purpose-built new tower, but simply to replace

195 Detail of the Palazzo del Capitanio, Padua, showing the civic clock (1437) now incorporated into the façade

the old one on the adjacent church. The master clock-maker chosen was Zuan Paolo Rainieri, together with his son, Zuan Carlo, citizens of Reggio Emilia, where they had already made a fine clock for their home town's own Torre Comunale. The new clock for San Marco was to be made in Reggio, and brought to Venice for final assembly.

Rainieri began to incur significant expenses in constructing the new clock after October 1493; on 21 October a Senate *terminazione* instructed the Provveditori al Sal to provide Rainieri with various materials, including 'azzuro e biancho' for pigments, as well as borax and sal ammoniac.[2] In February 1494 it was necessary to procure nearly 200 ducats' worth of copper, tin and iron, which was obtained by Daniele da Prato on behalf of the Captain of Brescia; it was followed by a consignment of 500 pounds of iron in July of the same year, to make the clock's structure. By November, Rainieri already had need of more materials, this time for 'smaltij [enamel], pesa grecha [?]', borax and 'refined tin', which was obtained by Carlo Valier, the Signoria's treasurer, at a total cost of 88 ducats.[3]

During the summer of 1495 consignments of lead and tin were again sent from Venice to Reggio, while in the following February Zuan Carlo acknowledged receipt of 100 ducats' worth of materials, 'to gild and silver the clock and other items in connection with it' ('per dorar e innarzontar l'horologio et altre cose pertinenti a quello'). By now, the work must have been almost complete, since gilding and silvering would have been the last operations of all.

It was only now, however, two years after Rainieri's appointment, that the Venetian Senate decided that, instead of simply replacing the old Sant'Alipio clock, a new tower would be built to house it instead. The Senate met on 3 November 1495; the opening words of their decision confirm that the manufacture of the clock itself was indeed far advanced: 'Essendo quasi infornito lo degno et honoratissimo horologio de esser posto sopra la piazza de san marcho' ('Since the noble and most honorable clock, which is to be positioned in the Piazza San Marco, is now almost finished . . .').[4] But the Senate was now aware of the wishes of the doge and Signoria, noting that 'since our Procurators of the church of San Marco are in agreement to accommodate the wishes of our Signoria in the matter of the location of the said clock, it will be positioned at the "mouth" of the *marzaria* . . . construction is to begin immediately in the said location'. There was no choice but to accept the loss of part of the old Procuracy building ('per tal fabrica se guastasse alcuna cosa delli procuratori'), and the Senate insisted that detailed,

careful accounts be kept of the building works and materials. In fact, only two bays of the Procuratie were to be demolished to provide land for the new Torre (figs 196, 197).

As usual, Marin Sanudo was on hand to provide us with an eyewitness account of the next stage: 'On 10 June [1496] they began to demolish the houses at the entrance to the Marzaria in the piazza of San Marco, where the *volto* is located . . . to form the foundations for a most excellent clock-tower . . . It will be the most beautiful in Italy'.[5] Malipiero's *Annali* confirm Sanudo's report: 'In this month of June 1496 a start was made on the foundations for the clock in the Piazza of San Marco at the Marzaria, and it will cost around 6,000 ducats.'[6] Sanudo's *volto* was the old archway in the colonnade, larger than all the others, which had given access to the Merceria, and which can be identified in Gentile Bellini's painting of the procession in the Piazza, also of 1496. The decision to build the tower was not without its critics; as a result of the costs of the War of Ferrara work on the Palazzo Ducale itself had temporarily ceased, as Malipiero again noted: 'azzo che no para che la Terra sia del tutto senza danaro'.[7]

A week after Sanudo watched the demolition works, Doge Agostin Barbarigo wrote to Rainieri in Reggio, pointing out that work had now started on site ('el loco dove el se ha, a poner se lavora cum ogni diligentia'); he instructed Rainieri to come to Venice urgently ('quanto più celeramente sia possibile'), together with the parts of the clock, so that he could see with his own eyes ('a veder cum lochio') the context in which it was now to be assembled, and so that Rainieri could also organise any additional works that might be necessary. Speed was urged on him so that abortive work was not undertaken, 'cum perdimento di tempo et spexa'.[8] On the following day Barbarigo drafted a letter of safe conduct for Rainieri, not simply for himself but also for his 'sotijs et famulis', 'throughout all of the necessary towns, lands, castles, forts, bridges, gates . . . rivers and waters', until he reached the capital.[9]

PROGRESS ON THE WORKS

The tower as finally completed was essentially a team effort. Although Rainieri's clock was the fundamental *raison d'être* for its construction, not only did the tower have to be designed to accommodate the particular requirements of his clock, but it was to be further elaborated with several elements that were not produced in Zuan Carlo's workshop across the Po plain. Among them were the decorations to the tower's façade, the

196 Gentile Bellini: detail of the *Procession in Piazza San Marco*, 1496, showing the location where the new Torre dell'Orologio was to be built

197 The Torre dell'Orologio from approximately the same viewpoint as Bellini's painting

figure sculptures and, lastly, the bell on the summit, together with the two famous figures known as the 'Moors'.

The design of the tower must have been finalised during the spring of 1496. With the clock itself largely complete, Codussi, if he was indeed the architect, had to incorporate the large circular face of the clock as the focal point of the design, and the dimensions of this face were the chief factors in determining the size and proportions of this centrepiece of the composition. The design of the rest of the tower must have been difficult, since to accommodate the elaborate mechanism of the clock, there were specific height requirements and the spatial needs of the primary mechanism. Nevertheless, this process progressed rapidly; design development must have taken place between the Senate decision in

236

November 1495 and the beginning of demolition on site in June 1496. Thereafter, construction proceeded equally rapidly, and the whole structure was erected in little more than a year.

The tower consists of five storeys or superimposed orders. The lowermost order forms a large, spacious archway, the top of which coincided with the level of the top of the façade of the old Procuracy building next to it;[10] its width corresponded to two of the narrow bays of the same Procuracy. Above this imposing arch – the dimensions of which are also very close to those of the portals on the façade of San Marco – there is a square storey containing the face of the clock, which when built rose above the level of the roofs of the adjacent Procuratie. Above this is a lower storey, in the centre of which is a niche containing the statue of the Virgin and Child, and above this in turn a further storey, slightly lower again, on the face of which was the prominent sculpted composition of the winged lion and the kneeling doge. Finally, the roof of the tower was not pitched but formed a raised platform on which was to stand the great bell and the two 'Moors' striking the hours with their hammers.

The tower is a rich and complex work, in which there is also a close mechanical interrelationship between Rainieri's clock and the other 'clockwork' features, that is, the 'Moors' and their bell, and the figures on the platform of the Virgin and Child. Indeed, the architecture of the tower really provides a classical framework for these various elements, consisting as it does chiefly of two broad, flanking pilasters, broken up by the friezes and cornices that define the diminishing storeys.

The bell on the summit was made by Simone 'Campanato' ('bell-maker') during the summer and autumn of 1497;[11] the materials were provided by the Arsenale, on the instructions of Gismondo (or Sigismondo) Alberghetto, the chief founder, and the bronze was formed from 7,670 pounds of copper and 2,948 pounds of tin, at a total cost of 682 ducats.[12]

This was an exceptionally busy period in the progress of the works. Not only was the bell being cast and the tower itself rapidly approaching completion, but another master, Ambrogio de le Anchore, probably the most skilful founder in the Arsenale, was casting the two famous figures for the top of the tower, which were to strike the bell. These 'ziganti', as they were then called, were complete by the end of October 1497, when Ambrogio was paid 180 ducats, a sum that included the cost of gilding the figures.[13] The supply of wax to form the moulds for the figures (to be made by the lost-wax process), however, was not debited until March 1499, well over a year later. The wax was supplied by

'Thomaso dal Sarasin, spicier' and had cost 100 ducats.[14] Ambrogio was also responsible for the elaborate iron frame that supports the bell.

On 1 December 1497 the bell was hauled to the top of the scaffold and installed on its frame; ten days later it was joined by the two 'ziganti'.[15] These 'giants' later became known as 'Moors' because, as the gilding wore away, the bronze developed its usual dark patina, and hence gave the figures their 'Moorish' appearance. Ambrogio was probably also responsible for the mechanism by which the 'Moors' are connected to the clock three storeys below, such that they rotate on their platforms and strike the hours on the bell with their hammers.

The decoration of the tower itself continued for some time. On the same day that Ambrogio was paid for the bell frame, 90 ducats' worth of copper was obtained, again from the Arsenale, with which to embellish the 'fazza [façade] de detta torre', and nearly a year later, on 1 September 1498, the nobleman Antonio Tron was paid for the supply of 'single and double gold [leaf]', as well as 'enamel of various colours in order that maistro Zuan Florentin and other masters may enamel [the façade]'. This was a costly exercise, and the materials and workmanship together were valued at nearly 500 ducats.[16] The pigments included quantities of expensive ultramarine (made from lapis lazuli) and many sheets of gold leaf for the surfaces of the two topmost storeys, both of which were clad almost entirely with these two luxury materials. The uppermost level has a background of ultramarine to represent the sky, with decorations of stars in gold leaf, while the level below, that of the Virgin and Child, has a repetitive pattern, again in gold and ultramarine.

The clock itself has a second face onto the Merceria; although considerably less elaborate than that onto the Piazza, it, too, was decorated with gold stars on a blue ground, with the sun's rays in the centre. Sigismondo Alberghetto was probably responsible for some of the other embellishments on the main façade, including the signs of the zodiac in relief, and the metal balustrade to the balcony with the Virgin and Child. The last major expenditure on the tower – (including the doramentij (gilding) of the clock – was not debited until as late as June 1499.[17]

On 1 February 1499 the tower was officially opened; once again Sanudo was on the spot to give us his account. The occasion was particularly notable because Doge Barbarigo was processing into the Piazza to make his ritual andata to vespers at Mauro Codussi's newly rebuilt (although not quite complete) church of Santa Maria

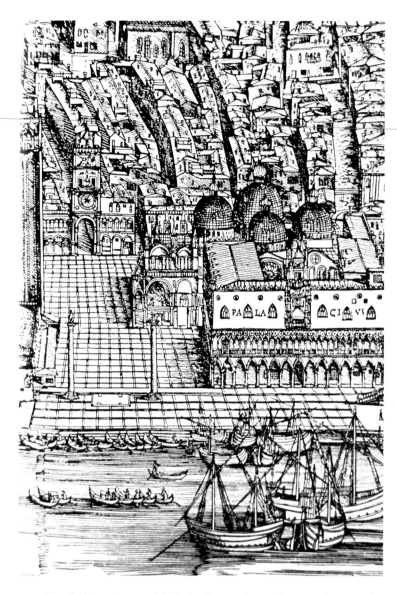

198 Detail from Jacopo de' Barbari's woodcut of 1500, showing the Piazzetta and Molo, with the newly completed Torre dell'Orologio in the background

Formosa. Sanudo tells us that 'for the first time the clock, which stands on the piazza, above the street that leads to the merceria, was uncovered and opened; it is made with great ingenuity and is very beautiful' (fig. 198).[18]

The Architect

As we noted above, the tower's architect remains highly elusive. Many writers have attributed the design to Codussi, although a few have dissented, including McAndrew, who inclined to the view that there was no one clear author.[19] Unfortunately, the cultural context serves to confuse rather than clarify the picture. The *proto* of San Marco at the time was Giorgio Spavento, but there is nothing about the tower's design that indicates his hand; at the same time, Rizzo was 'proto dil palazo' across the square, but there is even less about the tower's appearance that suggests Rizzo's involvement. It is also far distant from the refined, small-scale richness of Pietro Lombardo. Another possible contender might have been Bartolomeo Bon the Bergamasco (not the Bon of the Porta della Carta, who was long dead), and who had been appointed *proto* of the Provveditori al Sal on 20 August 1492. Bon, however, was away at sea during the period in which

238

the design must have been completed. Finally, there is the obscure figure of Bartolomeo Gonella, *proto* of the Procurators of San Marco *de supra*, and, in theory, the most likely candidate, since the tower was built on land in the Procurators' ownership and control. We might expect Gonella to have been responsible for the supervision of the construction, which certainly fell within his professional remit, but perhaps his very obscurity reflects the Signoria's lack of confidence in his design ability, such that they preferred to approach a far more creative, prominent master – Codussi – and then delegated the management of the site to Gonella.[20]

As the most creative architect in Venice, Mauro must have been an almost inescapable choice for the Signoria to make; by now, too, he had an impressive portfolio of completed works, including San Michele, the campanile of San Pietro in Castello, the Scuola Grande di San Marco and San Zaccaria. Codussi also had a minor connection with the site itself, in that, a few years earlier, in 1486–7, he had carved stone bases for three standards that were to rise in the Piazza directly in front of San Marco. They no longer survive, but according to Gentile Bellini's depiction they were simple, vertical plinths. Mauro's association with the Procurators thus already existed, and on several occasions in 1487 he had provided stone for works at the church.[21] Codussi was completing Santa Maria Formosa in this period, although in June 1495 he had been relieved of his post as *proto* at the Scuola Grande di San Marco, since the works were almost completed. Despite the complexity of the clock itself, the tower is architecturally quite simple, and Codussi's involvement, however briefly, remains the most likely of these several possibilities.

To reflect its role as a major new civic element, a conscious example of Renaissance *renovatio urbis*, the design had to be modern, representative not only of this philosophy of urban renovation, but because it was built to house a technical marvel, a product of the rational, scientific and enquiring mind, the mind of the new era. Codussi was an entirely appropriate master, since his own œuvre was not only classically based but inventive and ingenious as well. Certain details can also be linked with his work elsewhere, such as the cornice to the first order, which recalls San Zaccaria.

The Tower after 1500

On 8 February 1500 the Signoria ordered a summary of all the costs of the various elements associated with the clock.[22] They arrived at a total of 2,701 ducats, a sum that did not include the fabric of the tower. Of this sum,

just over 1,100 ducats had been spent on the 'ziganti' and their bell; the remainder was spent on the 'caxamento' (the housing or case) of the clock, and its surrounding decoration, the ornamentation of the Piazza façade and the three Magi and the Angel that formed part of the Ascension Day procession around the Virgin and Child, as well as the lesser façade to the Mercerie.

The Signoria decided to appoint a commission of experts to examine and agree the final account for the clock itself. These four experts were Spieraindio della Zecha (a goldsmith and medallist), Tomaso dai Obisi, Pencino dai Reloi (or 'dallj horologj', another clockmaker) and the familiar figure of Pietro Lombardo. By now the elder Rainieri had died, and the settlement was to be made with his son Zuan Carlo.[23]

In November the commission reported back to the Signoria, with a long list of the many elements of work, all individually valued, and with a total sum of 1,848 ducats. The priced schedule is comprehensive, encompassing the workings of the clock itself, the mechanisms of the planets and the signs of the zodiac, the 'astrolabij', the cornices and friezes of copper, the figures of the Magi and the Angel and all the surface decorations; it omits, however, the figurative elements noted in the first schedule, that is, the Virgin and Child, the 'Moors' and the bell, and also the sculpted stone figures of the Marcian lion and the figure of the doge. These last two elements, were, of course, made by others, by master stonemasons.[24]

On 20 November 1500 the Senate considered the request of Zuan Carlo for final settlement of the moneys that he claimed. The characteristically verbose record of the debate begins thus:

> Having made appearances on very many occasions before our Signoria, Zuan Carlo 'da rezo', maker of the clock here in the piazza of San Marco above the 'bocca di marzaria', requesting payment for its manufacture and the expenses that he has incurred, and for which he is still a creditor in the sum of 1,728 ducats according to the estimates made by the deputies, nonetheless is desirous to live and to die in this city, and is in agreement that the whole matter is referred to arbitration and to the wishes of our Signoria, [but] having the obligation to find the means of being able to maintain and support his family, not wishing for a single *soldo* on account of the said credit, and [wishing to] attend upon and regulate the said clock, that is, both he and his heirs and descendants, a duty that requires great knowledge and diligence . . . [and he has] to meet many expenses, amounting to some 40 ducats or more per year . . .[25]

The Senate noted Zuan Carlo's desire to stay in Venice and retain responsibility for the clock, which 'if it is allowed out of the hands that made it will fall into ruin'. They therefore made him an offer which he must have found extremely difficult to refuse. It consisted of two parts: first, in return for the cancellation of the debt, Zuan Carlo was offered one of the first *fontegarie* or flour concessions at the Fontego della Farina at Rialto, on the Riva del Vin. Second, in return for Zuan Carlo's obligation to 'keep, maintain and repair, all at his own expense, the said clock' he was offered a second flour concession at Rialto. There were thirty such concessions in all, generally offered to the public by auction, usually for a limited number of years.[26] This was a singular offer, though, and must have seemed an ideal means of making a very respectable and reliable income for Zuan Carlo and his family. He did accept, and remained in Venice for the remaining thirty years of his life, until 1531.

In the eventful year of 1500, a further decision was taken regarding the newly completed tower. The Senate, again supported by the Procurators of San Marco, decided to extend the fabric by the construction of two wings, one on either side. It is possible that such extensions had formed part of the original scheme; it may also have been the case that the tower was felt to be insufficiently stable and that the side wings would act as buttresses. Certainly the much lower Procuratie cannot have afforded a great deal of lateral restraint.[27]

On 11 January 1503 the Provveditori al Sal charged Pietro Lombardo with supplying a considerable quantity of 'squared marble, and of stone . . . to face the new houses built next to the *horologio* on the piazza'.[28] In fact, though, despite their modest extent, the new 'houses' were not completed until Ascension Day 1506. Although Pietro supplied stone and marble, there is no evidence that he designed these wings himself, and, here again, speculation surrounds their authorship. At this time Pietro was still *proto* at the Palazzo Ducale, having replaced the disgraced and disappeared Antonio Rizzo. In such a role he would have acquired large quantities of stone on a regular basis, and it would have been a simple matter to ask him to order further supplies for the wings of the tower. To build them, it was necessary to demolish further bays of the old Procuracy building; to the east of the new tower only three of these isolated bays had survived, but these were now promptly taken down, while a corresponding three bays were demolished on the west side.[29]

These side wings have four storeys, capped by a stone balustrade, which reflects that at the top of the tower itself. (The two storeys at the top, set back behind this balustrade, are eighteenth-century additions.) The design of these two wings, however, is far from satisfactory. The lowermost storey is contained by a frieze at the same level as the capitals on the main arch into the Merceria, but the next storey is defined by the frieze above the same arch, resulting in a squat mezzanine storey above the colonnade. The two upper floors, on the other hand, are squeezed into the height occupied by the large square bay of the clock face and this again produces one 'piano nobile' surmounted by a low attic storey below the crowning balustrade. The heights of the orders on the tower itself did not easily adapt to the more orthodox accommodation in the two side wings.

It is unlikely that these wings are the work of Lombardo, nor are they from the hand of Codussi, who died in 1504, before they were complete, and whose detailing is far more refined and self-assured. The elusive Gonella was still *proto* to the Procurators until his death in 1505, together with the better-known Spavento, and it may well have been the case that Gonella, having been perceived as insufficiently skilled to design the tower itself, was nevertheless considered sufficiently competent to deal with this essentially ancillary, less prestigious work.[30]

Image and Symbolism

The tower's rich façade embodies a number of powerful images. At first glance heterogeneous, collectively they represent a number of discrete but important facets of the image and iconography of the Republic in this period of a highly conscious (in this case rather self-conscious) sense of *civitas* and *renovatio urbis*.

The arch at the base forms a positive, purely practical link between the Piazza and the Merceria, but symbolically it also links nationalistic pride with the crowded commercial life-blood of the city, culminating in the banks and markets of Rialto. Its form is quintessentially triumphal, its architectural language clearly and confidently that of the Renaissance, with inset marble paterae very much in the Codussian manner. Across the architrave is the inscription IO PAV IO CAROL FIL REGIEN OP MID; that is, 'The work of Giovanni Paolo, Giovanni Carlo, his son, from Reggio, in 1499'.

The clock itself, on the next storey, is a triumph of complex mechanical art. The great circular face contains three concentric rings, the innermost of which is a blue disc, with gold stars to indicate the constellations, and a ball, representing the moon, that revolves around the centre and also on its own axis (fig. 193).

The ball is half black and half white, its own rotation thus indicating the lunar phases. In the next ring are the signs of the zodiac, formed in copper and enamelled with ultramarine, and with the symbols in gilded bronze relief. On the outermost ring, the twenty-four hours are incised in large Roman numbers in gold on marble; the hour is indicated by a gold sun on the end of a hand.[31]

The second storey contains perhaps the most complex symbolism. The chief element is the large semicircular balcony that breaks forward from the cornice and is surmounted by a boldly formed classical niche, in which are seated the Virgin and Child (fig. 199). Their sculptor is not known, and is not identified in the surviving accounts of the work; sometimes thought to be by Leopardi, the statue has also been attributed to the Lombardo workshop. The two little doors on either side play their special role during Ascension week, when they open to reveal the figure of the Angel Gabriel blowing a trumpet, followed by a procession of life-size figures of the three Magi, who genuflect to the Virgin and Child before disappearing through the doorway on the other side. Today the Ascension Day procession still takes place, but on other occasions the two side doors serve the more prosaic function of indicating the hours on one side and the minutes (in five – minute intervals) on the other.[32]

The Virgin and Child group provides the symbolic link to the basilica, which stands only metres away. Although in other respects the tower is essentially a civic structure, the Ascension Day procession ingeniously united the spiritual and the temporal in a uniquely Venetian manner. Ascension Day itself, *la Sensa*, was not simply a great religious festival, but since 1178 had also been the occasion for the famous Sposalizio del Mar, the ritual marriage of the doge to the sea, that most ancient and symbolic of festivals. It was also the occasion for a great and famous fair in the Piazza, where the world's traders could assemble and marvel at the scientific ingenuity of the tower and its sophisticated clock.

If the Virgin and Child group unites the spiritual and the temporal, then the next level of the tower firmly represents the institution of the Republic itself. Since 1797 this composition has been bereft of the figure of Doge Agostin Barbarigo, who formerly knelt in front of the winged lion, until he was destroyed by the iconoclastic Bonaparte. The design was very similar to the precedent that Doge Foscari had established at the Porta della Carta more than half a century earlier, although here the lion is reversed and Barbarigo's figure

(surprisingly small, according to seventeenth-century depictions) stood on the right. The lion (fig. 200), though, clearly derives from Bon's at the Porta della Carta, with its prominent wings and the open book held in his front paw; even the configuration of the tail is similar.[33]

The crowning 'Moors' have possessed their nickname for a long time. Francesco Sansovino described them thus in 1580, by which time their original gilding had already long worn off and not been replaced. The 'Moors' are in fact wild men, one old and one young, signifying the passage of time, from which none of us can escape, neither the poor and 'savage' (as represented here), nor the wealthy and educated. Although cast by Ambrogio at the Arsenale, their design is attributed to Paolo Savin (fig. 201).[34]

The entire assemblage of the tower represents the passage of time and its rites of passage, although the 'Moors' express the fleeting nature of temporal life in a particularly direct manner. They would draw the attention of the Senators to these inescapable facts every day when the bell was rung, and reminded them of their own brief sojourn on the thrones of power in the nearby palace. Unlike the iconography of the earlier Porta della Carta, therefore, triumphantly crowned by the universal image of Venice as the Republic of Justice, the iconography of the Torre culminates in a sculpted group representing not simply the technical ingenuity of the work but a salutary reminder of human vulnerability and the transitory nature of temporal power.

As a whole, though, the message of the Torre is remarkably clear: it was built by the Republic itself as a direct representation of its desire to enhance the prestige, splendour and image of the Serenissima to the city and to the world beyond. As at the Scala dei Giganti, Doge Barbarigo took advantage of the precedent set by Francesco Foscari in appropriating for himself the patronage of the work with his own physical representation. To emphasise further this ostentatious display of *civitas*, too, the tower was extensively decorated with the most costly finishes available: gold leaf and ultramarine, the same materials used to decorate the Porta della Carta and the basilica itself. Here again it is tempting to identify the influence of Barbarigo; despite the fact that the Republic was beset with financial concerns over the costs of the wars on the Terraferma, which were directly reflected in the notable scaling-down of work at the Palazzo Ducale itself, no expense was spared in the decoration of the Torre.

199   The Torre dell'Orologio: the platform with the aedicule of the Virgin and Child group

200   The Torre dell'Orologio: the lion of St Mark

Later History

On 27 September 1531, three decades after the completion of the tower and its remarkable clock, the
Consiglio dei Dieci met in the palace: they had a
problem. They reminded themselves of the conditions
of the contract with Zuan Carlo, by which he and his
successors were granted the two flour *fontegarie* at
Rialto, one in settlement of the account and the other
for the 'obligation di tener, governar et conciar [to
maintain, adjust and repair] ditto horologio continua-
mente'.

The problem was that Zuan Carlo had now died,
and not only were none of his heirs 'intelligente de tal
artificio' ('expert in this field'), but they no longer lived
in Venice anyway. The result was that the clock had
become 'mal governato', a fact not at all pleasing to the
Dieci, since, in addition to the great inconvenience of
an unreliable clock, the legal responsibility to maintain
it still rested with Raineri's descendants.

They therefore decided that the contract had to be
withdrawn, and with it the right to one of the two
fontegarie at Rialto. The post was now to be re-adver-
tised, in the hope that an appropriately qualified expert
('atta et sufficiente') would be forthcoming. He would
be interviewed by the Collegio and offered the *fonte-*

garia in lieu of a salary. To further entice such a master
to remain continuously available to adjust and maintain
the clock, he was to be offered the use of the house
next door, again formerly occupied by the Rainieri.[35]
A week later the Collegio confirmed the appointment
of Raffaele Pencino, either the same man or perhaps
the son of the same man, who, together with the other
commissioners, had evaluated the work of Zuan Carlo
back in 1500.

Twenty years later again, Jacopo Sansovino was asked
by the Procurators to conduct a survey of the condition of the tower, on the instructions of the Senate.
Sansovino had been *proto* of the Procurators since 1529,
and such work fell within the range of his duties.
Accompanying him on this inspection was Gieronimo
da Rezo, son of the late Zuan Carlo, the original maker
of the clock; Gieronimo, despite his apparent unsuit-
ability to become Zuan Carlo's successor as clock-
keeper, was felt to have useful knowledge of the clock
and its workings. It was, however, in a bad way: the
mechanism that rang the hours was 'malissimo in
ordine' (in fact, not working at all), while the 'raggio
che mostra le hore' (the hand marking the hours)
was completely broken. Major repairs were clearly
necessary.[36]

243

201   The Torre dell'Orologio: upper part of the tower

They seem to have been successful. Sansovino's own son Francesco, whose guide to the city was published in 1581, described the tower as we see it today, 'encrusted with the finest marbles' and with its various mechanisms apparently in good working order:

> the clock, that shows the hours, with the rays; the Angel with the trumpet, followed by the three Magi . . . [who] pass in front of the Virgin, they genuflect, and then enter by the other doorway by means of a turntable; two figures of bronze known popularly as Moors, between whom stands a bell, on which the figures beat the hours, each with a hammer . . .'[37]

Francesco concludes his description, justifiably, by noting that Zuan Carlo, from Reggio, was 'a man famous in mathematics, and with great experience in the making of such works'. It remains a tribute to Zuan Carlo and his father Zuan Polo that, despite many technical vicissitudes, the clock continues to provoke fascination and admiration today, and continues to fulfil its function five centuries after it was crafted.[38]

Conclusions

Changing Roles: The Proto and the Architect

THE ANCIEN RÉGIME AND THE CAREER OF BARTOLOMEO BON

Bartolomeo Bon was undoubtedly the most prominent mason and sculptor in Venice from around the mid-1420s until his death just after 1464. But he was never honoured with the title of *protomaestro*, nor was he employed by a government department or other public institution on such a basis, that is, that of a permanent salaried master in complete charge of a major building project.

The reason was largely a simple matter of chronology. Had he been born twenty or thirty years later, it is highly likely that he would have secured such a post, perhaps with the Republic itself, perhaps with one of the Scuole Grandi and their ambitious rebuilding programmes. As it was, his career embraces the last few decades of the *ancien régime*, with the coordination of the construction process largely in the hands of the master builder. His role thus differed in crucial respects from those of the masters of succeeding generations: Lombardo, Rizzo and, above all, Mauro Codussi.

Bon's first important commission, at Marin Contarini's new palace, was unusual because of Contarini's own particular role. Bon was essentially his father's junior partner and the workshop was initially employed on the basis of an annual salary, which was to be subdivided between the masters and their apprentices; this might suggest that the role of Zane and Bartolomeo was that of *proti* of the palace, but they had no responsibility for any trades other than their own, and, after a couple of years, Marin abandoned this system in favour of more traditional methods of payment: the 'elemental' one in the case of major individual pieces of work, and agreements based on simple rates for repetitive elements such as the carving of cornices.

The most important of Bartolomeo's mid-career commissions was the Porta della Carta. He was employed here solely to design and carve this one unique element of the Palazzo Ducale, again with no responsibility for any other ancillary trades or for the work of the builders and carpenters, who themselves were responsible for the structure that stands behind its stone façade.

The new Carità church, for which Bon provided most of the stonework, was essentially designed by the master builders, who were responsible for the erection of the whole fabric and for coordinating with Bon and with the master carpenters. At the Scuola della Misericordia, Bon's role was probably identical in principle to that at the Carità church; again, he provided stone for building-in by the master builders. Like the church, the Scuola is essentially a brick and timber structure, and the only unique element here was Bartolomeo's splendid bas-relief panel, carved for the main portal. In neither project was there a figure that we might identify as the architect in the modern sense of the term.

202 Jacopo Sansovino: detail of the Molo corner of the Biblioteca Marciana, begun in 1537, and completed by Vincenzo Scamozzi

By their nature, Bon's contributions of carved stone were episodic and fragmented, dependent on the programme and progress of the works.

If there was little possibility of continuity for the master mason on projects such as these, there was even less on more mundane projects such as the charity almshouses at the Corte Nova alla Misericordia, where the stonework was of such a simple, routine nature that it could have been provided by any competent stone-cutter in the city.

Two of Bon's later commissions were once again individual elements applied to a structure that had already been completed by others: the portal of the Madonna dell'Orto and the great west doorway of Santi Giovanni e Paolo. Both works were again contracted in the traditional elemental manner. Only Bartolomeo's last and most fragmentary work, the Ca' del Duca, might have been able to furnish definitive evidence that here, at last, he was appointed as the original designer of this great house – which he clearly was – and was also intended to be its superintending master. It was to be a project of sufficient size to justify the retention of Bon's services in such a capacity; more importantly, though, the distinctive character of its design indicates that this was to be a major work of architecture attributed to a single creative master. Bon's refusal to show his drawing to another master is a strikingly clear example of creative individuality and of his 'ownership' of the design.[1] Although Bartolomeo was well aware of the changes that were discernible in Venice in the 1460s, and was able to respond to them, he never designed and constructed the entire fabric of a major building project himself.

THE *PROTO* AND THE ARCHITECT: WHAT'S IN A NAME? THE EXAMPLE OF CODUSSI

To answer this question we must distinguish between the two fundamental aspects of the construction process, in this era as in any other: between the creative, design stage and the supervision of the building process. The *proto* is the figure who has emerged as the fulcrum in this shifting, developing matter of the relationships between those responsible for the design and construction process in this period.

Although the term simply means 'chief master',[2] the *proto* is certainly not *primus inter pares* on the fifteenth-century building site: he is often – at San Zaccaria and the Palazzo Ducale, for example – the designer and coordinating master of the entire process. Most fifteenth-century Venetian buildings – even well into the Renaissance – were still constructed under the responsibility of the master builder; in many cases they were the designers, too, but only in the qualified sense that they designed the basic structural shell, establishing its dimensions and general volumetric organisation. But we do not find such traditional masters responsible for the design of specialised and technically complex works such as San Zaccaria, Santa Maria Formosa or the façade of a major public project like the Scuola Grande di San Marco.

The vital shift of emphasis began in the 1460s, the result of a combination of three principal circumstances. One was that a series of large, expensive, even grandiose building projects was undertaken in this period by a number of public bodies and agencies, most of which required designers of great skill and experience; in the execution of these complex designs they also required considerable quantities of richly carved stone.

Parallel to these developments we find a desire first on the part of the Republic and later of other bodies to regularise the supervision of these projects, their accounts and procedures, by the appointment of a man who would provide essential administrative continuity and responsibility.

The third element was the developing appreciation of the role of the individual design master and the importance of ensuring that his design intentions were accurately and faithfully carried out. The appointment of Mauro Codussi at San Michele and of Pietro Lombardo at the Miracoli offer two dramatic examples of this power of highly focused individualised patronage as applied to – and which specifically 'adhered to' – a particular master, responsible for the integrated design and construction of an entire building. In these developing processes, the office of *proto* played a vital role, bringing stability and coordination, particularly valuable in the Venetian political context, where patrons were usually in office for only a very short period of time.

The first *proto* of whom we have any knowledge, Pietro Baseggio at the Palazzo Ducale in the 1340s, was unique at the time simply because the palace was the only very large-scale, complex project in the city that required such a master. (Baseggio was only referred to as *proto* in 1361, after his death; he is generally believed to have been the supervisor of construction but not necessarily the architect.) The construction of the Molo wing was exceptional in its structural ambition, in the complex programme of the sculpted decoration of its façades and in the decorative programmes of its interiors. It is not surprising, therefore, that we do not come across the post and its responsibilities again until the great wave of elaborate new building programmes in the middle and late decades of the fifteenth century.

The Procurators of San Marco employed their own *proti* at least from the 1460s, as did the Provveditori al Sal. It is easy to understand why these two institutions should have been in the vanguard in making such appointments, since they were both responsible for an important patrimony of properties. The practical roles of the two men were different, since the Procurators had direct responsibility for the upkeep and maintenance of the properties in their possession, whereas the Provveditori were essentially an executive agency directed by the Signoria or the Dieci. Nevertheless, both bodies saw the advantage of a role that in England was called something like 'surveyor of the fabric' or 'master of the works', their remit extending from routine surveys and inspections through periodic maintenance and repairs, to the occasional major new project.

The third office of *proto* was that re-established at the Palazzo Ducale in the late fifteenth century. As the scale and complexity of the works to the new east wing grew, in 1484 the title of chief master was elevated to that of full *proto* (as it had been back in the fourteenth century), when Rizzo was promoted into it. In contemporary documentation, however, Rizzo's title varied, and he is sometimes referred to as the *sorastante* (supervisor) of the works rather than the *proto*. Sanudo, for example, refers to Rizzo as 'soprastante Ant. Rizo Taiapiera con ducato 100 alano'; even after his second salary rise, Rizzo was still described in the decree that confirmed this rise as 'soprastante a la fabrica del palazzo'.[3]

Nevertheless, the conferring of the title of *protomaestro* by no means ensured outstanding architecture. Indeed, it did not necessarily ensure any architecture at all: it provided – principally – convenience and continuity on the part of the employing body. To a large extent these posts were routine, administrative roles; they were partly what one made of them, too, depending on the nature of the building projects, if any, undertaken during the period in question, and on the character and abilities of the incumbent (fig. 203).

The perceived modesty of their social status is also certainly partly responsible for their anonymity. Marin Sanudo rarely mentions the names of the masters engaged on major public building works during the long period covered by his voluminous diaries. However, it is equally clear that at times when an important outbreak of Republican *renovatio* coincided with the maturation of masters such as Codussi, Lombardo and, later, Jacopo Sansovino, then such posts pro-

vided excellent opportunities for a successful career. The extremely long professional life of Sansovino offers the finest example of the way in which a career could flourish given an exceptional gift and propitious circumstances: a Republic by then even more determined on outstanding works of urban *renovatio*. Even in his case, though, we must not forget that his forty-one years of service included many routine, minor surveying works. And on the rare occasion when things went wrong (as with the collapse at the Biblioteca Marciana in 1545), even his position was not invulnerable (fig. 202).

Back in the fifteenth century, Mauro Codussi's career allows us to appreciate the vicissitudes of the professional life of such a master in this period of flux. At San Michele, Mauro was employed specifically for his highly regarded skills in design; his abilities are extravagantly praised in his patrons' correspondence, and it is clear that he had a largely free hand in the development of the design of the church, which was probably unparalleled in Venice at the time.[4]

The technical requirements for Codussi's next project, the new bell-tower at the cathedral of San Pietro in Castello, were simplicity itself, but the result was as remarkable as the façade of San Michele; with a little imagination one can envisage the campanile rising on the islet behind the latter church, to complete a glittering ensemble, symbolising the new era and its new architectural language. That Codussi was in sole charge of the campanile is again made clear by the terminology of his appointment: he was 'magistro moreto lapicida et murario', both mason and builder (there was very little carpentry involved here), while to assist him was his partner and compatriot, 'magistrum jacobum de bergamo murarium sumptibus suis' ('Master Jacobo from Bergamo, builder, all at his own expense').[5]

Codussi's role at the Scuola Grande di San Marco was again as a *proto* with a regular monthly salary, to replace Lombardo; as at San Zaccaria, his skills in such a role were fully appreciated, and the completion of the Scuola further enhanced his reputation. At the Scuola Grande di San Giovanni Evangelista his responsibility was confined to the design and construction of a single element, the new staircase. There was no suggestion that his role was to be that of *proto*; the limited scope of the work could not justify such an appointment. Although Mauro was admitted as a member of the Scuola in 1498, he had still not completed the new staircase by the time of his death in 1504, so he clearly spent comparatively little time on it in the last six years of his life. Nevertheless, he was specifically charged with creating a staircase that would surpass his earlier work at the rival Scuola Grande di San Marco.[6]

204 Mauro Codussi: interior of the church of San Giovanni Grisostomo

In 1491 Codussi was commissioned to design and build the new parish church of Santa Maria Formosa; he was described, perhaps surprisingly, in the document of appointment as 'magistro Mauro quondam Martini de bergamo, murario, habitatore Venetijs in contrata sancti Proculi', that is, as a master builder, not a mason or *proto*. The use of the term *murario* indicates that the *banca* of the church required him to take responsibility for the entire construction process (as a *proto*, in a sense) and he would almost certainly have had a foreman builder under his direction. The church was not complete at his death, and work was concluded by his two sons, Domenico and Santino. At a settling-up with the two brothers in 1506, Mauro was referred to as 'magistri mori lapicide [stonemason] de codusis de lentina'.[7]

Codussi's reconstruction of the much smaller parish church of San Giovanni Grisostomo (fig. 204) was roughly contemporaneous with Santa Maria Formosa, and the organisation of its internal spaces (on a highly restricted site) offers an instructive comparison with the larger, wealthier foundation of Santa Maria Formosa. San Giovanni, too, remained unfinished at his death, and again the accounts were settled with his sons.

Mauro is again referred to here as a *lapicide*, and the arbitrators appointed to settle the account were both masons, the familiar figure of Zuane Buora, and Alvise Bossi. In the very last record relating to these accounts, on 3 November 1504, Mauro Codussi was referred to as an *architectus*, for the first, last and only time in his illustrious career.[8]

VENETIE MD: *The Imago Urbis*

In 1500 Jacopo de' Barbari's famous view of the city, triumphantly entitled VENETIE MD, represented an unequivocal celebration of the great metropolis, defining and definitive. Until modern aerial and satellite imagery, it had never been surpassed in its accuracy and comprehensive detail. If we bear in mind the turbulent geopolitical and economic events of the time, it can almost be read as a gesture of defiance, too, reasserting the image of the sea-city, unchallenged, unassailed.

De' Barbari's viewpoint, as if drawn from a hot-air balloon hovering somewhere to the south of San Giorgio Maggiore, permitted the city to be shown in

203 Jacopo Sansovino: detail of the Loggetta at the base of the campanile in Piazza San Marco, 1537–49

its unique context, both literally and metaphorically; its location in the centre of the lagoon rendered Venice regionally all-powerful, with Murano and the other northern satellites deferentially inferior; even Torcello was now a mere cipher, its glorious past lost below the waters.[9]

De' Barbari's anthropomorphic iconography is clear: most prominent are Mercury and Neptune, twin representatives of the elements of the Most Serene Republic. And although in reality many parts of the city were a characteristically teeming mass of late medieval humanity, the *volo d'uccello* viewpoint allows an Olympian detachment, a kind of visual apotheosis, in which God (and by implication, his Evangelist, too) looks down on his creation, unconcerned with its minor quotidian imperfections; and with the city surrounded by its God-given natural defences. Neptune guarded those waters, bustling with trading vessels, although a closer inspection also reveals the more representative activities of the *minuto popolo*, in the form of a regatta, rare evidence of a more humanitarian eye in this otherwise depersonalised image.

Much less prominent than the city, its lagoon and satellites, but again of great iconographic importance, is the Terraferma empire that frames the image along the top. This element of the bipartite Republic is represented by an idealised Arcadian fringe, with the great plain of the Veneto terminated by the craggy ranges of the Dolomites. Seraval is significantly identified by name, as the key to the northern passes, through which much of Venice's European trade was routed. De' Barbari's reputed patron, the German merchant, Anton Kolb, would have been familiar with this route.

This, then, was the mid-millennial metropolis, not perfect in detail, but (in theory) perfectible, and certainly perfectly located in this transcendent zone between land and sea, sea and sky. However, although de' Barbari's obsessive detail may appear to us almost pathologically precise, it is also, of course, utterly misleading as the representation of the reality of the city as a living organism. Where, for example, are the citizens who clogged the teeming quaysides and crowded around the stalls of the meat market in the Piazzetta? (Where, in fact, is the market itself?) The paucity of human figures in the panorama – the regatta is an almost unique exception – adds further to the idealised nature of the image, an almost deserted, mythical city.

As an image for dissemination abroad, however, which was almost certainly its primary function, this oddly depopulated yet clearly thriving city fulfilled an important role in spreading the *imago urbis*. We do not know how many copies were printed (nineteen survive, in two different states), but it was certainly intended for international distribution to advertise the fame and splendour of the sea-city, and to explain its miraculous context to those who had never seen it.

De' Barbari's extraordinary fidelity to Venice's built form cannot fail to indicate that this was a vast, densely packed, organic, medieval city, in which only a handful of modern interventions stand out by their rarity. What were the civic foci in 1500? The great expanses of Piazza and Piazzetta, of course, with San Marco symbolically located in the very centre of the panorama, and with the new Torre dell'Orologio as a beacon of the new *civitas*; the noble basins of the Arsenale with their ranks of shipbuilding sheds and the new land gate of gleaming marble; above all, perhaps, the Canalazzo, a sinewy artery of dignified order. But almost nothing else; even Rialto is only clearly identifiable at a first glance by its ancient, rickety timber bridge, and Rialto was the second hub of the city, fount of wealth and focus of international trade. Most of the rest of the city remained a sprawling collection of island parishes, with the largest *campi* (San Polo, Santa Maria Formosa) standing out as major social and cultural foci. As we have seen, the condition of Rialto epitomised the urban conflicts that afflicted the great medieval trading city, and the pitfalls that lay in the paths of those who wished to impose civic dignity and *renovatio urbis* on these almost infinitely complex, and seemingly intractable conflicts of interest. Venice's own *renovatio urbis* was to be a long, difficult and fragmented process, with some of its greatest triumphs – the churches of Palladio and Longhena, the great reclamations of the Zattere, the Fondamente Nuove and the Tereni Nuovi – still many decades in the future.

Postscript: The New Rome Achieved?

This question can be posited on a number of levels, some easier to analyse than others. In the sense that it was most widely understood in the fifteenth century, the concept of 'the new Rome' was applied by both Venetians and foreigners alike not to the classicisation of the fabric of the city itself, but rather to the Republican tradition, to the notion of a government based on law and justice. To these two principal parameters we should add the permanence of the institution of the state itself and its political stability, which derived, according to the Venetians themselves, directly from the first two attributes.

In 1450 Poggio Bracciolini, the Florentine scholar, had written a treatise entitled 'In praise of the Venetian

Republic'. As a Florentine, he was in a sense departing from the 'party line' as codified later by Machiavelli, according to which view the perfection of the rule of the 'Prince' (that is, the individual ruler) was the desired aim, rather than the stability that might be derived from government chaired by an elected head of state, presiding over a cabinet and an elected Senate, however distinguished the members of these bodies might be.[10]

In fact, particularly after the Terraferma expansion of the early fifteenth century, admiration of the Republic from abroad was frequently combined with a concern for the balance of power in Italy in general, the implication being that the Serenissima had thereby destabilised that power balance, despite the admirable institutions by which the Republic was governed. After the absorption of the Terraferma, though, the other south European powers began to appreciate that a new permanent equilibrium could be obtained, and was, in fact, now being consolidated: Venice as a counterfort to the power of Milan, and both of them territorial balances to the trans-Apennine ambitions of Florence and the papacy.

For much of the fifteenth century, Florence herself had remained under the powerful influence of Cosimo de' Medici, *pater patriae*, followed (after a brief interlude) by that of Lorenzo the Magnificent (fig. 205). Although the title was bestowed on Cosimo by later generations, the concept of a *pater patriae* was inconceivable within the Venetian republican system of government by an entire ruling class of nobles, who themselves elected all the highest offices of state, including the doge (*primus inter pares*) himself. One form of governmental stability, therefore, the elective gerontocracy of the Serenissima, could be directly compared with another, the enlightened, but 'semidespotic', dynastic power and influence of the Medici. In 1494, however, Lorenzo died, and after a couple of years, confusion and a lack of direction descended on the Tuscan capital. Until 1512 Florence was without its dominant dynasty, and a republican form of government was installed, based on the Venetian model. Venice, despite the financial crises of the early 1490s, appeared to be weathering these difficult times rather better than Florence, and it is in this immediate context that we can understand more clearly the sometimes rather fulsome writings of Marin Sanudo, patrician and patriot.[11]

It is worth recalling, however, the later views of another Florentine, Francesco Guicciardini, who, in his famous *Storia d'Italia*, published in 1561 (twenty years after his death), has much to say about the Italians' perception of the Dominante in the disastrous decade of

205   Palazzo Medici Riccardi, Florence: corner of the façade towards Via de' Martelli, with the Medici arms

Cambrai and Agnadello. Guicciardini, recreating Doge Leonardo Loredan's speech to the Senate in the critical month of September 1509, has Loredan recite the characteristic laudations to the Republic: 'equal justice, political freedom, Christian charity . . . God has guarded the destiny of Venetians . . . the bulwark and glory of Christianity for centuries'. Nevertheless, both Guicciardini himself and the Florentines in general remained highly ambivalent about the power of the

Republic and its pan-Italian role. On one hand, Guicciardini did not celebrate the Venetians' defeat at Agnadello, as did many others in Italy, and, as a republican, he retained enormous respect for the longevity and stability of the Dominante, perceived to be 'immortal' by many Italian states; on the other, he blamed the Republic for creating a situation in which northern Italy was now vulnerable to invasions from the barbarous north, across the Alps.[12]

The Venetian diarist Girolamo Priuli raised a series of issues to account for the disaster of Agnadello, among them the pride and arrogance of the Venetian senators, and the general corruption and licentious nature of Venetian society. To Priuli, the disaster was a divine warning to return to the stricter moral codes and moderate behaviour of the past, a view shared widely at the time, by, among others, his fellow diarist Sanudo. If the Venetians were to be 'new Romans' they must embrace the discipline, rigour and asceticism of the most successful of the classical rulers. A series of new sumptuary laws was one of the immediate, practical results of the defeat, while nobles such as Andrea Gritti (later doge) refused to take their salary as military commissioners, to set an example of personal sacrifice for the *res pubblica*.

However, since this book has been concerned with the physical manifestations of the *res pubblica* in this era, it is in this more direct sense that the physical achievements of 'the new Rome' during the late fifteenth century should be evaluated. As an institution, the Republic should have had certain profound advantages over dynastic rule, in its patronage of a long-term imperial rebuilding programme. It was a self-perpetuating oligarchy that had already outlived most other citystates in Europe by many decades, if not centuries. Venetian politicians were themselves used to thinking in terms of similarly long timescales, while their neighbouring principalities were concerned simply to ensure the survival of the role of their own houses through the next generation, whether they were d'Este, Sforza, Visconti, Carrara or even Medici.

This very stability, though, was a coin with two different faces. Although the winged lion on one side ensured the continuity and glory of the Republic of St Mark, on the other face was the portrait of the incumbent doge, heavily circumscribed in his freedom of action, enthroned – sometimes (and perhaps appropriately) uncomfortably – on his pyramid of power, all the other levels of which were also constrained by checks and balances of many kinds. Although the apparently endless succession of doges epitomised republican continuity, most of the other institutions of

state were predicated upon individual discontinuity, on the regular rotation of offices, on complex secret balloting, on procedures intended to ensure that no powerful cliques or factions could ever emerge to drive the Republic towards a more princely, authoritarian form of government. All these factors made works of urban improvement extremely difficult both to plan and execute.

As a patron, the Republic's head of state had significant powers of patronage, or, perhaps more accurately, of influence, but which also had to take account of the views of the Signoria, the Dieci and the Procurators of San Marco. Most executed projects were thus essentially the result of collective decision-making by these bodies, with which the doge himself generally concurred. On the other hand, there were occasions when his personal influence did have an important direct effect on such works, particularly if he had the forceful personality of a Francesco Foscari or an Agostin Barbarigo.[13]

As we have seen, many new projects were the result of urgent necessity and acts of God, among them the rebuilding of the *rio* wing of the Palazzo Ducale, the new Fondaco dei Tedeschi, the Procuratie Vecchie, the Scuola Grande di San Marco and the reconstruction of Rialto after 1514: all were the result of fires. Among the major projects that remain, though, the short list is extremely revealing. Those works that were built *ex novo* exhibit a remarkable clarity and consistency of purpose, despite their ostensibly rather different functions. To take the three most prominent state-funded examples, the Porta della Carta, the Arsenale gate and the Torre dell'Orologio: all three are triumphal arches, direct expressions of the republican ideal, the Roman ideal, in fact, since few building typologies are as redolent with classical, and by inference, with republican symbolism, as the triumphal arch, as the surviving examples in Rome, Verona and elsewhere so clearly attest.

Each of these three Venetian arches dignifies a certain aspect of the governance of the Serenissima. The Porta della Carta represents the Republic itself and its intimate identification with the concept of justice. The Arsenale gate represents the martial strength of the Serenissima, and is thus the most directly classical and 'Roman', both stylistically and iconographically. Finally, the Torre dell'Orologio encapsulates not only the concept of *civitas* and the civic dignity of the Piazza, but also represents the Republic's patronage of modern skills and technology. To the extent that these three crucial works represent pivotal aspects of the Republic's culture, then we can claim that, by degrees, the Serenissima did succeed in transforming the capital, or at least these important hubs within it, into a 'city of signs', a Renaissance capital where Republican imagery was harnessed to enhance the new Rome. We can extend this metaphorical application of the triumphal arch beyond these three works to encompass other prominent 'signs' of this period: the great west portal of Santi Giovanni e Paolo, for example, the façade of San Zaccaria, the main portal of the Scuola Grande di San Marco and the entrance screen of that of San Giovanni Evangelista. All of them are triumphal representations of a civic, religious or cultural organisation, contributing to a city that, by 1500, contained many such triumphal entrances, adding dignity and an enhanced sense of *civitas* to the squares in which they stand.

The 'myth of Venice' has been the subject of a great deal of analysis over the last two or three decades. Muir has emphasised the fact that 'partisans admired Venice's liberty, peacefulness and republican form of government. For the Venetians, "liberty" was not a matter of personal freedom, but rather of political independence from other powers'.[14] While undoubtedly true, this is not quite the whole story. Several further aspects of the 'myth' as identified by most modern scholars are, in fact, closely based on other aspects also created and nurtured by the Republic itself: religious piety, for example, and relative tolerance, as well as peace, republican government and stability. Our own contemporary understanding of the myth still tends to be associated, above all, with the Renaissance era, although, as Muir also points out, recognition of these qualities went back considerably earlier than the period generally understood by the term 'Renaissance'; Petrarch, for example, who lived in Venice for many years, wrote in 1364 of 'the one home today of liberty, peace and justice, the one refuge of honourable men'. These were again the qualities that the Republic promoted itself, and again went considerably further than a simple eulogising of political independence, vital though it was.

One specific aspect of the myth, the *primus inter pares* nature of the ducal office, had to be kept (or perhaps, should have been kept) under constant vigilant surveillance by the patriciate as a whole; as we have seen, the behaviour of such forceful doges as Foscari and Agostin Barbarigo attempted to push hard at some of the pre-established boundaries of ducal power and influence. Despite the myriad checks and balances, it had been remarkably easy for Barbarigo to enhance his personal power and prestige; again, in Muir's analysis, it took some decades to 'roll back' some of these images of individual privilege. An interesting example of one of the more direct (albeit subtle) ways to deflect attention away from the Roman aggrandisements of Barbarigo at the Scala dei Giganti was to be the addition of Sansovino's two great figures of Mars and Neptune, intentionally dwarfing the coronation ritual that took place beneath them, and reminding the spectators of the symbolic – and permanent – importance of the two elements of the Republic's empire, as a diversion from the carving of pompous, personalised Latin epithets on the columns beneath.[15]

In cultural terms, the debate over the classicisation or 'Romanisation' of Venice did not, of course, end with the century. Indeed, as we can see today, many of the city's more dramatic Renaissance urban interventions did not take place until well into the sixteenth century, assisted by the maturation of a triumvirate of remarkable architects, the *proto* Sansovino, together with Sanmicheli and Palladio. The scale of their buildings also increased significantly as the century progressed, along with a similarly increasing monumentality and theatricality in almost all of the arts, from the paintings of Tintoretto and Veronese to the church façades of Palladio and the music of the Gabrielli. The earlier fifteenth-century works were, by comparison, more subtly interventionist, although no less remarkable for all that; if Codussi's San Michele appears to us today less powerful and monumental than Palladio's San Giorgio (fig. 206), its intellectual and physical impact on the city's people and its fabric in 1470 was almost certainly greater.

The Scuole Grandi also continued to play a crucial role in *renovatio urbis*. The rich façades of those of San Marco and San Giovanni Evangelista (fig. 207) (and later San Rocco) proclaimed this role very publicly, as pillars of the community, pillars of marble and stone now, rather than of humble brick. The rivalry between them, though, was to drive them towards ever grander edifices, such that in the sixteenth century this spendthrift spiral was to bring at least one Scuola to the brink of bankruptcy and dishonour. The last stage in this process was to be epitomised on the one hand by the lavish opulence of San Rocco (fig. 209) and on the other by the conspicuously overweening ambition of the Scuola della Misericordia (fig. 208), still today a vast, unadorned *folie de grandeur* looming over the backwaters of Cannaregio.[16]

Attempts to build a new Rome: all these projects formed part of the same long-term pattern of urban development from the mid-fifteenth century to the end of the sixteenth. In the last few years of the fifteenth century, Domenico Morosini wrote an essay entitled 'De bene instituta re publica'.[17] It was largely a polemic against 'Foscarian' expansionism, and was sharply criti-

206 San Giorgio Maggiore from the Molo, by Andrea Palladio, begun in 1566, completed *circa* 1610 by Simon Sorella

cal of the Venetian constitution. His tract also contained recommendations for the physical development and beautification of his city as the heart of Venetian civilisation. In a sense Morosini was modernising the principles expounded by Alberti sixty years earlier, although his purpose was much more narrowly focused and, indeed, patriotic. Morosini urged a comprehensive programme of government-directed works of *renovatio urbis*, all to be expressive of the harmony, balance and wealth of the capital city. He was unequivocally prescriptive:

> Crooked streets should be straightened, narrow ones should be widened, those open spaces that give a beautiful view between the buildings . . . should be smoothed out, and should be adorned according to their settings and the houses in them. For such diligence requires no great labour and shows off the ornament and decoration of the city.[18]

Morosini's views were highly influential. He was a close friend of the enlightened doge Cristoforo Moro, patron

of Lombardo at San Giobbe, of Bernardo Bembo (himself promulgator of Alberti's philosophies) and of Pietro Delfin, patron of Codussi at San Michele. Elsewhere, Morosini writes that 'it is right for a well-instituted city to have experienced architects rather than unlearned and rough ones'.

In the decades before he wrote these words, Venice had indeed been gifted with experienced architects and not 'rough' ones: Lombardo and Codussi had led in the transformation of the city where Sansovino and Palladio were to follow, all of them contributing to the *genius loci*, to the refinement of the Dominante, and to the noble principle of *pro bono comunis*.

For a whole host of assorted and interconnected reasons, therefore – civic, liturgical, ambitious, political, patriotic, competitive – Venice's government and its other institutions developed programmes to change not simply the architectural style of the city but also its scale and its imperial character. If the new Rome was to be achieved in purely physical terms, it could be argued, then the Venetians did not achieve this condition until the end of the sixteenth century, with the giant orders

256

207   Scuola Grande di San Giovanni Evangelista: detail showing the entrance screen in the *campo*, with the eagle, symbol of the saint; probably by Pietro and Tullio Lombardo, 1478–81

208   The Scuola Grande della Misericordia: detail of the exterior, by Jacopo Sansovino, begun in 1532, and structurally completed *circa* 1588

209   The Scuola Grande di San Rocco: detail of the rear façade towards the Rio della Frescada, by Sante Lombardo

and looming pediments of Palladio; if, however, we retain the sense of the intellectual spirit of the new Rome, then we may fairly conclude that with this new sense of *civitas*, epitomised by rich, refined new public structures and monuments, and with the continuity of the Republic of Justice, then by the end of the fifteenth century the Republic was indeed fully justified in having carved on the Scala dei Giganti the symbolic letters SPQV, *Senatus Populus que Venetus*.

This city of Venice is a free city, a common home to all men, and it has never been subjugated by anyone, as have been all other cities . . . Its name has achieved such dignity and renown that it is fair to say that Venice merits the title 'Pillar of Italy' . . . It takes pride of place before all others in prudence, fortitude, magnificence, benignity and clemency; everyone throughout the world attests to this.

Marin Sanudo, *Laus urbis venetae*, Venice, 1493.

Appendix I

PEOPLE

I DOGES OF THE MOST SERENE REPUBLIC OF VENICE, 1400–1538

Michele Steno: 1 December 1400–26 December 1413
Tommaso Mocenigo: 7 January 1414–4 April 1423
Francesco Foscari: 15 April 1423–23 October 1457
Pasquale Malipiero: 30 October 1457–5 May 1462
Cristoforo Moro: 12 May 1462–9 November 1471
Niccolò Tron: 23 November 1471–28 July 1473
Niccolò Marcello: 13 August 1473–1 December 1474
Pietro Mocenigo: 14 December 1474–23 February 1476
Andrea Vendramin: 5 March 1476–6 May 1478
Giovanni Mocenigo: 18 May 1478–4 November 1485
Marco Barbarigo: 19 November 1485–14 August 1486
Agostin Barbarigo: 30 August 1486–20 September 1501
Leonardo Loredan; 2 October 1501–22 June 1521
Antonio Grimani: 6 July 1521–7 May 1523
Andrea Gritti: 20 May 1523–28 December 1538

2 *PROTOMAESTRI* TO DEPARTMENTS OF THE REPUBLIC'S GOVERNMENT

Proti to the Provveditori al Sal

Zuan Davanzo: ?–1470
Meneghin (Domenico) Bianco: 1470–73
Niccolò Pain: 1473–20 August 1492
Bartolomeo Bon, il Bergamasco: first recorded 1485; first recorded as *proto* 20 August 1492; died 1509
Pietro Bon: 1496–?1505
Note: Bartolomeo Bon was recorded as Pain's replacement on 23 December 1495, but had clearly been in post for some time (ASV, Provveditori al Sal, B. 6, f. 4, cc. 74t and 75).

Proti to the Procurators of San Marco

Antonio Zelega: ?–1470
Bartolomeo Gonella: 1470–?1505
Pietro Bon: 1505–1529 (death date)
Giorgio Spavento 1486 (first recorded)–1505 (died 17 April 1509)
Jacopo Sansovino: 7 April 1529–27 November 1570 (death date)
Note: there is clearly some overlapping of title and/or function in the case of some of the above. In particular, Spavento's role is unclear. He was recorded as *proto* to the Uffico alle Acque on 25 May 1500.

Proti dil palazzo

Antonio Rizzo: 'unofficial' *proto* 1468; full *proto* May 1484–1498
Pietro Lombardo: March 1499–1511 (died 1515)

Soprastante al Fontego dei Tedeschi

Antonio Abbondi (Scarpagnino): 4 February 1505

Provveditori al Sal for the reconstruction of the Fondaco dei Tedeschi

Francesco Garzoni
Alvise Emo
Andrea Magno
Marco Tiepolo
Pietro Lando
Alvise Sanudo

Proto dell'Ufficio alle Acque

Giorgio Spavento: 25 May 1500

3 PRINCIPAL ARCHITECTS, SCULPTORS AND ARTISTS IN VENICE IN THE FIFTEENTH AND EARLY SIXTEENTH CENTURIES

Abbondi, Antonio (lo Scarpagnino): born Milan, *circa* 1465–70; first recorded in Venice, 1505; died Venice, 26 November 1549

Bardi, Donato di Niccolò (Donatello): born Florence, *circa* 1382; died Florence, 13 December 1466

Bellini, Gentile di Jacopo: born Venice, 1429; died February 1507

Bellini, Giovanni di Jacopo: born Venice, *circa* 1430; died Venice, November 1516

Bellini, Jacopo di Niccolò: born Venice, *circa* 1400; died Venice, *circa* 1470–71

Bon, Bartolomeo di Zane: born Venice, *circa* 1400; first recorded in Venice, 1422; died Venice, between 1464 and 1467

Bon, Bartolomeo 'il Bergamasco': born Bergamo, *circa* 1450; died Venice, (?), 1508–9

Bon, Pietro: first recorded 1496; died Venice, 15 March 1529

Bon, Zane (Giovanni) di Bertuccio: born Venice, *circa* 1360; first recorded 1382; died Venice, 1442

Bregno, Antonio di Giovanni: family originally from Osteno or Righeggia, Lugano; born Como (?); first recorded in Venice, 1425; died 1457

Bregno, Giovanni-Battista di Roberto: born 1466–7; died after 1518

Bregno, Lorenzo di Roberto: born Verona, 1475–85; died Venice, 4 January 1525

Buora, Zane (Giovanni) di Antonio: born Osteno, Lugano before 1450; died Venice, 1513

Carpaccio, Vettor: first recorded in Venice, 1486; died Venice, 1525

Castelfranco, Giorgio da (Giorgione): born Castelfranco Veneto, *circa* 1478; died just before 25 October 1510

Codussi, Mauro: born Lenna (Lentina), Bergamo, *circa* 1440; died Venice, before 23 April 1504

Gambello, Antonio di Marco: first recorded in Venice, 1458; died 1481

Gambello, Vettor di Antonio: born Venice, *circa* 1460; died 1537

Grigi, Giovanni Giacomo di Guglielmo: first recorded 1554; died Venice (?), *circa* 1572

Grigi, Guglielmo (Viellmo) de' (di Giacomo): born Alzano, Bergamo, *circa* 1490; died Venice, *circa* 1533

Lombardo, Antonio di Pietro: born *circa* 1458; died Ferrara, *circa* 1516

Lombardo (Solari), Pietro di Martino: born Carona, Lugano, *circa* 1435; died Venice, June 1515

Lombardo, Sante di Tullio: born Venice 1504; died Venice, 1560

Lombardo, Tullio di Pietro: born *circa* 1455; died Venice, 17 November 1532

Masegne, Jacobello dalle: first recorded in Venice, 1383; died *circa* 1409

Masegne, Pier Paolo dalle: first recorded in Venice, 1383; died *circa* 1403

Rizzo, Antonio: born Verona, before 1440; died Cesena (?), *circa* 1499

Sansovino, Jacopo (Tatti): born Florence, baptised 2 July 1486; died Venice, 27 November 1570

Spavento, Giorgio: born Como; first recorded 1486; died Venice, 17 April 1509

Vecellio, Tiziano (Titian): born Pieve di Cadore, *circa* 1488–90; died Venice, 25 August 1576

Vivarini, Alvise di Antonio: born 1446; died between 1503 and 1505

Vivarini, Antonio di Michele ('da Murano'): born Murano, *circa* 1415 (?); died between 24 March 1476 and 24 April 1484

Vivarini, Bartolomeo di Antonio: born Murano, *circa* 1432; died *circa* 1499

Appendix II

DOCUMENTS

I   CONTRACT BETWEEN THE BON
WORKSHOP AND THE PROVVEDITORI AL SAL
FOR THE PORTA DELLA CARTA

Date: 10 November 1438
Source: ASV, Collegio dei Provveditori al Sal, vol. 3
(1411–1520), c. 8
Published: G. Lorenzi, *Monumenti per servire alla storia del
Palazzo Ducale* (Venice, 1868), document 159.

Jesus: MIIIIXXXVIII on the x day of November
Contract made by *maistro* Zuane Bom, stonemason and
Bortolamio his son. We have agreed with *missier* Tomado
Malipiero and his fellow Provveditori del Sal and of Rialto,
the price of 1700 gold ducats, with the manner and conditions written hereunder, as it appears in a document written
by his hand.
I, Zuane Bom, stonemason, of the parish of sam Marziliam,
and my son Bortolamio, declare to you, magnificent lords,
Provveditori dil Sal, for and in the name of the most Illustrious and ducal Signoria of Venexia, these contracts and
conventions, which we agree to, and which for you will be
observed by ourselves: and, *etiam*, for us by yourselves must
also be observed: that is, with regard to the great portal of
the Palazzo [Ducale] on the side next to the church of our
lord sam Marcho.
First, on your part, the above-mentioned magnificent lords,
you are to give and consign [to the Bon] the blocks of stone
for the said portal, that is, [to make] two buttresses, and the
upper order and that below. Adjacent to which you [the
Provveditori] are to provide the Rovigno stone for the lower
order [the plinth] of the said portal, such that the said lower

order abuts both one side and on the other in the same way,
and *etiam*, in the same manner, you are to give and consign
all of the marble stone [*sic*] in order to carve the figures
which in this said portal are to be fixed, and in the same
manner the pieces of marble foliage above the [upper] arch
of the said portal, to which are also to be fixed naked
cherubs, which are to be fitted in between the said foliage,
as can be seen on the drawing, and in the same way you are
to provide us with the marble stone to form the colonnettes
that are necessary, and above [is to be fixed the figure of]
sam Marcho in the form of a lion:
And on the other part, we, the above-mentioned Zuane Bom
and my son Bortolamio, promise to you, the abovementioned
magnificent lords, *ut supra*, to make and carve the said work,
with all of the decorations that are necessary for it, and with
the sam Marcho in the form of a lion, according to the image
on the drawing which was made for us, and which to yourselves, in your own hands, has been given and consigned; with
the intention that we are obliged to provide and place all of
the stone in addition to that specified *ut supra*, that is,
Rovigno stone and Verona stone: and the said sam Marcho
in the form of a lion we are to make and carve from our
Rovigno stone.
Next, we declare that we are required to form the tracery
with its arches, which will be carved in the same way both
within and without, with the intention that the said portal
with all of its decorations is to be as broad from one side to
the other as the space between the said church of *missier* sam
Marcho as far as [the wall of] the said Palazzo, and the said
portal with all of its decorations is to rise from ground level
as far as the uppermost plinth, and from there upwards we

are to make and carve a figure formed of our own marble, in the form of Justice, following the contents of the said drawing.

And if it pleases you that the said figure is to be carved 'in the round', that is, both within and without, we are in agreement to make and carve it thus.

And, *etiam*, that the said work is to be polished and pumiced and assembled together in a way and manner such that it appears fine. And all of the things that are our responsibility to put into the works, we are obliged to do so.

Item, we are obliged to complete the above-written works within eighteen months of the present date.

Item, we are obliged to arrange all of the transport of the said works to the site, where they are to be placed in the work, and the transport is to be at the expense of the city.

Provveditori al Sal:

Tommaso Malipiero

Antonio Marcello

Paolo Vallaresso

Marco Moro

10 November:

For the price of one thousand and six hundred gold ducats

On 15 November *sier* Filipo Chorer son of *missier* Polo, agrees to pledge 50 ducats

On 17 November *missier* Andrea Zulian agrees to pledge 50 ducats

On 18 November Bertuccio di Jacobello, stonemason of the parish of San Toma, agrees to pledge 50 ducats.

(Note: these three pledges were made in order for the Bon to purchase the remaining necessary stone.)

2   BON'S LACK OF PROGRESS AT THE PORTA DELLA CARTA

Date: 17 April 1442

Source: ASV, Provveditori al Sal, vol. 3 (1411–1520), c. 84

Published: Lorenzi, *Monumenti*, document 162

Copy of an aide-memoire of m[aestro] Zuane Bom with m[aestro] Bortolamio his son, the tenor of which is as follows: It is manifested to you, Lords Provveditori al Sal, that I, Zuane Bom, stonemason, and Bortolamio my son, are in agreement to complete the remainder of the work that is lacking at the great gate of the *palazzo*, within one year from this day, with this [condition]: that the pinnacles at the tops of the buttresses and the three angels that surround the sam Marcho in the centre, and around the upper aedicule we wish to give to you completed within the next three months from the present day; and from three months hence within a further two months we wish to complete and give to you the tracery that is necessary within the arch of the said portal and the other figures; the remainder of the works will be completed by the end of the year described above.

Unde, for the *spettabili et egregij* lords, that is, *missier* Biancho Dolfin, *missier* L. Venier, *missier* Vector Pasqualigo, the afore-mentioned having taken the above-written aide-memoire, are content and remain in accord; regarding the said duties, they [i.e., the Bon] have seen the tenor of the above aide-memoire and agree to observe the conditions, on penalty of a fine of one hundred gold ducats, with no other obstacle or exception to the sequestration of their own goods [to that value] by the lords provveditori al Sal and of Rialto.

3   THE GREAT WEST PORTAL AT SANTI GIOVANNI E PAOLO: BARTOLOMEO BON AND OTHERS

Date: April 1458 to February 1463 (=1464)

Source: Vicenza, Biblioteca Bertoliana, Cronaca della Chiesa e Convento de RR PP Predicatori de Santi Giovanni e Paolo di Venezia; MS G. 8. 29

Published: Gallo, document I

[Extract]

1458. 10 April.

Given for eight marble columns for the portal of the church 24 Ducats: = L. 148. 16

(Which were delivered from Torcello on 5 September of the year 1459, and the Convent paid for the transport costs)

Given to Antonio and Martino (masons) for carving rope mouldings for the portal of the church 10 Ducats = L. 62. 0. 0

Given to Jacobo who worked on the plinth of the portal: L. 5. 0. 0

Given to the same for working on 'quadrum Ostii' [?] 16 Ducats = L. 102. 4. 0

Given to the above stonemasons 2 Ducats = L. 12. 8. 0

1459. 24 April.

Given to master Bartholomeo stonemason for part of his labour, who was working on the portal of the Church 65 Ducats = L. 403. 0. 0

5 November: Given for working on the portal of the church from the first day of August until the fourth day of the month of November, on various items: L. 285. 10. 0

1460. 2 February. Given to master Giovanni from Milan for part of his labour 10 Ducats = L. 62. 0. 0

Given to master Bartholomeo, stonemason, in final payment of his salary for work on the portal of the church L. 186. 0. 0

1462. 4 November. Given to Antonio Paraboy who shipped stone from Rovigno for the portal of the church, one ducat = L. 6. 4. 0

8 November. Given to Domenico Fiorentino, stonemason, for part of the frieze of the church portal six ducats = L. 37. 4. 0

4   CONTRACT WITH BARTOLOMEO BON FOR THE PORTAL OF THE MADONNA DELL'ORTO

Date: 21 June 1460

Source: ASV, Scuole Piccole, B. 417, fasc. A, fol. 83

Published: Gallo, document II

In the name of God on the 21st day of June 1460
It is hereby manifested by ourselves, Rector and Governor and companions of the Scuola of Santa Maria and of San Cristofalo, that is, myself, Giacomo arnoldi as governor of the said scuola, and companions, that we are in agreement with s[er] Bartto[lomi]o de Zan bon, stonemason, to make a certain work for the entrance of the said church; the which work is shown in a drawing which we have in our hands, [and] we intend that there will be saints, such that, as it will appear to us, at the summit there will be one San Christo-fallo and in the centre our lady [sic], and the other carvings as shown on the said drawing, and we are in agreement that for the making of this work he is to receive for its manu-facture and all other expenses until the work is completed and installed, we are to give him two hundred and fifty gold ducats, that is, duc. CCL of gold. With this condition, that the said Bartt[olomi]o is obliged to receive half of this payment [from] the parish priest of Santa Maria delhortto, which is hereby seen to be one hundred and twenty-five ducats, that is, d. 125, all at his own risk, who will freely remain his debtor in the said sum; and of the balance he is to have duc. 40 now; of the remainder [i.e., 85 ducats], up to the sum of duc. 125, (which is the balance of the sum of ducats up to 250 ducats), he is to be given [payments] from time to time [as the work progresses] . . .

With this condition, that the said master is required to com-plete the said work within 15 months from today's date, fin-ished in all respects, and if it is not complete, then, for our interests, he will be required to give to the scuola duc. 50 of gold, intending that for our own part, we will keep our own obligations, declaring that the said promise made by the parish priest will be kept within two years, to ensure there is clarity between them, and if the money is not forthcom-ing from time to time, then on expiry of the time given to him [i.e., Bon] then he will not be obliged to pay the 50 ducats donation as above-written; and for clarity we coun-tersign below to confirm our agreement with that which is written above.

I, bartolamio son of Zuan bon, stonemason, am content with the above-written agreement.

5 PALAZZO GIUSTINIAN AT SAN MOISÈ: THE COSTS OF RECONSTRUCTION

Date: 1478
Source: ASV, Procuratori di San Marco de citra, B. 115, fasc. 17, p. 24
Summary of expenses on the reconstruction over the period 1477–8

Removal of demolition materials: L. 97. 16. 0
Sand: L. 85. 3. 0
Working of stone: L. 79. 17. 0
Timber (supply): L. 856. 12. 0
Carpenters: wages and salaries: L. 465. 0. 0
New roof tiles: L. 33. 11. 0
Unworked stone: L. 204. 2. 0

Nails, etc. (misc. ironwork): L. 60. 5. 0
Fresh water: L. 6. 7. 19
Metalwork for windows: L. 252. 10. 0
Bricks (supply): L. 653. 9. 0
Stonemasons: wages and salaries: L. 229. 12. 0
Windows of glass: L. 82. 0. 0
Terrazzo floors: L. 79. 16. 0
Wood-carving: L. 37. 12. 0
Builders: wages and salaries: L. 542. 16. 0
Lime (supply): L. 248. 17. 0
Minor expenses [spexe menude]: L. 201. 6. 0
Timber (supplies): L. 227. 16. 0
TOTAL expenses: L. 4444. 9. 0

6 SAN ZACCARIA: ANTONIO GAMBELLO AND HIS LOCUM

Date: 1477, 12 April
Source: ASV, San Zaccaria, b. 39 perg. (parchment contract)
Publlished: P. Paoletti, L'architettura e la scultura del Rinascimento in Venezia: ricerche storico-artistiche, 2 vols (Venice, 1893–7), pp. 71–2

1477, 12 April. These are the contracts and conventions newly made between the Monastery of Miss. San Zacharia of Venice, on the one part. And Maistro Antonio quondam Marco, protomaestro of the church of san Zacharia on the other part.

Whereas the above-written Maistro Antonio protomaestro and [sic] has to go to the Levant on the business of our Illustri-ous signoria of Venice, and for the time that he remains away from this city, he is obliged and hereby promises to comply, and to leave a good maistro [in his place], who fully under-stands the designs [in order] to make the templates for the master stonemasons so that they can work and lose no time, the which substitute maistro will be obliged to show the said designs only as he is asked [for them] by the above master masons, and to design them with good and correct propor-tions. The which maestro left [as replacement] for the said maestro Antonio proto is not to receive any money from our monastery for the design and drawing of the said details, which the above maestro Antonio will instruct [him to execute].

Etiam, for the time that the said maestro Antonio protho is away from this city, he is to receive no salary from our Monastery, and although XX master stonemasons and builders – or more, or fewer, as it appears to us to be necessary – will continue to work during this time, we are absolved from making any payment to the said maestro Antonjo protho. And of the work that [he] had completed up to now, and of the rent of the house in which he has been living, we desire and hereby state to the said maestro Antonio and his heirs that they are to have no further rights [in these matters]. And finally, he states to us that from this day he will make no further demands of us.
Item: He concedes [to us] the house in which he lives, with no rent, while he is away from this city, although he is obliged for such rent as may be due as above, and also [he is] to

provide a good, intelligent *maistro* who knows well all of the details necessary to work on our church.

Etiam, we declare that when it pleases God that the said *Maistro* Antonio returns to Venice, we desire and hereby confirm his salary in all respects as may be seen in the contracts and conventions first made between us, the which contracts we declare are to remain valid up to x [ten] years hence, beginning on the abovementioned date, one thousand . . . [*sic*]

MCCCCLXXVII On the xx day of April in the church of San Zaccaria. And for greater clarity and confirmation of the above contract there were called into the church all of the nuns of the monastery *etiam* there was also present the above *Maistro* Antonio *proto*.

I, marco, parish priest, (Stella [?] chaplain of the venerable nuns of san Zacharija), make public the above-written accord *de verbo ad verbum ut jacet*, and all of the nuns confirm it and *maistro* Antonio is also in agreement.

7 SAN ZACCARIA: APPOINTMENT OF MAURO CODUSSI AS *PROTO*

Date: 1483
Source: ASV, San Zaccaria, B. 31 (Fabbriche), c. 172

M[aestr]o moro our *proto* is to have on the XII June following: [in agreement with] the Reverend Mon. the abbess and the chamberlains and the nuns, also present *miss.* Piero donado, and *misser* Lorenzo Loredan with m[aestr]o Antonio: [he is] to be in charge of stonemasonry and the work of builders. And also that of carpentry; and he is to be paid for the time that he works in this city at the rate of LXXX ducats per annum.

Also present: the chamberlains Sammaritana Marcello, Camilla da Mula: and the abbess Lucia Donado.

8 THE SCUOLA GRANDE DI SAN MARCO: PIETRO LOMBARDO AND THE FAÇADE

Date: 18 November 1489
Source: ASV, Scuola Grande di San Marco, B. 136, loose papers, no. 30.
Published: Paoletti, *L'architettura*, p. 103; brief summary in P. Sohm, *The Scuola Grande di San Marco: The Architecture of a Venetian Lay Confraternity* (New York and London, 1982), document 52
Extracts:

MO.C.IIII LXVIIII on the 18th day of November in Venice
It is agreed that on this day a meeting and agreement took place between miss. Nicholo rizo as *vardian* [Guardian Grande] of the Schuola of *mess.* Sam marcho on the one part, and *maistro* piero lonbardo and *maistro* zuam buora, stonemasons and partners at the work of construction of the said schuola, on the other part, each of whom, in part and together, are obliged, without contradiction, to work all of the stone that is needed to complete the said works, as

appears in the drawing . . . with the exceptions solely of the large rectangular 'history' [narrative] relief panel, which is to be positioned centrally between the two windows [on the first floor], and *etiam* the large figure of san marcho in the form of a lion, which is to go at high level, together with the two figures that are [also] lacking, and which are to be placed at the very top; they are obliged to complete or have completed all of the other things by the end of the month of January next [i.e., of 1490], and that which remains by the end of the following month of February; and if they are not complete each one of them is in agreement to suffer the penalty of a deduction of 100 ducats as a discount on the price of the works as contracted, which is to be the sum of 1100 ducats excluding the 'history' relief panel, and thus if they do not attend to these conditions, they will be paid 1000 ducats for all of the works . . . [and] the said *miss.* Nicholo, the *vardian*, promises to give, on this day, 32 ducats in order to pay prioli, the owner of the maran [the ship that transported stone from Istria], and then to pay on a daily basis at the rate of 100 ducats every week . . .

9 THE SCUOLA GRANDE DI SAN MARCO: SUMMARY OF SURVIVING DOCUMENTS

Date: undated, but probably 1504
Source: ASV, Scuola Grande di San Marco, B. 77, Processi, fasc. 3.
Note: This is an extremely useful contemporary summary of crucial surviving documents regarding the construction of the Scuola, filed in B. 77. It was compiled shortly after the last document listed, in 1504. I have rearranged the entries solely to place them in chronological order. The first figure refers to the folio/document number as noted in the archive.

41. 1485: Timber ordered from Andrea Pasqualigo
28. 1487, 18 January [=1488]: Contract and agreement for the schuolla with the noble *ser* And[rea] Pasqualigo, son of *ser* Pietro, who agrees to supply a quantity of timber for the construction of the scholla
42. 1487, 30 January [=1488]: further timber supplies from *ser* Andrea Pasqualigo
34. 1488, 12 March: A contract and agreement in parchment written for the abovementioned scolla with m[aestro] zuanne candj and Marin [de Doimo] carpenters, to make [and install] the floor beams for the fabric of the said scolla, for the price and with the conditions as described in this agreement
29. 1489, 1 May: agreement made by the above scholla with m[aestro] Pietro Lombardo and m[aestr]o zuane Buora, stonemasons, for working stone for the construction of the works
36. 1489, 20 May: Document according to which the *Nobil Huomo ser* Andrea Pasqualigo is obliged to deliver to the scolla all of the timber necessary for the fabric, at the price and with the conditions as can be read in the said contract
31. 1489, 12 June: Certain receipts from And[rea], furnaceman, from Padua, in various sums, for the provision of stone and lime for the scolla

32. 1589 [*sic*], 13 July: copy of a *commandamento* issued by the office of the Giustizia Vecchia to the superintendents Pietro Lombardo and Zuane Buora, stonemasons, confirming the justice of their obligations regarding the delivery of stone to the said scolla

33. 1489, 15 July: Receipt in the sum of 25 ducats given to m[aestro] Zuanne Buxato from the above scolla on account for a cargo of stone for the fabric of the said scolla

30. 1489, 18 November: Text of another agreement between the scolla and the superintendents Pietro Lombardo and Zuanne Buora, stonemasons, for additional work to columns, and cornices and figures

35. 1489 [=1490], 19 February: text of agreement made by the above Zuanne Candj and marin de Doimo, carpenters, with certain other carpenters, to complete the construction of the [first] floor, according to the agreement with the scolla

19. 1490, 1 April: Another account of debit and credit with m[aestr]o Ieronimo and Domenego Moro, stonemasons, for works on the fabric of the chapel, the contents and sums of which are in the said [account]

20. 1490, 7 November: Agreement reached between the scolla on the one part and Pietro Lombardo and partners, *proti* and builders, on the other, on the occasion of works carried out to the above chapel

26. 1490 [=1491], 2 January: An account of debit and credit in semi-folio, entitled additional expenses on account of m[aestr]o moro de martin [Codussi], *proto*, in the total sum and contents as shown in the said document

27. [undated]: two other similar accounts in debit and credit in various separate folios, relating to the above m[aestr]o moro de martin, *proto* of the fabric of the said scholla

25. 1491, 26 May: An account assigned to *ser* Alessandro [Maffei?] for timber for the fabric of the Chapel

18. 1491 until 1499: an account of debit and credit for timber and the expenses of carpenters in connection with the making of benches, and the Chapel, and beams, in the total sum and with the contents described therein

24. 1492, 1 September: A debit account of m[aestr]o Giosafat lovato and m[aestr]o Anto[nio] de luca Burato on account of the works in the sums as described therein

23. 1492 [=1493], 8 February: text and agreement and contract made by the scholla . . . with m[aestr]o marco [?moro], stonemason, for pink and black stone to make the pavement for the scholla

22. 1493, 13 April: Receipt from *ser* Andrea Pasqualigo son of *ser* Piero for 50 ducats received from the scolla for part of the timber for the works

21. 1493, 19 April: Text of an agreement made by the scolla . . . with m[aestr]o Bernardin de Rigo and Domenego Rosina according to which the said [masters] are obliged to provide many pieces of unworked stone for the works on the Chapel, on behalf of m[aestr]o moro de martin, *proto*

14. 1502, 13 [?]: Text of an agreement made by the scolla . . . with nicolo di marco, carpenter, known as zotto [=*zoppo*, lame], for him to make all of the benching for the scolla, with a note of various moneys paid on account

15. 1502, 22 May: Another text of an agreement made by the above scolla with the above-written Nicolo, carpenter, to make another length of benching for the scolla . . . with a receipt from the above for the remainder of the money

17. 1502 [=1503], 10 January: Text of an agreement made by the scolla written with m[aestr]o luca, stonemason of san zane e polo to make a portal above the hall of the scolla similar to that to the albergo, for the sum of 60 ducats

16. 1504: an account of debit and credit for timber for the manufacture of the benching above-written, in the sum of, and according to the contents, written therein.

10   THE SCUOLA GRANDE DI SAN MARCO: CODUSSI AND RIZZO ARE APPOINTED TO EVALUATE THE WORK OF PIETRO LOMBARDO

Date: 1490, 7 November
Source: ASV, Scuola Grande di San Marco, B. 136
Published: Paoletti, *L'architettura*, p. 103; L. Puppi and L. Olivato Puppi, *Mauro Codussi* (Milan, 1977), p. 259; brief summary in Sohm, *The Scuola Grande di San Marco*, document 57

Misser Alvise de Dardani, the *vardian* [Guardian Grande] of the schuola of *miser* San Marcho and his companions, presiding over the said schuola, on the one part, and *misser* Piero Lonbardo and *ser* Zuan Buora and *miser* Bartolomio de Domenego, stonemason, on the other part, are all in accord regarding a compromise agreement in respect of all that the said masters have done in addition to that shown on the contracted drawing and similarly, regarding that which is lacking in the work as shown on the contracted drawing; thus are appointed as arbitrators in word and deed *more veneto*, *ser* Antonio Rizo and maistro Moro [Codussi] of San Zacharia, stonemason, who, having *ut supra* once heard the statements, will adjudicate regarding the above-mentioned matters, as it will appear reasonable and in accordance with their conscience, having none other than God to advise them, and the said parties promising to accept the conclusion of the said judgement. And I, Marcho Pelegrin, have written the above by consent of both parties. And it is countersigned below by the said *messer* the *vardian* and companions.

I, Aluise de Dardani, *vardian* of the scuolla of *messer* San Marco am in agreement *ut supra* and thereby promise to honour [the agreement]

I, Piero Lombardo and companions, we are in agreement with all the above-written.

11   THE PALAZZO DUCALE: FUNDING FOR RECONSTRUCTION

Date: 1484 [=1485], 10 February
Source: ASV, Provveditori al Sal, B. 59, C. 93t.

MCCCCLXXXIIII on the X day of February
Terminazione of the Illustrious Signoria:
That the moneys for [repairs to] the *lidi*, 500 ducats, are to be expended on the building of the *palazzo*.

The undersigned lord Councillors have decreed that, from the 900 ducats from the Provveditori al Sal, allocated every month for works to the littoral . . . 500 ducats per month are to be allocated to the building of the palace . . .

Ducal Councillors:

Dom[enico] mauroceno
Io[hannis] contareno
Ant[onio] Marcello
Franc[esco] de priolis
Leon[ardo] loredan
Marco foscolo

12   THE PALAZZO DUCALE: ANTONIO RIZZO NEGOTIATES A SALARY RISE

Date: 1491, 10 October
Source: ASV, Magistrato al Sal, Notatorio 2, c. 6.
Published: D. Pincus, *The Arco Foscari: The Building of a Triumphal Gateway in Fifteenth Century Venice* (New York and London, 1976), document 21; Lorenzi, *Monumenti*, p. 106; also A. M. Schulz, *Antonio Rizzo, Sculptor and Architect* (Princeton, 1983), p. 131

The magnificent Signori, *missier* Hieronimo Malipiero, *missier* Piero da Mosto, *missier* Zanoto Quirini, *missier* Francesco Nani and *missier* Andrea Venier, most dignified Provveditori al Sal, seeing the instructions issued by the Most Illustrious Signoria, and having heard and understood *maistro* Antonio Rizo, who has explained that being deputed as the surveyor to the fabric of the Palazzo to carve the figures and to do all of the other necessary things for the said fabric, with his salary amounting to one hundred and twenty-five ducats [per annum], on which he is unable to live, nor is he able to make provision for his old age, nor for his family, since he has had to close and abandon his own workshop, to continue which would have resulted in intolerable fatigue; [but] with which his own workshop would have enabled him to have tripled his salary. He is requesting that he receives a salary that is sufficient, so that he may continue to work with a good spirit and as faithfully as he has worked up to now; and having seen how diligently he has proceeded with the said works, and his intolerable fatigue, as by experience one can see by examination of the said works; and since it is necessary for the satisfactory completion and beauty of the said works, that he is able to persevere with a good heart and soul, in order to satisfy the instructions of the Signoria *ut supra*, all [of us] are in agreement and have determined that the said *maistro* Antonio is to receive from this Office each year and every year at the rate of two hundred gold ducats per year for payment of his salary and efforts on the fabric of the said Palazzo, in order for the expeditious continuation and attention to all of the things that are necessary.

13   THE PALAZZO DUCALE: PIETRO LOMBARDO IS APPOINTED AS *PROTO*

Date: 1499, 9 March
Source: ASV, Senato, Deliberazioni, vol. XIII; Magistrato al Sal,

Notatorio, vol. 2, c. 32v.
Published: N. Erizzo, *Relazione storico-critica sulla Torre dell' Orologio di San Marco in Venezia*, 2nd edn. (Venice, 1866), document II; Pincus, *The Arco Foscari*, document 28

Decree of the Most Excellent Senate in which is nominated *m[aestr]o* Pietro Lombardo as *Proto* of the *palazzo* in substitution for *m[aestr]o* Ant[onio] Rizzo: MCCCCLXXXXVIIII on the VIIII March

Having absented himself from this our city Maestro Antonio Rizo, deputed *olim* surveyor to the fabric of the *palazzo*, the which [post] was held with a salary of CXXV ducats per year, and being necessary to provide for the administration of the said works, Maistro Pietro Lombardo has been nominated and substituted, a man highly skilled in his craft, and who, with great diligence and study has attended to the progress of the works from 16 May last up to the present date; it can be seen by experience that he has not lacked, but has attended to all of the things pertinent to his office; it is just and convenient that for his labours and works, he should receive the remuneration and reward that he merits, and especially since he has left his own workshop; and *post posto* every other thing in order to serve and demonstrate to all his virtue and capability; therefore, for this reason, the above-written Lord Councillors have deliberated and decreed unanimously and thus do now deliberate and decree that the said M[aestr]o Piero Lombardo is to have for his salary each year and at the annual rate the same money as was paid to the said M[aestr]o Ant[onio] Rizo, 120 ducats, the which salary is intended to commence from the day in which he began to work at our Pallazo, which was the XVI day *ut supra* of the month of May above-written, such that with a good heart and spirit he may persevere and attend to the construction of the above works. And together [unanimously], the Magnificent Lords, the Heads of the Most Excellent Council of Ten, [hereby] make this above-written deliberation and decree

Councillors:

Victor Caotorta
Faustinus de cha da Pesaro
Paulus Barbaro
Luchas Civranus
Marinus Antonius Maurocenus *aeques* (*cavalier*)
Leonardus Mocenigo

(Note: By a further decree made by the Council of Ten on 21 March 1499, Lombardo was to be paid by the Provveditori al Sal from the salt funds: ASV, Magistrato al Sal, Notatorio, vol. 2, c. 33. There is no clear explanation for the 5-ducat discrepancy in the document noted above.)

14   THE TORRE DELL'OROLOGIO: THE DECISION TO CONSTRUCT THE TOWER

Date: 3 November 1495
Source: ASV, Procuratori di San Marco *de supra*, B. 64, Processo, no. 141, c. 1

1495 on the third day of November in Libro XII of the Most Excellent Pregadi . . .

Since the most worthy and honourable clock that is to be positioned in the *piazza* of san Marco is approaching completion, it is necessary to construct the place where it is to be most conveniently sited, and whereas our procurators of the church of san marco are in agreement to accommodate the wishes of our Signoria as to the place where the said clock is to be positioned; that is, above the mouth [*bocha*] of the *marzaria*, it is opportune to provide the means for this to take place; and therefore:

It is hereby decreed that an immediate start is to be made on the construction of the said work, and all of the necessary decoration, at the expense of our Signoria and [it is] to proceed with all diligence, and with no further delay, and which is to proceed with the minimum of damage to the works already in place, in order that the above clock is placed in the work; We also declare that if in order to construct the said works any damage is caused to the [property] of the said procurators [i.e., parts of the Procuratie Vecchie] it is to be restored at the expense of our above-mentioned Signoria. We further declare that clear and accurate accounts are to be kept of the moneys expended in the said construction, and other decorations to the said clock.

15   COMPLETION OF THE TORRE DELL'OROLOGIO IN PIAZZA SAN MARCO

Date: 20 November 1500
Source: ASV, Procuratori di San Marco *de supra*, B. 64 (Processi), 141, c. 6t.

1500, 20 November in Pregadi
Having made appearances on very many occasions before our Signoria, Zuan Carlo da rezo, the maker of the clock here in the *piazza* of s. Marco at the mouth of the *marzaria*, requesting payment for its manufacture and the expenses that he has incurred, and for which he is still a creditor in the sum of 1728 ducats according to the estimates made by the deputies, *tamen* [he] is desirous to live and to die in this city, and is content to submit all of the matter to arbitration, and to the wishes of our Signoria, having the obligation to find the means of keeping and sustaining himself and his family, not wishing for a single soldo on account of the said credit, and [wishing] to maintain and attend upon the said clock, both he and his heirs and descendants, the which work requires great diligence and study, and in addition to which in order to keep it working effectively requires at least two *famiglj* [assistants or apprentices], and to meet many other expenses, which amount to some 40 ducats a year and more, all of which he has to meet himself.

It is agreed that, first, for the sake of Justice and Equity of this present situation, *de inde*, to conserve and maintain such a fine and ingenious work, which, if it is allowed out of the hands that made it, will fall into ruin, his request is to be expedited: however:

It is decreed that by the authority of this Council it is agreed that for the satisfaction of the said 1728 ducats which the Signoria *ut supra* are to give to him, *etiam*, for the obligation continually to keep, maintain and repair the said clock, all at his own expense, it has been offered and will be given and conceded to the said Zuan Carlo, his heirs and descendants, two of the first *fontegarie* . . . at our flour warehouse at Rialto, with no further burdens or obligations; one of which is in satisfaction of the moneys and the other for the obligation noted above, and he is to remain living where he is at present, with no reduction [in the rent?], as is just and appropriate . . .

16   THE TORRE DELL'OROLOGIO: A CONTEMPORARY INVENTORY

Date: 1531
Source: ASV, Procuratori di San Marco *de supra*, Archivio della Fabbriceria di San Marco: Processi: Horologio de piazza – chiesa, no. CXXXXI
Published: Erizzo, *Relazione*, document IV

Inventory of the Clock of San Marco, consigned by the procurators *de supra* to the new custodian of the Tower, Raffaele Pencino, from Padua:

1   Our Lady, with her throne, with four angels, stars, friezes and balcony, all decorated
2   Item: the clock face towards the *piazza*, with its XII celestial signs, and seven planets above and below, with all of its degrees, letters and stars
3   Item: the four astrolabes with their mechanisms, in the four tondi surrounding the clock-face, all finished and decorated
4   Item: friezes and cornices of copper towards the *piazza*, among them large and small, totalling 125 [linear] feet
5   Item: two small doorways with two angels
6   Item: plates of enamelled copper in the main front façade, with their fixings, weighing 1200 pounds
7   Item: the Most Serene Prince, with his banner, and with his *balle* [?], and 2 no. crosses, fixed onto the large and small bells
8   Item: the sun with its rays, facing the *marzaria*, with a Samharco [*sic*] in the centre and a sun's head at the top
9   Item: the great bell and the small bell, with the two giants complete
10   Item: the casement and the decoration of the clock positioned within the tower, with its columns, cornices, friezes and plinths; and the Clock within the said casement, all plated with tin, and with all of the mechanisms
11   Item: the movement of the clock, with the motion of the VII planets, above and below, with all of the cogs and necessary mechanisms
12   Item: the three Magi, with an angel with its trumpet, and *mantissa*, and with all the necessary mechanisms and movements

Notes and References

ABBREVIATIONS

ASV	Archivio di Stato di Venezia
B., b.	*busta*, envelope of documents
BMV	Biblioteca Nazionale Marciana, Venice
C. , c.	*carta*, sheet or folio
Canc. Inf.	Cancelleria Inferiore, the Lower Ducal Chancery
Cod.	*codice*, codex
Coll.	Collegio
Comm.	Commessaria, estate commission
Cons. d. X	Consiglio dei Dieci, the Council of Ten
Delib.	*deliberazione*, debate
Fasc.	*Fascicolo*, bundle of documents
Fol., fols	folio, folios
L., libr.	*Libro, libretto*: a book or booklet
MC	Maggior Consiglio
Provv. Sal	Provveditori al Sal, the Salt Commissioners
PSMdC	Procurators of San Marco *de citra*
PSMdS	Procurators of San Marco *de supra*
PSMdU	Procurators of San Marco *de ultra*
Quad	*Quaderno*, a small notebook
r	*recto*
Reg.	*Registro*, register
Sen.	Senato
Sez. Not.	Sezione notarile, notarial archive
SG Carità	Scuole Grande di Santa Maria della Carità
SGSGE	Scuola Grande di San Giovanni Evangelista
SGSM	Scuola Grande di San Marco
SG Mis.	Scuola Grande della Misericordia
SGSR	Scuola Grande di San Rocco
t.	*tergo*, back
v	verso

CHAPTER ONE

1 Among the standard works, see F. C. Lane, *Venice: A Maritime Republic* (Baltimore and London, 1973); also J. R. Hale, ed., *Renaissance Venice* (London, 1974); among the essays in the latter, particularly useful is N. Rubinstein, 'Italian reactions to Terraferma expansion in the 15th century', pp. 197–217. An accessible summary is D. S. Chambers, *The Imperial Age of Venice, 1380–1580* (London, 1970). See also the encyclopaedic *Storia di Venezia: dalle origini alla Caduta della Serenissima*, 12 vols (Rome, 1992–8); and G. Arnaldi and M. P. Stocchi, eds, *Storia della cultura veneta*, 6 vols (Vicenza, 1976–86).

2 There are three contemporary accounts of the War of Chioggia: that of Rafain Caresini in *Rerum italicarum scriptores*, vol. XII (Bologna, 1923); that of Galeazzo Gattari, in ibid., vol. XVII; and that of Daniele di Chinazzo in *Monumenti storici*, vol. XX (Venice, 1939).

3 Lane, *Venice*, pp. 228–9.

4 Lane, *Venice*, pp. 225–34.

5 For the domestic economy in the fifteenth century, see G. Luzzatto, *Storia economica di Venezia dal XI al XVI secolo* (Venice, 1995), pp. 173–85. For the state's income from taxes and duties, ibid., pp. 186–94.

6 E. Concina, *L'Arsenale della Repubblica di Venezia: tecniche e istituzioni dal medioevo all'età moderna* (Milan, 1984). For the shipbuilding industry, F. C. Lane, *Venetian Ships and Shipbuilders of the Renaissance*, new edn (Baltimore and London, 1992); and R. C. Davis, *Shipbuilders of the Venetian Arsenal* (Baltimore and London, 1991).

7 For Rialto, see R. Cessi and A. Alberti, *Rialto: l'isola, il ponte, il mercato* (Bologna, 1934; facs. reprint 1988); and

D. Calabi and P. Morachiello, *Rialto: le fabbriche e il ponte* (Turin, 1987).

8 The secondary literature on the Piazza is extensive. For a useful historical analysis, with plans and elevations, see G. Samonà et al., *Piazza San Marco: l'architettura, la storia, le funzioni* (Venice, 1970). For the sixteenth century, see especially M. Morresi, *Piazza San Marco: istituzioni, poteri e architettura a Venezia nel primo Cinquecento* (Milan, 1999). See also ibid., pp. 11–35, for the Procuratie Vecchie.

9 For the loss of the Eastern capital, see D. M. Nicol, *Byzantium and Venice: A Study in Diplomatic and Cultural Relations* (Cambridge, 1988), pp. 381–407.

10 Luzzatto, *Storia economica*, pp. 165–6. The costs of wars and of the 'routine' defence of the Terraferma empire were enormous. In a single year, 1432, the latter cost more than 1 million ducats to defend; the war against the Carrara in the years 1404–6 cost 2 million ducats; the *conquista* (i.e., the further expansion) of the Terraferma empire over the period 1428–38 cost 7 million ducats, and the Turkish war of the early 1470s cost 1.2 million ducats per annum. In order to help fund the last of these, in 1463 the Republic instituted the *decima*, a tithe based on the estimated value of real estate, itself the result of a property register, the *catastico*. Between 1463 and 1479 the Republic resorted to the *decima* no fewer than 40 times, on each occasion raising approximately 75–80,000 ducats. All of these figures from J.-C. Hocquet, *Denaro, navi e mercanti a Venezia, 1200–1600* (Rome, 1999), pp. 34 et seq. (with further bibliography). Even in times of peace, regular defence costs were substantial; in the 1490s these typically amounted to 170,000 ducats per annum for military wages; 90,000 ducats for *castellani* and provisions; and 100,000 for the Arsenale, totalling 360,000 ducats per annum (These last figures from Hocquet, ibid., citing M. Knapton, 'I rapporti fiscali tra Venezia e la terraferma', *Archivio veneto*, CXVII, 1981).

11 Lane, *Venice*, pp. 290–91; Luzzatto, *Storia economica*, pp. 218–21; see also F. C. Lane, *I mercanti di Venezia* (Turin, 1982), pp. 219–36. For the recovery of the spice trade after 1500, see Lane, *I mercanti*, pp. 195–203; Luzzatto, *Storia economica*, pp. 228–38. See also F. C. Lane and R. C. Mueller, *Money and Banking in Medieval Venice*, 2 vols (Baltimore and London, 1985–97).

12 The Cambrai crisis: see all of the general histories of the Republic; also F. Gilbert, 'Venice in the crisis of the League of Cambrai', in Hale, ed., *Renaissance Venice*, pp. 274–92.

13 See note 11 above. See also E. Concina, *Fondaci: architettura, arte e mercatura tra Levante, Venezia e Alemagna* (Venice, 1997).

14 See especially P. Maretto, *L'edilizia gotica veneziana* (Rome, 1961); E. Arslan, *Venezia gotica* (Milan, 1970).

15 R. J. Goy, *The House of Gold: Building a Palace in Medieval Venice* (Cambridge, 1993). For a general survey of the treatment of façades, marble cladding, etc., see W. Wolters, *Architektur und Ornament: Venezianischer Bauschmuck der Renaissance* (Munich, 2000), especially pp. 50–61.

16 Palazzo Medici, by Michelozzo, was begun in 1444, Alberti's Palazzo Rucellai *circa* 1453 and Palazzo Strozzi by Benedetto da Maiano in 1489. In Venice, Ca' Dario dates from *circa* 1487, Codussi's Palazzo Lando (Corner Spinelli) from *circa* 1490 and Palazzo Loredan (later Vendramin Calergi) from *circa* 1502–4. For Alberti, see F. Borsi, *Leon Battista Alberti* (Oxford, 1977). For further detail of the complex dating of Palazzo Rucellai, see R. Tavernor, *On Alberti and the Art of Building* (New Haven and London, 1998), pp. 7–97, with bibliography. Ca' Dario has a truly Renaissance-inspired inscription on the façade, URBIS GENIO IOANNES DARIUS, dedicated to the 'spirit of the city'.

17 D. Howard, *Venice and the East: The Impact of the Islamic World on Venetian Architecture, 1100–1500* (New Haven and London, 2000).

18 The painting is cited by Giorgio Vasari in his *Lives of the Artists*, first complete English edn, trans. J. Foster (London, 1878), vol. II, p. 48.

19 *De re aedificatoria* (Florence, 1485); first Italian edn, trans. Pietro Lauro (Florence, 1546); first English edn, trans. Giacomo Leoni (London, 1726). Venice remained a vital hub for the dissemination of architectural ideas via its European domination of the printing industry; see especially M. Lowry, *Il mondo di Aldo Manuzio: affari e cultura nella Venezia del Rinascimento* (Rome, 2000). For a concise survey of Venice's importance in European information communications generally, see P. Burke, 'Early modern Venice as a center of information and communications', in J. Martin and D. Romano, eds, *Venice Reconsidered: The History and Civilization of an Italian State, 1297–1797* (Baltimore and London 2000), pp. 389–419. See especially the table of published architectural treatises, pp. 409–10.

20 In the early fifteenth century, artistic links were closer than architectural ones; links between Florence and Padua were particularly strong. Pietro Lamberti and Nanni di Bartolo worked in the Santo in 1430, and three years later Filippo Lippi also worked there. Ten years later he was followed by Donatello. Padua received a number of illustrious exiles from Florence, including Cosimo de' Medici, before he moved on to Venice. For Codussi, see L. Puppi and L. Olivato Puppi, *Mauro Codussi* (Milan, 1977).

21 C. R. Mack, *Pienza: The Creation of a Renaissance City* (Ithaca, NY, and London, 1987); G. Gerboni Baiardi et al., eds, *Federigo da Montefeltro: lo stato, le arti, la cultura*, 3 vols (Rome, 1986); M. L. Polichetti, *Il Palazzo di Federigo da Montefeltro* (Urbino, 1985).

22 For Michelozzo, see M. Ferrara and F. Quinterio, *Michelozzo di Bartolomeo* (Florence, 1984). For his visit to Venice, see Vasari, *Lives*, vol. I, p. 497.

23 On the humanists, see M. King, *Umanesimo e patriziato a Venezia nel quattrocento*, 2 vols (Rome, 1989); for summaries of the careers of Girolamo Donà, see pp. 532–5; for Ermolao Barbaro, pp. 460–62; for Bernardo Bembo, pp. 482–8. For Bembo, see also V. Cian, 'Per Bernardo Bembo', *Giornale storico della letteratura italiana*, XXVIII (1896); A. della Torre, 'La prima ambasce-

ria di Bernardo Bembo a Firenze', *Giornale storico della letteratura italiana*, XXV (1900). For Ermolao Barbaro, see V. Branca, 'Ermolao Barbaro and late quattrocento Venetian humanism', in Hale, ed., *Renaissance Venice*, pp. 218–43.

24 Filarete (Antonio Averlino), *Trattato di architettura*, ed. A. M. Finoli and L. Grassi (Milan, 1972) [Florence, Biblioteca Nazionale, Cod. Magliabechiana II, I, 140]. Filarete was in Venice in 1449. For his involvement at the Ca' del Duca, see below, pp. 136–9. For a concise summary of Filarete's work and influence, see J. Onians, *Bearers of Meaning: The Classical Orders in Antiquity, the Middle Ages and the Renaissance* (Princeton, 1990), pp. 50–61.

25 V. Fontana, *Fra Giovanni Giocondo, architetto, 1432–1515* (Vicenza, 1988); Francesco di Giorgio Martini, *Trattati di architettura, ingegneria e arte militare*, ed. C. Maltese (Milan, 1967). In 1492 Giocondo illustrated a manuscript of Francesco's treatise for the court at Naples: see F. P. Fiore and M. Tafuri, eds, *Francesco di Giorgio architetto* (Milan, 1993).

26 E. Concina, *Storia dell'architettura di Venezia dal VII al XX secolo* (Milan, 1995), p. 123.

27 Mack, *Pienza*.

28 For the planning of Ferrara, see T. Dean, *Land and Power in Late Medieval Ferrara: The Rule of the Este, 1350–1450* (Cambridge, 1988); also A. F. Marciano, *L'età di Biagio Rossetti: Rinascimento di casa d'Este* (Ferrara, 1991). For Milan, see G. Lubkin, *A Renaissance Court: Milan under Galeazzo Maria Sforza* (Berkeley, CA, and London, 1994). For Sansovino at San Marco, see D. Howard, *Jacopo Sansovino: Architecture and Patronage in Renaissance Venice* (New Haven and London, 1975); and M. Morresi, *Jacopo Sansovino* (Venice, 2000).

29 For the orientalist influences, see Howard, *Venice and the East*, passim.

30 For the Scuola Grande di San Marco, see below, pp. 191–215. For Brunelleschi's early works, see H. Klotz, *Filippo Brunelleschi: The Early Works and the Medieval Tradition* (New York and London, 1990); G. Marchini, *Giuliano da Sangallo* (Florence, 1942).

31 The site of the Dominican house was given to the order in 1234 by Doge Iacopo Tiepolo, who owned extensive marshy land in this part of the city. Land for the Franciscans was given two years later; it was also marshy, and part of it was occupied by a pond known as the Lago Badoer.

32 See especially P. Sohm, *The Scuola Grande di San Marco, 1437–1550: The Architecture of a Venetian Lay Confraternity* (New York and London, 1982); and excerpts from 'Il Sogno di Caravia' by Alessandro Caravia (1541), trans. R. MacKenney in D. S. Chambers and B. Pullan, eds, *Venice: A Documentary History, 1450–1630* (Oxford and Cambridge, MA, 1992), pp. 213–16. For the rivalries between the Scuole Grandi, see also M. Tafuri, *Venice and the Renaissance*, trans. J. Levine (Cambridge, MA, and London, 1989), pp. 81–97; and B. Pullan, *Rich and Poor in Renaissance Venice: The Social Institutions of a Catholic*

State (Cambridge, MA, and Oxford, 1971), pp. 33–62, 84–98, and especially pp. 99–131.

33 Marin Sanudo, *De origine, situ et magistratibus urbis Venetae, ovvero La città di Venetia*; as *La città di Venetia*, ed. A. C. Arico (Milan, 1980), pp. 85–90. For analysis of the Venetian constitution, see G. Maranini, *La costituzione di Venezia*, 2 vols (Florence, 1927; new paperback edn, 1974); see especially vol. II, pp. 273–324. For the State Archives, see A. da Mosto, *Archivio di Stato di Venezia: indice generale*, 2 vols (Rome, 1937–40). There are also summaries in *Guida generale degli archivi di stato italiani*, 4 vols (Rome, 1994): M. F. Tiepolo, 'Archivio di Stato di Venezia', ibid., vol. IV, pp. 859–1148 (hereafter 'Tiepolo, *Guida generale*').

34 Maranini, *La costituzione*, vol. I, pp. 262–314; Sanudo, *La città di Venetia*, pp. 100, 243; da Mosto, *Archivio*, vol. I, p. 34; Tiepolo, *Guida generale*, p. 894. See also ASV, Sen., Delib., vol. XIII, and ASV, Provv. Sal, Notatorio 2.

35 See below, p. 41 et seq.

36 The Senate appointed Lombardo as *proto* at the Doge's Palace in 1499; this was ratified by the Consiglio dei Dieci, who confirmed that he was to be paid out of the 'salt fund': ASV, Sen., Delib., vol. XIII.

37 Maranini, *La costituzione*, vol. I, pp. 207–40, 332–64; vol. II, pp. 35–130. Also Sanudo, *La città di Venetia*, pp. 145–52; F. Sansovino and G. Martinioni, *Venetia, città nobilissima et singolare . . .*, 2 vols (Venice, 1663; new facs. edn, 1968); da Mosto, *Archivio*, vol. I, p. 29; Tiepolo, *Guida generale*, p. 887.

38 Maranini, *La costituzione*, vol. II, pp. 385–444; Sanudo, *La città di Venetia*, pp. 98–100, 241–3. For a new evaluation of the identity of the Maggior Consiglio at the end of the fifteenth century, see S. Chojnacki, 'Identity and ideology in Renaissance Venice: the third *Serrata*', in Martin and Romano, eds, *Venice Reconsidered*, pp. 263–94.

39 Sanudo, *La città di Venetia*, pp. 104–6; da Mosto, *Archivio*, vol. I, p. 25. The best overall study of the roles and duties of the Procurators is R. C. Mueller, 'The Procurators of San Marco in the 13th and 14th centuries: a study of the office as a financial and trust institution', *Studi veneziani*, XIII (1971), pp. 105–220.

40 Sansovino and Martinioni, *Venetia*, vol. I, p. 297.

41 Howard, *Sansovino*. For the two Bon, see M. Tafuri, *Venice and the Renaissance*, p. 219, note 3. See also the career of Spavento, who held the office of *proto* from 1486 to his death in 1509.

42 Sanudo, *La città di Venetia*, pp. 107–8, 245–6; da Mosto, *Archivio*, vol. I, p. 142.

43 R. J. Goy, *Chioggia and the Villages of the Venetian Lagoon: Studies in Urban History* (Cambridge, 1985), p. 68. For salt revenues in the fifteenth century, see Hocquet, *Denaro*, especially pp. 73–102.

44 Sanudo, *La città di Venetia*, pp. 107–8.

45 ASV, Provv. Sal, B. 6, fasc. 3 (1411–1520), c. 8.

46 For the Provveditori, see ASV, Provv. Sal, B. 6, cc. 20t, 21; for diversion of funds to the Doge's Palace, see ASV, Provv. Sal, B. 59, c. 93t. Considerable revenues still derived from salt duty; in the 1460s they were in the

order of 165,000 ducats (approximately 1 million lire) per annum; see Luzzatto, *Storia economica*, p. 192; Hocquet, *Denaro*, pp. 17 et seq.

47 For the customs house, see ASV, Provv. Sal, B. 60, c. 271t (1525), when 332 ducats were spent on repairs. ASV, Provv. Sal, B. 6 ('Parti') contains many examples of such expenditure.

48 ASV, Provv. Sal, B. 59, c. 132t. For an attempt at summarising the offices of *proto* to the Procurators and others, see Appendix I, no. 2. Pain's term of office seems to have overlapped with that of Bon, who is first recorded as *proto dil sal* in 1485.

49 For Rizzo, see below, pp. 219–28.

50 The Piovego: Sanudo, *La città di Venetia*, pp. 123, 258; da Mosto, *Archivio*, vol. I, p. 178; Tiepolo, *Guida generale*, p. 979. For examples of the role of the Piovego in supervising and controlling construction activity, see ASV, Piovego, B. 4, fol. 1, covering the period 1517–21.

51 Sanudo, *La città di Venetia*, pp. 109–10, 247; da Mosto, *Archivio*, vol. I, p. 178.

52 Sanudo, *La città di Venetia*, pp. 136–7, 266–7.

53 Sanudo, *La città di Venetia*, p. 252.

CHAPTER TWO

1 C. Tentori, *Della legislazione veneziana* (Venice, 1792), pp. 95, 121.

2 The two essential studies of Rialto are: R. Cessi and A. Alberti, *Rialto: l'isola, il ponte, il mercato* (Bologna, 1934; facs. reprint 1988); and D. Calabi and P. Morachiello, *Rialto: le fabbriche e il ponte* (Turin, 1987), especially part 1, pp. 5–170.

3 For the encroachment of the loggia by the market traders, see Calabi and Morachiello, *Rialto*, p. 35. For a later record from 1487, see ASV, Provv. Sal, B. 60, p. 24; and ASV, Sen., Terra, Reg. 10, c. 70v.

4 Calabi and Morachiello, *Rialto*, p. 11; citing ASV, MC, Leona, c. 75v.

5 ASV, MC, Leona, c. 92v (29 December 1397).

6 ASV, MC, Leona, c. 87 (28 March 1396).

7 ASV, Sen., Misti, LV, cc. 3v et seq. (11 March 1424); cited in Cessi and Alberti, *Rialto*, p. 61.

8 ASV, Sen., Misti, LV, c. 30 (2 June 1424).

9 Calabi and Morachiello, *Rialto*, pp. 25, 36. See also D. Howard, *Venice and the East: The Impact of the Islamic World on Venetian Architecture, 1100–1500* (New Haven and London, 2000), pp. 117–18; P. Fortini Brown, *Venetian Narrative Painting in the Age of Carpaccio* (New Haven and London, 1988), p. 268. *Plus ça change* . . . the problems of congestion at Rialto span the centuries. As I write this, the *comune* is engaged in a struggle with traders to relocate some of the stalls from the Ruga dei Oresi into the Campo della Bella Vienna, yet again to ease congestion at the bridge foot.

10 ASV, Provv. Sal, B. 6, fasc. 4, c. 23.

11 ASV, Provv. Sal, B. 59, c. 164t (20 October 1487): 'essendo il rialto uno dei piui nobeli luogi di questa cita'.

12 ASV, Provv. Sal, B. 59, c. 169.

13 ASV, Sen., Terra, Reg. 10, c. 70v.

14 ASV, Provv. Sal, B. 59, c. 194t.

15 Calabi and Morachiello, *Rialto*, p. 29. See especially E. Concina, *Fondaci: architettura, arte e mercatura tra Levante, Venezia e Alemagna* (Venice, 1997), pp. 119–24. The *fondaco* survived until the nineteenth century, when it was demolished and the adjacent canal reclaimed. The front block facing the Grand Canal contained the offices, while the central archway led into the long narrow central *cortile*, flanked by two rows of *fontegarie*. See also ASV, Provv. alle Biade, B. 2, reg. 4. Much of the same ground as Concina's *Fondaci* is covered in summary by the same author in 'I fondaci del medioevo veneziano', in F. Valcanover and W. Wolters, eds, *L'architettura gotica veneziana. Atti del Convegno Internazionale di Studio: Venice, 27–9 November 1996* (Venice, 2000), pp. 131–8.

16 ASV, Provv. Sal, B. 59, c. 278.

17 L. B. Alberti, *De re aedificatoria* (Florence, 1485), Book VIII, chapter VI.

18 ASV, Provv. Sal, B. 60, c. 146; the costs of the fish stalls were given as 759 lire (27 April 1511).

19 M. Sanudo, *De origine, situ et magistratibus urbis Venetae, ovvero La città di Venetia*; as *La città di Venetia*, ed. A. C. Arico (Milan, 1980), p. 110.

20 ASV, Provv. Sal, B. 6, fasc. 4, c. 41.

21 Calabi and Morachiello, *Rialto*, p. 177, citing G.-B. Galliciolli, *Delle memorie venete antiche, profane ed ecclesiastiche*, 8 vols (Venice, 1795), I, v, pp. 143–6, and the Savina chronicle (BMV, MSS It., cl. VII, no. 134, c. 189r). Also Sanudo, *La città di Venetia*, p. 21.

22 ASV, Sen., Terra, Reg. 4, cc. 83 and 87; see also Calabi and Morachiello, *Rialto*, p. 178, and Cessi and Alberti, *Rialto*, p. 169.

23 For the shops, see Calabi and Morachiello, *Rialto*, p. 182. This is the condition of the bridge as illustrated by both Carpaccio in 1494 and de' Barbari in 1500. An annual rent of 500 lire was raised: Cessi and Alberti, *Rialto*, p. 169.

24 ASV, Provv. Sal, B. 6, fasc. 4, cc. 119t, 120, 120t. See also ASV, Provv. Sal, B. 61, reg. 4, c. 184v.

25 ASV, Provv. Sal, B. 6 fasc. 4, c. 163; cited in Cessi and Alberti, *Rialto*, pp. 171–2.

26 ASV, Coll., reg. 12, c. 32v (18 November 1475); cited in Calabi and Morachiello, *Rialto*, p. 180.

27 There is an excellent summary of the history of the Fondaco dei Tedeschi in E. Concina, *Fondaci*, pp. 152–81. See also H. Simonsfeld, *Der Fondaco dei Tedeschi in Venedig und die deutsch-venetianischen Handelsbeziehungen*, 2 vols (Stuttgart, 1887). For the decision to proceed with reconstruction, see M. Sanudo, *I diarii*, ed. R. Fulin et al., 58 vols (Bologna, 1879–1903), vol. VI, 131 (4 February 1505). See also J. McAndrew, *Venetian Architecture of the Early Renaissance* (Cambridge, MA, and London, 1980), pp. 434 et seq.; Howard, *Venice and the East*, pp. 129–31.

28 Sanudo, *I diarii*, vol. VIII, 97.

29 ASV, Provv. Sal, Parti del Collegio dil Sal, reg. 4, c. 166.

30 Concina, *Fondaci*, pp. 202–17. For summaries of the career and importance of Bernardo Bembo and other leading humanists of this period, see M. King, *Umanesimo e patriziato a Venezia nel quattrocento*, 2 vols (Rome, 1989), passim., but especially vol. II, pp. 482–8.

31 Spavento's appoinment was confirmed two days later in the records of the Provveditori al Sal: ASV, Provv. Sal, B. 60, p. 86.

32 For a concise summary of 'what is known' about the construction of the new Fondaco, see Concina, *Fondaci*, pp. 169 et seq.

33 Sanudo, *I diarii*, vol. VII, 30 (15 March 1507). For a note on the funding that was necessary to support such rapid reconstruction, see below, p. 58.

34 Concina, *Fondaci*, p. 154.

35 There is an extensive bibliography on the frescos at the Fondaco by Titian and Giorgione, beginning with Giorgio Vasari (*Lives of the Artists*, first complete English edn, trans. J. Foster, London, 1878, vol. II, pp. 398–9, Giorgione, and vol. V, p. 384, Titian). See also T. Pignatti, 'Giorgione e Tiziano', in *Tiziano*, exhibition catalogue (Venice, 1990), pp. 68–76, with further bibliography. For a more detailed discussion of the design of the *cortile* and other elements, see McAndrew, *Venetian Architecture*, pp. 434 et seq. The rhythm of paired windows on the façade of the Fondaco is a reflection of the internal planning; each room has a central fireplace, flanked by a window on either side. The mullion between the paired windows thus represents the cross wall between the rooms. A row of tall Venetian chimneys also formerly enlivened the skyline.

36 McAndrew, *Venetian Architecture*, p. 443. On 12 May 1508 the Republic published its new 'house rules' for the German merchants who were to occupy the new Fondaco: see D. S. Chambers and B. Pullan, eds, *Venice: A Documentary History, 1450–1630* (Oxford, 1992), pp. 329–40. The rooms were available to rent on an annual basis, those on the first and second floors at 12 ducats per annum, those on the top floor at 8 ducats. The Fondaco was managed on behalf of the Republic by three officials known as *Visdomini*: Sanudo describes their roles and duties in *La città di Venetia*, pp. 273–4.

37 All the relevant documents are in ASV, Procuratori di San Marco *de citra* (hereafter PSMdC), B. 26. Michiel's will is in B. 26, b. 1, and the building records are in B. 26, b. 9.

38 ASV, PSMdC, B. 26, b. 9.

39 See also P. Maretto, *La casa veneziana nella storia della città* (Venice, 1986), p. 348.

40 G. Gianighian and P. Pavanini, *Dietro i palazzi: tre secoli di architettura minore a Venezia, 1492–1803* (Venice, 1984), pp. 68–9; Maretto, *La casa veneziana*, p. 381.

41 For all the above, see ASV, PSMdC, B. 54, fasc. XXVI (Comm. Giorgio Baseggio).

42 ASV, PSMdC, B. 54, quad. 2 (1418–90).

43 For all of the above, see ASV, PSMdC, B. 54, fasc. XXVI.

44 For the well, see ASV, PSMdC, B. 53, fasc. 7, c. 1.

45 The later history of the site is rather complex. In 1504–5 an adjacent site, which occupied the land between the Corte Nova and the end wall of the Scuola Vecchia della Misericordia, was itself redeveloped. It was completed in 1505; thus from this date onwards our own 1440s Corte Nova was really the Corte Vecchia. The portal, which today forms the entrance to the remains of the first Corte Nova, is itself an assemblage, which incorporates material from the entrance of the first Corte Nova as well as the inscription of 1505 from the second development. See G. Fabbri, ed., *La Scuola Grande della Misericordia* (Venice, 1999), p. 23, with references on pp. 60–61, and maps on pp. 102–3.

46 For the estates of India Formenti and Dandola Caroso, see ASV, PSMdC, B. 133, fasc. 1, 4 and 5.

47 ASV, PSMdC, B. 115 (Comm. Francesco Giustinian), fasc. 17. See Appendix II, document 5.

48 For detailed further bibliography, see E. Arslan, *Venezia gotica* (Milan, 1970), p. 323 and note 48; also P. Paoletti, *L'architettura e la scultura del Rinascimento in Venezia: ricerche storico-artistiche*, 2 vols (Venice, 1893–7), p. 44, note 9. There is a *stemma* on the façade that Rizzi has dated to the reconstruction *circa* 1474: A. Rizzi, *Scultura esterna a Venezia* (Venice, 1987), p. 110 (San Marco no. 77).

49 See note 46 above.

50 For all of the above, see ASV, PSMdC, B. 115, fasc. 17, cc. 1–24.

51 For the five cottages, see ASV, PSMdC, B. 115, fasc. 17, supplementary account on cc. 26–33.

52 The name of the family and their chapel is frequently, but incorrectly, Italianised to Emiliani. However, the Miani, like the Vitturi, were an ancient Venetian clan, some branches of which were noble. For the use (and status) of marble in this period, see J. Strupp, 'The color of money: use, cost and aesthetic appreciation of marble in Venice *c.* 1500', *Venezia Cinquecento*, V (1993), pp. 7–32.

53 All the Miani chapel documentation is in ASV, PSMdC, B. 67, which is filed together with B. 65 and 66. There is a paper copy of Margherita's will in fasc. 4. The Miani chapel was nearly built elsewhere: as F. Corner records (*Notizie storiche delle chiese e monasteri di Venezia e di Torcello*, Padua, 1756 [facs. edn, Bologna 1990], p. 643), the chapel was to be built either at San Michele or San Francesco della Vigna. However, 'Non essendovi dunque contiguo al Monastero di San Francesco sito opportuno per collocarla, fu con la più nobile magnificenca eretta a canto della Chiesa di San Michele, ed abbellita con fini marmi Orientali'.

54 The chapel has suffered serious structural difficulties over the centuries as a result of this vulnerable location, exacerbated in recent times by the *moto ondoso* of numerous powered boats. It is at present (2003–5) being restored by the Venice in Peril Fund.

55 The building accounts are located thus: ASV, PSMdC, B. 67: lib. no. 19 (quad. 1, cc. 1–45): 1527–9; quad. 2: 1530–32; quad. 3: 1533–4. Contrary to some accounts, de' Grigi did not die in 1530; he was certainly active until the summer of 1533.

56 For all of the above, see ASV, PSMdC, B. 67, quad. 1, especially cc. 10 and 13; quad. 2, especially c. 1. For a survey of the various marbles used in Venetian construction, see L. Lazzarini, 'I materiali lapidei dell'edilizia storica veneziana', *Restauro e Città*, II/3–4 (1986), pp. 84–92; and L. Lazzarini on San Marco in R. Polacco, ed., *Storia dell'arte marciana: l'architettura* (Venice, 1997), pp. 309–26. See also the summary on marble cladding in W. Wolters, *Architektur und Ornament: Venezianischer Bauschmuck der Renaissance* (Munich, 2000), pp. 50–61. For the construction of the Miani chapel cupola, see L. Cicognara, A. Diedo and G.-A. Selva, *Le fabbriche più cospicue di Venezia misurate, illustrate ed intagliate dai membri della Veneta Reale Accademia di Belle Arti*, 2 vols (Venice, 1815–20), vol. 1, fig. 164.

57 ASV, PSMdC, B. 67, quad. 3, c. 2.

58 ASV, PSMdC, B. 67, quad. 3, c. 38.

CHAPTER THREE

1 For the building accounts, see ASV, SG Carità, B. 227, no. 104. The works took place between June 1443 and about mid-January 1444.

2 See below, p. 192.

3 For the funding of the reconstruction of the Fondaco, see ASV, Provv. Sal, B. 60, c. 164 (Cons. d. x and Zonta, 19 April 1505).

4 See below, pp. 159–60. See also F. Corner, *Notizie storiche delle chiese e monasteri di Venezia e di Torcello* (Padua, 1758; facs. edn, Bologna 1990), pp. 42–5.

5 See, for example, the lists of *elemosine* in the building accounts of San Zaccaria and the Carità church.

6 For further comment on the Scuola Grande di San Marco, see P. Sohm, *The Scuola Grande di San Marco, 1437–1550: The Architecture of a Venetian Lay Confraternity* (New York and London, 1982), pp. 13–19. For detailed discussion of the constitutions of the Scuole, see B. Pullan, *Rich and Poor in Renaissance Venice: The Social Institutions of a Catholic State: to 1620* (Oxford and Cambridge, MA, 1971), pp. 40–62; and Sohm, *The Scuola Grande di San Marco*, pp. 6–19.

7 Sohm, *The Scuola Grande di San Marco*, p. 10; and ASV, Cons. d. x, Misti, Reg. 22, fol. 124r.

8 H. A. Millon, 'I modelli architettonici nel rinascimento', in Millon and V. M. Lampugnani, eds, *Rinascimento da Brunelleschi a Michelangelo: la rappresentazione dell'architettura* (Milan, 1994), pp. 19–73, with excellent illustrations of many of the finest models of the era. It should be noted that the term *modello* in contemporary documentation can have two or three meanings: it can refer to a permanent physical model of wood, a more temporary 'sketch' model or simply a drawing.

9 ASV, San Zaccaria, B. 31, c. 4. See p. 169 below.

10 ASV, San Zaccaria, B. 31, c. 7.

11 D. Calabi, *Il mercato e la città* (Venice, 1993), p. 241. For the Fondaco dei Tedeschi, see E. Concina, *Fondaci: architettura, arte e mercatura tra Levante, Venezia e Alemagna* (Venice, 1997), pp. 152–81.

12 For the Florentine experience, see R. Goldthwaite, *The Building of Renaissance Florence* (Baltimore and London, 1980), passim. See also C. L. Frommel, 'Sulla nascita del disegno architettonico', in Millon and Lampugnani, eds, *Rinascimento*, pp. 101–21. Among the extensive work on drawings in this era, see J. Ackerman, 'Architectural practice in the Italian Renaissance', in his *Distance Points: Essays in Theory and Renaissance Art and Architecture* (Cambridge, MA, 1991), pp. 361–78; W. Lotz, *Studies in Italian Renaissance Architecture* (Cambridge, MA, 1977).

13 ASV, Sez. Not., Atti Ferro Vittore, B. 541.

14 ASV, Provv. Sal, vol. 3, c. 8. See also below, pp. 113–14.

15 As, for example, the Molo window contract and some of the freestanding figure sculptures at the Porta della Carta.

16 For masons' templates (*sagome* or *modani*), see T. E. Cooper, 'I modani', in Millon and Lampugnani, eds, *Rinascimento*, pp. 494–500.

17 For the 'classifications' of rich and poor in the Scuole Grandi, see especially B. Pullan, *Rich and Poor*, pp. 63–83. The issue of citizenship is a complex one, and varied over time. For a recent analysis, see J. Grubb, 'Elite citizens', in J. Martin and D. Romano, eds, *Venice Reconsidered: The History and Civilization of an Italian State, 1297–1797* (Baltimore and London, 2000), pp. 339–64. The class of *cittadini* was numerically quite small, and it seems unlikely that anything other than a minority of the construction industry's members were 'full' *cittadini*. Among them, however, there may have been some well-established craftsmen who ran a substantial *bottega* of their own. (As we see, the largest group in the construction industry were day workers.) An even smaller minority of the citizen class comprised the *cittadini originari*. It is generally reckoned that nobles and citizens together probably accounted for around 8–10 per cent of the city's population. *Cittadini originari* did not usually engage in 'mechanical labour' and most were lawyers, civil servants, doctors, notaries and traders. See further comments in J.-C. Hocquet, *Denaro, navi e mercanti a Venezia, 1200–1600* (Rome, 1999), pp. 303–10. In his words, the *cittadini originari* 'erano più cittadini degli altri' (p. 304). Grubb, however, concludes that as a class the *cittadinanza* remained 'inchoate and ill-defined'. See also E. Muir, *Civic Ritual in Renaissance Venice* (Princeton, 1981), pp. 38–44. There is considerable further analysis in D. Romano, *Patricians and Popolani: The Social Foundations of the Venetian Renaissance State* (Baltimore and London, 1987). For a discussion of the *arti* and politics, see R. MacKenney, 'Corporazioni e politica nel medioevo a Venezia', in G. Gianighian, ed., *Ricerche venete, I: Venezia tardomedioevale* (Venice, 1989), pp. 87–130.

18 ASV, SGSM, Reg. 19 bis, fol. 9.

19 Sohm, *The Scuola Grande di San Marco*, pp. 6–19.

20 For Giovanni Bellini, there are several references in ASV, SGSM, B. 202; for Gentile, see ibid., B. 135. For Bellini's career in general, see R. Goffen, *Giovanni Bellini* (New Haven and London, 1989). For Gentile's

visit to Constantinople, see P. Fortini Brown, *Venetian Narrative Painting in the Age of Carpaccio* (New Haven and London, 1988), pp. 54–5, 68, 196, 206. See also J. Raby, *Venice, Dürer and the Oriental Mode* (Totowa, NJ, 1982).

21 For the Florentine organisations, see Goldthwaite, *The Building of Renaissance Florence*, especially pp. 242–54. There is a useful summary of the Venetian building crafts system in S. Connell Wallington, 'Il cantiere secondo i dati d'archivio', in F. Valcanover and W. Wolters, eds, *L'architettura gotica veneziana. Atti del Convegno Internazionale di Studio: Venice, 27–9 November 1996* (Venice, 2000), pp. 35–52. See also S. Connell, 'Gli artigiani dell'edilizia', in G. Gianighian, ed., *Ricerche venete*, II: *dal medioevo al tardo Rinascimento* (Venice, 1993), pp. 31–92.

22 See below, p. 73.

23 For a general discussion of foreigners in Venice, see D. S. Chambers and B. Pullan, eds, *Venice: A Documentary History, 1450–1630* (Oxford and Cambridge, MA, 1992), part VIII, pp. 325–52.

24 For the Gruato, see S. Connell, *The Employment of Sculptors and Stonemasons in Venice in the Fifteenth Century* (London and New York, 1988), pp. 84–5, 214–51; for Luca Taiamonte, ibid., pp. 18, 32–3, 98, 215; for the dal Vescovo, ibid., pp. 96, 99. Connell also provides a partial list of foreign masters in Venice. The following names, from my own researches, provide single examples from each of the principal towns in Istria: Alegreto da Cataro, Ambroxio da Fiume (Rijeka), Antonio da Brioni, Felipo di Marco Bena da Orsera, Zane da Trau, Martino da Sebenico and Zian di Martino da Ruigno (Rovigno). For Giorgio da Sebenico, see D. Howard, 'San Michele in Isola: re-reading the genesis of the Venetian Renaissance', in J. Guillaume, ed., *L'Invention de la Renaissance* (Paris, 2004), pp. 27–42.

25 A handful of other masters from the Terraferma include Franzescho and Griguol, both from Padua, Antonio Visentin, Zane Rizzo da Verona, and Mattio, Cristoffolo and Martin da Bressa (Brescia). We should also mention the significant, if rather elusive Giorgio da Sebenico: see A. M. Schulz, 'Giorgio da Sebenico and the workshop of Giovanni Bon', in *Juraj matejev Dalmatinac*, ed. M. Prelog (Zagreb, 1982), pp. 72–92.

26 Antonio, Venturin and Bortolamio da Bergamo were all builders at Palazzo Giustinian in 1477; Piero da Bergamo was a mason on the same project; see above, pp. 51–2.

27 For the *maestri comacini* in Florence, see Goldthwaite, *The Building of Renaissance Florence*, pp. 247–8.

28 For all of the above, see P. Paoletti, *L'architettura e la scultura del Rinascimento in Venezia: ricerche storico-artistiche*, 2 vols (Venice, 1893–7); W. Wolters, *La scultura gotica veneziana*, 2 vols (Venice, 1976). For earlier observations, see J. Pope-Hennessey, *Italian Gothic Sculpture*, 3rd edn (London, 1985), pp. 46–7, 216–17, 220–21, 283–4. See also A. M. Schulz, *Niccolò di Giovanni Fiorentino and Venetian Sculpture of the Early Renaissance*

(New, York 1978). Nicolò di Pietro ('il pela') was in Venice circa 1416–23; he died in Florence in 1456. Pietro di Niccolò Lamberti (b. Arezzo, 1393) was in Verona in 1430; in 1434 he contracted with Marin Contarini to carve fireplaces for the Ca' d'Oro, but died shortly afterwards. Nanni di Bartolo (b. Florence) was in Verona in 1424, then in Venice.

29 See the *mariegole* (statutes) of the stonemasons' guild, para. 45 (1456): Venice, Biblioteca Correr, MSS Correr, IV, no. 150.

30 For various modifications to the *mariegole* in this period, see Connell, *The Employment of Sculptors and Stonemasons*, pp. 72–9.

31 ASV, Coll., Notatorio, 1481–9, c. 121.

32 For typical entry requirements of the guilds, see the original *mariegole* of the stonemasons (15 September 1307): ASV, Giustizia Vecchia, B. 1, reg. 1, cc. 222–3; and G. Monticolo, *I capitolari delle arti veneziane*, 3 vols (Rome, 1896–1914), vol. III, pp. 244 et seq. For the concerns of the masons in 1491, see G. Caniato and M. dal Borgo, *Le arti edili a Venezia* (Rome, 1990), p. 167. See also note 30 above.

33 For the Bon, see Schulz, *Niccolò di Giovanni*; also A. M. Schulz, 'The sculpture of Giovanni and Bartolomeo Bon and their workshop', *Transactions of the American Philosophical Society*, LXVIII/3 (1978). For a recent concise summary of Bartolomeo's career, see W. Wolters, 'Ipotesi su Bartolomeo Buon architetto', in Valcanover and Wolters, eds, *L'architettura gotica*, pp. 273–9.

34 For examples of stonemasons' companies, see Connell, *The Employment of Sculptors and Stonemasons*, pp. 36–53; for the Pizolo, see R. J. Goy, *The House of Gold: Building a Palace in Medieval Venice* (Cambridge, 1993), pp. 119–20; for Zuane (de Martin) Bello at San Zaccaria, see ASV, San Zaccaria, B. 31, cc. 33 et seq.

35 See below, p. 99–100. See also Goy, *The House of Gold*, pp. 68, 151–3, 208.

36 For the Frison, see Goy, *The House of Gold*, pp. 70, 176, 178–9; for the Taiamonte, see especially Connell, *The Employment of Sculptors and Stonemasons*, pp. 30–34.

37 For the dal Vescovo and Gruato clans, see note 24 above. See also the family tree of the former clan in Connell, 'Gli artigiani', p. 49.

38 For Piero Alegro, see ASV, Santa Maria della Carità, parte terza (documenti cartacei), B. 3, cc. 51, 52t; for Alegreto, see ASV, SGSM, B. 136; for Palazzo Giustinian, see ASV, PSMdC, B. 115, fasc. 17.

39 For San Zaccaria, see ASV, San Zaccaria, B. 31, especially cc. 201–2; for the Scuola Grande di San Marco, see ASV, SGSM, B. 136, where there is an unnumbered contract dated 1 May 1489 in which they are referred to as 'taiapiera chonpagnj'.

40 For the Busetto, see ASV, SGSM, B. 77, fasc. 3, list of documents no. 33 (15 July 1489); for the Pramaior company, see ASV, PSMdC, B. 269 bis, L. IV, cc. 18t, 19 and 22t.

41 For the career of Niccolò Luxe, see as follows: at the Ca' d'Oro: ASV, PSMdC, bis, L. IV, cc. 47t, 48, 56; for

the Carità: ASV, Santa Maria della Carità, parte terza (documenti cartacei), B. 3, cc. 46t, 51t, 55t–56; for Corte Nova, ASV, PSMdC, B. 54, fasc. XXVI; for the Madonna dell'Orto, ASV, PSMdC, B. 189, fasc. 6; for San Zaccaria, ASV, San Zaccaria, B. 31, c. 10. For extensive further detail of lesser masters, see Paoletti, *L'architettura*, and Connell, *The Employment of Sculptors and Stonemasons*, both passim.

42 For Pantaleon, see as follows: Corte Nova: ASV, PSMdC, B. 54, fasc. XXVI; for the Carità church, ASV, Santa Maria della Carità, parte terza (documenti cartacei), B. 3, c. 55t; for the Scuola Grande della Carità, ASV, SG Carità, B. 227, no. 104, cc. 2t, 5 and 12.

43 Among many examples, see Antonio di Martini's contract at the Ca' d'Oro in 1431: Goy, *The House of Gold*, pp. 217–23 and appendix 7; from ASV, PSMdC, B. 169 bis, misc. papers no. 3. For the work of Griguol at the Scuola Grande di San Marco, see below, p. 195 et seq. The statutes of the *mureri* make it very clear that they should not undertake any work that is the responsibility of the *marangoni* and vice versa. The statutes of 1606 have been published in Gianighian, ed., *Ricerche venete*, II, pp. 159–211; see especially pp. 173–4. For the *mureri*, see also Caniato and Dal Borgo, *Le arti edili*, pp. 117–40.

44 For carpenters at the Ca' d'Oro, see ASV, PSMdC, B. 269 bis, L. IV, cc. 41t and 42; for the Carità, see ASV, Santa Maria della Carità, parte terza (documenti cartacei), B. 3, cc. 51, 52t. For the guild of *marangoni*, see also Caniato and Dal Borgoz, *Le arti edili*, pp. 179–96.

45 This sequence of operations is particularly clearly evident at the Carità church: see below, pp. 119–25.

CHAPTER FOUR

1 Leon Battista Alberti, *De re aedificatoria* (Florence, 1485), Book II, chapter IX.

2 F. Sansovino and G. Martinioni, *Venetia, città nobilissima et singolare . . .* , 2 vols (Venice, 1663; new facs. edn, 1968), vol. I, p. 383.

3 S. Connell, *The Employment of Sculptors and Stonemasons in Venice in the Fifteenth Century* (London and New York, 1988), pp. 89–95. For the Istrian quarries, see also G. Sebesta, 'Gli edifici e l'uomo', in G. Caniato and M. dal Borgo, eds, *Le arti edili a Venezia* (Rome, 1990), pp. 262–8. Caniato and Dal Borgo, eds, *Le arti edili*, is the essential secondary work for all this material, with many primary sources also cited and reproduced. See also the chapter on the *arte dei tagiapiera* in ibid., pp. 159–78.

4 G. Monticolo, *I capitolari delle arti veneziane*, 3 vols (Rome, 1896–1914), vol. III, p. 254.

5 For San Zaccaria, see below, p. 178. For the conditioning of stone, see (*inter alia*) A. Palladio, *I quattro libri dell'architettura* (Venice, 1570), Book I, chapter 3, p. 7.

6 For the 'clans' see Connell, *The Employment of Sculptors and Stonemasons*, pp. 95–6.

7 F. C. Lane, *Venetian Ships and Shipbuilders of the Renais-*

sance, new edn (Baltimore and London, 1992), p. 53. See also ASV, Sen., Misti, reg. 47, cc. 152–4.

8 ASV, PSMdC, B. 54, quad. 2.

9 ASV, San Zaccaria, B. 31, c. 5.

10 ASV, San Zaccaria, B. 31, c. 19.

11 ASV, SG Carità, B. 227, fasc. 104, c. 4.

12 ASV, San Zaccaria, B. 31, cc. 19, 47 and 70.

13 ASV, SGSM, B. 77, fasc. 3, c. 63.

14 ASV, SGSR, B. 423, cc. 7–24; for the consignment of 1527, ibid., but no *carta* number.

15 ASV, PSMdC, B. 67, lib. 19, c. 10.

16 ASV, PSMdC, B. 54 (Comm. Baseggio), reg. 2, fasc. XXVI.

17 ASV, San Zaccaria, B. 31, c. 26.

18 ASV, San Zaccaria, B. 31, c. 26.

19 Cited by R. Gallo in 'L'architettura di transizione dal gotico al Rinascimento e Bartolomeo Bon', *Atti del Istituto Veneto di Scienze, Letteratura ed Arti*, CXX (1961–2), pp. 201–2, doc. 1.

20 ASV, SG Carità, B. 227, fasc. 104, c. 4.

21 ASV, San Zaccaria, B. 31, c. 47.

22 ASV, PSMdC, B. 67, lib. 19, c. 10.

23 ASV, SGSR, B. 423, cc. 37v–43v.

24 ASV, PSMdC, B. 67, lib. 19, c. 13.

25 ASV, SGSR, B. 423 (loose, unnumbered folio).

26 Caniato and Dal Borgo, eds, *Le arti edili*, p. 75. Also Sebesta, 'Gli edifici', in ibid., pp. 268–73.

27 Caniato and Dal Borgo, eds, *Le arti edili*, p. 76.

28 Caniato and Dal Borgo, eds, *Le arti edili*, pp. 76–7.

29 Caniato and Dal Borgo, eds, *Le arti edili*, p. 80: ASV, MC, Delib., reg. 12, 'Clericus Civicus', c. 95.

30 ASV, MC, Delib., reg. 13, 'Phronesis', c. 41.

31 ASV, Avogaria di Comun, reg. 21, 'Neptunus', c. 142v.

32 ASV, MC, Delib., reg. 17, 'Spiritus', c. 12v.

33 Caniato and Dal Borgo, eds, *Le arti edili*, p. 77.

34 ASV, Cassier della bolla ducale, 'Grazie', reg. 3, c. 13v.

35 ASV, Quarantia al Criminal, reg. 16, 'Liber partum', XXIIII, c. 69.

36 ASV, Compilazione leggi, B. 105, no. 743.

37 ASV, Sen., Misti, reg. 42, c. 112.

38 ASV, MC, Delib., reg. 21, 'Leona', c. 72.

39 ASV, MC, Delib., reg. 22, 'Ursa', c. 20v.

40 ASV, Sen., Misti, reg. 57, c. 115v.

41 ASV, Compilazione leggi, B. 105, no. 757.

42 R. J. Goy, *The House of Gold: Building a Palace in Medieval Venice* (Cambridge, 1993), p. 105.

43 Goy, *The House of Gold*, pp. 195, 197, from ASV, PSMdC, B. 169 bis, L. IV, cc. 2 and 39.

44 ASV, PSMdC, B. 54, fasc. XXVI.

45 ASV, SG Carità, B. 227, fasc. 104, c. 5.

46 ASV, San Zaccaria, B. 31, c. 168.

47 ASV, San Zaccaria, B. 31, c. 172.

48 ASV, PSMdC, B. 133 (Comm. India Formenti), fasc. 4.

49 ASV, Sez. Not., Canc. Inf., Misti, atti diversi, B. 122 (Atti Marevidi).

50 For the Corner clan and the Ca' del Duca, see J. R. Spencer, 'The Ca' del Duca in Venice and Benedetto Ferrini', *Journal of the Society of Architectural Historians*, XXX (1971).

51 ASV, PSMdC, B. 54, fasc. XXVI.

52 For all of the above, see ASV, Santa Maria della Carità, parte terza (documenti cartacei), B. 3, cc. 47–55t.

53 Corner's original ten-year period of exile must have been significantly reduced to enable him to trade again as early as 1462.

54 ASV, San Zaccaria, B. 31, cc. 39, 42 and 90.

55 ASV, PSMdC, B. 26, b. 8.

56 ASV, San Zaccaria, B. 31, c. 174. For brick sizes and moulds, see Caniato and Dal Borgo, eds, *Le arti edili*, pp. 106–7, with further archive references.

57 Treviso had become a permanent Venetian possession as early as 1339, Padua only in 1404.

58 ASV, SGSM, B. 136, doc. 31.

59 At Corte Nova in Castello most bricks came from Treviso or Ferrara.

60 The price of small bricks also fluctuated significantly. Prices typically ranged from 5 to 6 lire per thousand from the 1440s to the end of the century; there had been peaks earlier, though, and at the Ca' d'Oro a price as high as 9 lire was recorded in 1429.

61 ASV, Santa Maria della Carità, parte terza (documenti cartacei), B. 3, c. 55t.

62 ASV, San Zaccaria, B. 31, cc. 168 and 174.

63 For roof tiles, see, for example, ASV, Santa Maria della Carità, parte terza (documenti cartacei), B. 3, cc. 51 and 56t; San Zaccaria, B. 31, c. 42.

64 ASV, San Zaccaria, B. 31, c. 6.

65 ASV, SG Carità, B. 227, fasc. 60, c. 1t.

66 ASV, PSMdC, B. 115, fasc. 17, c. 6.

67 ASV, SS Giovanni e Paolo, busta 'M', fasc. 22, c. 113.

68 Marin Sanudo, *De origine, situ et magistratibus urbis Venetae, ovvero La città di Venetia; as La città di Venetia*, ed. A. C. Arico (Milan, 1980), p. 211. For a useful discussion on carpentry, see M. Piana, 'La carpenteria lignea veneziana nei secoli XIV e XV', in F. Valcanover and W. Wolters, eds, *L'architettura gotica veneziana. Atti del Convegno Internazionale di Studio: Venice, 27–9 November 1996* (Venice, 2000), pp. 73–81.

69 Goy, *The House of Gold*, pp. 124, 235; from ASV, PSMdC, B. 169 bis, L. IV, c. 56t.

70 Giovanni q. Costantin was the first member of the house of Priuli to be elected a Procurator of San Marco, in 1453: Sansovino and Martinioni, *Venetia*, vol. I, pp. 182, 304.

71 Priuli's name has an extraordinary variety of spellings, including Priollo and Brioli; Dom Agostin at the Carità church refers to him as de Broilo. There was a very large, specialised vocabulary for describing the sizes and purposes of elements of timber: the essential reference here is E. Concina, *Pietre, parole, storia: glossario della costruzione nelle fonti veneziane (sec. XV–XVIII)* (Venice, 1988), with extensive archival references.

72 ASV, SG Carità, B. 227, fasc. 104, cc. 3 and 12.

73 ASV, PSMdC, B. 54, quad. II.

74 ASV, San Zaccaria, B. 31, c. 103.

75 ASV, San Zaccaria, B. 31, c. 104.

76 L. Puppi and L. Olivato Puppi, *Mauro Codussi* (Milan, 1977), p. 191; and ASV, San Zaccaria, B. 31, c. 219.

77 ASV, San Zaccaria, B. 31, c. 234.

78 ASV, SGSM, B. 77, fasc. 3, c. 7.

79 See above, pp. 52–5; ASV, PSMdC, B. 67 (Comm. Margherita Miani), lib. 19 (quad. 1), passim.

80 ASV, San Zaccaria, B. 31, c. 71.

81 Goy, *The House of Gold*, p. 184.

82 ASV, PSMdC, B. 26 (Comm. M. Michiel), b. 9 (loose, unnumbered folio).

83 Goy, *The House of Gold*, pp. 181–2; ASV, PSMdC, B. 169 bis, L. IV, cc. 18t, 19 and 22t.

84 See note 80 above.

85 G. Tassini, *Curiosità veneziane, ovvero origini delle denominazioni stradali di Venezia*, 4th edn (Venice, 1887; reprinted 1964), p. 659, citing ASV, MC, Delib., reg. 17, 'Spiritus' (1331).

86 ASV, San Zaccaria, B. 31, c. 12.

87 ASV, PSMdC, B. 169 bis, L. IV, cc. 46t and 47. For lime kilns, see Sebesta, 'Gli edifici e l'uomo', in Caniato and Dal Borgo, eds, *Le arti edili*, pp. 273–7. See also 'Fornaci per calce di tipo tradizionale', in ibid., pp. 109–16.

88 ASV, PSMdC, B. 169 bis, L. IV, cc. 46t and 47.

89 ASV, SGSM, B. 220, no.1, c. 12.

90 Caniato and Dal Borgo, eds, *Le arti edili*, pp. 92 et seq.

91 ASV, San Zaccaria, B. 31, c. 13.

92 For Gambello at San Zaccaria, see ASV, San Zaccaria, B. 31, c. 8; for Codussi, ibid., c. 172. For Codussi at the Scuola Grande di San Marco, see ASV, SGSM, B. 136 (several loose, unnumbered folios), and ibid., reg. 16 bis, fols 35–36t. See also S. Connell, 'Gli artigiani dell'edilizia', in G. Gianighian, ed., *Ricerche venete, II: dal medioevo al tardo Rinascimento* (Venice, 1993), pp. 73–80, with considerable detail of wages and salaries.

93 For Niccolò Pain, see ASV, Provv. Sal, B. 59, c. 132t. For Bon the Bergamasco, see ASV, Provv. Sal, B. 6, fasc. 4, cc. 75–75t.

94 For Rizzo's rise, see ASV, Provv. Sal, B. 6, fasc. 4, c. 75t; also discussed by A. M. Schulz, *Antonio Rizzo, Sculptor and Architect* (Princeton, 1983), p. 131. See Appendix II, document 12. See also ASV, Provv. Sal, Notatorio, B. 2, c. 6. For Lombardo as proto, see ASV, Sen., Delib., vol. XIII, and Provv. Sal, Notatorio, B. 2, cc. 32–3.

95 For details of salaries, there is a copy in ASV, Provv. Sal, B. 6, fasc. 4, cc. 74t, 75 and 76t. For Bellini at the Maggior Consiglio, see R. Goffen, *Giovanni Bellini* (New Haven and London, 1989), pp. 263 et seq., and notes 11, 13, 17, 20, 22.

96 For the Molo window, see ASV, Sez. Not., Atti Ferro Vittore, B. 541. For Lombardo at the Scuola Grande di San Marco, see ASV, SGSM, B. 136, doc. 30. For Vivarini, see ASV, Santa Maria della Carità, parte terza (documenti cartacei), B. 3, c. 57. For Antonio Vivarini, see also F. d'Arcais, *Antonio Vivarini* (Milan, 1966); J. Steer, *Antonio Vivarini: His Art and Influence* (Cambridge, 1982). There is a useful summary, also by Steer, in *Encyclopedia of Italian Renaissance and Mannerist Art*, ed. J. Turner, 2 vols (London and New York, 2000), vol. II, pp. 1782–4.

97 For the Madonna dell'Orto, see ASV, Scuole Piccole, B. 417, fasc. 'A', fol. 83. For the portal of Santi Giovanni

98 Bon's original contract for the Porta does not refer to a fine, but the *zetola* of 1442 does: see below, p. 109; and Appendix II, doc. 1. See also, *inter alia*, Zane Bon's first contract with Marin Contarini in 1423, and further examples, below, p. 131.

99 For Raverti at the Ca' d'Oro, see ASV, PSMdC, B. 269 bis, misc. fragments, no. 20; also ibid., L. III, cc. 5t, 10t; L. IV, cc. 10t, 44t. For Bon at the Madonna dell'Orto, see note 97 above. For de' Grigi at San Michele, see ASV, PSMdC, B. 67, quad. III, c. 38. P. Sohm, *The Scuola Grande di San Marco, 1437–1550: The Architecture of a Venetian Lay Confraternity* (New York and London, 1982), doc. 79; P. Paoletti, *L'architettura e la scultura del Rinascimento in Venezia: ricerche storico-artistiche*, 2 vols, Venice, 1893–7, p. 106.

100 Luca di Pietro: ASV, SGSM, B. 77, fasc. 3 (summary list), and ibid., doc. 16 (10 January 1502 [=1503]). See also Sohm, *The Scuola Grande di San Marco*, docs 47 and 53.

101 ASV, SGSM, B. 77, fasc. 3, cc. 6 and 8.

102 ASV, PSMdC, B. 189, fasc. 4.

103 ASV, Santa Maria della Carità, parte terza (documenti cartacei), B. 3, cc. 46, 46t, 47, 49, 50.

104 ASV, San Zaccaria, B. 31, c. 154 (Buora) and cc. 24 and 28 (Bertuccio). Connell has compiled a schedule of such elements in 'Gli artigiani', pp. 79–80.

105 ASV, Santa Maria della Carità, parte terza (documenti cartacei), B. 3, c. 52t; ASV, SGSM, B. 77, fasc. 3, c. 6.

106 The Miani chapel: ASV, PSMdC, B. 67, quad. III, c. 34; the Ca' d'Oro: ASV, PSMdC, B. 269 bis, L. IV, c. 58.

107 Corte Nova: ASV, PSMdC, B. 26, b. 9, 'spese di fabbriche': unnumbered fragment; ASV, SGSM, B. 136: unnumbered schedule of documents.

108 ASV, SG Carità, B. 227, fasc. 104, c. 5.

109 ASV, San Zaccaria, B. 31, cc. 20, 201, 202. See note 104 above.

110 Sohm, *The Scuola Grande di San Marco*, doc. 54 (ASV, SGSM, B. 136, 'conti diversi', doc. 19).

111 Goy, *The House of Gold*, p. 96.

112 Sohm, *The Scuola Grande di San Marco*, doc. 108 (ASV, SGSM, B. 77, fasc. 3, doc. 22).

113 The Ca' d'Oro: ASV, PSMdC, B. 269 bis, L. III, c. 4; L. IV, c. 7t; Corte Nova alla Tana: ASV, PSMdC, B. 26, b. 9 (unnumbered fragment); Corte Nova in Cannaregio: ASV, PSMdC, B. 53, fasc. 7. The same system was used at the Scuola Grande di San Marco in 1487, when Griguol agreed to be paid one third of a ducat per square *passo*: Sohm, *The Scuola Grande di San Marco*, doc. 40.

114 ASV, San Zaccaria, B. 31, cc. 22, 29, 214, 223. See also Connell, 'Gli artigiani', pp. 80–81, and table on p. 84.

115 See case studies below. For the hospital at San Barnaba, see ASV, PSMdC, B. 32 (Comm. Bertuccio da Ca' da Pesaro), fasc. 9 (unnumbered sheets). For the training of apprentices, see Connell, *The Employment of Sculptors and Stonemasons*, pp. 55–64.

116 See note 115 above.

117 For the Ca' d'Oro: ASV, PSMdC, B. 269 bis, L. IV, c. 39. For the Giudecca hospital: ASV, PSMdC, B. 53, b. 8.

118 ASV, SG Carità, B. 227, fasc. 104, cc. 6, 7 and 15.

119 ASV, San Zaccaria, B. 31, cc. 1, 14, 15, 21, 23, 24, etc.

120 ASV, PSMdC, B. 115, fasc. 17, cc. 3, 8, 13, 15, 22. See also note 114 above.

121 Goy, *The House of Gold*, pp. 92–8.

122 Sohm, *The Scuola Grande di San Marco*, especially pp. 116–17 and 131–44, with notes and references.

123 The Miani chapel: ASV, PSMdC, B. 67 (together with BB. 65, 66): quad. I (=libretto no. 19), quad. II and quad. III. See also ASV, SGSM, B. 220, no.1, 'spese 1534–5'. A word of caution needs to be added regarding wage levels as late as the 1520s, since a degree of inflation probably eroded some of the perceived increases in day-wage rates. See F. C. Lane and and R. C. Mueller, *Money and Banking in Medieval Venice*, 2 vols (Baltimore and London, 1985–97); for the overall economic context, see G. Luzzatto, *Storia economica di Venezia dal XI al XVI secolo* (Venice, 1995), pp. 221–38.

CHAPTER FIVE

1 For the careers and works of the two Bon, see S. Connell, *The Employment of Sculptors and Stonemasons in Venice in the Fifteenth Century* (London and New York, 1988), passim; R. J. Goy, *The House of Gold: Building a Palace in Medieval Venice* (Cambridge, 1993); W. Wolters, *La scultura gotica veneziana*, 2 vols (Venice, 1976); A. M. Schulz, 'The sculpture of Giovanni and Bartolomeo Bon', *Transactions of the American Philosophical Society*, LXVIII/3 (1978), pp. 1–81. See also W. Wolters, 'Ipotesi su Bartolomeo Buon architetto', in F. Valcanover and W. Wolters, eds, *L'architettura gotica veneziana. Atti del Convegno Internazionale di Studio: Venice, 27–9 November 1996* (Venice, 2000), pp. 273–80.

2 Goy, *The House of Gold*, passim.

3 Goy, *The House of Gold*, pp. 108–16, 122–32.

4 For Contarini's three successive master builders, see Goy, *The House of Gold*, pp. 102–6, 195–7, 240–43.

5 For the pendant tracery at the Ca' d'Oro, see Goy, *The House of Gold*, pp. 154–62; for the archive reference, see ASV, PSMdC, B. 269 bis, L. IV, c. 7, cc. 20t and 21.

6 The essential secondary bibliography for the Porta della Carta: F. Zanotto, *Il Palazzo Ducale di Venezia*, 4 vols (Venice, 1842–6); G. Lorenzi, *Monumenti per servire alla storia del Palazzo Ducale* (Venice, 1868); L. Planiscig, *Venezianischer Bildhauer der Renaissance* (Vienna, 1921); E. Arslan, *Venezia gotica* (Milan, 1970); S. Sinding Larsen, *Christ in the Council Hall: Studies in the Religious Iconography of the Venetian Republic* (Rome, 1974); D. Pincus, *The Arco Foscari: The Bulding of a Triumphal Gateway in Fifteenth Century Venice* (New York and London, 1976); Wolters, *La scultura gotica veneziana*; S. Romano, *The Restoration of the Porta della Carta*, trans. A. Clarke and P. Rylands (Venice and London, 1980); J. Pope-Hennessey, *Italian Gothic Sculpture*, 3rd edn (London, 1985).

For a new, concise summary of the story of the construction of the Molo and Piazzetta wings, see U. Franzoi, 'Per la storia del Palazzo: origini e sviluppi', in G. Romanelli, ed., *Palazzo Ducale: storia e restauri* (Venice, 2004), pp. 81–126. According to Franzoi (p. 124), there was always an entrance to the Palazzo in this location, which must therefore always have provided the most direct route from the Piazza/Piazzetta to the ducal apartments.

7   ASV, MC, Delib., vol. 'Ursa', 1415–54, c. 42v. See also Lorenzi, *Monumenti*, doc. 148. For a recent detailed discussion of the Molo and Piazzetta façades, see M. Schuller, 'Il Palazzo Ducale di Venezia: le facciate medioevali: storia, costruzione, effetti cromatici', in Valcanover and Wolters, eds, *L'architettura gotica veneziana*, pp. 351–427, with numerous measured drawings and structural analyses. See also the further observations by M. Schuller, 'Le facciate medievali: storia, costruzione, effetti cromatici', in Romanelli, ed., *Palazzo Ducale*, pp. 235–46. See also Franzoi in note 6 above.

8   There are many different attributions for the *Judgement of Solomon*; see Sinding Larsen, *Christ in the Council Hall*, pp. 167 et seq. Wolters ascribes the work to Bon, as do others, while Jacopo della Quercia and Nanni di Bartolo are other attributions cited by Pope-Hennessey in *Italian Gothic Sculpture*, p. 283.

9   Howard has identified a link between the tall, inset form of the Porta della Carta and earlier Islamic examples such as the Sultan Hassan mosque in Cairo (1356–9): D. Howard, *Venice and the East: The Impact of the Islamic World on Venetian Architecture, 1100–1500* (New Haven and London, 2000), pp. 181–3.

10 ASV, Provv. Sal, B. 6, fasc. 3, c. 81. Also Lorenzi, *Monumenti*, p. 66. See also Pincus, *The Arco Foscari*, doc. 2.

11 ASV, PSMdC, B. 189 (Comm. B. Morosini), fasc. 4. Steffanino's contract for the Morosini chapel is dated 7 April 1442. His carpenter partner here was the familiar figure of Cristoforo Candio, member of a prominent family of builders and carpenters.

12 ASV, Santa Maria della Carità, parte terza (documenti cartacei), B. 3.

13 *Felza*: the term is translated by Pincus as a plate of lead forming part of a roof covering. The better-known popular meaning (with various spellings) is as the canvas covering of the cabin of a gondola or other small boat. E. Concina, in *Pietre, parole, storia: glossario della costruzione nelle fonti veneziane (sec. XV–XVIII)* (Venice, 1988), has *felce* meaning the intrados, the inner or lower surface of an arch and this is closer to its meaning here. (There would have been no point in finishing the upper surfaces of these rooms with very expensive lead cladding since they already stood within the pre-existing structure of the Palazzo.) The phrases as a whole read 'voltarla in felze'; in other words, they were to be vaulted not with stone ribs but with plain surfaces, rather like canvas or other sheeted material.

14 See note 13 above. *Chroxere* are cross-vaults.

15 For a more detailed discussion, see Pincus, *The Arco Foscari*, passim. The whole process of building the loggia

and arch was very slow and protracted. See also A. M. Schulz, *Antonio Rizzo, Sculptor and Architect* (Princeton, 1983), pp. 98 et seq.

16 ASV, Provv. Sal, B. 6, fasc. 3 (1411–1520), c. 8. See also Lorenzi, *Monumenti*, doc. 159. See also Appendix II, document 1.

17 Romano, *The Restoration of the Porta della Carta*, p. 23.

18 For the contract with the dalle Masegne, see ASV, Sez. Not., Atti Ferro Vittore, B. 541.

19 See above, chapter four.

20 ASV, Provv. Sal, B. 6, fasc. 3, c. 84, and Lorenzi, *Monumenti*, doc. 162. The aide-memoire begins with the words 'Io. Zuane Bom [*sic*] taiapiera e Bortolamio mio fio'. This was probably a mere formality of the text, however, and there is strong evidence that Zane was illiterate. At the Ca' d'Oro all the surviving relevant documents are signed by Bartolomeo alone, even though at this time his father was head of the workshop and (as far as we know) was healthy and able-bodied. See Appendix II, document 2.

21 ASV, Provv. Sal, B. 6, fasc. 3, c. 84, and Lorenzi, *Monumenti*, doc. 162. The three Provveditori cited in the note were Biancho Dolfin, Vetor Pasqualigo and L. Venier.

22 See note 29 below.

23 See below, p. 119 et seq.

24 See below, p. 125–6.

25 For the *Sensa* (Ascension Day) and the many other processions, see F. Sansovino and G. Martinioni, *Venetia, città nobilissima et singolare . . .*, 2 vols (Venice, 1663; new facs. edn, 1968), vol. I, pp. 492–525; an entire chapter is devoted to these rituals. See also E. Muir, *Civic Ritual in Renaissance Venice* (Princeton, 1981), especially pp. 119–34.

26 For further discussion of the iconography, see S. Romano, 'History and critical analysis', in Romano, *The Restoration of the Porta della Carta*, pp. 15–27; and Sinding Larsen, *Christ in the Council Hall*, pp. 167 et seq.

27 Sansovino and Martinioni, *Venetia*, vol. I, p. 319.

28 The inscription on Foscari's monument includes the triumphant summary of his 'conquests': 'Turbatores quietis compescui, Brixiam [Brescia], Bergomum, Ravennam, Cremam Imperio adiuxi vestri', For a discussion of the votive images employed by doges in their iconography, see W. Wolters, 'L'autocelebrazione della repubblica', in *Storia di Venezia: dalle origini alla Caduta della Serenissima*, 12 vols (Rome, 1992–8), vol. IV.

29 A brief summary of some of the attributions for the *Virtues*: *Charity* (top left): no clear attributions; perhaps by Bregno or an assistant of Bon. The figure is not carved at the rear. Fiocco attributed it to 'Giovanni di Martino' (G. Fiocco, 'I Lamberti a Venezia', in *Dedalo*, VIII, 1927–8, pp. 432–58), G. Mariacher to Bregno ('New light on Antonio Bregno', *Burlington Magazine*, XCI, 1950); *Prudence* (top right): from a different hand from the other three. Usually ascribed to a Tuscan master, although Lorenzetti suggested Bregno in *Venice*, p. 243. It is also not carved in the round; *Temperance* (lower left): similar in style to *Fortitude*. Sometimes

given to Bon himself, although other attributions have included Giorgio da Sebenico (by Romano, *The Restoration of the Porta della Carta*), to Lamberti (by Lorenzetti) and to Bregno by Pope-Hennessey (*Italian Gothic Sculpture*). Influences from Jacopo della Quercia and Ghiberti are detectable, although this does not preclude Bon himself as author. L. Planiscig (*Venezianischer Bildhauer der Renaissance*, Vienna, 1921) also attributed it to Bregno, Fiocco to Pietro Lamberti; *Fortitude*: attributions are mostly as for *Temperance*. Again Pope-Hennessey favours Bregno, as does Planiscig; Lorenzetti and Fiocco again suggested Lamberti, while Mariacher proposes 'a Tuscan'. See also the discussions by Wolters in *La scultura gotica veneziana*. The crowning *Justice* on the pinnacle is now almost universally given to Bon himself. For further discussion of the use of Marcian imagery and symbolism, see D. Rosand, *Myths of Venice: The Figuration of a State* (Chapel Hill, NC, 2001). For the symbolism of the winged lion and the *Justice*, see also Muir, *Civic Ritual*, pp. 114–17.

30 A. Forcellini, 'Sui restauri delle principali facciate del Palazzo Ducale di Venezia', in *L'ingegneria a Venezia* (Venice, 1887), cited by Romano in *The Restoration of the Porta della Carta*, p. 34. The closer I have examined Ferrari's present lion, the less 'medieval' it looks: the lean, muscular form and the pose of the head have little in common, for example, with the slightly later (original) lion at the Arsenale gate or in the depictions by Carpaccio, Bellini, et al. The Porta della Carta figure thus appears to be a rather free nineteenth-century 'interpetation'.

31 See p. 146.

32 The 'sam Marcho in forma de liom' is, of course, cited in the contract of 1438; see note 30 above.

33 The putti, both at Ca' Foscari and on the Porta, are 'proto-Renaissance' figures, as John McAndrew has observed (*Venetian Architecture of the Early Renaissance*, Cambridge, MA, and London, 1980, p. 3). Foscari's monument in the Frari also embodies a mixture of traditional Venetian Gothic elements and Renaissance details. The latter are most clearly seen in the Corinthian capitals and pedestals. Probably carved *circa* 1466–70, it is often attributed to Antonio and Paolo Bregno.

34 Romano, *The Restoration of the Porta della Carta*, p. 18.

35 The sword and scales were lost in 1853, but probably replaced in the restoration of 1879–83; see Antonelli, 'Restorations', in Romano, *The Restoration of the Porta della Carta*, p. 31.

36 Pope-Hennessey, *Italian Gothic Sculpture*, p. 222, following P. Paoletti, *L'architettura e la scultura del Rinascimento in Venezia: ricerche storico-artistiche*, 2 vols (Venice, 1893–7), p. 39, note 1. See also Arslan, *Venezia gotica*, p. 253, note 145. This course of events still appears illogical, but not entirely impossible; perhaps the *Justice* was considered a high priority and was installed early. Howard has suggested (in correspondence) that Pope-Hennessey may have obtained his interpretation from Paoletti.

37 K. Hempel and G. Hempel, 'A technical report on the condition of the Porta della Carta', in Romano, *The Restoration of the Porta della Carta*, pp. 37–9.

38 Again, see Bellini's depiction in the *Procession in the Piazza*. Bellini was perhaps more lavish in his depiction than the reality; he shows gold decoration to the figures of Foscari and the lion, to the plinth/architrave below them; to the arrises of the flanking pinnacles; to the Foscari *scudo*; to the wave decoration, and to Bon's capitals. Restoration has confirmed, however, that there was gilding to the leaves of the frieze, to the inner surfaces of the canopies of the four *Virtues*, to the capital that supports the crowning *Justice*, and to the window tracery.

39 ASV, Coll., Notatorio, vol. III, c. 177 (31 January 1453 (= 1452 mv). See also ASV, PSMdS, B. 77, Processo 180.

40 ASV, Sen., Terra, reg. 5 (1463–7), c. 50 (August 1463).

41 For the Carità church, see pp. 119–26; for Corte Nova in Cannaregio, see pp. 48–50.

42 Translation and interpretation by Pincus in *The Arco Foscari*, p. 108 and doc. 7. See also Lorenzi, *Monumenti*, doc. 185. Pincus's translation reads in part: 'it was understood by the Doge [that] the four fifths which was set aside for such work was paid for the figures and the considerable amount of work already executed. And that so much worthy work for a little thing would not remain uncompleted'. The translation is rather awkwardly phrased, and (understandably, perhaps) retains nearly as many ambiguities as the original text.

43 Zanotto, *Il Palazzo Ducale*, vol. I, p. 76. Selvatico also broadly agrees with Zanotto, although few scholars retain his dates today.

44 Schulz, *Antonio Rizzo*, pp. 32 et seq., 152–9. This general chronology is supported by Franzoi in 'Per la storia del Palazzo', in Romanelli, ed., *Palazzo Ducale*, pp. 81–126.

45 For some comments on Calendario, see L. Puppi, 'Geografia di un crinale: Filippo Calendario tra storia e leggenda', in Valcanover and Wolters, eds, *L'architettura gotica veneziana*, pp. 99–103. A further fascinating attempt to 'pin down' the character of Calendario is L. Puppi, 'Vischiosità della leggenda e levità della storia', in Romanelli, ed., *Palazzo Ducale*, pp. 145–54. Puppi attempts (quoting Umberto Eco) to establish 'una verità probabile attraverso la serie di errori sicuri'.

46 In the National Gallery, London.

47 This was the work of Gian-Antonio Selva in 1807–11. Currently there are plans to restore the church following the recent transfer of the teaching Accademia into the former hospital of the Incurabili on the Zattere nearby. The transfer will enable the Gallerie to expand the exhibition space considerably into the former teaching studios on the ground floor of the complex.

48 For a few notes on early history, see G. Tassini, *Curiosità veneziane, ovvero origini delle denominazioni stradali di Venezia*, 4th edn (Venice, 1887; reprinted 1964), pp. 133–4.

49 The building accounts are in ASV, Santa Maria della Carità, parte terza (documenti cartacei), B. 3. Dom

Agostin's text begins on c. 45. The chief secondary sources on the church are: Paoletti, *L'architettura*; F. Fogolari, 'La chiesa di Santa Maria della Carità di Venezia', *Archivio veneto-tridentino*, XV (1924), pp. 57–119; see also A. M. Schulz, 'The sculpture of Giovanni and Bartolomeo Bon and their workshop', *Transactions of the American Philosophical Society*, LXVII/ 3 (June 1970). For the later history, especially Palladio's work here, see E. Bassi, *Il convento della Carità*, Corpus palladianum, VI (Vicenza, 1971). See also S. Connell, 'Gli artigiani dell'edilizia', in G. Gianighian, ed., *Ricerche venete*, II: *Dal medioevo al tardo Rinascimento* (Venice, 1993), especially pp. 67–73.

50 There are several arithmetical errors in the accounts, and Dom Agostin's summary on the last page is approximately 30 ducats adrift from the correct total from the individual folios. The nobleman Lorenzo Soranzo was the 'procurator' or sponsor of the project and perhaps kept more reliable accounts himself; but the 'libro grando' referred to by Dom Agostin is lost. Cc. 30 et seq. contain a list of *elemosine* or charitable donations towards the works. Fogolari (cited in note 49 above) seems to have regarded Dom Agostin as the 'architect' of the building, although this was certainly not the case in the generally understood meaning of the term.

51 ASV, Santa Maria della Carità, parte terza (documenti cartacei), B. 3, c. 45. For the long saga of the porch and rights of access to the adjacent Scuola, see P. Sohm, *The Scuola Grande di San Marco, 1437–1550: The Architecture of a Venetian Lay Confraternity* (New York and London, 1982), pp. 299–301 and doc. 130.

52 ASV, Santa Maria della Carità, parte terza (documenti cartacei), B. 3, c. 45t.

53 ASV, Santa Maria della Carità, parte terza (documenti cartacei), B. 3, c. 45t. Steffanino also worked at the Morosini chapel at the Madonna dell'Orto at about the same time: see ASV, PSMdC, B. 189, especially fasc. 4, 6 and 11. The bricks were provided by Marco Corner. He also supplied San Zaccaria in the later 1450s and 1460s: see below, p. 175.

54 For a summary of the career of the two Bon, see Connell, *The Employment of Sculptors and Stonemasons*, pp. 8–23. For the Bon at the Ca' d'Oro, see Goy, *The House of Gold*, passim. See also W. Wolters, 'Ipotesi su Bartolomeo Buon architetto', in Valcanover and Wolters, eds, *L'architettura gotica veneziana*, pp. 273–80.

55 For Bartolomeo at the Porta della Carta, see above, pp. 102–19.

56 The total value of Bon's work here was approximately 1,800 ducats, slightly more than that of his contribution towards Marin Contarini's new palace at Santa Sofia.

57 The windows were later used as models for some windows carved by Bertuzi (Bertuccio) di Iacomo at San Zaccaria: see below, p. 175, and ASV, San Zaccaria, B. 31, c. 24.

58 ASV, Provv. Sal, vol. 3 (1411–1520), c. 84.

59 ASV, Provv. Sal, vol. 3 (1411–1520), c. 8.

60 ASV, Santa Maria della Carità, parte terza (documenti cartacei), B. 3, cc. 46, 46t.

61 As late as 1463 Bon and his partner Pantaleon were being pressed to complete their obligations at the Doge's Palace: ASV, Sen., Terra, reg. 5, c. 50. See above, p. 116.

62 ASV, Santa Maria della Carità, parte terza (documenti cartacei), B. 3, cc. 46t, 47, 47t and 48.

63 See note 53 above. See also ASV, Scuole Piccole, B. 417, fasc. 'A', fol. 83, for Bon's work at the Madonna dell'Orto.

64 ASV, Santa Maria della Carità, parte terza (documenti cartacei), B. 3, cc. 47t and 48.

65 ASV, Santa Maria della Carità, parte terza (documenti cartacei), B. 3, cc. 48t and 49.

66 ASV, Santa Maria della Carità, parte terza (documenti cartacei), B. 3, c. 49. The relief panel is now kept in the small sacristy of the church of Santa Maria della Salute.

67 ASV, Santa Maria della Carità, parte terza (documenti cartacei), B. 3, cc. 48t, 49 and 49t.

68 See Pincus, *The Arco Foscari*.

69 ASV, Santa Maria della Carità, parte terza (documenti cartacei), B. 3, c. 49t. The bank was run by Francesco Balbi and his brothers: see Lane, *I mercanti*, especially pp. 19–22 and 100–07; and Mueller, *The Venetian Money Market*. Francesco Balbi died in 1470, aged 84: G. Luzzatto, *Storia economica di Venezia dal XI al XVI secolo* (Venice, 1995), p. 214.

70 ASV, Santa Maria della Carità, parte terza (documenti cartacei), B. 3, c. 51.

71 ASV, Santa Maria della Carità, parte terza (documenti cartacei), B. 3, c. 51.

72 ASV, Santa Maria della Carità, parte terza (documenti cartacei), B. 3, c. 52t.

73 For Niccolò at the Ca' d'Oro, see ASV, PSMdC, B. 260 bis, *libretti di spese*, no. IV. See also Goy, *The House of Gold*, pp. 187, 189, 219–20, 222.

74 ASV, San Zaccaria, B. 31, c. 10.

75 ASV, Santa Maria della Carità, parte terza (documenti cartacei), B. 3, c. 50t.

76 ASV, Santa Maria della Carità, parte terza (documenti cartacei), B. 3, cc. 52 and 52t.

77 ASV, Santa Maria della Carità, parte terza (documenti cartacei), B. 3, cc. 52 and 52t.

78 ASV, Santa Maria della Carità, parte terza (documenti cartacei), B. 3, cc. 51t and 52. The *cambanilitij* or 'turrets' ('kiosks') are characteristic features of the façades of most later Gothic churches in Venice: see Santo Stefano as well as the more elaborate versions at the Frari and Santi Giovanni e Paolo. Bon himself probably provided the smaller, simpler ones on the façade of the Scuola Vecchia della Misericordia.

79 A. Canaletto, *The Grand Canal from the Church of the Carità* (circa 1730; Royal Collection, Windsor).

80 ASV, Santa Maria della Carità, parte terza (documenti cartacei), B. 3, c. 52t.

81 ASV, Santa Maria della Carità, parte terza (documenti cartacei), B. 3, cc. 53, 53t, 54 and 57.

82 ASV, Santa Maria della Carità, parte terza (documenti cartacei), B. 3, cc. 51t and 54. Ercole del Fiore was the adopted son of the painter Jacobello del Fiore (*circa.*

1370–1439), who worked in the hall of the Maggior Consiglio at the Palazzo Ducale during the years 1409–15. Little is known of Ercole, other than his work at the Carità.

83 ASV, SG Carità, B. 227, no. 60; B. 3, no.10.

84 ASV, Santa Maria della Carità, parte terza (documenti cartacei), B. 3, cc. 55 and 55t.

85 ASV, Santa Maria della Carità, parte terza (documenti cartacei), B. 3, cc. 55 and 55t.

86 ASV, Santa Maria della Carità, parte terza (documenti cartacei), B. 3, cc. 55 and 55t. This was the Pantaleon who became Bartolomeo's formal partner.

87 ASV, Santa Maria della Carità, parte terza (documenti cartacei), B. 3, cc. 56 and 56t.

88 ASV, Santa Maria della Carità, parte terza (documenti cartacei), B. 3, cc. 56 and 56t. Donatello remained in Padua until his return to Florence *circa* 1455, two years after his *Virgin and Child* was completed for the Carità. He already had a notable reputation and had completed the famous equestrian statue of the *condottiere* Gattamelata, begun in 1446, and which stands in front of the 'Santo', the church of Sant'Antonio in Padua.

89 Antonio Vivarini was already well known to the monastery. In 1446, ten years earlier, he had painted the 'Carità triptych', now in the Accademia, Venice. At the final account, Vivarini was paid extra by the Carità; in their own words 'per la fatura . . . de la nuova pala duc. 180 de pato facto e 20 dati super el pato per humanita che vene . . . duc. 200' ('for the making of the new altarpiece 180 ducats as previously contracted, and an additional 20 ducats as a charitable gesture, making 200 ducats in all'). See also note 78 above.

90 The west portal of Santo Stefano: U. Franzoi and D. di Stefano, *Le chiese di Venezia* (Venice, 1976), pp. 333–5; Arslan, *Venezia gotica*, p. 324, also notes its uniquely rich and extravagant extrados. Wolters, 'Ipotesi', in Valcanover and Wolters, eds, *L'architettura gotica veneziana*, p. 275, dates the portal to *circa* 1430; he also notes that, like the façade of Santi Giovanni e Paolo, the lower part of that of Santo Stefano was also to be decorated in an integral manner. He believes that this lower part, below the stone string course (which itself is integrated with the portal), was originally painted.

91 The Scuola Vecchia della Misericordia: the decision to rebuild the façades is cited by Sohm, *The Scuola Grande di San Marco*, p. 312, from Paoletti, *L'architettura*, p. 91. Wolters, 'Ipotesi', in Valcanover and Wolters, eds, *L'architettura gotica veneziana*, dates the façade from the decade between the decision in 1441 and 1451. See also the same author's *La scultura gotica veneziana*, cat. no. 250. The original attribution of the tympanum of the façade to Bon was given by Sansovino in 1581 (Sansovino and Martinioni, *Venetia*, vol. I, p. 286): 'Ha la fabrica vecchia sopra il portone la statua di nostra Donna di marmo, con bell'aria, belle mani, e con panni molto ben intesi, e fu scolpita da Bartolomeo, che fece il Portone di Palazzo [the Porta della Carta]'. A. M. Schulz has attributed the two angels on the portal to Giorgio da Sebenico: 'Giorgio da Sebenico

and the workshop of Giovanni Bon', in *Juraj Matejev Dalmatinac*, ed. M. Prelog (Zagreb, 1982), pp. 72–92. See also G. Fabbri, ed., *La Scuola Grande della Misericordia di Venezia* (Venice, 1999).

92 The sculptures at the Frari: Wolters, 'Ipotesi', in Valcanover and Wolters, eds, *L'architettura gotica veneziana*, pp. 273–80.

93 ASV, Santa Maria della Carità, parte terza (documenti cartacei), B. 3, c. 46.

94 For an account of the first stages of the restorations of the church, which began in 1969, see A. Clarke and P. Rylands, *The Church of the Madonna dell'Orto* (London, 1977); see also L. Moretti, *La chiesa della Madonna dell'Orto in Venezia* (Turin, 1981); the final stage of cleaning and restoration of the façade was concluded in 1995. See also UNESCO, *Venice Restored, 1966–1986* (Milan, 1991), pp. 24–8. On the façade of the church is a bas-relief panel with the arms of the Tiberio; it thus dates from the foundation of the church: A. Rizzi, *Scultura esterna a Venezia* (Venice, 1987), p. 275, Cann. no. 185.

95 For Zane Bon's will, see ASV, Sez. Not., Test. T. Pavoni, B. 797, no. 270. Zane left 1 ducat to the parish priest of San Marziale and 5 ducats to the Servites, whose nunnery was also nearby.

96 ASV, PSMdC, B. 189, fasc. 4 and 11.

97 For Morosini's will, see ASV, PSMdC, B. 189. His chapel is in the third bay on the left of the nave; the monastic cloisters occupy the right side beyond the right flank wall of the aisle. Morosini's chapel was later followed by those of the Contarini (1462) and Valier (1520).

98 ASV, PSMdC, B. 189, fasc. 6, c. 22.

99 Zane Bon died between August and 25 November 1443.

100 ASV, PSMdC, B. 189, fasc. 6, c. 26.

101 For the contract, see ASV, Scuole Piccole, B. 417, fasc. 'A', c. 83. See also Appendix II, document 4. The membership of the Scuola also included the artists Alvise Vivarini and Giovanni Bellini.

102 Connell, *The Employment of Sculptors and Stonemasons*, pp. 68–9, and R. Gallo, 'L'architettura di transizione dal gotico al Rinascimento', *Atti del Istituto Veneto di Scienze, Letteratura ed Arti*, CXX (1961–2), pp. 198–201. Gallo also published excerpts from the accounts (ibid., doc. III), which can be found in full in ASV, Scuole Piccole, B. 417, fasc. 'A', cc. 88–9 and 96–7.

103 ASV, Scuole Piccole, B. 417, fasc. 'A', c. 96v. Wolters, 'Ipotesi', in Valcanover and Wolters, eds, *L'architettura gotica veneziana*, p. 277.

104 The omission of the *Virgin* from the lunette may be explained by the fact that it is instead occupied by a fine slab of porphyry, a rare and highly regarded stone. It was perhaps donated to the church and the lunette adapted accordingly. The columns appear very short, and stand on tall, rather boxlike plinths, reminding us of other examples elsewhere, where recycled columns were used: the portico of the Scuola Grande di San Marco, for instance (see below, p. 208).

105 Sansovino and Martinioni, *Venetia*, vol. I, p. 163.

106 Schulz, *Antonio Rizzo*, p. 65. She claims that 'none of the figures that do adorn the portal was executed by, or under Bon', despite the almost universal agreement that Bon carved the *St Christopher*; the documentary evidence indicates that Bon was paid almost all the contracted sum by October 1461. This last fact does, however, perhaps support my suggestion that his own figures of the *Annunciation* were not quite complete at the time of his death, i.e., when work was apparently stalled awaiting the arrival of the columns. Schulz attributes the *Angel* to Rizzo and the *Virgin* to Niccolò di Giovanni Fiorentino (ibid., pp. 161–3 and 185, both with detailed historiography). Gallo ('L'architettura di transizione'), however, retains Bon's authorship for all three figures. Schulz is also certain that the *St Christopher* is the work of Niccolò, and dates it to 1465–7, although there is no documentary evidence. Neither Rizzo nor Niccolò are mentioned in the accounts of payments for the portal.

107 Schulz, *Antonio Rizzo*, p. 65.

108 For the Ca' del Duca, see above, pp. 136–8. See also note 103 above.

109 Gallo, 'L'architettura di transizione', pp. 192–4, 201–2 and doc. 1. See also Appendix II, document 3, in the present volume. The document itself is in Vicenza, Biblioteca Bertoliana, Cronaca della chiesa e convento di SS Giovanni e Paolo del R. P. Fra Rocco Curti; MS. G. 8.29. The portal was formerly traditionally attributed to Antonio Gambello.

110 Gallo, 'L'architettura di transizione', pp. 192–4, 201–2 and doc. 1.

111 Noted by Ennio Concina in *L'Arsenale della Repubblica di Venezia: tecniche e istituzioni dal medioevo all'età moderna* (Milan, 1984), p. 63 and note 85. He has suggested a possible common source for the columns of the Arsenale gate and the portal of Santi Giovanni e Paolo.

112 For the Ca' del Duca, the following two works are essential: J. R. Spencer, 'Filarete and the Ca' del Duca', *Journal of the Society of Architectural Historians*, XXXV/3 (1976), pp. 219–22; L. Beltrami, *La Ca' del Duca sul Canal Grande ed altre reminiscenze sforzesche a Venezia* (Milan, 1900). For some recent comments on Bon's role here, see Wolters, 'Ipotesi', in Valcanover and Wolters, eds, *L'architettura gotica veneziana*, pp. 277–9. See also McAndrew, *Venetian Architecture*, pp. 12–15.

113 Spencer, 'Filarete and the Ca' del Duca'; and Beltrami, *La Ca' del Duca*, pp. 30, 36. In this case the *modello* is likely to have been a drawing rather than a physical model.

114 For comments on the rustication, see W. Wolters, *Architektur und Ornament: Venezianischer Bauschmuck der Renaissance* (Munich, 2000), pp. 68–9; and McAndrew, *Venetian Architecture*, p. 14.

115 See note 112 above.

116 In the *Trattato*, Filarete described his palace as 'built in a swampy [or marshy] and boggy place . . . The water was brackish and emptied into the sea in many places, but there were many noble buildings here': *Trattato*,

XXI, 169v, 170r. Translated by J. R. Spencer (New Haven and London, 1965), and cited by McAndrew, *Venetian Architecture*, pp. 12, 14. Ferrini was in Venice in 1449, 1458 and 1459, and almost certainly on other occasions as well.

117 There are manuscript copies of the *Trattato* in the Biblioteca Nazionale in Florence and in the Biblioteca Nazionale Marciana, Venice. The latter is a Latin translation, which was acquired by the library at Santi Giovanni e Paolo in 1525.

CHAPTER SIX

1 M. Sanudo, *De origine, situ et magistratibus urbis Venetae, ovvero La città di Venetia*; as *La città di Venetia*, ed. A. C. Arico (Milan, 1980), p. 36.

2 F. Sansovino and G. Martinioni, *Venetia, città nobilissima et singolare . . .* , 2 vols (Venice, 1663; new facs. edn, 1968), vol. I, p. 366.

3 E. Concina, *L'Arsenale della Repubblica di Venezia: tecniche e istituzioni dal medioevo all'età moderna* (Milan, 1984), p. 51. Concina's is the most provocative and perceptive of several books on the Arsenale; see also G. Bellavitis, *L'Arsenale di Venezia* (Venice, 1983), and M. Nani Mocenigo, *L'Arsenale di Venezia* (Venice, 1939).

4 ASV, Sen., Terra, reg. 4, cc. 62–62t; for Pietro Bon, see ASV, Coll., Notatorio, reg. 9, cc. 176, 178t; and Sen., Terra, reg. 5, c. 167.

5 D. Malipiero, 'Annali', ed. F. Longo, in *Archivio Storico Italiano* (1844), p. 651.

6 Savina's Chronicle: Paris, Bibliothèque Nationale, MSS It. 2108, c. 2693; cited by Concina, *L'Arsenale*, p. 51 and note 21.

7 Malipiero's *breve*, as cited by Sansovino and Martinioni (*Venetia*, vol. II, p. 578), and by Concina (*L'Arsenale*, p. 51) reads: 'me duce Pax patriae data est'. The description 'totus moderatus' is from F. Filelfo, *Epistolae* (Venice, 1492), and cited by E. Garin, *L'umanesimo italiano* (Bari, 1965), p. 59.

8 Concina, *L'Arsenale*, p. 54.

9 For the printing claim, see Sansovino and Martinioni, *Venetia*, vol. II, p. 578, and 'Cronico veneto', p. 49.

10 For San Zaccaria, see pp. 167–89. See also J. McAndrew, *Venetian Architecture of the Early Renaissance* (Cambridge, MA, and London, 1980), pp. 17–23.

11 C. Bollani, 'De creatione Serenissimi atque illustrissimi principis Christofori Mauri . . .', in BMV, MSS Lat., cl. 14, cod. 252 (= 4718), c. 870. For Capodilista, see BMV, MSS Lat., cl. 14, cod. 2 (= 4590), c. 21v. Both are cited by Concina, *L'Arsenale*, p. 72, notes 38 and 39.

12 For the arch at Pola, see G. Traversari, *L'arco dei Sergi* (Padua, 1971); and McAndrew, *Venetian Architecture* p. 19. For Falconetto, see Concina, *L'Arsenale*, p. 60. For further discussions of this humanist network, see ibid., pp. 58–60. Falconetto's drawing of the Pola arch is in London, Royal Institute of British Architects, vol. XII, c. 10r.

13 For Andrea Corner, Sforza and the Ca' del Duca, see above, pp. 136–8, and J. R. Spencer, 'The Ca' del Duca

in Venice and Benedetto Ferrini', *Journal of the Society of Architectural Historians*, XXX (1971), pp. 1 et seq. See also Concina, *L'Arsenale*, pp. 64, 67–8; and also L. Beltrami, *La Ca' del Duca sul Canal Grande ed altre reminiscenze sforzesche a Venezia* (Milan, 1900).

14 Concina, *L'Arsenale*, p. 68 and note 100.

15 J. R. Spencer, ed., *Filarete's Treatise on Architecture* (New Haven and London, 1975); A. Averlino [Filarete], *Trattato di architettura*, ed. A. M. Finoli and L. Grassi (Milan, 1972). A further possibility is Luciano di Martino da Laurana, best known for his association with the palace of Federigo da Montefeltro at Urbino. However, the earliest definitive record of Laurana dates from 1464, when he was at Fano. For the arch at Naples, see note 17 below; see also Concina, *L'Arsenale*, p. 60.

16 See below, p. 146. Concina (*L'Arsenale*, p. 63 and note 85) suggests that the columns for both works came from the same source, i.e., Torcello, since 'they appear so similar'. See the *Hypnerotomachia Poliphili* by 'Francesco Colonna', first published by Aldo Manuzio in Venice in 1499. For a new edn, see G. Pozzi and L. A. Ciapponi, eds (Padua, 1980). For a discussion of the significance of the numerous architectural illustrations in the *Hypnerotomachia*, see also P. Fortini Brown, *Venice and Antiquity: The Venetian Sense of the Past* (New Haven and London, 1996), pp. 207–19; and J. Onians, *Bearers of Meaning: The Classical Orders in Antiquity, the Middle Ages and the Renaissance* (Princeton, 1990), pp. 207–15.

17 For the Naples arch, see G. L. Hersey, *The Aragonese Arch at Naples, 1443–1475* (New Haven and London, 1973). Also associated with the Castel Nuovo arch are Pietro da Milano, Francesco Laurana, Paolo Romano and the Catalan Pere Joan. Pisanello's influence is also particularly notable. Many Venetian masons would have been familiar with the Roman arch at Pola, because it was near the Istrian stone quarries.

18 Fortini Brown, *Venice and Antiquity*, pp. 109–10. For the dates of construction, see ASV, Sen., Terra, reg. 4, c. 62 (20 January 1457 mv [= 1458]), and Sen., Terra, reg. 4, c. 143 (24 April 1460). See also P. Paoletti, *L'architettura e la scultura del Rinascimento in Venezia: ricerche storico-artistiche*, 2 vols (Venice, 1893–7), p. 140; and R. Gallo, 'La porta d'ingresso dell'Arsenale e i leoni del Pireo', in *Rivista mensile della città di Venezia* (Venice, 1925), pp. 323–33. According to Sanudo, there were normally only two *provveditori*, 'degni patritij', but they received no salary.

19 Malipiero's funerary monument at Santi Giovanni e Paolo, by Pietro Lombardo, is a very rich, ornate work, again perhaps indicative of his personal taste. It combines a Gothic canopy (a traditional Venetian feature) with a framing in the form of a much more Florentine aedicule. It was carved by Pietro Lombardo *circa* 1470, and has a very close family resemblance to the portal at San Giobbe: see p. 163 below. See (inter alia) McAndrew, *Venetian Architecture*, pp. 118 et seq.

20 Few writers to date have commented on the oversized lion; perhaps it was simply made as large (and imposing) as possible. It is one of very few to have escaped

Napoleon's iconoclastic purges, probably because it was not accompanied by the figure of the doge. For a detailed discussion of the symbolism and iconography, see R. Lieberman, 'Real architecture, imaginary history: the Arsenale gate as Venetian mythology', *Journal of the Warburg and Courtauld Institutes*, LIV (1991), pp. 117–26. For further observations on the lion, see also A. Rizzi, *Scultura esterna a Venezia* (Venice, 1987), p. 67 and note 55.

21 '. . . to enhance the beauty and practicality not only of this place, but also of the city': ASV, Sen., Terra, reg. 4, c. 143v (24 May 1460); for the acquisition of the land, see Sen., Terra, reg. 5, c. 175r (18 January 1467 [= 1466 mv]).

22 '. . . a [public] square in front of the said Arsenale, to provide beauty and prestige, to the effect that the prospect of this work will also give it dignity and beauty': ASV, Coll., Notatorio, reg. 11, c. 19 (24 March 1468).

23 Sansovino and Martinioni, *Venetia*, vol. 1, p. 367.

24 See E. Zucchetta, 'The Arsenal', in UNESCO, *Venice Restored, 1966–1986* (Milan, 1991), pp. 54–5; see also G. Tassini, *Curiosità veneziane, ovvero origini delle denominazioni stradali di Venezia*, 4th edn (Venice, 1887; reprinted 1964), pp. 38–9.

25 There are also two fine studies of the operations within the Arsenale: R. C. Davis, *Shipbuilders of the Venetian Arsenal* (Baltimore and London, 1991); and F. C. Lane, *Venetian Ships and Shipbuilders of the Renaissance*, new edn (Baltimore and London, 1992).

CHAPTER SEVEN

1 The standard work on Codussi is L. Puppi and L. Olivato Puppi, *Mauro Codussi* (Milan, 1977); still useful is L. Angelini, *Le opere in Venezia di Mauro Codussi* (Milan, 1945), although not all of the attributions are accepted today. For the Roman arena at Verona, see also Sebastiano Serlio, *The Five Books of Architecture* (London, 1611; facs. edn, New York, 1982), Book III, chapter 4, fol. 34; for the amphitheatre at Pola, ibid., fol. 36.

2 For San Michele, see Puppi and Olivato Puppi, *Mauro Codussi*, pp. 18–39, with comprehensive notes and references. For stylistic observations, see also J. McAndrew, *Venetian Architecture of the Early Renaissance* (Cambridge, MA, and London, 1980), pp. 236–61. For Donà and Delfin, see also below, p. 158. For the roles of both men in Venetian humanist circles, see M. King, *Umanesimo e patriziato a Venezia nel quattrocento*, 2 vols (Rome, 1989), especially vol. II, pp. 523–7.

3 It is also worth recalling the flat, square rustication on the lowermost order of the base of the Ca' del Duca (see pp. 136–8 above), built a few years earlier, and which Codussi must have seen. Codussi may have been familiar with the treatise of Filarete, although whether he travelled to Florence, Pienza or Urbino is not known. Urbino is a fairly short distance from Rimini,

however. Clarke, in *The Roman House*, p. 232, has dated the Roman inscription at Urbino to later than 1474.

4 See below, pp. 157–9.

5 For the campanile of San Pietro, see McAndrew, *Venetian Architecture*, pp. 263–7; Puppi and Olivato Puppi, *Mauro Codussi*, pp. 45–8. For the new interpretation of the scope of Codussi's work at San Pietro, see D. Howard, *Venice and the East: The Impact of the Islamic World on Venetian Architecture, 1100–1500* (New Haven and London, 2000), pp. 94–5 and notes 158–62. For archival references, see P. Paoletti, *L'architettura e la scultura del Rinascimento in Venezia: ricerche storico-artistiche*, 2 vols (Venice, 1893–7), vol. I, p. 101, 'misc. di documenti', nos 67–9. See also ASV, Mensa patriarchale, B. 60, Reg. di cassa, vol. I, fol. 35. For a note on the *stemme* on the façades of the campanile, see A. Rizzi, *Scultura esterna a Venezia* (Venice, 1987), p. 162, Castello, catalogue nos 10 and 11.

6 Puppi and Olivato Puppi, *Mauro Codussi*, p. 178. For further notes on the career of Girardi, see F. Corner, *Notizie storiche delle chiese e monasteri di Venezia e di Torcello* (Padua, 1756), pp. 18–19. Corner describes him as 'Umile, e austere per se, sollicito e benigno cogli altri'.

7 Corner, *Notizie storiche*, p. 180. See also V. Meneghin, *San Michele in Isola di Venezia*, 2 vols (Venice, 1962), vol. II, p. 310. King (*Umanesimo*, pp. 523–7) puts Delfin's birth date as 1444. For the early history of the church, see Corner, *Notizie storiche*, pp. 637–45.

8 F. Sansovino and G. Martinioni, *Venetia, città nobilissima et singolare . . .* , 2 vols (Venice, 1663; new facsimile edn, 1968), vol. II, p. 593. For Delfin's writings see King, *Umanesimo*, vol. II, pp. 526–7. There is also extensive correspondence with Savonarola, Ermolao Barbaro and his cousins Domenico and MarcAntonio Morosini.

9 M. Sanudo, *De origine, situ et magistratibus urbis Venetae, ovvero La città di Venetia*; as *La città di Venetia*, ed. A. C. Arico (Milan, 1980), pp. 178–9 [BMV, Cod. Cicogna 970, cc. 23–4].

10 Paoletti, *L'architettura*, vol. II, pp. 165–6.

11 ASV, Sez. Not., Canc. Inf., B. 124 (Protocollo di Bernardo Morosini), c. 72v.

12 ASV, Monasteri soppressi: San Michele in Isola, B. 3 (Testamenti), c. 27. Girolamo Donà (*circa* 1456–20 October 1511): for works, see King, *Umanesimo*, pp. 532–5.

13 ASV, Monasteri soppressi: San Michele in Isola, B. 4 (Testamenti) c. 27v.

14 Loredan drafted his will on 15 June 1513, three months before he was killed: see Puppi and Olivato Puppi, *Mauro Codussi*, p. 182. For archival references, see ASV, Sez. Not., Canc. Inf., Misc. Testamenti, B. 29, no. 3045. See also ASV, Monasteri soppressi: S Michele in Isola, B. 3 (Testamenti), cc. 40v–45r. For the Priuli chapel, see J. Fletcher and R. Mueller, 'Bellini and the bankers: the Priuli altarpiece for San Michele in Isola, Venice', *Burlington Magazine*, vol. CXLVII (January 2005).

15 ASV, Mensa Patriarcale, B. 69.

16 See above, p. 158.

17 See note 6 above. See also Corner, *Notizie storiche*, pp. 42–5, although he errs regarding Codussi's reconstruc-

tion of the church, claiming that, following its earlier reconstruction in 1105, 'Durò per quattro e più secoli intatta la Chiesa, finche nell'anno 1689, essendo stata da una violenta scossa di terremoto in gran parte atterrata'. He states that it was then rebuilt with 'due facciate di marmo'. The two façades were in fact constructed in 1542 (that to the *rio*) and 1604 (that to the *campo*).

18 There is a brief summary of Grimani's extraordinary career in Sansovino and Martinioni, *Venetia*, vol. II, p. 592. He was doge for one year, two months and two days.

19 Despite general acceptance, there is no secure documentation to confirm Codussi as the architect of Palazzo Lando (later Corner Spinelli); see also E. Bassi, *Palazzi di Venezia: admiranda urbis Venetae* (Venice, 1976), pp. 386–95. The house was bought from the Lando by Zuanne Corner in 1542 after the disastrous fire at his own palace at San Polo. It was modernised internally by Sanmicheli shortly afterwards: P. Gazzola, *Michele Sanmicheli* (Venice, 1960), pp. 148–50 and figs 225, 226. See also P. Davies and D. Hemsoll, *Sanmicheli* (Milan, 2004).

20 The great house was certainly complete by 1509, since it was described in that year by Girolamo Priuli in his 'Diarii': in *Rerum Italicarum Scriptores* (Bologna, 1938), vol. IV, p. 254.

21 Puppi and Olivato Puppi, *Mauro Codussi*, p. 222, citing part of the text of his will.

22 For a stylistic analysis of Pietro's ducal monuments, see McAndrew, *Venetian Architecture*, pp. 118–33. All three are today in SS Giovanni e Paolo, although that to Niccolò Marcello was originally in the now lost church of Santa Marina.

23 For the early history of San Giobbe, see Corner, *Notizie storiche*, pp. 283–8; see also McAndrew, *Venetian Architecture*, pp. 134–43; F. Finotto, *San Giobbe* (Verona, 1994), passim; U. Franzoi and D. di Stefano, *Le chiese di Venezia* (Venice, 1976), pp. 108–11. For a detailed bibliography of San Bernardino at San Giobbe, see R. Goffen, *Piety and Patronage in Renaissance Venice: Bellini, Titian and the Franciscans* (New Haven and London, 1986), appendix 1 and note 1, p. 249. According to Corner: 'Arrivò frattanto nell'anno 1443 in Venezia per seminarvi la parola di Dio l'Apostolico uomo San Bernardino da Siena . . . v'attrasse un mirabil concorso di persone per venerarne la santità, fra quali Cristoforo Moro Senatore . . . [che] contrasse un così stretto legame di riverente amicizia col Sant'uomo, che nell'anno susseguente alla di lui canonizzazione celebrata solennemente da Niccolò Papa V nell'anno 1450, volle a proprie spese inalzargli nella chiesa di san Giobbe una magnifica Cappella'.

24 McAndrew, *Venetian Architecture*, p. 141.

25 Almost all aspects of the history, architecture and sculptures of the Miracoli church are covered in the very fine new monograph edited by Mario Piana and Wolfgang Wolters, *Santa Maria dei Miracoli a Venezia: la storia, la fabbrica, i restauri* (Venice, 2003); see especially

A. Schiavon, 'Santa Maria dei Miracoli: una fabbrica "cittadina"' (pp. 3–16); A. Niero, 'La Madonna dei Miracoli nella storia della pietà veneziana: breve profilo' (pp. 17–40). Still important is R. Lieberman, *The Church of Santa Maria dei Miracoli in Venice* (New York, 1972). See also McAndrew, *Venetian Architecture*, pp. 150–81; Corner, *Notizie storiche*, pp. 334–6.

26 For Diedo, see King, *Umanesimo*, pp. 214, 218 and especially pp. 523–5.

27 McAndrew, *Venetian Architecture*, p. 156.

28 Sanudo, *La città di Venetia*, p. 26: 'una chiesia nuovamenta fabricata di una nostra Donna antichissima, che era su una strata ivi, che fece miracoli, et *cotidie* tanti ne fanno ch'e cossa incredibile a veder li arzenti, et statue vi sono, et il corso della zente che fa dir ogni zorno messe. Quivi e sta' fatto d'elemosina – non e cinque anni – una bellissima chiesia torniata di marmi, lavorata all'anticha con porfidi, et serpentini, coverta di piombo.' For the suggested influence, see E. Concina, *Storia dell'architettura di Venezia dal VII al XX secolo* (Milan, 1995), p. 133. Other suggested influences are the Scrovegni chapel in Padua and the Mascoli chapel in San Marco. Concina himself has also proposed the Malatesta church at Rimini.

29 McAndrew, *Venetian Architecture*, pp. 144–9; Paoletti, *L'architettura*, p. 222.

30 See below, p. 202. See also P. Sohm, *The Scuola Grande di San Marco, 1437–1550: The Architecture of a Venetian Lay Confraternity* (New York and London, 1982), doc. 57.

31 See below, p. 231. For the Badoer-Giustinian chapel, see the new monograph by A. M. Schulz, *La cappella Badoer-Giustinian* (Florence, 2003). There is an excellent brief survey of the sculptures (following their recent restoration) in S. Onda, *La chiesa di San Francesco della Vigna: guida artistica* (Venice, 2003), pp. 93–111. The chapel has attracted high praise for centuries. Sansovino (*Venetia*, vol. I, p. 49): 'tutta coperta di figurette di mezzo rilievo con ricchi fregij marmi, & di bronzi: la quale per Grandezza di corpo, & bellezza di sito e molto honorata'.

CHAPTER EIGHT

1 Among the surprisingly small number of secondary sources on the history of San Zaccaria are the following: B. Cecchetti, 'Documenti per la storia della fabbrica della chiesa di San Zaccaria', *Archivio Veneto*, XXXI (1886), pp. 459–96; P. Paoletti, *L'architettura e la scultura del Rinascimento in Venezia: ricerche storico-artistiche*, 2 vols (Venice, 1893–7); L. Angelini, *Le opere in Venezia di Mauro Codussi* (Milan, 1945); N. Carboneri, 'Mauro Codussi', in *Bollettino CISA 'Andrea Palladio'*, V/2 (1964), pp. 188–98; U. Franzoi and D. di Stefano, *Le chiese di Venezia* (Venice, 1976); J. McAndrew, *Venetian Architecture of the Early Renaissance* (Cambridge, MA, and London, 1980); L. Puppi and L. Olivato Puppi, *Mauro Codussi* (Milan, 1977). An important new contribution

is G. Radke, 'Nuns and their art: the case of San Zaccaria in Renaissance Venice', *Renaissance Quarterly*, no. 44 (2001), pp. 430–59. For the ducal *andate* to San Zaccaria (and elsewhere), see E. Muir, *Civic Ritual in Renaissance Venice* (Princeton, 1981), especially pp. 221–3.

2 Paoletti, *L'architettura*, vol. I, pp. 61–2; F. Sansovino and G. Martinioni, *Venetia, città nobilissima et singolare . . .*, 2 vols (Venice, 1663; new facs. edn, 1968), vol. I, p. 82.

3 The apse was 'edificadho e fatto nuovamente': ASV, San Zaccaria, B. 9; Paoletti, *L'architettura*, vol. I, p. 63.

4 Some chronicles claim that the church was severely damaged by fire in the 1450s, in which were claimed the lives of 100 nuns (cited by McAndrew, *Venetian Architecture*, p. 24), although other sources (e.g., G. Tassini, *Curiosità veneziane, ovvero origini delle denominazioni stradali di Venezia*, 4th edn, Venice, 1887; reprinted 1964, p. 297) record an identical loss of life in a much earlier fire of 1105. F. Corner (*Notizie storiche delle chiese e monasteri di Venezia e di Torcello*, Padua, 1756, p. 130) also records the fire of 1105 ('un terribile incendio'), but not the fate of the nuns. Sansovino (*Venetia*, vol. II, 'Cronico veneto', p. 22) puts the fire in 1106, but does not mention the much later one in the 1450s, nor do the building accounts from 1456 make any mention of such a recent tragedy.

5 Despite the clear provenance of the plan of San Zaccaria, it is interesting to note that neither of the great Benedictine churches in the Venetian Terraferma, Praglia and Follina (the latter rebuilt by Tullio Lombardo after *circa* 1490), have such a plan. It was not only highly unusual in Italy, therefore, but was also complex and expensive to construct. As Sansovino notes (*Venetia*, vol. I, p. 84), the church 'fu finita in due volte, ma con diversa manieria d'Architettura'. For discussion of the plan forms, see M.-A. Winkelmes, 'Form and reform: illuminated Cassinese reform-style churches in Renaissance Italy', *Annali di Architettura*, VIII (1996), pp. 61–84.

6 ASV, San Zaccaria, B. 31 (it is not in fact a *busta*, an envelope or bundle, but a large bound ledger). See also S. Connell's important summary in 'Gli artigiani dell'edilizia', in G. Gianighian, ed., *Ricerche venete*, II: *Dal medioevo al tardo Rinascimento* (Venice, 1993), pp. 73–84, 90–92.

7 ASV, San Zaccaria, B. 31, c. 42: 'per resto de hognij suo provision e raxon facta dacordo fin questo di che el de prinzipiar i pati nuovj appar per carta facta per man de ser marco de mearij nodaro'.

8 ASV, San Zaccaria, B. 31, c. 7.

9 ASV, San Zaccaria, B. 31, c. 4. Niccolò Bernardo remained the banker of the nunnery for at least some years. The nunnery also bought timber from him: ibid., B. 31, c. 1, the very first entry in the account book. The other private bankers in this period were Luca Soranzo, Bernardo Ciera and Francesco and Bernardo Balbi: F. C. Lane, *I mercanti di Venezia* (Turin, 1982), p. 135. The Bernardo bank had been founded in 1430. It later passed under the direction of Andrea Garzoni. It col-

lapsed in the 'crash' of 1499, but reopened (and failed again) in 1500 (Lane, ibid., p. 220; from M. Sanudo, *I diarii*, vol. II, 391). The nunnery received donations from many sources, including papal indulgences: Corner, *Notizie storiche*, p. 131.

10 ASV, San Zaccaria, B. 31, c. 4

11 ASV, San Zaccaria, B. 31, c. 7. The document actually refers to 'dessegnj' in the plural, so the work may perhaps have included some details, profiles of stonework, or even alternatives for some parts of the work.

12 The new model, made in 1466, however, was described as 'uno designo facto de nuovo de legname', in the singular; the reference to it is added to the bottom of ASV, San Zaccaria, B. 31, c. 7, out of chronological sequence.

13 For a summary of these works, see Paoletti, *L'architettura*, vol. I, pp. 64–7; see also McAndrew, *Venetian Architecture*, p. 27 (plan).

14 ASV, San Zaccaria, B. 31, c. 24.

15 ASV, San Zaccaria, B. 31, c. 10. See also R. J. Goy, *The House of Gold: Building a Palace in Medieval Venice* (Cambridge, 1993), pp. 187, 189 and 219–20.

16 ASV, San Zaccaria, B. 31, c. 29, and Paoletti, *L'architettura*, vol. I, pp. 64–7, 69 and 71–4.

17 ASV, Santa Maria della Carità, parte terza (documenti cartacei), B. 3, cc. 48t, 49, 50t.

18 Goy, *The House of Gold*, pp. 232–4; see also ASV, PSMdC, B. 269 bis: libretti di spese no. IV, cc. 57t and 58.

19 ASV, San Zaccaria, B. 31, c. 64. For detail of the many descriptive terms for sizes and lengths of timbers, see E. Concina, *Pietre, parole, storia: glossario della costruzione nelle fonti veneziane (sec. XV–XVIII)* (Venice, 1988), pp. 59–60 and elsewhere.

20 ASV, San Zaccaria, B. 31, cc. 65–7 and 73. See also Paoletti, *L'architettura*, vol. I, p. 65; and S. Connell, *The Employment of Sculptors and Stonemasons in Venice in the Fifteenth Century* (London and New York, 1988), p. 176.

21 ASV, San Zaccaria, B. 31, c. 72. Much of the timber was bought from Zuan Morexin (Morosini) and Benedetto Donato.

22 For the roof tiles, see ASV, San Zaccaria, B. 31, c. 42; for Polo the carpenter, ibid., c. 88; for Niccolò Luxe, the blacksmith, ibid., c. 83; and for the *festa* on completion of the roof, ibid., c. 13.

23 For records of all of these decorations, see ASV, San Zaccaria, B. 31, c. 95.

24 ASV, San Zaccaria, B. 31, cc. 96 and 98.

25 For the choirstalls, see ASV, San Zaccaria, B. 31, c. 118.

26 For the Ca' d'Oro, see Goy, *The House of Gold*, pp. 103, 118, 140 and 151. For the Doge's Palace, see G. Zuccolo, *Il restauro statico nell'architettura di Venezia* (Venice, 1975), pp. 60–61.

27 ASV, San Zaccaria, B. 31, c. 6.

28 The 'smaller' piles were still $1\frac{1}{2}$ Venetian feet in diameter, that is, almost exactly half a metre. The larger ones cost 17 lire per hundred, the smaller L. 8.10.0.

29 ASV, San Zaccaria, B. 31, c. 6. Almost 5,000 of these planks were required in total; again the source was

Lorenzo da Bergamo. These were squared planks sawn by carpenters, unlike the piles, which were not sawn, but were simply 'de-barked', sharpened stakes.

30 ASV, San Zaccaria, B. 31, cc. 11 and 14.

31 ASV, San Zaccaria, B. 31, cc. 21 and 23. See Concina, *Pietre, parole, storia*, p. 145.

32 ASV, San Zaccaria, B. 31, c. 8. All were paid out of the account with the banker Niccolò Bernardo.

33 ASV, San Zaccaria, B. 31, c. 18. The usual rate was 10 lire per 1,000. There were 7,500 recorded as 'prede rosse de padoana' but cost the same rate.

34 For all of these deliveries, see ASV, San Zaccaria, B. 31, cc. 5, 12 and 13.

35 ASV, PSMdC, B. 54 (Comm. Baseggio), quad. III. See also Connell, *The Employment of Sculptors and Stonemasons*, p. 33.

36 ASV, San Zaccaria, B. 31, c. 20; and Connell, *The Employment of Sculptors and Stonemasons*, pp. 33–4 and 98.

37 ASV, San Zaccaria, B. 31, c. 20, and Connell, *The Employment of Sculptors and Stonemasons*, p. 274.

38 ASV, San Zaccaria, B. 31, c. 24.

39 ASV, San Zaccaria, B. 31, c. 26; also Puppi and Olivato Puppi, *Mauro Codussi*, p. 67. According to Paoletti (*L'architettura*, vol. I, p. 68), the Ammiana columns were originally destined for San Marco.

40 Some of the nuns, or at least the abbess herself, went to inspect the columns on 21 July 1458, before the purchase was concluded: ASV, San Zaccaria, B. 31, c. 8.

41 The *comune* of Torcello had prohibited the removal of stone in the fourteenth century, a prohibition that was renewed in 1424 and yet again in 1441, but it was clearly fighting a lost cause. In 1429 the *podestà* of Torcello complained directly to the doge himself, Francesco Foscari, about this continuing plunder: Connell, *The Employment of Sculptors and Stonemasons*, p. 137; and M. Corner, *Scritture sopra la laguna*, ed. G. Pavanello (Venice, 1919), p. 77.

42 McAndrew, *Venetian Architecture*, p. 32.

43 ASV, San Zaccaria, B. 31, cc. 27–8.

44 ASV, San Zaccaria, B. 31, cc. 35 and 70.

45 ASV, San Zaccaria, B. 31, cc. 19 and 45.

46 ASV, San Zaccaria, B. 31, c. 47.

47 ASV, San Zaccaria, B. 31, c. 52. On the rent of a house in Rovigno: on 18 January 1461 the nunnery rented a house for two years for about 4 ducats. A similar rental was taken up again in 1476 (ibid., c. 140), and on a third occasion, in 1484, one at Orsera, a few miles up the coast: ibid., c. 164.

48 ASV, San Zaccaria, B. 31, cc. 52–61, 65–7 and 70.

49 ASV, San Zaccaria, B. 31, cc. 109, 111 and 113. The accounts up to 1464/5 were kept by *gastaldo* Giovanni di Benedetto. His successor, Jacopo Gebellin, began his term with a new ledger, now lost, but which had a total of *spese* amounting to 2,424 ducats. Gebellin was sacked in 1473 on suspicion of financial irregularities, but the case was finally resolved in 1480, when Gebellin was ordered to repay 400 ducats back to the convent. His successor in turn, Antonio Foscolo,

reverted to using di Benedetto's original ledger, as we see today: Connell, 'Gli artigiani', in Gianighian, ed., *Ricerche venete*, II, pp. 75–6.

50 For the new model, see ASV, San Zaccaria, B. 31, c. 7.

51 ASV, San Zaccaria, B. 31, c. 120.

52 For the costs of building the Ca' d'Oro, see Goy, *The House of Gold*, pp. 244–6 and Appendix 1.

53 ASV, San Zaccaria, B. 31, cc. 122–5, 129 and 131–3.

54 For the capitals, ASV, San Zaccaria, B. 31, cc. 134, 136, 142 and 144.

55 For the contract signed by Gambello just before he went abroad, see ASV, San Zaccaria, B. 39 (perg.); and Paoletti, *L'architettura*, vol. 1, pp. 71–2. See also Appendix II, document 6.

56 ASV, San Zaccaria, B. 31, cc. 149–51 and 153–4.

57 ASV, San Zaccaria, B. 31, c. 152. The dal Vescovo were an important clan of stone dealers: see Connell, *The Employment of Sculptors and Stonemasons*, p. 96, for a genealogical table and further details of their activities. See also Connell, 'Gli artigiani', in Gianighian, ed., *Ricerche venete*, II, p. 49.

58 For the bishop of Brescia's columns, see Paoletti, *L'architettura*, vol. 1, p. 68.

59 ASV, San Zaccaria, B. 31 c. 154.

60 For the death of Gambello and his will, see ASV, Coll., Notatorio (1474–81), and Paoletti, *L'architettura*, vol. 1, p. 95. The pension given to his widow was a reflection of his services to the Republic: 'defuncti in servitijs nostri'; the record also notes 'in quanta paupertate post se dimiserit relictam suam cum Grandi numero filiorum'.

61 ASV, San Zaccaria, B. 31, cc. 160–63.

62 McAndrew, *Venetian Architecture*, pp. 34 and 37.

63 ASV, San Zaccaria, B. 31, c. 164.

64 ASV, San Zaccaria, B. 31, c. 162.

65 ASV, San Zaccaria, B. 31, c. 167.

66 P. Paoletti, *La Scuola Grande di San Marco* (Venice, 1929), p. 16, note 5.

67 ASV, San Zaccaria, B. 31, c. 172. See also Puppi and Olivato Puppi, *Mauro Codussi*, p. 191. For Codussi at San Michele: ibid., pp. 32, 177–8; see also Appendix II, document 7.

68 ASV, San Zaccaria, B. 31, c. 168.

69 Puppi and Olivato Puppi, *Mauro Codussi*, p. 58.

70 ASV, San Zaccaria, B. 31, c. 172. The entry reads: 'm[aestr]o moro nostro proto die aver adj XII zugno chel se haconza con la reverendissima madona labadesa e chamerlenghe e done prexente miss. Piero donado, E missier loredan q. m[esser] Ant[onio] a lavorar si de taiapiera E de murer E quelo son a far de marangon e die haver per el tempo el stara in la tera a raxon de duc. LXXX alano'. See Appendix II, document 7.

71 For Loredan's bricks: ASV, San Zaccaria, B. 31, c. 175.

72 ASV, SGSM, B. 136, loose unnumbered folio; Paoletti, *L'architettura*, pp. 102–3. See also P. Sohm, *The Scuola Grande di San Marco, 1437–1550: The Architecture of a Venetian Lay Confraternity* (New York and London, 1982), p. 268 (docs 49, 52, 53). See also below, p. 198.

73 For comments on Bernardo's role in Codussi's other projects, see especially Puppi and Olivato Puppi, *Mauro Codussi*, pp. 22, 42 (note 104), 58 and 194.

74 ASV, San Zaccaria, B. 31, c. 167. Laziero was paid for carving vaulting ribs on 2 May and 20 June 1483.

75 ASV, San Zaccaria, B. 31, c. 176. The stone consisted of two 'cargoes', that is, two *maran*-loads, and cost 44 ducats.

76 ASV, San Zaccaria, B. 31, cc. 177–8, 182 and 185.

77 ASV, San Zaccaria, B. 31, c. 176.

78 ASV, San Zaccaria, B. 31, c. 187 (Codussi's visit) and c. 172 and c. 190 for Zuan and Bernardo.

79 ASV, San Zaccaria, B. 31, cc. 221, 224 and 230.

80 ASV, San Zaccaria, B. 31, c. 195.

81 For work on the stone for the façade, ASV, San Zaccaria, B. 31, cc. 201–2. For Jacopo della Costa, see Puppi and Olivato Puppi, *Mauro Codussi*, p. 191.

82 ASV, San Zaccaria, B. 31, cc. 214 and 216.

83 ASV, San Zaccaria, B. 31, cc. 233 and 249. The larger slab of porphyry cost 10 ducats, much more costly than Istrian stone.

84 ASV, San Zaccaria, B. 31, cc. 213, 216 and 220.

85 ASV, San Zaccaria, B. 31, c. 225.

86 ASV, San Zaccaria, B. 31, c. 239. Some of the lead was bought from Benedetto di Simone. The three consignments totalled approximately 180 sheets in all, and the price was considerable, further evidence of the high quality of specification for the church as a whole.

87 ASV, San Zaccaria, B. 31, c. 255.

88 For the accounts of the sacristy, ASV, San Zaccaria, B. 31, cc. 234, 238, 240 and 245.

89 The open colonnade has long since been filled in, and is thus recorded in several eighteenth-century engravings. At the back of the cloister was a garden or orchard, which survived at least until Merlo's view of 1696 (copies in Museo Civico Correr, Venice, and Bibliothèque Nationale, Paris).

90 We have no evidence of Codussi visiting Florence, although he may well have done so; while in Ravenna, though, it is highly likely that he visited Rimini to see Alberti's church for the Malatesta.

91 Sansovino and Martinioni, *Venetia*, vol. 1, p. 84.

CHAPTER NINE

1 J. McAndrew, *Venetian Architecture of the Early Renaissance* (Cambridge, MA, and London, 1980), p. 361; P. Sohm, *The Scuola Grande di San Marco, 1437–1550: The Architecture of a Venetian Lay Confraternity* (New York and London, 1982), p. 140. Sohm is an essential secondary source, with many archival sources also published.

2 There is one reference to it in ASV, Cons. d. X, Misti, reg. 11, fol. 49r. See also Sohm, *The Scuola Grande di San Marco*, doc. 1.

3 ASV, Cons. d. X, Misti, reg. 12, fol. 1r. See also ASV, SGSM, B. 122, fasc. D, c. 9. An extract of the same text in ASV, SGSM, B. 77, fasc. 3, fol. 3, reads: 'Essendo in

la salla dila nostra scolla a sa.+ [Santa Croce] assem-
bladij xxxto di nostri fradelli appresso m. lo vardian e
suo compagnij, el qual m. lo vardian dimando licenzia
a i predittj de poder comenzar a lavorar la casa della
nostra scuola a SS Zuanne pollo, i qual tutti a una vose
disse . . . [chel] ditto lavorar devesse principiar': Sohm,
The Scuola Grande di San Marco, doc. 2.

4 For the extent of the plot and the lagoon shore, see
de' Barbari's view of 1500.

5 ASV, SGSM, reg. 15 bis, fol. 8; Sohm, *The Scuola Grande
di San Marco*, doc. 4.

6 ASV, SGSM, reg. 15 bis, fol. 9; P. Paoletti, *La Scuola
Grande di San Marco* (Venice, 1929), p. 13.

7 ASV, SGSM, B. 122, fasc. D, cc. 10–13; Sohm, *The Scuola
Grande di San Marco*, doc. 7.

8 ASV, SGSM, reg. 16 bis, fol. 9; and B. 122, fasc. C, c. 31.
See also Paoletti, *La Scuola Grande di San Marco*, p. 14;
W. Wolters, *La scultura gotica veneziana*, 2 vols (Venice,
1976), p. 291; P. Paoletti, *L'architettura e la scultura del
Rinascimento in Venezia: ricerche storico-artistiche*, 2 vols
(Venice, 1893–7), vol. I, p. 40.

9 Sohm, *The Scuola Grande di San Marco*, pp. 86–7.

10 Erizzo: BMV, It., Classe LVI, no. 8636. See also Sanudo,
'Vite de' Dogi', in BMV, It., Classe VII, cod. CXXV
(7640), fol. 176r.

11 ASV, Cons. d. X, Misti, reg. 12, fols 5r and 7.

12 Bon carved the tympanum bas-relief of the *Madonna
della Misericordia* (London, Victoria and Albert
Museum), and was almost certainly responsible for the
windows, *campanilitij* ('tabernacles') and other elements
of carved stonework, when the Scuola was partially
rebuilt after 1441: Paoletti, *L'architettura*, vol. I, p. 91;
R. J. Goy, *The House of Gold: Building a Palace in
Medieval Venice* (Cambridge, 1993), pp. 111–12, 115, 154
and 228; Wolters, *La scultura gotica veneziana*, p. 197, who
attributes the design to Bon but the execution to his
workshop.

13 For the bas-relief and a summary of attributions, see
Wolters, *La scultura gotica veneziana*, pp. 291–2; also Paoletti, *L'architettura*, vol. I, pp. 102–7, 175–7; and Sohm,
The Scuola Grande di San Marco, p. 85. If Bon's portal
was not the main (south) entrance it was possibly the
portal at the north end, facing the lagoon. It was of
some size (9 Venetian feet high and 6¼ feet wide). The
relief panel, though, must surely have been located
above the main land entrance.

14 Sohm, *The Scuola Grande di San Marco*, p. 88.

15 For works to the interior, see ASV, SGSM, B. 122, fasc.
C, c. 32; and SGSM, reg. 16 bis, fol. 12.

16 Felix Fabri, *Evagatorum in Terrae Sanctae* . . . , ed. C. D.
Hassler (Stuttgart, 1849).

17 ASV, Cons. d. X, Misti, reg. 15, fol. 152r.

18 For Jacopo Bellini, see ASV, SGSM, reg. 16 bis, fol. 35;
Gentile Bellini, ibid., fol. 36; Giovanni Bellini, ibid., fol.
38; Bartolomeo Vivarini, ibid., fol. 37; Lazzaro Bastiani,
ibid., fol. 38. See also P. Fortini Brown, *Venetian Narrative Painting in the Age of Carpaccio* (New Haven and
London, 1988), pp. 47, 269. See also Sohm, *The Scuola
Grande di San Marco*, pp. 87–8 and docs 18–23.

19 Malipiero, 'Annali', in *Archivio storico italiano*, ed. A.
Sagredo, parts 1 and 2 (1843–4), p. 675.

20 For the Senate's meeting on 16 April, see ASV, SGSM,
reg. 16 bis, fol. 56r; and SGSM, B. 122, fasc. C, c. 3. See
also Paoletti, *L'architettura*, p. 102, and Sohm, *The Scuola
Grande di San Marco*, p. 98.

21 ASV, Cons. d. X, Misti, reg. 22, fol. 24r. For 1487: ibid.,
reg. 23, fol. 111; see also SGSM, B. 52 (loose, unnumbered folio).

22 Most of the documents are in ASV, SGSM, B. 77 and
B. 136. B. 77 also contains a contemporary list sum-
marising the papers from the period 1485–1504: see
Appendix II, document 9.

23 ASV, SGSM, reg. 16 bis, fol. 56r. The use of the term
proto is interesting, if rather hesitant: see below, pp.
248–9.

24 ASV, SGSM, B. 77, fasc. 3, c. 6. Also Sohm, *The Scuola
Grande di San Marco*, p. 268.

25 The fire began at the altar in the chapter hall, at the
north end, farthest from the *albergo* and the façade onto
the *campo*. See Malipero, 'Annali', VII, parts 1 and 2,
p. 675; cited by Sohm, *The Scuola Grande di San Marco*,
p. 98 and note 50.

26 ASV, SGSM, B. 122, fasc. 'C', cc. 4–5. Also Sohm, *The
Scuola Grande di San Marco*, doc. 36. The *provveditori*
were required to 'determenar el bixogna [sic] dela dita
fabricha con quele menor spexe e sparagno ['tight-
fistedness'] ed interesso che ala prudenzia de quellj
sara posibele'. The *provveditori* were Giacomo Feletto,
Bortolamio Penzin, Domenico de Piero, Alvise de'
Dardani and Giacomo Bon.

27 ASV, SGSM, B. 136 (loose, unnumbered folio).

28 ASV, SGSM, B. 121, cc. 1–4. Also Sohm, *The Scuola
Grande di San Marco*, doc. 38: 'dicti fratres concedunt
dictis de dicta Scola locum ubi erat eorum rasura';
'dicta Scola ut possint ampliare dictam Scolam in latus
versus eorum Refectorium pedibus quinque'; 'possint
in capite suae Scolae extra muros dicta Scolae con-
struire eorum Capellam'.

29 ASV, SGSM, B. 77, fasc. 5, c. 11; ibid., B. 122, fasc. 2, c.
38.

30 ASV, Cons. d. X, Misti, reg. 22, fol. 124r (20 April 1485);
ibid., reg. 23, fol. 111, and SGSM, B. 52 (unnumbered
folio): 8 June 1487. On both occasions 100 new
members were admitted.

31 ASV, SGSM, B. 77, fasc. 3, c. 5. Extract in Sohm, *The
Scuola Grande di San Marco*, doc. 40.

32 ASV, SGSM, B. 77, fasc. 3, c. 5: 'per le qual el ditto die
aver ognj altro pagamento duc. 25 per sua fadiga'.

33 ASV, SGSM, B. 77, fasc. 3, c. 6: 'se debia meter do man
de cholone soto le travadure dela dita schuola, 5 per
banda che saremo cholone 10 oltra 4 meze che vano
ai muri do per lista'.

34 ASV, SGSM, B. 77, fasc. 3, c. 7. Sohm (*The Scuola Grande
di San Marco*) identifies (wrongly, I think) these six
largest *bordonali* as 'corresponding exactly to the width
of the lower hall'; they do not precisely, since the internal width is 7 *passi* and 4 feet. The transverse beams
would not, in any case, span the full width of the hall

but would be of two lengths, jointed above the *barba-cani*. The six 'spine' beams, though, carry the largest loads and would have been required on site for fixing before the others.

35 ASV, SGSM, B. 77, fasc. 3, no. 34, altered to no. 26. Extract in Sohm, *The Scuola Grande di San Marco*, doc. 44. It is a formal contract, signed and notarised. The carpenter was to employ 'sufficientj maistrj dei mior de questa terra'; a high standard of work was clearly expected.

36 ASV, SGSM, B. 77, fasc. 3, no. 34, altered to no. 26. 'Li sia pagatj de setemana in setemana i lavorentj segondo che i havera merita'.

37 ASV, SGSM, B. 52, fasc. 3, c. 7; A. Caravia, 'Il *Sogno* di Caravia', in D. S. Chambers and B. Pullan, eds, *Venice: A Documentary History, 1450–1630* (Oxford and Cambridge, MA, 1992), pp. 213–16, and in M. Tafuri, *Venice and the Renaissance*, trans. J. Levine (Cambridge, MA, and London, 1989), pp. 81–3.

38 ASV, SGSM, B. 77, fasc. 3, c. 6: 'se obliga piagnete da nuova e repolir tutj j travj vechj che . . . erano nela fabricha vechia e stropare [plug, or fill cracks] quelj dove era i petenelj con diligenza per tal che i siano ben, e che i ditj parera nuovj [so that they appear as new]'.

39 ASV, SGSM, B. 136, doc. 29, and Paoletti, *L'architettura*, pp. 102–3; 'et chompir lopra che i Ano prenzipiado Et chontinuar el lavor chon sollizitudine Et tal lavor abia luogo piuj breve che sia possibell'.

40 Sohm, *The Scuola Grande di San Marco*, pp. 268–9.

41 McAndrew, *Venetian Architecture*, pp. 150–81.

42 ASV, SGSM, B. 136, no. 30. See also Appendix II, document 8.

43 For further discussion on the roles of Lombardo and Codussi, see Sohm, *The Scuola Grande di San Marco*, pp. 113–17 and 122–44; for Codussi, see also L. Puppi and L. Olivato Puppi, *Mauro Codussi* (Milan, 1977), pp. 61, 73, 196–203; L. Angelini, *Le opere in Venezia di Mauro Codussi* (Milan, 1945), p. 49. The extraordinarily rapid timescale for completing the works seems to be supported by the very high levels of payment, 100 ducats per week (for ten weeks?); a further 32 ducats was allocated immediately for transport costs. The other masons cited by name are Ieronimo Meschin and Domenico Moro. For Bon at the Porta della Carta, see pp. 102–19. De' Barbari in 1500 shows the two soldiers and Marcian lion still missing. For the parapet sculptures, see Wolters, *La scultura gotica veneziana*, p. 289.

44 ASV, SGSM, B. 77, fasc. 3, c. 10. See also ASV, SGSM, B. 136, no. 19 (1 April 1490); summary in Sohm, *The Scuola Grande di San Marco*, doc. 54. Moro was almost certainly one of Lombardo's 'team', but the flank wall itself was a virtually self-contained piece of work, much of it linear and repetitive.

45 ASV, SGSM, B. 136, no. 19. The 'san marcho' on the façade ('su la porta') refers to the re-fixing of Bon's bas-relief.

46 ASV, SGSM, B. 136, no. 35. The main text reads that they are due only 75 ducats since some work was still incomplete. Sohm's reading has 40 ducats of work to com-plete, but if the original contract sum was maintained, there remained 60–70 ducats' worth still to be executed.

47 For the roof covering: ASV, SGSM, reg. 16 bis, fol. 18r. For the debt of 1,000 ducats, see SGSM, B. 46, fasc. 1, and Sohm, *The Scuola Grande di San Marco*, doc. 56.

48 ASV, SGSM, B. 136; published in Puppi and Olivato Puppi, *Mauro Codussi*, p. 259. See also Appendix II, document 10.

49 ASV, SGSM, B. 136, no. 26.

50 ASV, Cons. d. X, Misti, reg. 24, fol. 201r; Sohm, *The Scuola Grande di San Marco*, doc. 58.

51 See note 49 above.

52 ASV, SGSM, B. 77; Puppi and Olivato Puppi, *Mauro Codussi*, p. 259.

53 ASV, SGSM, reg. 16 bis, fol. 25; Sohm, *The Scuola Grande di San Marco*, doc. 63.

54 ASV, SGSM, B. 136. There seem to be two documents listing the work completed by Griguol; one is the remeasurement of the brickwork, published by Sohm, *The Scuola Grande di San Marco*, doc. 64, and dated 15 December 1493. Sohm records this as doc. 5 in B. 136. However, there is a second schedule, also in B. 136, numbered no. 5, and undated, with a different list of works. These are not wall-building works, but other works to the façade such as the fixing of stone; see below, pp. 206–7.

55 ASV, SGSM, B. 135 (no folio number); Sohm, *The Scuola Grande di San Marco*, doc. 62. See also Fortini Brown, *Venetian Narrative Painting*, especially pp. 291–5. The Bellini document is published on p. 292.

56 For the memorandum of 1486, see ASV, SGSM, B. 121, cc. 1–4; Sohm, *The Scuola Grande di San Marco*, doc. 38.

57 For discussions of the design of the two stairs at the Scuole Grandi di San Marco and di San Giovanni Evangelista, see also Puppi and Olivato Puppi, *Mauro Codussi*, pp. 202–3, 218–21; McAndrew, *Venetian Architecture*, pp. 363 (San Marco) and 364–74 (San Giovanni Evangelista).

58 See Jacopo de' Barbari (1500); also note 57 above.

59 See note 57 above.

60 F. Sansovino and G. Martinioni, *Venetia, città nobilissima et singolare . . .* , 2 vols (Venice, 1663; new facs. edn, 1968), vol. I, p. 286.

61 T. Temanza, *Vite de' più celebri architetti e scultori veneziani* (Venice, 1778); cited by McAndrew, *Venetian Architecture*, p. 363, and Puppi and Olivato Puppi, *Mauro Codussi*, p. 202.

62 ASV, SGSM, reg. 16 bis, fols 35v–36r.

63 ASV, SGSM, reg. 16 bis, fol. 37r.

64 ASV, SGSM, reg. 16 bis, fol. 36v; Puppi and Olivato Puppi, *Mauro Codussi*, p. 259.

65 The façade was still not yet complete: the two soldiers and the lions were not in place.

66 ASV, SGSM, B. 77, fasc. 3, fols 1–2; summary in Sohm, *The Scuola Grande di San Marco*, doc. 72. See also note 54 above.

67 ASV, SGSM, B. 77, fasc. 3, fols 1–2. Griguol was also paid 'per portar' three *chanpanieli*, which are usually 'tabernacles', probably those for the north façade, which was still essentially Gothic in appearance, with a profiled parapet;

68 ASV, SGSM, B. 77, fasc. 3, fols 1–2. Also Paoletti, *L'architettura*, p. 105: 'el die far e compir segondo la forma de lacordo zioe calcinar e bianchizar dentro e fuora si de sotto come de sora e de fuora [*sic*] . . . tuta la scuolla preditta de san marco'. Some of the work listed as complete in the above document, dated 29 October 1495, is carried forward from the earlier schedule of 15 December 1493, e.g., the measurement of 1,165 *passi quadrati* of brickwork at the rate of 3 *passi* per ducat.

69 ASV, SGSM, B. 122, fasc. D, fols 29–36. This chapel was built by the monastery, not the Scuola, and stood to the east of the chapter hall and the stairs.

70 ASV, SGSM, reg. 17, fol. 19: Sohm, *The Scuola Grande di San Marco*, doc. 78. In the same period, on 10 January 1503, Luca de Piero was commissioned to carve a portal for the *sala capitolare* to match that to the *albergo*. He was to be paid 60 ducats: see ASV, SGSM, B. 77, fasc. 3, fol. 16. It is not clear whether this was executed to a design by Codussi, whose permanent employment here had ended eight years earlier. However, the present portal is strongly Codussian in character. Luca was to complete the work by the end of March, yet another very short programme. None of the secondary sources cited in this chapter offers an opinion.

71 ASV, SGSM, B. 135 (no folio number); Sohm, *The Scuola Grande di San Marco*, doc. 80; see also SGSM, reg. 17, fols 28 and 34. For the painting cycles, see R. Goffen, *Giovanni Bellini* (New Haven and London, 1989), pp. 268–9 and appendix 3, pp. 272–3. The uncompleted work was the *Preaching of San Marco in Alexandria* (Milan, Brera). See also note 55 above.

72 ASV, SGSM, reg. 17, fol. 27; Sohm, *The Scuola Grande di San Marco*, doc. 81.

73 ASV, SGSM, reg. 17, fols 65–9. For Giovanni Bellini, see note 71 above. His 'historia' is cited in SGSM, reg. 17, fol. 60.

74 ASV, SGSM, reg. 17, fols 85–6. The ceiling was not completed until 1535: SGSM, B. 77, fasc. 3, no. 22.

75 Pietro Casola, *Viaggio di Pietro Casola a Gerusalemme* (Milan, 1885), p. 12; Sansovino and Martinioni, *Venetia*, vol. I, p. 286. Casola was, in fact, a priest from Milan travelling to the Holy Land via Venice.

76 See especially McAndrew, *Venetian Architecture*, pp. 150–81. For the Miracoli church, see M. Piana and W. Wolters, eds, *Santa Maria dei Miracoli a Venezia: la storia, la fabbrica, i restauri* (Venice, 2003), passim.

77 The western part of the façade would have been even richer if the projected *instoria granda* had been executed. For further discussion of the relief panels, see Sohm, *The Scuola Grande di San Marco*, pp. 131 et seq.; also S. B. McHam, *The Chapel of St Anthony at the Santo and the Development of Venetian Renaissance Sculpture* (Cambridge, 1994), pp. 37, 42, 96–7, 104 and 112.

78 Sohm attributes conclusively the *sala capitolare* windows to Codussi, chiefly on the basis of the 'embedded' columns, and is inclined to attribute the *albergo*

windows to him as well: *The Scuola Grande di San Marco*, p. 138.

79 We have seen many other examples of the reuse of columns and capitals from elsewhere: for example, at the Ca' d'Oro, the Arsenale gate, San Zaccaria, etc. See also Sohm, *The Scuola Grande di San Marco*, pp. 149–53, where the portal's ceremonial role is discussed.

80 The present Marcian lion, like that on the Porta della Carta, is by Luigi Ferrari (late nineteenth century), and replaces that destroyed by Napoleon in 1797. *Circa* 1481 Pietro Lombardo carved the tympanum of *St John Blessing the Confratelli* for the Scuola Grande di San Giovanni Evangelista; the Carità relief similarly shows the *Virgin* surrounded by a group of *confratelli*, while that by Bon, formerly at the Misericordia, also depicts this same theme.

81 For further observations on lions flanking entrances, see Sohm, *The Scuola Grande di San Marco*, pp. 172–8.

82 Sohm, *The Scuola Grande di San Marco*, pp. 170–71; also McHam, *The Chapel of St Anthony at the Santo*, pp. 96–7.

83 Wolters, *La scultura gotica veneziana*, p. 289; Sansovino and Martinioni, *Venetia*, vol. I, p. 286.

84 Sohm is hesitant about the interpretation of the putti and the lamb representing the Passion: *The Scuola Grande di San Marco*, p. 181.

85 Sohm, *The Scuola Grande di San Marco*, pp. 178–9, although he does not mention the symbolism of the phoenix in the context of the Scuola's own history.

86 McAndrew, *Venetian Architecture*, pp. 118–33; A. M. Schulz, *Antonio Rizzo, Sculptor and Architect* (Princeton, 1983), p. 117.

87 Puppi and Olivato Puppi, *Mauro Codussi*, pp. 46, 48, 50, 187–90, 257–8.

88 See chapter 9 above.

89 Se above, pp. 206–7.

90 For the Ca' d'Oro, see Goy, *The House of Gold*, pp. 216–22; for the Carità church, see above, pp. 119–26.

91 ASV, SGSM, B. 136 (no folio number).

92 See note 37 above.

93 For the building sagas of the other Scuole Grandi, especially San Rocco, see Tafuri, *Venice and the Renaissance*, pp. 81–97. For Sansovino's experiences, see D. Howard, *Jacopo Sansovino: Architecture and Patronage in Renaissance Venice* (New Haven and London, 1975), pp. 96–110. See also G. Fabbri, ed., *La Scuola Grande della Misericordia di Venezia* (Venice, 1999).

94 Francesco Sansovino's own words are that the Scuole Grandi 'rappresentarono anco un certo modo di governo civile, nel quale i cittadini, quasi in propria Repubblica, hanno i gradi & gli honori secondo i meriti, and le qualità loro' (*Venetia*, vol. I, p. 282).

95 See above, p. 202.

CHAPTER TEN

1 The earthquake of 1512 was serious and was (much later) described by Sansovino as a 'Terremoto horribile, per lo quale vanno a terra case, and campanili, & cag-

giono cinque statue marmoree dalla cima della Chiesa di San Marco (F. Sansovino and G. Martinioni, *Venetia, città nobilissima et singolare . . .* , 2 vols, Venice, 1663; new facs. edn, 1968, vol. II, 'Cronico veneto', p. 55).

2 See above, p. 58.

3 D. Calabi and P. Morachiello, *Rialto: le fabbriche e il ponte* (Turin, 1987), pp. 41–9, with archive references.

4 The fire of 1479 was also fairly serious, and located in approximately the same part of the palace; Sansovino again: 'Fuoco notabile in palazzo, arde le stanze del Doge, con una cuba [cupola] della Chiesa di San Marco, & si salva la Sala dei Pregadi' (*Venetia*, vol. II, 'Cronico veneto', p. 52).

5 See note 4 above. For an eyewitness account of the fire, see G. Lorenzi, *Monumenti per servire alla storia del Palazzo Ducale* (Venice, 1868), p. 92, doc. 198 (Marin Sanudo, MS of the 'Vite de' Dogi' [BMV]).

6 Lorenzi, *Monumenti*, p. 92, doc. 198.

7 Lorenzi, *Monumenti*, p. 93, doc. 198.

8 D. Malipiero, 'Annali', ed. F. Longo, in *Archivio storico italiano*, II (1844), p. 674: 'la mazor parte sentiva de no spender più de 6,000 ducati in reparar el palazzo, per la stretezza de i tempi; ma dapuo' e sta ressolto de farlo tutto da nuovo'. Also cited in A. M. Schulz, *Antonio Rizzo, Sculptor and Architect* (Princeton, 1983), pp. 82–4, 126–8.

9 Lorenzi, *Monumenti*, p. 93, doc. 198.

10 Lorenzi, *Monumenti*, doc. 199.

11 J. McAndrew, *Venetian Architecture of the Early Renaissance* (Cambridge, MA, and London, 1980), pp. 82–3.

12 ASV, Mensa patriarchale, B. 69, Reg. di Cassa; see also P. Paoletti, *L'architettura e la scultura del Rinascimento in Venezia: ricerche storico-artistiche*, 2 vols (Venice, 1893–7), vol. II, p. 101; and L. Puppi and L. Olivato Puppi, *Mauro Codussi* (Milan, 1977), p. 257.

13 ASV, San Zaccaria, B. 31, c. 173r. See also B. Cecchetti, 'Documenti per la storia della fabbrica della chiesa di San Zaccaria', *Archivio veneto*, XXXI (1886), pp. 495–6. The attribution to Codussi for the design of the east wing (or at least the canal façade) is given with some conviction by W. Wolters in *The Art of Renaissance Venice*, with Norbert Huse (Chicago, 1990), p. 27. His justification must remain stylistic, however, since there is no firm documentation, and he follows here the view of T. Hirthe, 'Mauro Codussi als Architekt des Dogenpalastes', *Arte veneta*, no. 36 (1982), pp. 31–44. Although a case can be made for Codussi's initial design involvement on the *rio* façade, his connection with the works on site must have been tenuous, given his commitments elsewhere and given the fact that he had no official role at the palace.

14 McAndrew, *Venetian Architecture*, pp. 112–43.

15 Schulz, *Antonio Rizzo*, pp. 8–9.

16 Schulz, *Antonio Rizzo*, especially pp. 8–15 and 80–81.

17 ASV, Provv. Sal, B. 59 (Notatorio reg. 1), cc. 58, 58t. See also Schulz, *Antonio Rizzo*, pp. 11, 43, 64. Despite her comment (p. 43) that 'in this or a subsequent siege . . . he was wounded', it is clear from the record that Rizzo was wounded in the second siege of Scutari.

18 ASV, Provv. Sal, B. 59 (Notatorio reg. 1), cc. 58, 58t and 61.

19 *Terminazione* of the Pregadi, cited in ASV, Provv. Sal, B. 59 (Notatorio reg. 1), c. 61.

20 Schulz agrees that 'perhaps it is as much to [the governors of] Venice's appreciation of his patriotism as to his artistic merit that Rizzo owed the subsequent commission for the Tomb of Doge Nicolò Tron and his eventual appointment to the post of *protomaestro* of the Ducal Palace' (*Antonio Rizzo*, p. 43). It was hardly 'eventual', however, since it was in February that his pension was granted while his appointment at the Doge's Palace followed only a few months later.

21 M. Sanudo, 'Vite de' Dogi', in Lorenzi, *Monumenti*, p. 93, doc. 198; see also p. 94, doc. 202; and Malipiero, 'Annali', ed. Longo, p. 674. See also Paoletti, *L'architettura*, vol. II, p. 144.

22 *Terminazione* of the Signoria on 10 February 1485 (= 1484 mv). Copy in ASV, Provv. Sal, B. 59 (Notatorio), c. 93t. See also Appendix II, document 11.

23 ASV, Provv. Sal, B. 59, c. 114t.

24 Sansovino in *Venetia*, vol. I, p. 320. Sansovino also famously attributes the east wing and its façades to Bregno: 'la faccia del Palazzo Ducale . . . cominciata dal Doge Marco Barbarigo, & finita da Agostino suo fratello e successore, fu opera d'Antonio Bregno Architetto, and Prothomaestro del Palazzo'.

25 *Terminazione* of the Maggior Consiglio on 11 November 1485: Lorenzi, *Monumenti*, p. 121, doc. 250; Schulz, *Antonio Rizzo*, p. 147.

26 Biblioteca Civica Correr, Venice, MS Cicogna 3533: the doge was 'conduto nel duchal palazzo et insta lordene decreto in la sua eletione in sopra la scala del ditto palazzo aceptato per i consiglierij et capi di 40 jurado la sua promissione per el nobel homo zuanne da leze menor conseglier posto fu la veta et per el nobel homo piero memo major conseglier posto fu la bareta duchal sopra il capo'.

27 Marin Sanudo, 'De magistratibus urbis', in 'Cronachetta': BCV, MS Cicogna 969, c. 43v: published in *La città di Venetia (De origine, situ et magistratibus urbis Venetae), 1493–1530*, ed. A. C. Arico (Milan, 1980), p. 88: 'Poi vien . . . in Palazzo dove è la Signoria con li 41 che l'aspetta, et al patto della scala de piera dal più zovene Conseier li vien messo la veta in testa, et dal più vecchio la barretta ducal di gran precio'.

28 P. Casola, *Viaggio di Pietro Casola in Gerusalemme* (Milan, 1885), p. 7.

29 M. Sanudo, *I diarii*, ed. R. Fulin et al., 58 vols (Bologna, 1879–1903), vol. I, 821; Schulz, *Antonio Rizzo*, p. 90.

30 Sanudo, *I diarii*, vol. IV, 134, for the coronation of Leonardo Loredan.

31 The Scala is not precisely on the axis of the loggia: see below.

32 For the ducal coronation, see Marin Sanudo, *De origine, situ et magistratibus urbis Venetae, ovvero La città di Venetia*; as *La città di Venetia*, ed. A. C. Arico (Milan, 1980), pp. 88–9. See also especially E. Muir, *Civic Ritual in Renaissance Venice* (Princeton, 1981), pp. 207 et seq., and pp.

282–9. For the ducal oath, see ASV, Coll., Cerimoniale, I, fol. 4v. For coronations generally, see A. da Mosto, *I dogi di Venezia nella vita pubblica e privata* (Milan, 1960), pp. xxii–xxxi. For the later coronation of Antonio Grimani, see Sanudo, *I diarii*, vols xxx, 479–90, and xxxi, 7–11; and for that of Andrea Gritti, ibid., vol. xxxiv, 155–85.

33 Schulz, *Antonio Rizzo*, pp. 145–52, and figs 173–84. She goes to considerable lengths to play down the personalisation of Barbarigo's works at the palace, especially the Scala. Her observations on the Arco Foscari do not take full account of Foscari's own remarkable precedent at the palace (in terms of personal influence on design and symbolism) at the Porta della Carta. The suggestion that 'references to victory [on the Scala] must be applied . . . not to the person of Agostino Barbarigo, but to his office, and, in other places, to the Venetian government' again flies directly in the face of the cult of personal laudation that accompanied his reign, and which he encouraged strongly. It barely needs emphasising that Barbarigo's initials and arms are scattered liberally over the building, particularly the *cortile* façade. Muraro's interpretations here are considerably more convincing. Muir (*Civic Ritual*, pp. 265 et seq.) draws the same conclusions as Muraro (and myself) as to Barbarigo's flagrant representations of personal aggrandisement. For plans, etc., see Schulz, *Antonio Rizzo*, figs 167–72. See also L. Cicognara, A. Diedo and G.-A. Selva, *Le fabbriche più cospicue di Venezia misurate, illustrate ed intagliate dai membri della Veneta Reale Accademia di Belle Arti*, 2 vols (Venice, 1815–20), vol. II, pl. 56. For M. Muraro, see 'La scala senza giganti', in *Essays in Honor of Erwin Panofsky*, ed. M. Meiss (Zurich, 1960), vol. I, pp. 350–70.

34 Sanudo, *I diarii*, vol. IV, 181–4. Later in the same denouncement, Antonio Loredan refers to Barbarigo as 'diabolical', with 'detestable avarice and insatiable cupidity'. According to Sanudo, there were 200 testimonies against him.

35 See note 33 above.

36 ASV, Provv. Sal, B. 59, Notatorio, c. 202; see also D. Pincus, *The Arco Foscari: The Building of a Triumphal Gateway in Fifteenth Century Venice* (New York and London, 1976), doc. 19; Lorenzi, *Monumenti*, doc. 225. The phraseology of this short document is somewhat ambiguous; nowhere is the stair precisely identified. Schulz (*Antonio Rizzo*, p. 150) claims that the Gruato record 'does not concern the Scala dei Giganti. This can be inferred from the fact that the ends of the steps referred to in the document were to be morticed into the wall, while the ends of the steps to the Scala dei Giganti are flush with the walls of the balustrade.' The dismissal is not totally convincing: the method of construction could well have changed during the course of the works or in later restorations. The Gruato stair was clearly very richly detailed, and appears to fit the description of the Scala dei Giganti in other respects.

37 ASV, Coll., Notatorio, 1481–9, c. 121; Lorenzi, *Monumenti*, doc. 214; Schulz, *Antonio Rizzo*, p. 129. The four ducal councillors were Luca Navagero, Fantin 'de cha de pexaro', Zaccaria Barbaro and Benedetto Trevisan. However, for attempts by Venetian masons to restrict or exclude foreign masters in the city, see S. Connell, *The Employment of Sculptors and Stonemasons in Venice in the Fifteenth Century* (London and New York, 1988), pp. 75 et seq. (with further references).

38 Copy in ASV, Provv. Sal, B. 59, Notatorio, c. 166t; Lorenzi, *Monumenti*, doc. 217.

39 ASV, Provv. Sal, B. 60, Notatorio, c. 6; Lorenzi, *Monumenti*, doc. 229; Pincus, *Arco Foscari*, doc. 21. It reads in part: 'et visto quanto diligentemente si ha portato cerca ditta fabrica et li suo intolerabil fatige, come per experientia si puol veder per le opere fatte . . . et azo che perseverar possa cum bon cuor et animo al bisogno di quella volendo satisfar ai comandamenti Ducali *ut supra* tutti concordemente hanno terminato che ditto maistro Antonio haver debia da questo Officio (dil Sal) ogni anno et in raxon di anno duc. Dusento doro per sua mercede salario et fatiche per la fabricha dil ditto Palazzo'. See Appendix II, document 12.

40 Decree of the Cons. d. x and Zonta: Lorenzi, *Monumenti*, doc. 238. There is also a copy in ASV, Provv. Sal, B. 59, Notatorio, c. 73t: 'el quarto de la spexa mensual fina qui facta largamente sara bastante'.

41 Sanudo, *I diarii*, vol. I, 205; Malipiero, 'Annali', ed. Longo, p. 699.

42 Cons. d. x and Zonta; also ASV, Provv. Sal, B. 59, Notatorio, cc. 74t and 75. See also Lorenzi, *Monumenti*, doc. 239. Among those retained after this 'culling' of staff were Alvise de Domenego, *taiapiera* (stonemason), at 13 soldi a day; his responsibilities included 'a tegnir conto di piere cotte e calcina venia dischargade a palazzo parsse ai Signori al sal de dar duc. Do al mexe attendando ale ditte cosse'. Bertuci, *taiapiera*, was also retained at 18 soldi a day, 'per solicitar le maistranze et per andar in Istria per trazer piere vive per il palazzo'; there were also Zuan da Spalato at 24 soldi a day and Michiel Naranza at 17 soldi. The last had been injured, but was retained partly for charitable reasons: 'per ess. Mal conditionato . . . per haver perso mezi I piedi'.

43 Lorenzi, *Monumenti*, doc. 240.

44 Sanudo, *I diarii*, vol. I, 927 et seq. See also Lorenzi, *Monumenti*, doc. 198.

45 This new wing did not represent the whole of the east wing that we see today, but rather the northern and central sections only. The extent of the 'Rizzo' wing can be seen clearly on the *cortile* façade, where there is a break in the roof profile and a different pattern of fenestration on the top storey. The remainder of the east wing, as far as its junction with the *liagò* of the Molo wing, was built in the sixteenth century. For Pietro's fireplaces, see U. Franzoi, T. Pignatti and W. Wolters, *Il Palazzo Ducale di Venezia* (Treviso, 1990); and W. Wolters, *Architektur und Ornament: Venezianischer Bauschmuck der Renaissance* (Munich, 2000), pp. 164–7.

46 Lorenzi, *Monumenti*, docs 250, 251. On 1 October 1498 Lombardo was instructed to transport two slabs of

marble to the Palazzo: ASV, Provv. Sal, B. 61, Notatorio, vol. 3, c. 124v: 'Mo. Piero Lombardo deputado ala Fabricha del Palazo novo' was to take the stone to 'sancto Vitalle, ben poi extimade per nui et tansato il prexio di esse prie'.

47 ASV, Sen., Delib., XIII, and Provv. Sal, B. 60, Notatorio, vol. 2, c. 32v: 'cum salario ducatorum centum viginti in anno et ratione anni'. See Appendix II, document 13. See also Pincus, *Arco Foscari*, doc. 28; N. Erizzo, *Relazione storico-critica sulla Torre dell'Orologio di San Marco in Venezia*, 2nd edn (Venice, 1866), doc. 2. The Senate decree begins: 'Havendosse absenta da questa cita nostra Maistro Antonio Rizo deputado olim soprastante ala fabricha dil palazzo qual fo tolto cum salario de ducati CXXV al anno, et essendo sta necessario proveder al governo di la fabricha predicta, fu nominato et substituito Maistro Piero Lombardo homo nel arte sua sufficientissimo'.

48 ASV, Provv. Sal, B. 60, Notatorio, vol. 2, c. 32v. See also Pincus, *Arco Foscari*, doc. 27.

49 ASV, Provv. Sal, B. 60, Notatorio, vol. 2, c. 34. Spavento had as yet received no extra money for these works beyond his normal remit because of this dispute: 'mai de la faticha sua habuto pagamento alchuno per la divisione era tra i tre stimadori deputati cum sacramento e Antonio Rizo qual non se contentava de la stima facta per essi deputati'.

50 ASV, Provv. Sal, B. 60, Notatorio, vol. 2, c. 59.

51 ASV, Provv. Sal, B. 60, Notatorio, vol. 2, c. 85.

52 ASV, Provv. Sal, B. 60, Notatorio, vol. 2, c. 105.

CHAPTER ELEVEN

1 The essential secondary bibliography for the Torre is not extensive. The chief documentary source is N. Erizzo, *Relazione storico-critica sulla Torre dell'Orologio di San Marco in Venezia*, 2nd edn (Venice, 1866). Also useful are P. Paoletti, *L'architettura e la scultura del Rinascimento in Venezia: ricerche storico-artistiche*, 2 vols (Venice, 1893–7); L. Puppi and L. Olivato Puppi, *Mauro Codussi* (Milan, 1977); J. McAndrew, *Venetian Architecture of the Early Renaissance* (Cambridge, MA, and London, 1980); and G. Samonà et al., *Piazza San Marco: l'architettura, la storia, le funzioni* (Venice, 1970). See also M. Muraro, 'The Moors of the Clock-tower of Venice', *Art Bulletin*, LXVI (1984), pp. 603–9.

2 Puppi and Olivato Puppi, *Mauro Codussi*, p. 208, citing Erizzo, *Relazione*.

3 ASV, PSMdS, B. 64, Processi, no. 141, fasc. 1 (scritture pella costruzione del fabricato dal 1495–1571), c. 8t. This is a long list of expenses over the period to January 1500. The total cost given is D. 2701. 5. 22 (2, 701 ducats, L. 5.22.0).

4 ASV, PSMdS, B. 64, Processi, no. 141, fasc. 1, c. 1 (a copy of the decree of the Senate); see also ASV, Sen., Terra, Terminazioni, XII. See Appendix II, document 14.

5 M. Sanudo, *I diarii*, ed. R. Fulin et al., 58 vols (Bologna, 1879–1903), vol. I, 205.

6 D. Malipiero, 'Annali', ed. F. Longo, in *Archivio storico italiano*, II (1844), VII.

7 Puppi and Olivato Puppi, *Mauro Codussi*, p. 168.

8 Ducale dated 16 June 1496: copy also in ASV, PSMdS, B. 64, Processi, no. 141, fasc. 1.

9 Letter of safe passage: ASV, PSMdS, B. 64, Processi, no. 141, fasc. 1, c. 3. The Rainieri arrived in Venice within a month, together with the clock, the *Angel* and the figures of the *Three Magi*. See also A. Bristot, 'The Clock Tower', in UNESCO, *Venice Restored, 1966–1986* (Milan, 1991), pp. 185–6.

10 See de' Barbari's view of 1500 for the relationship between the tower and the old Procuracy building.

11 Puppi and Olivato Puppi, *Mauro Codussi*, p. 210, imply that the date of completion of the bell was around December 1496, but it must have been in 1497: see below.

12 ASV, PSMdS, B. 64, Processi, no. 141, fasc. 1, c. 8t. The copper and tin, of course, were the component elements of bronze. The sum of 682 ducats was entered into the debit account on 2 June 1497.

13 ASV, PSMdS, B. 64, Processi, no. 141, fasc. 1, c. 8t: 'Mo. Ambruoxo . . . dale anchore per far di Ziganti et comprar oro da dorar, per tutto D.180'. Ambrogio's nickname derived from his chief occupation at the Arsenale. The gilding wore off and apparently was not replaced. In *Venetia, città nobilissima et singolare . . .* (2 vols, Venice, 1663; new facs. edn, 1968) Francesco Sansovino described them as bronze, not gilded bronze. See also Muraro, 'The Moors'.

14 ASV, PSMdS, B. 64, Processi, no. 141, fasc. 1, c. 8t: '4 marzo 1499 per officio di camerlengj de comun alla cassa have ser Thomaso dal Sarasin spicier per cera per far la forma di zigant1'.

15 E. Vio, 'La Torre dell'Orologio', in Samonà et al., *Piazza San Marco*, p. 139, citing Paoletti, *L'architettura*, vol. II, pp. 189–90. See also Muraro, 'The Moors'.

16 ASV, PSMdS, B. 64 (Processi), no. 141, fasc. 1, cc. 8t and 9. For Fiorentini, see also Paoletti, *L'architettura*, vol. II, p. 190.

17 ASV, PSMdS, B. 64 (Processi), no. 141, fasc. 1, cc. 8t and 9.

18 Sanudo, *I diarii*, vol. II, 396: 'in questo zorno primo de febrer a hora andava el Principe per piazza, er andar a vespero a Santa Maria Formosa, fo aperto e scoperto la prima volta lorologio ch'e su la piazza, sopra la strada va in Marzaria, fato cum gran inzegno, et belisimo'.

19 McAndrew, *Venetian Architecture*, pp. 389–94.

20 McAndrew, *Venetian Architecture*, pp. 389–94; also Puppi and Olivato Puppi, *Mauro Codussi*, pp. 210–11.

21 ASV, PSMdS, Cassier Chiesa, reg. 1; and Puppi and Olivato Puppi, *Mauro Codussi*, pp. 195–6.

22 ASV, PSMdS, B. 64 (Processi), no. 141, fasc. 1, c. 5.

23 Speraindio was Sperandio Savelli, from Mantua. He was in Venice in the years 1496–1504, and formerly worked on the clock tower of San Petronio in Bologna.

24 ASV, PSMdS, B. 64 (Processi), no. 141, fasc. 1, cc. 7, 7t, 8 and 8t; transcribed from ASV, Sen., Delib., vol. XIII, c. 157. See also Erizzo, *Relazione*, p. 153, and Vio, 'La

Torre', pp. 139–40. The document is translated by Goy in D. S. Chambers and B. Pullan, eds, *Venice: A Documentary History, 1450–1630* (Oxford and Cambridge, MA, 1992), pp. 394–6.

25 ASV, PSMdS, B. 64 (Processi), no. 141, fasc. 1, c. 6t, with a copy also on c. 29. See Appendix II, document 15.

26 D. Calabi and P. Morachiello, *Rialto: le fabbriche e il ponte* (Turin, 1987), pp. 29–30.

27 Puppi and Olivato Puppi, *Mauro Codussi*, p. 211; Vio, 'La Torre', p. 139.

28 Paoletti, *L'architettura*, vol. II, p. 189. The document reads in part: 'marmori quadri e de la piera viva . . . per investir le chaxe nove fabrichade apresso lo horologio sopra la piazza'. Lombardo 'debia in questa cita cercar, dove se trova marmi et piere de le qualita soprascritta'.

29 See, for example, the view of Venice by G. Merlo (1696), before the uppermost terraces were added by Massari in 1755. Massari also strengthened the base of the tower by the insertion of eight circular columns at ground level to reduce the rather excessive spans of the stone lintels above the colonnade. The only original columns are thus those immediately flanking the archway.

30 McAndrew, *Venetian Architecture*, pp. 394–6.

31 The clock had to be large enough to be read from some distance; in its originally intended location it would have been legible for much of the length of the Piazza, and in its final location it could be read by nobles entering or leaving the Porta della Carta.

32 According to McAndrew (*Venetian Architecture*, p. 385), these figures were added in the nineteenth century.

33 Paoletti thought that Rizzo might have had a role in the composition of the doge and winged lion, especially since the work at the Palazzo had fallen off significantly in this period; see note 34 below.

34 A. M. Schulz, *Antonio Rizzo, Sculptor and Architect* (Princeton, 1983), p. 116. Although dismissed by Schulz, Roberto Cessi also suggested that Rizzo may have designed the 'Moors': *Medioevo e umanesimo*, II (1979), pp. 11–13. Se also Muraro, 'The Moors'. Muraro has proposed the reading of the 'Moors' as 'wild men'. Paolo Savin is recorded as the author of the figure of *St John the Baptist* in the Zen chapel in San Marco.

35 ASV, PSMdS, B. 64 (Processi), no. 141, fasc. 1, c. 35. There is a further copy in ibid., fasc. 2, entitled 'Simili [i.e., 'scritture'] relative alla Macchina dal 1500 al 1681'. See Appendix II, document 16.

36 SV, PSMdS, B. 64 (Processi), no. 141, fasc. 1, c. 39. For much more detail of the rather troubled later history of the clock and its mechanism, see ibid., fasc. 2. There is also a useful summary of Massari's and other later works in Puppi and Olivato Puppi, *Mauro Codussi*, pp. 208–14.

37 Sansovino and Martinioni, *Venetia*, vol. I, p. 317. The tower and clock have been restored more than once in recent times, notably in 1975 and 1993–6.

38 E. Vio, 'Le Procuratie Vecchie' in Samonà et al., *Piazza San Marco*, pp. 143–9; Sanudo, *I diarii*, vol. XIV, 305. Both clock and tower have been undergoing a further highly protracted restoration as this book is being written; the completion of the restoration of the tower itself is currently programmed for Spring 2006.

CONCLUSIONS

1 See above, p. 000. The incident is recounted in several works, including J. McAndrew, *Venetian Architecture of the Early Renaissance* (Cambridge, MA, and London, 1980), p. 12; S. Connell, *The Employment of Sculptors and Stonemasons in Venice in the Fifteenth Century* (London and New York, 1988), p. 21. See also especially L. Beltrami, *La Ca' del Duca sul Canal Grande ed altre reminiscenze sforzesche a Venezia* (Milan, 1900). Benedetto Ferrini, Sforza's own architect, wrote that Bon 'non me vole dar el desegnio perche dice vorebe luy havere lhonore et lutile'. Antonio Guidobono, Milanese ambassador to Venice, had no better success: 'quello maystro Bartolomeo tagliapetra non li ha voluto dare el dessigno che ha facto in carta de la fazata'.

2 *Proto*: one of the earliest uses of the term in Venice is in reference to the reconstruction of the Molo wing of the Doge's Palace: 'cum protis magistri murariis et marangonis nostri Comunis sale Maioris Consilij fiende': cited in D. Howard, *Venice and the East: The Impact of the Islamic World on Venetian Architecture, 1100–1500* (New Haven and London, 2000), p. 242, note 13.

3 See above, pp. 219–21. ASV, Magistrato al Sal, Notatorio, vol. 2, c. 6.

4 L. Puppi and L. Olivato Puppi, *Mauro Codussi* (Milan, 1977), pp. 177–83. For the monastic correspondence regarding his employment at San Michele, see E. Martene, *Veterum scriptorum et monumentorum . . . amplissima collectio*, 3 vols (Paris, 1724). There are extracts in Puppi and Olivato Puppi, *Mauro Codussi*, pp. 257–8.

5 ASV, Mensa Patriarchale, B. 69, Reg. di Cassa. See also P. Paoletti, *L'architettura e la scultura del Rinascimento in Venezia: ricerche storico-artistiche*, 2 vols (Venice, 1893–7), vol. II, p. 101.

6 For Codussi's admission to the Scuola Grande di San Giovanni Evangelista, see ASV, SGSGE, B. 6 (Mariegole). For the purchase of the land on which to build Codussi's staircase, see ASV, SGSGE, Reg. 140. cc. 302r–308v. In 1504, the year of Codussi's death, the Scuola successfully petitioned the Consiglio dei Dieci to suspend distribution of charity so that the stair could be completed: ASV, Cons. d. X, Misti, Reg. 30, c. 66v.

7 Venice, Archivio Parrocchiale di S. Maria Formosa, fondo pergamene. For the reference of 1506 to Mauro, see ASV, Sez. Not., Canc. Inf., Atti Zanetto Bonetti; also Paoletti, *L'architettura*, vol. II, p. 115.

8 ASV, Sez. Not., Canc. Inf., Atti Zanetto Bonetti.

9 There is an extensive (mostly recent) bibliography on de' Barbari: see especially C. Balistreri-Trincanato and D. Zanverdiani, *Jacopo de Barbari: il racconto di una città* (Venice, 2000), itself with extensive bibliography. See also D. Howard, 'Venice as a dolphin: further investiga-

tions into Jacopo de' Barbari's view', in *Artibus et Historiae*, XVIII/35 (1997); G. Mazzariol and T. Pignatti, *La pianta prospettica di Venezia del 1500 disegnata da Jacopo de' Barbari* (Venice, 1962); S. Biadene, G. Romanelli and C. Tonini, *A volo d'uccello: Jacopo de' Barbari e le rappresentazioni di città dell'Europa del Rinascimento* (Venice, 1999). See also the important detailed discussion by J. Schulz, 'Jacopo de' Barbari's view of Venice: mapmaking, city views and moralizing geography before the year 1500', *Art Bulletin*, LX (1978), pp. 456 et seq. For an analysis of the aquatic aspects of the myth of Venice with special emphasis on the lagoon context, see E. Crouzet-Pavan, 'Towards an ecological understanding of the myth of Venice', in J. Martin and D. Romano, eds, *Venice Reconsidered: The History and Civilization of an Italian State, 1297–1797* (Baltimore and London, 2000), pp. 39–64.

10 Poggio Braccolini, 'In laudem rei publicae Venetorum', in *Opera omnia* [facs. of the 1538 edn], ed. R. Furbini, 4 vols (Turin, 1964–9), vol. II, pp. 917–37.

11 For the Medici, see, for example, J. R. Hale, *Florence and the Medici: The Pattern of Control* (London and New York, 1977), especially pp. 35–48 (Cosimo), pp. 49–75 (Lorenzo). There is an extensive further bibliography. See also, for example, F. Cardini, ed., *Lorenzo il Magnifico* (Rome, 1992); N. Rubinstein, *The Government of Florence under the Medici* (Oxford, 1966); N. Rubinstein, ed., *Florentine Studies: Politics and Society in Renaissance Florence* (Florence, 1968).

12 F. Guicciardini, *Storia d'Italia*, ed. S. Menchi, 3 vols (Turin, 1971), vol. II, pp. 781–89. For a detailed discussion of Guicciardini's view of the myth of Venice, see R. Finlay, 'The Myth of Venice in Guicciardini's *History of Italy*: Senate orations on princes and the Republic', in E. E. Kittell and T. F. Madden, eds, *Medieval and Renaissance Venice* (Urbano and Chicago, 1999), pp. 294–326. See also W. J. Bouwsma, *Venice and the Defense of Republican Liberty: Renaissance Values in the Age of the Counter-Reformation* (Berkeley and Los Angeles, 1968), pp. 57, 69. As Findlay notes, Guicciardini, like many other Italian commentators, had a 'deeply ambivalent' attitude towards the Republic, whose chief characteristics could be seen equally as positive attributes or dangerous precedents. For example, the very longevity and stability of the Serenissima, could be seen as threat-

ening – by this very stability – to the constantly fluctuating fortunes and cycles of peace/upheaval that characterised most other Italian city states. For a broader discussion of the limits of Republicanism in the Terraferma empire, see also E. Muir, 'Was there Republicanism in the Renaissance Republics? Venice after Agnadello', in Martin and Romano, eds, *Venice Reconsidered*, pp. 137–67.

13 On the extent of these powers, see G. Maranini, *La costituzione di Venezia*, 2 vols (Florence, 1927), passim.

14 E. Muir, *Civic Ritual in Renaissance Venice* (Princeton, 1981), p. 17.

15 For comprehensive discussion on ritual and procession, see Muir, *Civic Ritual*, passim, and D. Queller, *Il patriziato veneziano: la realtà contro il mito* (Rome, 1987), pp. 17–51.

16 For a highly perceptive discussion on *renovatio urbis* (some from later decades, i.e., the early and mid-sixteenth century), see M. Tafuri, *Venice and the Renaissance*, trans. J. Levine (Cambridge, MA, and London, 1989), passim, but especially pp. 81–97 for the Scuole Grandi, and pp. 1–15: '*Memoria et Prudentia*: patrician mentalities and *res aedificatoria*'.

17 Domenico Morosini, *De bene instituta re publica*, ed. C. Finzi (Milan, 1969). For a summary of Morosini's career, see M. King, *Umanesimo e patriziato a Venezia nel quattrocento*, 2 vols (Rome, 1989), pp. 601–3. See also G. Gozzi, 'Domenico Morosini e il *De bene instituta re publica*', *Studi veneti*, XII (1970), pp. 405–58.

18 Morosini, *De bene instituta re publica*, pp. 134–5. See also Tafuri, *Venice and the Renaissance*, pp. 104–5; also Gozzi, 'Domenico Morosini'. Morosini's urban precepts may be directly compared with some of those of Alberti in *De re aedificatoria*, especially Book VIII, chapter VI. He was less narrowly prescriptive than Morosini, however, noting that 'if the City is noble and powerful the Streets should be straight and broad, which carries an air of Greatness and Majesty; but if it is only a small Town or Fortification, it will be better, and as safe, not for the Streets to run strait to the Gates; but to have them wind about sometimes to the Right, sometimes to the Left' (translation from the Giacomo [James] Leoni edn, London, 1755, p. 75).

Glossary

albergo
A small hall on the upper floor of a Scuola Grande (q.v.) where the governing board sat; it was also the room from which charity was dispensed

altana
A roof terrace, built of timber, supported on brick columns

andeo, andido, andito
A covered route, i.e., a portico or colonnade

androne
The lower great hall of a Venetian palace; the term is also used of the lower hall in a Scuola Grande

arpese
Metal cramp for holding stones together, usually of iron, and held in place using molten lead

Arsenale
The shipyards in the eastern district of Castello, where the Republic's navy was constructed and maintained

arte
One of the legally registered trade guilds

banca
Literally a 'bench', a ruling committee, for example, of the Scuole Grandi and other organisations; the same term is used for the commercial banks at Rialto

barco
Upper gallery in a church, usually above the west end of the nave, where the choir was located

bordonal
A massive timber beam, usually of oak or larch, roughly square in section, and used to support the lesser beams of a floor; typical dimensions are 240–390 mm in section

botega, bottega
A craftsman's workshop, usually integrated with his house

Ca' or Cà
The usual Venetian abbreviation of 'casa' or 'casa da stazio', the principal residence of a Venetian noble clan or family

cadena, caena
Literally, a chain: a tie beam of timber, often the lowest chord of the truss of a roof; also a metal tie rod used to stabilise church vaults and roofs.

calle, callesella
The usual Venetian term for a street in the city, and its diminutive

campaniliti (various spellings)
Stone 'tabernacles' (or 'kiosks') on the tops of the façades of Venetian Gothic churches, often housing statues

campo, campiello
A Venetian square and its diminutive; all Venetian squares are so called, other than the Piazza and Piazzetta of San Marco and (occasionally) that at Rialto

Canalazzo
The Grand Canal

caneva
A boathouse

cantinella
A small, narrow section of timber, used as laths to form partition walls or as decoration to ceilings; usually of larch or fir

canton
Venetian term for the external corner or angle of a building

casada
A noble family or clan

cavanna
A small inlet of water or dock

chiave
A timber beam, usually of fir or larch, smaller than a *bordonal*;

297

the typical beam supporting an upper floor; a *chiavesella* was smaller, typically approximately 90 mm square in section

chiodo
A nail

cipollino
A type of fine, light grey marble, so-called (*cipolla* = onion) from the figuring, which resembles that of an onion

Collegio
Also known as the Serenissima Signoria: the uppermost level of Venetian government or cabinet, presided over by the doge

Consiglio dei Dieci (Council of Ten)
The supreme body controlling state security, and the highest court of appeal in the Venetian Republic

contado
The rural territory surrounding a town or city; the two were mutually dependent, the *contado* providing the city with food and provisions, the city providing secure shelter and defence of its territory

cortile
An enclosed courtyard, usually of a Venetian palace

cotto
Brickwork (from *pietra cotta* = brickwork)

desegno, dissegno
A 'design', usually a drawing on paper or parchment, but sometimes used to describe a three-dimensional model

Dogado
The original heartland of the Venetian state, comprising the lagoon and the coastal territories from Chioggia as far as Grado

doge
The head of state of the Most Serene Republic; he was a patrician, was elected by the Maggior Consiglio and reigned for life

ducato
The gold ducat, foundation of the Venetian monetary system. The ducat was of highly refined gold, and in the late fifteenth century had a value corresponding to L.6.4.0, or 124 soldi (see lira). The ducat was recognised over much of Europe

Dogana
Customs house

Erberia
The vegetable market at Rialto

fante
An apprentice of a master craftsman

fenestrer
A window-maker

ferramenta
Ironwork, as produced in a smithy; for building construction the *fabbro* (smith) produced nails, chains, tie rods, locks and bars and grilles for windows, etc.

fondaco, fontego
A warehouse; in Venice the term is usually applied to the bases of foreign merchants in the city (e.g., 'dei Tedeschi', 'dei Turchi'), which also offered accommodation and other facilities for expatriates

fondamenta
A quay

fondamento (occasionally fondamenta)
The foundation of a structure

fornaxa, fornace
A kiln for firing bricks and tiles, or for making glass

Giustizia Vecchia
A government body responsible, *inter alia*, for the registration and monitoring of the trade guilds in the city

gorna
A rainwater gutter

gotico fiorito ('florid Gothic')
The architectural style characteristic of the city from the very late fourteenth century until about 1460–70. Its clearest manifestation is in the design of the façades of noble palaces

lido
One of the long, narrow islands that separate the lagoons along the Venetian coast from the Adriatic, and protect the lagoon settlements from floods and storms. The 'Lido di Venezia' is one of many such *lidi*

lire, soldi, denari
Pounds, shillings and pence; the Venetian monetary system used for all day-to-day transactions and for paying wages, etc. As in the former system in the United Kingdom, there were 12 denari in a soldo, and 20 soldi in one lira. Sometimes called lira *di piccoli* since there was also a much larger money of account, the lira *a grossi*

loggia
A colonnaded structure often used as a meeting place, providing shelter form the elements

magazen
A storage warehouse

Maggior Consiglio
The 'Great Council' of the Republic, consisting of all adult male noblemen who were eligible to attend and vote; the Maggior Consiglio elected all the other highest organs of state

Magistrato alle Acque
The 'magistracy of the waters': the agency responsible for the maintenance of the lagoon, canals and sea defences

manovalo, manoal
An unskilled manual labourer on a construction site

maran
A cargo vessel, used to carry stone from the quarries in Istria to the city

marangono (da casa)
A carpenter-joiner

Mariegola
The statutes and governing regulations of the Venetian guilds, all of which had to be legally registered with the Giustizia Vecchia

Marzaria, Merceria
A group of streets connecting the Piazza San Marco with the markets and banks at Rialto; the city's principal commercial centre

mesola, mexola
Corbel or bracket

murer
A bricklayer or general building contractor: the term literally means 'wall builder'

ocio, occhio

The circular window ('eye') frequently seen on the main façade of Venetian churches in the late Gothic period

orto

An orchard

palazzo

A palace; the Venetian noble palace is sometimes also referred to as 'Ca', abbreviated from Casa da stazio

parlatorio

The 'parlour' in a nunnery, where it was possible to receive visitors

Pescheria

The fish market at Rialto

piede, passo

The Venetian units of length: 1 foot (*piede*) was equivalent to 347 mm; 5 feet comprised 1 *passo*

piera, pietra, piera viva

Stone; *piera da leto*: bedding slabs at the base of a wall; *piera cotta*: brickwork (literally 'fired stone'); *piera negra*: the grey stone from Verona sometimes used for columns, vaulting ribs and capitals

Piovego

The department of government responsible for issuing permits for construction, for the maintenance of building lines and the paving of streets

pòrtego

The central great hall of a Venetian palace, almost always on the first floor or *piano nobile*

pozzo

A Venetian well; Venetians did not take water from underground aquifers, but instead from tanks containing filtered rainwater

Pregadi

The Venetian Senate

Procurators of San Marco

Senior officials responsible for the management and maintenance of the shrine of San Marco and other state properties on the Piazza and Piazzetta; the Procurators *de citra* and *de ultra* were responsible for managing estates and bequests in the two 'halves' of the city

proto, protomaistro

A permanent, salaried master responsible for the overall management of a substantial building project

Provveditori al Sal

The Salt Commissioners, responsible for managing the state's revenues from its salt monopoly. They also funded many public building works as directed by the highest offices of state

rio

One of the city's minor canals

Rivo alto, Rialto

The 'high bank' that was, according to legend, the earliest part of the city to be settled; Venice's commercial hub, its centre for banking, insurance and retail and wholesale markets

ruga

An important city street, usually with shops and commercial functions; the term is said to derive from the French *rue*

sagoma

A template for the carving of stone profiles

sala capitolare

The chapter hall of the Scuole Grandi, the imposing hall on the first floor where general assemblies of members were held, and masses conducted

salizzada

A paved street, i.e., a street paved from an early date and therefore one of the most important in the city's network

scalini, schalini

Steps; also sometimes the base course of stonework in a wall or façade

Scuola Grande

A lay charitable confraternity; originally three, they eventually numbered seven

Senato

The Senate or upper house, the more formal title of the Pregadi

sestiere

One of the six districts in which the city is divided, three on each side of the Grand Canal: Castello, San Marco and Cannaregio (north/east); and Dorsoduro, Santa Croce and San Polo (south/ west)

sotoportego

A covered passageway, with a building constructed above

squero

A yard for the construction and repair of small boats

taiapiera, tagiapiera

A stonemason

tegola

A clay roof tile

terazer

A terrazzo-layer; terrazzo is an ancient and characteristic Venetian floor finish

Terraferma

The Venetian territories on the Italian mainland

tola, tavola

A plank of timber, such as those used for flooring, usually of fir, larch or beech

tolpo

A timber pile for forming foundations, usually of oak

trave

A timber beam

verier

A glassmaker, based on the island of Murano

zattaron

A decking of timber planks, placed on top of the timber piles that form a building's foundations

Zecca

The state mint, based at San Marco, where all coinage was struck

Bibliography

Ackerman, J. S., 'The cloisters of San Zaccaria', in J. McAndrew, *Venetian Architecture of the Early Renaissance*, Cambridge, 1980, pp. 554–9

——, 'Observations on Renaissance church planning in Venice and Florence', in *Florence and Venice: Comparisons and Relations*, ed. S. Bertelli, N. Rubinstein and C. H. Smyth, 2 vols, Florence, 1980, vol. II, pp. 287–308

——, *Distance Points: Essays in Theory and Renaissance Art and Architecture*, Cambridge, MA, 1991

Alberti, L. B., *De re aedificatoria*, Florence, 1485; first English edn, trans. G. Leoni, London, 1726 (second edn, 1738; third edn, 1755)

Ames-Lewis, F., *Drawing in Early Renaissance Italy*, New Haven and London, 1981

——, *New Interpretations of Italian Renaissance Painting*, London, 1994

——, *The Intellectual Life of the Early Renaissance Artist*, New Haven and London, 2000

Angelini, L., *Le opere in Venezia di Mauro Codussi*, Milan, 1945

——, *Bartolomeo Bon, e Guglielmo d'Alzano, architetti bergamaschi in Venezia*, Bergamo, 1961

Antonelli, V., 'Restorations of the Porta della Carta since 1797', in Romano, *The Restoration*, pp. 29–36

Arcais, F. d', *Antonio Vivarini*, Milan, 1966

Architettura e Utopia nella Venezia del Cinquecento, exhibition catalogue, Milan, 1980

Arnaldi, G., G. Cracco and A. Tenenti, eds, *Storia di Venezia*, vol. III: *La formazione dello stato patrizio*, Rome, 1997

Arnaldi, G., and M. P. Stocchi, eds, *Storia della cultura veneta*, 6 vols, Vicenza, 1976–86

Arslan, E., *Venezia gotica*, Milan, 1970

Averlino, A. [Filarete], *Trattato di architettura*, ed. A. M. Finoli and L. Grassi, Milan, 1972

Balistreri-Trincanato, C., and D. Zanverdiani, *Jacopo de Barbari: il racconto di una città*, Venice, 2000

Baron, H., *The Crisis of the Early Italian Renaissance: Civic Humanism and Republican Liberty in an Age of Classicism and Tyranny*, 2 vols, Princeton, 1955

Bassi, E., *Appunti per la storia del Palazzo Ducale di Venezia*, Vicenza, 1962

——, *Il convento della Carità*, Corpus palladianum, VI, Vicenza, 1971

——, *Palazzi di Venezia: admiranda urbis venetae*, Venice, 1976

——, *Tracce di chiese veneziane distrutte*, Venice, 1997

Baxandall, M., *Painting and Experience in Fifteenth Century Italy*, Oxford, 1972

Bellavitis, G., 'La condizione spaziale di Venezia nell'opera prima di Mauro Coducci', *Psicon*, III (1976), pp. 109–15

——, *L'Arsenale di Venezia*, Venice, 1983

Beltrami, L., *La Ca' del Duca sul Canal Grande ed altre reminiscenze sforzesche a Venezia*, Milan, 1900

Biadene, S., G. Romanelli and C. Tonini, C., *A volo d'uccello: Jacopo de' Barbari e le rappresentazioni di città dell'Europa del Rinascimento*, Venice, 1999

Bigaglia, G., *La chiesa della Madonna dell'Orto in Venezia*, Venice, 1937

Boni, G., 'Santa Maria dei Miracoli in Venezia', *Archivio veneto*, XXXIII (1887)

Borsi, F., *Leon Battista Alberti*, Oxford, 1977

Boschini, M., *La Carta del Navegar Pitoresca*, Venice, 1660

Bouwsma, W. J., *Venice and the Defense of Republican Liberty: Renaissance Values in the Age of the Counter-Reformation*, Berkeley and Los Angeles, 1968

Bracciolini, Poggio, Gianfrancesco, 'In laudem rei publicae Venetorum', in *Opera omnia*, ed. R. Furbini, 4 vols, Turin, 1964–9

Branca, V., 'Ermolao Barbaro and late quattrocento Venetian humanism', in Hale, ed., *Renaissance Venice*, pp. 218–43

Brenzoni, R., *Fra Giovanni Giocondo, veronese*, Florence, 1960

Bristot, A., 'The Clock-tower', in UNESCO, *Venice Restored, 1966–1986*, Milan, 1991, pp. 185–6

Burke, P., *Tradition and Innovation in Renaissance Italy*, London, 1974

——, 'Early modern Venice as a center of information and communications' in Martin and Romano, eds, *Venice Reconsidered*, pp. 389–419

Cadorin, G., *Pareri di XV architetti e notizie storiche intorno al Palazzo Ducale di Venezia*, Venice, 1838

Caffi, M., *I Solari, artisti Lombardi nella Venezia*, Milan, 1885

——, 'Guglielmo Bergamasco ossia Vielmo Vielmi di Alzano, architetto e scultore del secolo XVI', *Nuovo archivio veneto*, second series, vol. III (1892)

Calabi, D., and P. Morachiello, *Rialto: le fabbriche e il ponte*, Turin, 1987

——, *Il mercato e la città*, Venice, 1993

——, 'The location of the banking system: Venice between the XVI and XVII centuries', in *Cities of Finance*, ed. H. A. Diedericks and D. Reeder, Oxford and New York, 1996, pp. 237–50

Caniato, G., and M. Dal Borgo, *Le arti edili a Venezia*, Rome, 1990

Caravia, Alessandro, *Il Sogno*, Venice 1541

Carboneri, N., 'Mauro Codussi', *Bollettino CISA 'Andrea Palladio'*, VI/2 (1964), pp. 188–98

Cardini, F., ed., *Lorenzo il Magnifico*, Rome 1992

Caresini, Rafain, 'Cronica', in *Rerum Italicarum Scriptores*, vol. XII (Bologna 1923)

Casola, P., *Viaggio di Pietro Casola in Gerusalemme*, Milan, 1885

Cassini, G., *Piante e vedute prospettiche di Venezia, 1479–1855*, Venice, 1971

Cecchetti, B., 'Documenti per la storia della fabbrica della chiesa di San Zaccaria', *Archivio veneto*, XXXI (1886), pp. 459–96

——, 'La facciata della Ca' d'Oro dello scalpello di Giovanni e Bartolomeo Buono', *Archivio veneto*, XXXI (1886), pp. 201–4

Cennini, Cennino d'Andrea, *The Craftsman's Handbook: 'Il Libro dell'Arte'*, trans. D. V. Thompson, New York, 1960

Cessi, R., *Deliberazioni del Maggior Consiglio di Venezia*, 3 vols, Bologna, 1931–50

——, *Storia della Repubblica di Venezia*, Milan and Messina, 2 vols, 1944–6

——, and Alberti, A., *Rialto: l'isola, il ponte, il mercato*, Bologna, 1934; facsimile reprint 1988

——, Medioevo e umanesimo, II, 1979

Chambers, D. S., *The Imperial Age of Venice, 1380–1580*, London, 1970

——, and B. Pullan, eds, *Venice: A Documentary History, 1450–1630*, Oxford and Cambridge, MA, 1992

——, C. Clough and M. Mallett, eds, *War, Culture and Society in Renaissance Venice: Essays in Honour of John Hale*, London, 1993

Chinazzo, Daniele de, 'Cronaca della Guerra de' Veneciani e Genovesi', in *Monumenti Storici*, Venice 1939, vol. XX

Chojnacki, S., 'In search of the Venetian patriciate: families and factions in the 14th century', in Hale, ed., *Renaissance Venice*, pp. 47–90

——, 'Identity and ideology in Renaissance Venice: the third Serrata', in Martin and Romano, eds, *Venice Reconsidered*, pp. 263–94

Cian, V., 'Per Bernardo Bembo', in *Giornale Storico della Letteratura italiana*, XXVIII, 1896

Cicogna, E. A., *Delle iscrizioni veneziane, raccolte ed illustrate*, 6 vols, Venice, 1824–53

Cicognara, L., A. Diedo and G.-A. Selva, *Le fabbriche più cospicue di Venezia misurate, illustrate ed intagliate dai membri della Veneta Reale Accademia di Belle Arti*, 2 vols, Venice, 1815–20

Clarke, A., and P. Rylands, *The Church of the Madonna dell'Orto*, London, 1977

Clarke, G., *Roman House – Renaissance Palaces*, Cambridge, 2003

Clough, C. H., ed., *Cultural Aspects of the Italian Renaissance: Essays in Honour of Paul Oskar Kristeller*, Manchester and New York, 1976

Cohn, S. K., and S. A. Epstein, eds, *Portraits of Medieval and Renaissance Living: Essays in Memory of David Herlihy*, Ann Arbor, 1996

Cole, A., *Art of the Italian Renaissance Courts*, London, 1995

Colonna, F., *Hypnerotomachia Poliphili*, ed. G. Pozzi and L. A. Ciapponi, Padua, 1980

Concina, E., *L'Arsenale della Repubblica di Venezia: tecniche e istituzioni dal medioevo all'età moderna*, Milan, 1984

——, *Pietre, parole, storia: glossario della costruzione nelle fonti veneziane (sec. XV–XVIII)*, Venice, 1988

——, *Le chiese di Venezia: l'arte e la storia*, Udine, 1995

——, *Storia dell'architettura di Venezia dal VII al XX secolo*, Milan, 1995

——, *Fondaci: architettura, arte e mercatura tra Levante, Venezia e Alemagna*, Venice, 1997

——, 'I fondaci del medioevo veneziano', in Valcanover and Wolters, eds, *L'architettura gotica veneziana*, pp. 131–8

Connell, S., *The Employment of Sculptors and Stonemasons in Venice in the Fifteenth Century*, London and New York, 1988

——, 'Gli artigiani dell'edilizia', in Gianighian, ed., *Ricerche venete*, II: *Dal medioevo al tardo Rinascimento*, pp. 31–92

Connell Wallington, S., 'Il cantiere secondo i dati d'archivio', in Valcanover and Wolters, eds, *L'architettura gotica veneziana*, pp. 35–52

Cooper, T. E., 'I modani', in Millon and Lampugnani eds, *Rinascimento*, pp. 494–500

Corner, F., *Ecclesiae Venetae antiquis monumentis nunc etiam primum editis*, Venice, 1749

——, *Ecclesiae Torcellanae*, Venice, 1756

——, *Notizie storiche delle chiese e monasteri di Venezia e di Torcello*, Padua, 1756; facsimile edn, Bologna, 1990

——, *Scritture sopra la laguna*, ed. G. Pavanello, Venice, 1919

Costa, M. dalla, and C. Feiffer, *Le pietre dell'architettura veneta e di Venezia*, Venice, 1981

Cozzi, G., 'Domenico Morosini e il "de bene re publica"', *Studi veneziani*, XII (1970)

——, and M. Knapton, *Storia della Repubblica di Venezia dalla Guerra di Chioggia alla riconquista della Terraferma*, Turin, 1986

Cracco, G., and G. Ortalli, eds, *Storia di Venezia*, vol. I: *Origini, età ducale*, Rome, 1995

——, eds, *Storia di Venezia*, vol. II: *L'età del Comune*, Rome, 1995

Crouzet-Pavan, E., *Sopra le acque salse: espaces, pouvoir et société à Venise à la fin du Moyen Age*, 2 vols, Rome, 1992

——, *Venise triomphante: les horizons d'un mythe*, Paris, 1999

——, 'Towards an ecological understanding of the myth of Venice', in Martin and Romano, eds, *Venice Reconsidered*, pp. 39–64

Davies, P., and D. Hemsoll, *Sanmicheli*, Milan, 2004

Davis, J. C., *The Decline of the Venetian Nobility as a Ruling Class*, Baltimore, 1962

Davis, R. C., *Shipbuilders of the Venetian Arsenal*, Baltimore and London, 1991

Dean, T., *Land and Power in Late Medieval Ferrara: The Rule of the Este, 1350–1450*, Cambridge, 1988

Dellwing, H., 'Die Kirchen S Zaccaria im Venedig', *Zeitschrift für Kunstgeschichte*, vol. XXXVII (1974), pp. 224–34

——, *Die Kirchen Baukunst des späten Mittelalters in Venetien*, Worms, 1990

Demus, O., *The Mosaics of San Marco*, 4 vols, Chicago and London, 1984

Dorigo, W., *Venezia origini: fondamenti, ipotesi, metodi*, 2 vols, Milan, 1983

——, *Venezia romanica: la formazione della città medievale fino all'età gotica*, 2 vols, Sommacampagna, Verona, 2003

Ell, S. R., 'Citizenship and immigration in Venice 1350–1500', PhD dissertation, University of Chicago, 1976

Erizzo, N., *Relazione storico-critica sulla Torre dell'Orologio di San Marco in Venezia*, 2nd edn, Venice, 1866

Fabbri, G., ed., *La Scuola Grande della Misericordia di Venezia*, Venice, 1999

Fabri, F., *Evagatorum in Terrae Sanctae*, ed. C. D. Hassler, Stuttgart, 1849

Ferrara, M., and F. Quinterio, *Michelozzo di Bartolomeo*, Florence, 1984

Filarete [Antonio Averlino], *Filarete's Treatise on Architecture*, ed. J. R. Spencer, New Haven and London, 1975

Filelfo, F., *Epistolae*, Venice, 1492

Finlay, R., 'The myth of Venice in Guicciardini's *History of Italy*: Senate orations on princes and the Republic', in Kittell and Madden, eds, *Medieval and Renaissance Venice*, pp. 294–326

Finotto, F., *San Giobbe*, Verona, 1994

Fiocco, G., 'I Lamberti in Venezia', in *Dedalo*, 1927–8, pp. 287–314, 343–76, 432–58

Fiore, F. P., and M. Tafuri, *Francesco di Giorgio architetto*, Milan, 1993

Fletcher, J., and R. Mueller, 'Bellini and the bankers: the Priuli altarpiece for San Michele in Isola, Venice', *Burlington Magazine*, vol. CXLVII (January 2005)

Fogolari, F., 'La chiesa di Santa Maria della Carità di Venezia', *Archivio veneto-tridentino*, XV (1924), pp. 57–119

Fogolari, G., *I Frari e i Santi Giovanni e Paolo a Venezia*, Milan, 1939

Fontana, G.-J., *Venezia monumentale: i palazzi*, Venice, 1865; reprinted 1967

——, *Venezia monumentale: i templi*, Venice, 1863

Fontana, V., *Fra Giovanni Giocondo, architetto, 1432–1515*, Vicenza, 1988

Forcellini, A., 'Sui restauri delle principali facciate del Palazzo Ducale di Venezia', in *L'ingegneria a Venezia*, Venice, 1887, pp. 14-et seq.

Forlati, F., 'Il Fondaco dei Tedeschi', *Palladio*, IV (1940)

Fortini Brown, P., *Venetian Narrative Painting in the Age of Carpaccio*, New Haven and London, 1988

——, *Venice and Antiquity: The Venetian Sense of the Past*, New Haven and London, 1996

Foscari, A., 'La costruzione della chiesa agostiniana di Santo Stefano', in *Gli agostiniani a Venezia e la chiesa di Santo Stefano*, ed. M. Mattei et al., Venice, 1997, pp. 121–58

Foscari, L., *Affreschi esterni a Venezia*, Milan, 1936

Francesco di Giorgio Martini, *Trattato di architettura, ingegneria e arte militare*, ed. C. Maltese, Milan, 1967

Franzoi, U., 'La Scala dei Giganti', *Bollettino dei Musei Civici veneziani*, IV (1965)

——, 'Per la storia del Palazzo: origini e sviluppi', in Romanelli, ed., *Palazzo Ducale*, pp. 81–126

——, and D. di Stefano, *Le chiese di Venezia*, Venice, 1976

——, T. Pignatti and W. Wolters, *Il Palazzo Ducale di Venezia*, Treviso, 1990

Frommel, C. L., 'Sulla nascità del disegno architettonico', in Millon and Lampugnani, eds, *Rinascimento*, pp. 101–21

Galliciolli, G.-B., *Delle memorie venete antiche, profane ed ecclesiastiche*, 8 vols, Venice, 1795

Gallo, R., 'La porta d'ingresso dell'Arsenale e i leoni del Pireo', *Rivista mensile della città di Venezia*, Venice, 1925, pp. 323–33

——, 'L'architettura di transizione dal gotico al Rinascimento', *Atti del Istituto Veneto di Scienze, Letteratura ed Arti*, CXX (1961–2), pp. 198–201

Garin, E., *L'umanesimo italiano*, Bari, 1965

Gazzola, P., *Michele Sanmicheli*, Venice, 1960

Gerboni Baiardi, G., et al., *Federigo da Montefeltro: lo stato, le arti, la cultura*, 3 vols, Rome, 1986

Gianighian, G., ed., *Ricerche venete, I: Venezia tardomedioevale: istituzioni e società nella storiografia angloamericana*, Venice, 1989

——, ed., *Ricerche venete, II: dal medioevo al tardo Rianscimento: ricerche di storia del costruire a Venezia*, Venice, 1993

——, and P. Pavanini, *Dietro i Palazzi: tre secoli di architettura minore a Venezia, 1492–1803*, Venice, 1984

Giannetto, N., *Bernardo Bembo: umanista e politico veneziano*, Florence, 1985

Gilbert, F., 'Venice in the crisis of the League of Cambrai', in Hale, ed., *Renaissance Venice*, pp. 274–92

Gilmore, M., 'Myth and reality in Venetian political theory', in Hale, ed., *Renaissance Venice*, pp. 431–44

Goffen, R., *Piety and Patronage in Renaissance Venice: Bellini, Titian and the Franciscans*, New Haven and London, 1986

——, *Giovanni Bellini*, New Haven and London, 1989

Goldthwaite, R., *The Building of Renaissance Florence*, Baltimore and London, 1980

Goy, R. J., *Chioggia and the Villages of the Venetian Lagoon: Studies in Urban History*, Cambridge, 1985

——, *Venetian Vernacular Architecture: Traditional Housing in the Venetian Lagoon*, Cambridge, 1989

——, *The House of Gold: Building a Palace in Medieval Venice*, Cambridge, 1993

——, 'To the glory of God: building the church of S. Maria della Carità, Venice, 1441–54', *Architectural History: Journal of the Society of Architectural Historians of Great Britain*, XXXVII (1994), pp. 1–23

——, *Venice: The City and its Architecture*, London and New York, 1997

Gozzi, G., 'Domenico Morosini e il *De bene instituta re publica*', *Studi veneti*, XII (1970), pp. 405–58

Gramigna, A.S.-P., *Scuole di arti e mestieri e devozione a Venezia*, Venice, 1981

Griffiths, A., 'Bartolomeo Vivarini', MA thesis, Courtauld Institute, University of London, 1976

Grubb, J., 'Elite citizens', in Martin and Romano, eds, *Venice Reconsidered*, pp. 339–64

Guicciardini, F., *Storia d'Italia*, ed. S. S. Menchi, 3 vols, Turin 1971

Hale, J. R., *Florence and the Medici: The Pattern of Control*, London and New York, 1977

——, ed., *Renaissance Venice*, London, 1974

——, *War and Society in Renaissance Europe*, London, 1985

——, *The Civilization of Europe in the Renaissance*, London, 1993

Hempel, K., and Hempel, G., 'A Technical Report on the Condition of the Porta della Carta', in Romano, *The Restoration*, pp. 37–9

Hersey, G. L., *The Aragonese Arch at Naples, 1443–1475*, New Haven and London, 1973

Heydenreich, L. H., 'Il bugnato rustico nel Quattrocento e Cinquecento', *Bolletino CISA*, II (1960), pp. 40–41

Hirthe, T., 'Mauro Codussi als Architekt des Dogenpalastes', *Arte veneta*, no. 36 (1982), pp. 31–44

Hocquet, J. C., *Il sale e la fortuna di Venezia*, Rome, 1990

——, *Denaro, navi e mercanti a Venezia, 1200–1600*, Rome, 1999

Horster, M., *Andrea del Castagno*, Oxford, 1980

Howard, D., *Jacopo Sansovino: Architecture and Patronage in Renaissance Venice*, New Haven and London, 1975

——, 'Venice as a dolphin: further investigations into Jacopo de' Barbari's view', *Artibus et historiae*, XXXV (1997), pp. 101–12

——, *Venice and the East: The Impact of the Islamic World on Venetian Architecture, 1100–1500*, New Haven and London, 2000

——, *The Architectural History of Venice*, new edn, New Haven and London, 2002

——, 'San Michele in Isola: re-reading the genesis of the Venetian Renaissance', in *L'Invention de la Renaissance*, ed. J. Guillaume, Paris, 2003, pp. 27–42

Humfrey, P., *The Altarpiece in Renaissance Venice*, New Haven and London, 1993

——, *Painting in Renaissance Venice*, New Haven and London, 1995

——, and R. Mackenney, 'The Venetian trade guilds as patrons of art in the Renaissance', *Burlington Magazine*, CXXVIII (1986), pp. 317–30

King, M., *Umanesimo e patriziato a Venezia nel quattrocento*, 2 vols, Rome, 1989; first published as *Venetian Humanism in an Age of Patrician Dominance*, Princeton, 1986

Kittell, E. E., and T. F. Madden, eds, *Medieval and Renaissance Venice*, Urbana and Chicago, 1999

Klotz, H., *Filippo Brunelleschi: The Early Works and the Medieval Tradition*, New York and London, 1990

Knapton, M., 'I rapporti fiscali tra Venezia e la terraferma', *Archivio veneto*, CXVII (1981)

Lane, F. C., *Venice and History: The Collected Papers of Frederic C. Lane*, Baltimore, 1966

——, *Venice: A Maritime Republic*, Baltimore and London, 1973

——, *I mercanti di Venezia*, Turin, 1982

——, *Venetian Ships and Shipbuilders of the Renaissance*, new edn, Baltimore and London, 1992

——, and R. C. Mueller, *Money and Banking in Medieval Venice*, 2 vols, Baltimore and London, 1985–97

Lazzarini, L., *Studio scientifico sullo stato di conservazione delle pietre e dei marmi della Porta della Carta di Venezia*, Padua, 1979

——, 'I materiali lapidei dell'edilizia storica veneziana', *Restauro e Città*, II/3–4 (1986), pp. 84–92

——, *Pietra d'Istria: genesi, proprieta e cavatura della pietra di Venezia*, in preparation

——, and R. Strassoldo, 'I marmi colorati del Palazzo', in Romanelli, ed., *Palazzo Ducale*

Lazzarini, V., 'Filippo Calendario, l'architetto della tradizione del Palazzo Ducale', *Nuovo archivio veneto*, new series, IV (1894)

Lieberman, R., *The Church of Santa Maria dei Miracoli in Venice*, New York, 1972

——, *Renaissance Architecture in Venice, 1450–1540*, Cambridge, MA, and London, 1980

——, 'Real architecture, imaginary history: the Arsenale gate as Venetian mythology', *Journal of the Warburg and Courtauld Institutes*, LIV (1991), pp. 117–26

Lorenzetti, G., *Venezia e il suo estuario: guida storico-artistica*, Rome, 1926

——, *La Scuola Grande di San Giovanni Evangelista a Venezia*, Venice, 1929

Lorenzi, G., *Monumenti per servire alla storia del Palazzo Ducale*, Venice, 1868

Lotz, W., *Studies in Italian Renaissance Architecture*, Cambridge, MA, 1977

Lowry, M., *Il mondo di Aldo Manuzio: affari e cultura nella Venezia del Rinascimento*, second edn, Rome, 2000; first published as *The World of Aldus Manutius: Business and Scholarship in Renaissance Venice*, Oxford, 1979

Lubkin, G., *A Renaissance Court: Milan under Galeazzo Maria Sforza*, Berkeley, CA, and London, 1994

Luzio, A., and R. Renier, 'Di Pietro Lombardo, architetto e scultore veneziano', *Archivio storico dell'arte*, I (1888), pp. 433–8

Luzzatto, G., *I prestiti della repubblica di Venezia nei secoli XII–XV*, Padua, 1929

——, *Il debito pubblico della Repubblica di Venezia dagli ultimi decenni del sec. XII alla fine del XV*, Milan and Varese, 1963

——, *Storia economica di Venezia dal XI al XVI secolo*, Venice, 1995

Mack, C. R., *Pienza: The Creation of a Renaissance City*, Ithaca, NY, and London, 1987

Mackenney, R., *Tradesmen and Traders: The World of the Guilds in Venice and Europe, c. 1250–1650*, Totowa, NJ, 1987

——, 'Corporazioni e politica nel medioevo a Venezia', in Gianighian, ed., *Ricerche venete*, I: *Venezia tardomedioevale*, pp. 87–130

Malipiero, D., 'Annali', first edn, F. Longo, 1564; new edn, F. Longo, in *Archivio storico italiano*, II (1843–4)

Mallett, M., 'Venice and the War of Ferrara, 1482–84', in *War, Culture and Society*, ed. D. Chambers et al., London, 1993, pp. 57–72

Mallett, M. E., and J. R. Hale, *The Military Organization of a Renaissance State: Venice, c. 1400–1617*, Cambridge, 1984

Malsburg, R. von der, 'Die Architektur der Scuola Grande di San Rocco in Venedig', Ph.D. dissertation, Heidelberg University, 1976

Manno, A., *I mestieri di Venezia: storia, arte e devozione delle corporazioni dal XIII al XVIII secolo*, Cittadella, 1995

——, *Palazzo Ducale: guida al Museo dell'Opera*, Venice, 1996

——, ed., *Il poema del tempo: i capitelli del Palazzo Ducale di Venezia: storia e iconografia*, Venice, 1999

Maranini, G., *La costituzione di Venezia*, 2 vols, Florence, 1927; new paperback edn, 1974

Marchini, G., *Giuliano da Sangallo*, Florence, 1942

Marciano, A. F., *L'età di Biagio Rossetti: Rinascimento di casa d'Este*, Ferrara, 1991

Maretto, P., *L'edilizia gotica veneziana*, Rome, 1961

——, *La casa veneziana nella storia della città*, Venice, 1986

Mariani, S., 'Vita e opere dei proti Bon, Bartolomeo e Pietro', dissertation, IUAV, Venice, 1982–3

Marichaer, G., 'Le opere di Mauro Codussi a Venezia', *Ateneo veneto* (1945)

——, 'New light on Antonio Bregno', *Burlington Magazine*, XCII (1950), pp. 123–8

——, 'Pietro Lombardo a Venezia', *Arte veneta*, IX (1955), pp. 38–52

——, *The Ducal Palace of Venice*, Rome, 1956

——, *Il Palazzo Vendramin Calergi a Venezia*, Venice, 1965

Martene, E., *Veterum scriptorum et monumentorum . . . amplissima collectio*, 3 vols, Paris, 1724

Martin, J., and D. Romano, eds, *Venice Reconsidered: The History and Civilization of an Italian State, 1297–1797*, Baltimore and London, 2000

Martineau, J., and C. Hope, eds, *The Genius of Venice, 1500–1600*, exhibition catalogue, London, 1983

Mazzariol, G., and T. Pignatti, *La pianta prospettica di Venezia del 1500 disegnata da Jacopo de' Barbari*, Venice, 1962

McAndrew, J., *Venetian Architecture of the Early Renaissance*, Cambridge, MA, and London, 1980

McHam, S. B., *The Chapel of St Anthony at the Santo and the Development of Venetian Renaissance Sculpture*, Cambridge, 1994

Meneghin, V., *San Michele in Isola di Venezia*, 2 vols, Venice, 1962

Millon, H., and V. M. Lampugnani, eds, *Rinascimento da Brunelleschi a Michelangelo: la rappresentazione dell'architettura*, Milan, 1994

Miozzi, E., *Venezia nei secoli: la città*, Venice, 1957

Molmenti, P., *La storia di Venezia nella vita privata*, 2nd edn, 3 vols, Turin, 1880

Monticolo, G., *I capitolari delle arti veneziane*, 3 vols, Rome, 1896–1914

Moretti, L., *La chiesa della Madonna dell'Orto in Venezia*, Turin, 1981

Morosini, D., *De bene instituta Re Publica*, ed. C. Finzi, Milan, 1969

Morresi, M., *Piazza San Marco: istituzioni, poteri e architettura a Venezia nel primo cinquecento*, Milan, 1999

——, *Jacopo Sansovino*, Venice, 2000

Moschini, G. A., *Guida per la Città di Venezia*, 2 vols, Venice, 1815

Moschini, V., *I Vivarini*, Milan, 1946

Mosto, A. da, *Archivio di Stato di Venezia: indice generale*, 2 vols, Rome, 1937–40

——, *I dogi di Venezia nella vita pubblica e privata*, Milan, 1960

Mueller, R. C., 'The Procurators of San Marco in the 13th and 14th centuries: a study of the office as a financial and trust institution', *Studi veneziani*, XIII (1971), pp. 105–220

——, 'The role of bank money in Venice, 1300–1500', *Studi veneziani*, new series, III (1979)

——, 'L'imperialismo monetario veneziano nel quattrocento', *Società e storia*, VIII (1980)

——, 'Effetti della Guerra di Chioggia sulla vita economica e sociale di Venezia', *Ateneo veneto*, new series, XIX (1981), pp. 27–41

——, *The Venetian Money Market: Banks, Panics, and the Public Debt 1200–1500*, Baltimore and London, 1997

Muir, E., *Civic Ritual in Renaissance Venice*, Princeton, 1981

——, 'Was there republicanism in the Renaissance Republics?: Venice after Agnadello', in Martin and Romano, eds, *Venice Reconsidered*, pp. 137–67

Munman, R., 'Giovanni Buora: the "missing" sculpture', *Arte veneta*, XXX (1976)

Muraro, M., 'La scala senza giganti', in *Essays in Honor of Erwin Panofsky*, ed. M. Meiss, Zurich, 1960, pp. 350–70

——, 'The Moors of the Clock-tower of Venice and their sculpture', *Art Bulletin*, LXVI (1984), pp. 603–9

Muratori, S., *Studi per una operante storia urbana di Venezia*, Rome, 1959

Nani Mocenigo, M., *L'Arsenale di Venezia*, Venice, 1939

Nicol, D. M., *Byzantium and Venice: A Study in Diplomatic and Cultural Relations*, Cambridge, 1988

Niero, A., 'La Madonna dei Miracoli nella storia della pietà veneziana: breve profilo', in Piana and Wolters, eds, *Santa Maria dei Miracoli*, pp. 17–40

Norwich, J. J., *A History of Venice*, Harmondsworth, 1982

Olivato, L., 'Precisazione archivistica a Mauro Codussi', *Arte lombarda*, II (1969), pp. 151–3

Onda, S., *La chiesa di San Francesco della Vigna: guida artistica*, Venice, 2003

Onians, J., *Bearers of Meaning: The Classical Orders in Antiquity, the Middle Ages and the Renaissance*, Princeton, 1990

Orlandini, G., *La Capella Corner nella chiesa dei Santi Apostoli in Venezia*, Venice, 1914

Padoan, E., 'Il Fondaco dei Tedeschi a Venezia', *Emporium*, issue 90 (1939), pp. 287–92

Paganuzzi, G.-B., *Iconografia delle trenta parocchie di Venezia*, Venice, 1821

Palladio, A., *I quattro libri dell'architettura*, Venice, 1570

Pallucchini, R., *I Vivarini: Antonio, Bartolomeo, Alvise*, Venice, 1962

Paoletti, P., *L'architettura e la scultura del Rinascimento in Venezia: ricerche storico-artistiche*, 2 vols, Venice, 1893–7

——, *La Scuola Grande di San Marco*, Venice, 1929

Pavanini, P., 'Abitazioni popolari e borghesi nella Venezia cinquecentesca', *Studi veneziani*, new series, v (1981), pp. 63–126

Pazzi, P., *La chiesa di San Giovanni Evangelista a Venezia*, Venice, 1985

Pemble, J., *Venice Rediscovered*, Oxford, 1995

Perocco, G., and A. Salvadori, *Civiltà di Venezia*, 3 vols, Venice, 1973–6

Piana, M., 'La carpenteria lignea veneziana nei secoli XIV e XV', in Valcanover and Wolters, eds, *L'architettura gotica veneziana*, pp. 73–82

——, and W. Wolters, eds, *Santa Maria dei Miracoli a Venezia: la storia, la fabbrica, i restauri*, Venice, 2003

Pignatti, T., *Piazza San Marco*, Novara, 1958

——, *Palazzo Ducale*, Novara, 1964

——, *The Golden Age of Venetian Painting*, Los Angeles, 1979

——, *Le scuole di Venezia*, Milan, 1981

——, 'Giorgione e Tiziano', in *Tiziano*, exhibition catalogue, Venice, 1990, pp. 68–76

Pincus, D., *The Arco Foscari: The Building of a Triumphal Gateway in Fifteenth Century Venice*, New York and London, 1976

——, 'Hard times and ducal radiance', in Martin and Romano, eds, *Venice Reconsidered*, pp. 89–136

Planiscig, L., *Venezianischer Bildhauer der Renaissance*, Vienna, 1921

Plant, M., 'Mauro Codussi: the presence of the past in Venetian Renaissance architecture', *Arte veneta*, XXXVIII (1984)

Polacco, R., ed., *Storia dell'arte marciana: l'architettura*, Venice, 1997

Polichetti, M. L., *Il Palazzo di Federigo da Montefeltro*, Urbino, 1985

Pope-Hennessey, J., *Italian Renaissance Sculpture*, New York, 1958

——, *Italian Gothic Sculpture*, 3rd edn, London, 1985

Priuli, G., 'I diarii, 1494–1512', in *Rerum Italicarum Scriptores*, Bologna, 1938, vol. IV

Pullan, B., *Crisis and change in the Venetian economy in the 16th and 17th century*, London, 1968

——, *Rich and Poor in Renaissance Venice: The Social Institutions of a Catholic State: to 1620*, Oxford and Cambridge, MA, 1971

——, 'The occupations and investments of the Venetian nobility in the middle and late 16th century', in Hale, ed., *Renaissance Venice*, pp. 379–408

Puppi, L., 'Per Tullio Lombardo', *Arte lombarda*, XXXVI (1972), pp. 100–3

——, 'Geografia di un crinale: Filippo Calendario tra storia e leggenda', in Valcanover and Wolters, eds, *L'architettura gotica veneziana*, pp. 99–103

——, 'Vischiosità della leggenda e levità della storia', in Romanelli ed., *Palazzo Ducale*

——, and L. Olivato Puppi, *Mauro Codussi*, Milan, 1977

Queller, D., *Il patriziato veneziano: la realtà contro il mito*, Rome, 1987

Quill, S., *Ruskin's Venice: The Stones Revisited*, Aldershot, 2000

Raby, J., *Venice, Dürer and the Oriental Mode*, Totowa, NJ, 1982

Radke, G., 'Nuns and their art: the case of San Zaccaria in Renaissance Venice', *Renaissance Quarterly*, no. 44 (2001), pp. 430–59

Redford, B., *Venice and the Grand Tour*, New Haven and London, 1996

Rizzi, A., *Scultura esterna a Venezia*, Venice, 1987

Robertson, G., *Giovanni Bellini*, Oxford, 1968

Romanelli, G., *La Scuola Grande di San Rocco*, Milan, 1994

——, ed., *Palazzo Ducale: storia e restauri*, Venice, 2004

——, et al., eds, *A volo d'uccello: Jacopo de' Barbari e la rappresentazione di città nell'Europa del Rinascimento*, Venice, 1999

Romano, D., *Patricians and Popolani: The Social Foundations of the Venetian Renaissance State*, Baltimore and London, 1987

Romano, S., *The Restoration of the Porta della Carta*, trans. A. Clarke and P. Rylands, Venice and London, 1980

Rosand, D., *Myths of Venice: the Figuration of a State*, Chapel Hill, NC, 2001

Rubinstein, N., *The Government of Florence under the Medici*, Oxford, 1966

——, ed., *Florentine Studies: Politics and Society in Renaissance Florence*, Florence, 1968

——, 'Italian reactions to Terraferma expansion in the 15th century', in Hale, ed., *Renaissance Venice*, pp. 197–217

Ruskin, J., *The Stones of Venice*, 3 vols, London, 1851–3

Sagredo, A., *Sulle consorterie delle arti edificative in Venezia*, Venice, 1856

Salzman, F., *Building in England down to 1540*, Oxford, 1952

Sammartini, T., and G. Crozzoli, *Decorative Floors of Venice*, London, 1999

Samonà, G., et al., *Piazza San Marco: l'architettura, la storia, le funzioni*, Venice, 1970

Sansovino, F., and G. Martinioni, *Venetia, città nobilissima et singolare . . .* , 2 vols, Venice, 1663; new facsimile edn, Venice, 1968

Sanudo, M., *De origine, situ et magistratibus urbis Venetae, ovvero La città di Venetia*; as *La città di Venetia*, ed. A. C. Arico, Milan, 1980

——, *I diarii*, ed. R. Fulin et al., 58 vols, Bologna, 1879–1903

——, *Vite dei dogi*, Città di Castello, 1906

——, *I diarii: pagine scelte*, ed. P. Margaroli, Vicenza, 1997

Schiavon, A., 'Santa Maria dei Miracoli: una fabbrica "cittadina"', in Piano and Wolters, eds, *Santa Maria dei Miracoli*, pp. 3–16

Schuller, M., 'Il Palazzo Ducale di Venezia: le facciate medioevali', in Valcanover and Wolters, eds, *L'architettura gotica veneziana*, pp. 235–46

——, 'Le facciate medievali: storia, costruzione, effetti cromatici', in Romanelli, ed., *Palazzo Ducale*, pp. 235–46

Schulz, A. M., 'The sculpture of Giovanni and Bartolomeo Bon and their workshop', *Transactions of the American Philosophical Society*, LXVII/ 3 (June 1978), pp. 1–81

——, 'The Giustiniani chapel and the art of the Lombardo', *Antichità viva*, XVI/2 (1977), pp. 27–44

——, *Niccolò di Giovanni Fiorentino and Venetian Sculpture of the Early Renaissance*, New York, 1978

——, 'Giorgio da Sebenico and the workshop of Giovanni Bon', in *Juraj Matejev Dalmatinac*, ed. M. Prelog, Zagreb, 1982, pp. 72–92

——, *Antonio Rizzo, Sculptor and Architect*, Princeton, 1983

——, *Giambattita and Lorenzo Bregno: Venetian Sculpture in the High Renaissance*, Cambridge, 1991

——, *La cappella Badoer-Giustinian*, Florence, 2003

Schulz, J., *Venetian Painted Ceilings of the Renaissance*, Berkeley, CA, 1968

——, *The Printed Plans and Panoramic Views of Venice*, Florence, 1970

——, 'Jacopo de' Barbari's view of Venice: map making, city views and moralizing geography before the year 1500', *Art Bulletin*, LX (1978), pp. 425–74

Sebesta, G., 'Gli edifici e l'uomo', in Caniato and Dal Borgo, *Le arti edili a Venezia*, pp. 259–307

Semenzato, C., 'La pianta prospettica di Venezia di Jacopo de' Barbari', *Arte veneta*, XVII (1963), p. 214

Serlio, S., *The Five Books of Architecture*, London, 1611; facsimile edn, New York, 1982

Shelby, L. R., 'Medieval masons' templates', *Journal of the Society of Architectural Historians*, XXX (1971), pp. 140–54

Simonsfeld, H., *Der Fondaco dei Tedeschi in Venedig und die Deutsch–Venetianischen Handelsbeziehungen*, 2 vols, Stuttgart, 1887

Sinding Larsen, S., *Christ in the Council Hall: Studies in the Religious Iconography of the Venetian Republic*, Rome, 1974

Sohm, P., *The Scuola Grande di San Marco, 1437–1550: The Architecture of a Venetian Lay Confraternity*, New York and London, 1982

Spencer, J. R., 'The Ca' del Duca in Venice and Benedetto Ferrini', *Journal of the Society of Architectural Historians*, XXX (1971)

——, *Filarete's Treatise on Architecture*, New Haven and London, 1965

——, 'Filarete and the Ca' del Duca', *Journal of the Society of Architectural Historians*, XXXV/3 (1976), pp. 219–22

Spufford., P., *Handbook of Medieval Exchange*, London, 1986

Steer, J., *Alvise Vivarini: His Art and Influence*, Cambridge, 1982

Stefanutti, U., *La Scuola Grande di San Marco*, Venice, 1960

Storia di Venezia: dalle origini alla Caduta della Serenissima, 12 vols, Rome, 1992–8

Strupp, J., 'The color of money: use, cost and aesthetic appreciation of marble in Venice c. 1500', *Venezia Cinquecento*, V (1993), pp. 7–32

Tafuri, M., *Venice and the Renaissance*, trans. J. Levine, Cambridge, MA, and London, 1989

Tassini, G., *Alcuni Palazzi ed antiche edifici di Venezia*, Venice, 1879

——, *Curiosità veneziane, ovvero origini delle denominazioni stradali di Venezia*, 4th edn, Venice, 1887; reprinted Venice, 1964

Tavernor, R., *On Alberti and the Art of Building*, New Haven and London, 1998

Temanza, T., *Vite de' piu celebri architetti e scultori veneziani*, Venice, 1778

Tentori, C., *Della legislazione veneziana*, Venice, 1792

Thornton, P., *The Italian Renaissance Interior*, London, 1991

Tiepolo, M.-F., 'Archivio di Stato di Venezia', in *Guida generale degli archivi di stato italiani*, 4 vols, Rome, 1994, vol. IV

Torre, A. della, 'La prima ambasceria di Bernardo Bembo a Firenze', *Giornale storico della letteratura italiana*, XXV, 1900

Tramontin, S., *La chiesa di Santa Maria dei Miracoli*, Venice, 1959

——, *San Giovanni Grisostomo*, Venice, 1968

Traversari, G., *L'arco dei Sergi*, Padua, 1971

Trincanato, E. R., *Venezia minore*, Milan, 1948

——, *Palazzo Ducale, Venezia*, Novara, 1969

——, *La casa veneziana delle origini*, Venice, 2000

Turner, J., ed., *Encyclopedia of Italian Renaissance and Mannerist Art*, 2 vols, London and New York, 2000

Ufficio Tecnico dei Musei Civici Veneziani, *Palazzo Ducale: restauro conservativo della facciata fronte Piazza*, Venice, 2000

UNESCO, *Venice Restored, 1966–1986*, Milan, 1991

Urbani di Gheltof, G. M., *Guida storica-artistica della Scuola di San Giovanni Evangelista*, Venice, 1895

Valcanover, F., 'Titians Fresken am Fondaco dei Tedeschi', *Giorgione a Venezia*, Milan, 1978, pp. 130–42

——, and W. Wolters, eds, *L'architettura gotica veneziana. Atti del Convegno Internazionale di Studio: Venice, 27–9 November 1996*, Venice, 2000

Vasari, G., *Le vite de' piu eccellenti architetti, pittori e scultori italiani*, ed. G. Milanesi, 9 vols, Milan, 1878–85; first complete English edn, trans. J. Foster, 5 vols, London, 1878

Ventura, A., *Nobiltà e popolo nella società veneta del Quattrocento e Cinquecento*, Milan, 1993

Vio, E., 'Le Procuratie Vecchie', in Samonà et al., *Piazza San Marco*, pp. 143–9

——, 'La Torre dell'Orologio', in Samonà et al., *Piazza San Marco*, pp. 138–41

White, J., *Art and Architecture in Italy, 1250–1400*, 3rd edn, New Haven and London, 1993

Wilde, J., *Venetian Art from Bellini to Titian*, Oxford 1974; new paperback edn, 1995

Winkelmes, M.-A., 'Form and reform: illuminated Cassinese reform-style churches in Renaissance Italy', *Annali di architettura*, VIII (1996), pp. 61–84

Wirobisz, A., 'L'attività edilizia a Venezia nel XIV e XV secolo', *Studi veneziani*, VII (1965), pp. 307–43

Wittkower, R., *Architectural Principles in the Age of Humanism*, London, 1960

Wolters, W., *La scultura gotica veneziana*, 2 vols, Venice, 1976

——, *Architektur und Ornament: Venezianischer Bauschmuck der Renaissance*, Munich, 2000

——, 'Ipotesi su Bartolomeo Buon architetto', in Valcanover and Wolters, eds, *L'architettura gotica veneziana*, pp. 273–80

——, and N. Huse, *The Art of Renaissance Venice*, Chicago, 1990

Zanetti, V., *Guida di Murano e delle celebri sue fornaci vetrarie*, Venice, 1866

Zanotto, F., *Il Palazzo Ducale di Venezia*, 4 vols, Venice, 1842–6

Zava Boccazzi, F., *La basilica dei Santi Giovanni e Paolo in Venezia*, Venice, 1965

Zompini, G. G., *Le arti che vanno per via nella città di Venezia*, Venice, 1753

Zorzi, A., *Venezia ritrovata, 1895–1939*, Milan, 1995

——, *Venezia scomparsa*, Venice, 1971; new paperback edn, 2001

Zuccolo, G., *Il restauro statico nell'architettura di Venezia*, Venice, 1975

Photograph Credits

All illustrations are by the author, with the exception of the following:

Museo Civico Correr, Venice: 9, 31, 59, 60, 72, 73; Gallerie Nazionali delle Marche, Urbino: 21; Camerafoto, Venice: 32, 129, 205; Archivio di Stato, Venice: 35, 58, 66, 67; Accademia delle Belle Arti, Venice: 42, 95, 194; Victoria and Albert Museum, London: 61, 105; Bibliotheque Nationale de France, Paris: 63; Dijon Library: 64; Giacomelli, Venice: 70; Mario Piana: 79; National Gallery, London: 99; Alinari, Florence: 178; British Museum, London: 185

Index

310